The Roots of Thinking

The Roots of THINKING

Maxine Sheets-Johnstone

TEMPLE UNIVERSITY PRESS

PHILADELPHIA

Temple University Press, Philadelphia 19122
Copyright © 1990 by Temple University. All rights reserved
Published 1990
Printed in the United States of America

Library of Congress Cataloging-in-Publication Data
Sheets-Johnstone, Maxine.
    The roots of thinking / Maxine Sheets-Johnstone.
        p.   cm.
    Includes bibliographical references.
    ISBN 0-87722-711-X cloth (alk. paper)
    ISBN 0-87722-769-1 paperback
    1. Philosophical anthropology.   2. Thought and thinking.   3. Concepts.
4. Mind and body.   5. Human evolution.   I. Title.
BD450.S4355   1990
128—dc20   89-29681
                                                          CIP

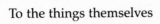

To the things themselves

Contents

vii

Acknowledgments

Major parts of Chapter 3—"On the Origin of Counting: A Re-Thinking of Upright Posture"—were presented at the 65th annual meeting of the American Association for the Advancement of Science, San Francisco, California, June 1984. The complete paper was subsequently requested for inclusion in a volume of original essays edited by Mary LeCron Foster and Jayne Botscharow (linguistic and physical anthropologists, respectively): *The Life of Symbols* (Boulder, Colo.: Westview Press, 1990). Chapter 6—"On the Origin of Language"—originally appeared in *North Dakota Quarterly* 51/2 (Spring 1983). Major parts of Chapter 7—"Hominid Bipedality and Sexual Selection Theory"—originally appeared in *Evolutionary Theory* 9 (July 1989). Chapter 8—"On the Conceptual Origin of Death"—originally appeared in *Philosophy and Phenomenological Research* 47/1 (September 1986). Major parts of Chapter 14—"Methodology: The Genetic Phenomenology Strand"—were presented in a paper, "What Was It Like to Be Lucy?" given at the 58th annual meeting of the American Philosophical Association, Long Beach, California, March 1984.

Part I

Overview

1

The Thesis, the Method, and Related Matters

And what is *thinking*?—Well, don't you ever think? Can't you observe yourself and see what is going on? It should be quite simple. You do not have to wait for it as for an astronomical event and then perhaps make your observation in a hurry.

LUDWIG WITTGENSTEIN

THE THESIS

This book is about conceptual origins. In particular, it addresses the question of the conceptual origin of fundamental human practices and beliefs that arose far back in evolutionary human history: tool-making, counting, consistent bipedality, language, the concept of death, engraving and painting. Typically, answers to questions about origins—how a verbal language originated, how counting began, for example—take for granted the very concepts basic to the practice, the concept of oneself as a sound-maker in the case of language, for instance, or the concept of numbers in the case of counting. Insofar as fundamental human practices and beliefs entail concepts, and insofar as concepts entail some form of thinking, a proper account of the origin of any particular human practice or belief must necessarily give an account of thinking, that is, an account of the standard in terms of which the relevant concepts were forged. The thesis of this book is that in each case the living body served as a semantic template. Concepts were either generated or awakened by the living body in the course of everyday actions such as chewing, urinating, striding, standing, breathing, and so on. As everyday actions gave rise to new concepts, so new concepts gave rise to new possibilities, new possibilities to new ways of living, and new ways of living to the establishment finally of those revolutionary new practices and beliefs that are definitive of hominid evolution. The broad thesis of this book is thus that there is an indissoluble bond between hominid thinking and hominid evolution, a bond cemented by the living body.

Evidence supporting hominid evolution is based on fossil and artifactual remains. To date, discovered remains span roughly a period of three and a half million years. At the near end, cave paintings dating as far back as thirty thousand years testify to the hominid practice of drawing. At the far end, skeletal segments dating as far back as three and a half million years document the appearance of the earliest yet known hominids on the evolutionary scene, that is, the appearance of creatures who began walking upright. In between are stone artifacts testifying to the practice of hominid tool-using and tool-making, fossil remains attesting to the possibility of certain linguistic practices, artifactual and fossil remains testifying to hominid burial practices. A progressive and comprehensive examination of the evidence—from upright posture and tool-using/tool-making to burial sites and cave paintings—points decisively and at every step to a thinking creature. Hominid evolution was shaped by hominid thinking.

There would seem to be no difficulty in accepting that fact. For example, it is natural to suppose that ancestral hominids who made stone tools thought of shaping them with respect to their intended future use. They did not just take any stone to begin with, for instance, any more than they mindlessly whacked away at the stone they took with any other stone. Thoughtful preparation and shaping informed the process of making a stone tool, obviously so where a particular form was duplicated over and over again. Data gathered by field primatologists strongly support the disposition to impute thinking to ancestral tool-making hominids. A female chimpanzee who is going to fish for termites, for example, will choose not just any twig and proceed to strip it of leaves, but will choose a twig of a certain girth and pliancy before shaping it to her intended use.[1] It seems, then, not only natural but justifiable to credit ancestral hominids with thinking. The problem is with what is *not* natural, indeed with what might appear utterly foreign and in need of rigorous and thorough-going substantiation and validation: crediting hominids with thinking corporeally.

The thesis that thinking is modeled on the body is actually supported by the same evidence that supports hominid evolution. Concepts fundamental to hominid thinking have their origin in animate form and in the tactile–kinesthetic correlates of behaviors regularly attributed to our hominid ancestors on the basis of fossil and artifactual evidence. Stone implements, burial remains, cave paintings, skeletal fragments, all attest not just to various behaviors such as upright posture and locomotion, tool-making, and pictorial depiction —or suggest others, such as the possibility of language and counting —but attest to specific tactile–kinesthetic concepts subtending the behaviors or generated by them: the concept of edges, of death, of numbers, or of oneself as a sound-maker, for example. Hominid thinking thus developed not through divine decree or interplanetary machinations but in the course of organic evolution. And reciprocally, as indicated above, hominid evolution was shaped by hominid thinking. The cognitive impetus for the cultivation and establishment of those behaviors shaping the development of a hominid style of living originated in bodily concepts entailed in animate form and tactile–kinesthetic experience. Just as without evolution there would be no human thinking, so without thinking, there would have been no hominid evolution.

The key to an understanding of the dynamics of the reciprocal relationship between hominid thinking and hominid evolution lies in deepened understandings of the body, specifically, in corporeal analyses of a hominid animate form and tactile–kinesthetic body. By *animate form* is meant a species-specific body with all its various spatial conformations, and attendant everyday postures, modes of locomotion, movements, and gestures. In broad terms, animate form is equivalent to the spatiality of the body in all its dimensions. The *tactile–kinesthetic body* is the sentiently felt body, the body that knows the world through touch and movement. It is not the body that simply *behaves* in certain observed or observable ways, but the body that resonates in the first-person, lived-through sense of any behavior. It is the experienced and experiencing body. The thesis that thinking is modeled on the body thus links thinking to spatial and sentient–kinetic life.

This fresh approach to an understanding of thinking attempts to crack the noetic code by tracing its evolutionary roots, at the same time recognizing and bypassing traditional schisms embedded in the received wisdom of twentieth-century thought. Such an approach asks different questions because it starts not only from the beginning, but with what is obvious in the beginning. Seminal evolutionary changes in practice and belief that mark the historical development of hominids were made possible not by "a greater intelligence" or "a more sophisticated consciousness" but concretely by new ways of thinking. In each instance, conceptual touchstones necessarily provided the impetus: the concept of sound, of articulatory gestures, and of oneself as a sound-maker necessarily anchored the invention of a verbal language; the concept of numbers necessarily anchored the invention of counting; the concept of edges and of flaking (one stone with another) necessarily anchored the invention of stone tool-making; the concept of punctuated existence necessarily anchored a belief in death; the concept of drawing necessarily anchored the inventions of engraving and painting. The question is, Where did these concepts come from— the concept of *edges*?, of *flaking*?, of a *spoken language*?, of *numbers*?, of a *punctuated existence*?, of *drawing*?

In evolutionary terms, new ways of perceiving the world and acting within it were discovered. At their origin, they were more properly the result of accident than design—more like the female Japanese macaque's original discovery that washing sweet potatoes before eating them rid them of abrasive sand particles (a practice that spread throughout the troop)[2] than like reflective manoeuvres on the order of think-tank physics or brainstorm problem-solving. Yet however accidental the circumstances of discovery, new ways of perceiving and acting took root only in moments of conceptual insight. In each instance, insight was generated in tactile–kinesthetic experience, which is to say by the tactile–kinesthetic body—the body that through touch and movement distinguishes not only a rubble of stones from no rubble at all as it walks the earth, or the making of sound from no making of sound as it conceals itself from danger, but the body that distinguishes a sharp-edged stone from a blunt one, a quadrupedal stride from a bipedal one, a touching of lips in making the sound *m* from a touching of lips in making the sound *p*, and so on. That sensorily felt and sensorily feeling body was the cognitive source of those fundamental and preeminently human concepts that shaped human thinking and human evolution. That body functioned as a semantic template. It was the standard upon which each new practice or system of beliefs was forged.

An original bodily logos can be demonstrated ontogenetically as well as phylogenetically. Though anchored in paleoanthropological case studies, Part II of this book will present evidence in both historical modes. It will detail how the roots of thinking are engendered in bodily life, that is, how concepts fundamental to human life originated and originate in animate form and the tactile–kinesthetic body.

An original bodily logos can be substantiated theoretically as well as ontogenetically and phylogenetically, in the sense that whether esteemed rudimentary or highly complex in any particular instance, thinking necessarily originated and evolved in accordance with a conceptual standard of some kind. What is thought is in other words structured in and by some previously experienced system(s) of meanings. This explains why, quite apart from its etymology, recognition can be designated a fundamental mode of thinking and why children can learn a verbal language. They learn it on the basis of the system of meanings already engendered in past perceptual experiences. They thereby recognize a heretofore nonverbal world in another, verbal one. Casual reflection shows that numbers function as just such a previously experienced system of meanings in forms of mathematical thinking, that perceptual experience functions as just such a previously experienced system of meanings in dream-thinking and in imagic thought generally, that words function as just such a previously experienced system of meanings in linguistic thinking, that bodily powers function as just such a previously experienced system of meanings in kinetic thinking. This is why mathematician, dancer, dreamer, and speaker, for example, may each be said to think *in* something, in something not uncommonly designated a particular kind of language. Casual reflection and the analogy to verbal language, however, can lead to ill-founded simplifications as well as incomplete explanations. The evidential propriety of designating the medium of thought to be a language in each case, for example, remains unsubstantiated. Of greater concern here is the fact that what casual analysis and the analogy to verbal language leave unexplained is precisely the conceptual source of the specified language. Numbers, for instance, cannot simply be taken for granted in an explanation of mathematical thinking. The *concept* of numbers must be accounted for just as must the concept of bodily powers, of language, of pictorial depiction, and so on. The task of the paleoanthropological case studies in Part II is to show how the most basic system of meanings—the original conceptual standard upon which both rudimentary and advanced forms of hominid thinking were forged—was a system of corporeal meanings. Analysis of the hominid evolutionary record will show that basic human concepts, including those of word and number, ultimately revert to the body as semantic template. What was—and is—originally thought was—and is—founded on a bodily logos.

There are two major forms of opposition to the thesis stated above. The first may be succinctly identified with an all-encompassing, steadfast belief in cultural relativism, the second with the all-encompassing, steadfast practice of thinking dualistically and reducing biologically. Each form of opposition will be critically examined at length in Part III, in Chapters 10 and 11 respectively. Readers who are curious about how the opposition is put to rest, or skeptical that it can be, are invited to turn to the later chapters before proceeding to the paleoanthropological case studies of Part II. Only a brief acknowledgment of the issues raised by the two forms of opposition will be given here.

The notion of getting back to the conceptual origins of human thought goes against academically popular dogma. Cultural relativism decrees permanent servitude to the practices and beliefs of one's own current culture: since there is no way of thoroughly detaching oneself from that culture, there is no way of obtaining a point of view on it. There is thus no way of analyzing the layers of meaning—the strata of thought—embedded in its practices and beliefs. In brief, cultural relativists adhere to the belief that it is impossible to "get back." They would thus declare the roots of thinking unexposable. What is shown in detail in Chapter 10 is that the various theoretical obstacles placed in the way of getting back are all in a robust biological sense biodegradable. Given animate form and the tactile–kinesthetic body, and given bona fide evolutionary theory and sound reasoning therefrom, the obstacles disintegrate.

The division of life into "the mental" and "the physical" has a long Western history. The division is held in place by academic practice: minds are treated by philosophers, bodies are treated by scientists, and rarely do the twain ever meet. The consequences are sizable when it comes to understanding our evolutionary past, in particular the "mental" capacities of reconstructed fossil hominid forms or the "mental" capacities signified by their artifacts. Since in the traditional divisional scheme of things bodies provide little more than a dumb show of movement and minds are privileged shrines vouchsafed to humans alone, any resemblance between ancestral hominids and present-day ones is purely physical. Add to this mere physical resemblance the clear-cut privileging of minds over bodies so far as *thinking* is concerned, and the bodily behaviors of reconstructed hominid creatures readily become empty shells of "doings," doings that in fact are subject to the same explanatory canon as that applied regularly to all nonhuman animals. That is, although they are clearly *hominids*, these reconstructed ancestral forms are not members of the *human* species. Thus, unless lower mental processes can be shown *not* to explain their behavior—their burial practices, for instance, or their tool-making, each of which, it should be noted, has correlates among nonhuman animals—no "higher mental processes" can be postulated of the reconstructed hominids any more than they can be postulated of any other nonhuman animals.

Metaphysical dualism and academic practice similarly give rise to a piecemeal, reductive approach to the body. Separate physical characters are singled out and their separate evolutionary histories told, each one in turn being given an adaptive role. Little if any acknowledgment is given of anything beyond the physical. What Chapter 11 shows is that the failure to think in "persistent wholes"—to tie one's thinking to intact living organisms—is to do injustice to the living, intact creatures in question. It shows that with the academic institutionalization of metaphysical dualism, the body is not given its due. At the same time, it shows through a reexamination of Darwin's three major writings on evolution that an institutionalized dualism is nowhere to be found in the original formulations of evolution theory, and that the present-day practice of reading Darwin in a highly selective manner—a practice nowhere acknowledged or methodologically justified—is a further way of failing to give the body its due. In sum, what Chapter 11 suggests is that academically propagated creatures—in essence, mindless bodies on the one hand and disembodied minds on the other—are unnatural species.

THE METHOD

Access to the conceptual lifeworld of ancestral hominids is had initially through a hermeneutic methodology, a methodology that is in every sense complementary to traditional paleoanthropological methodologies. It is important to document this complementarity concretely if briefly at this point since in spite of Thomas Kuhn's well-known and widely accepted analysis of scientific practice,[3] hermeneutical analyses are at times misunderstood as antithetical to scientific accounts. Where they are so misunderstood, it is first of all because whether viewed primarily as a mode of critical inquiry, type of philosophy, or critical theory,[4] hermeneutics is erroneously construed as a subjective enterprise or methodology.[5] But hermeneutical analyses are not

subjective fantasies. Not only did Kuhn persuasively show the hermeneutical nature of all science—in simplified terms, *interpretation* of data
is fundamental—but Milford Wolpoff, a paleoanthropologist, specifically pointed out the indispensable if obvious role of interpretation.
In a discussion of the nature of paleoanthropology as a science, he
jocularly, but all the more emphatically, averred that "data does not
speak for itself; I have been in rooms with data and listened very carefully. The data never said a word."[6] Moreover neurobiologist Gunther
Stent doubly argued—on the basis of his analysis of the function of
neuronal networks and his methodological appraisal of David Marr's
currently prominent analysis of visual perception—that hermeneutics
is both a necessary dimension of methodological inquiry in the human
sciences because of the degree of complexity of those sciences relative to the physical sciences, and the basic process by which visual
meanings are structured. In Stent's words, hermeneutics is the "activity" by which visual perception is achieved. Taken together, these
several assessments clearly indicate that, were hermeneutical analyses
merely subjective reportings, virtually all human knowledge would
be "merely subjective."[7]

What is essential to point out in addition is that hermeneutical
methodology is not to be confused with hermeneutical critical theory.[8]
While it may be that "very great skepticism needs to be shown [by
paleoanthropologists and archaeologists] to the critical or hermeneutic
theory of Habermas," as anthropologist John Hall warned,[9] hermeneutic *methodology* concerns itself with local problems of interpretation, not with the problem of interpretation in general. Hence, in their
acknowledgment and use of hermeneutic methodology, paleoanthropologists and archaeologists need not concern themselves with the
more specifically philosophical underpinnings of interpretive theory.

As a methodology, hermeneutics is best described as an elucidation of that system of double meanings that comes into play wherever
interpretations are made.[10] Whether it be a fossil interpreted with reference to a once-living creature,[11] a tool with reference to a certain
activity or "representative process,"[12] a monument with reference to
an idealized belief structure, or a text with reference to an historical
happening, the item in question—the original thing itself or datum—
is progressively explicated through a complex system of double meanings arising from the fact that at each turn, the data play a double role:
the original datum is interpreted; that interpretation becomes a datum
and is in turn interpreted; and so on. That this hierarchy of interlocking interpretations exists in paleoanthropology and archaeology

is patently evident in the different levels at which controversy takes place and in the fact that dispute at any one level affects all others. In the case of fossil bones, for example, interpretational disputes arise at the level of dating, of species designation, of inferred behavior, or of adaptational relationships, and their effect is always multilevel.

Given this methodological perspective, hermeneutical explications are clearly not exercises in fancy but are grounded in a hierarchy of interpretations traditionally beginning (so far as ancestral hominids are concerned) with fossil or otherwise dated evidence, and ending precisely with those behaviors and evolutionary meanings that fossil bones, tools, monuments, and texts, for example, are seen concretely by paleoanthropologist and archaeologist alike to memorialize: that is, upright walking, the fashioning of implements, the construction of buildings symbolizing particular beliefs, and the invention and use of a language respectively.

There is a collateral paleoanthropological hermeneutics that is often utilized to flesh out or support the traditional one. In this hermeneutics, extant human and/or nonhuman behavior is appropriated as original data and used analogically in the reconstruction of ancestral hominid life. Specifically, interpretational extrapolations are made from data on extant nonhuman primates, on primitive hunter–gatherer peoples, and/or on social carnivores. At first glance, the resulting hierarchy of interpretations might appear less complex, in fact single-level: an original, known datum—an aspect in the life of present-day chimpanzees, for example—is interpreted, and that interpretation serves as datum for interpreting what is unknown—that is, a conjectured, corresponding aspect in the life of ancestral hominids. But the collateral hermeneutical structure is not usually so simple. In the seed-eater model of early hominid life, for instance, extrapolations having to do with the skeletal form—cranial and postcranial —of gelada baboons are the basis for reconstructions first about the diet of ancestral hominids, and ultimately about their basic behavioral patterns and capabilities all the way from upright posture to verbal language.[13]

Whether based on a traditional or collateral paleoanthropological hermeneutics—or on both—what *full-scale* hermeneutical analyses provide to paleoanthropological reconstructions is a more substantial and more finely structured bridge from original datum to associated conjectured behaviors, and from associated conjectured behaviors to their expanded and often complex evolutionary significance. They do this through an uncovering of that conceptual terrain engendered by or essential to the behavior both as a corporeal reality—a once actually lived-through event—and as a habitual life pattern—a consistent, established manner of acting. Traditional hermeneutical methodology is in other words carried one step further to generate *corporeal analyses*. The corporeal analyses are in essence a working backward from data —stone tools, cave paintings, primordial language, primitive counting systems, even the advent of upright posture—to the hominid body that produced them. Using archaeologist Lewis Binford's terms,[14] they are a working backward from *statics*—the posture, the painting, the language, the numbers—to *dynamics*, in this case *corporeal* dynamics. Full-scale hermeneutical analyses are in fact inherently linked to precisely the kind of methodology Binford called for to produce Middle Range Theory: "a paradigmatic frame of reference for giving meaning to selected characteristics of the archaeological record."[15]

Binford did not specify from what tradition, logical positivist or other, the new frame of reference—the new "cognitive device" as he has called it—must come, but clearly, the hominid body is just such a new frame of reference. By turning behavior and/or artifact into corporeal data for further interpretation, corporeal analyses uncover a conceptual terrain. Concepts engendered in the advent of upright posture, for example, or entailed in the making of stone tools, are brought to light. The new paradigmatic frame of reference reveals its remarkable explanatory scope, power, and coherency in filling out cognitive dimensions inherent in conjectured behaviors and in the production of artifacts. Indeed, it reveals its explanatory scope, power, and coherency in filling out the conceptual structures that establish the behaviors as habitual life patterns to begin with—language, for example, or burial practices—and that make the artifactual productions possible in the first place. In short, when the traditional or collateral hermeneutical process is carried one step further so as to take full account of the living body, the source and standard of fundamental hominid concepts are no longer a terra incognita in need of mapping; the map takes palpable shape.

Yet it is not sufficient merely to affirm certain relationships, for example to point out a functional replacement of teeth by tools in accounting for the conceptual development of stone tool-making. It is necessary to show in a precise way how each particular concept would arise, thus how the concept of teeth as tools would arise and correlatively, how the concept of a stone as a potential tool would arise. A full-scale paleoanthropological hermeneutics thus needs further evidential grounding through a method akin to genetic phenomenology.

The label *genetic* is not a surreptitious attempt to soften up phenomenology for logical positivist consumption. Neither is it a bold attempt to make a philosophical dent in the bastions of genetic research—to slip an alien foot unobtrusively through the laboratory door as it were. To begin with, the label is not purloined; it is philosopher Edmund Husserl's, and though nowhere defined specifically, its meaning has clearly nothing to do with genes per se but with what genes represent: the *origin* of something. For Husserl, the origin of concern is the origin of *meaning*, the everyday meanings of human life, which build up over time such that, like archaeological sedimentations, semantic deposits of the past are hidden under topmost, immediately apparent layers. In broad terms, Husserl's purpose in using the term is to distinguish a phenomenological *typology* of experienced meanings—what he terms a static phenomenology—from a phenomenological *history* of experienced meanings—a genetic phenomenology. In more exacting terms, his aim is to show how, through the method of genetic phenomenological analysis, the origin of human meanings can be ultimately exposed, to the end that fundamental concepts— of *world, Nature, space, time, animate organism, social community*, for example—and fundamental concepts in domains of human knowledge such as mathematics, are *evidentially* clarified.[16] With the grounding of basic human concepts in the everyday realities of human experience, human knowledge is securely tethered to its experiential moorings. Fundamental concepts are no longer assumed or taken for granted in scientific discourse but are firmly anchored in concrete structures of human experience. As is evident, Husserl's concerns in this matter are contemporary, not paleoanthropological, but his method may clearly be put in the service of paleoanthropology.[17] A very brief example will show why.

From a methodological viewpoint, the primary hermeneutical step that generates a corporeal analysis is something of an intuitive *fait accompli* with respect to stone tool-making. As suggested above, a readily self-evident relationship between a particular aspect of the body and stone tools is intuitively recognized by many researchers and in fact is consistently remarked upon even though an empirically demonstrated association between teeth and tools has not been shown.[18] To affirm that stone tools replaced teeth for processing food, for example, puts forth a certain understanding—an *interpretation*— of stone tools that is at the edge of a full-scale hermeneutics. The inchoate existential interpretation is akin to traditional interpretations which specify the age of a stone tool, for instance, or its geographical location relative to a certain area. Unlike the latter interpretations, however, the former one remains unsubstantiated empirically: what is the experiential and in effect conceptual basis for the replacement of teeth by tools? Why not a replacement by knuckles or feet, for example? To answer simply that upright posture freed the hands for tool-making constitutes neither an analysis nor an explanation of the connection between stone tools and teeth—any more than the affirmation, "tool-making freed the teeth for sound-making," constitutes an analysis and explanation of a connection between sounds and words. What is needed is a phenomenological analysis that can show a conceptual linkage, even a rational connection, between stone tools and teeth. That the connection is conceptual, and that it has an experiential base and can thus be empirically anchored in the realities of everyday corporeal life, are obvious but neglected facts.

Chapters 13 and 14 of the book spell out both the hermeneutical and the phenomenological strands of the methodology in detail. They clarify the methodology and at the same time resolve methodological issues. Chapter 13 in particular details the need for a full-scale hermeneutical paleoanthropology that rightfully and explicitly recognizes itself at the interface of the natural and human sciences, and in turn recognizes that hominid fossils are at once items discovered in a landscape and sensed relics of once-living kindred forms. Chapter 14 in particular answers to the core methodological problem inherent in the attempt to describe experienced meanings in creatures other than one's own immediate kind. The key question with respect to that problem, the question of establishing sufficient similarity in point of view, is shown to be properly answered through the procedures of bracketing and of corporeal scanning. The procedure of bracketing involves suspending typical twentieth-century cultural meanings to the end that the sedimented physiognomic character of things comes to light. As the chapter documents, the procedure is not that far removed either from certain everyday human behaviors or behavioral possibilities, or from certain scientific investigatory procedures. Corporeal scanning involves an examination of animate form and the tactile–kinesthetic body with respect to concepts subtending or generated by "the facts": stone tool-making, cave paintings, a belief in death, and so on. As might be apparent, the initial stage in the process of corporeal scanning is implicitly exemplified by the connection paleoanthropologists intuitively draw between teeth and stone tools. Like the procedure of bracketing, corporeal scanning has specific affinities with certain common scientific investigatory procedures. Together the two procedures of bracketing and corporeal scanning effect a "corporeal reduction" through which relevant concepts are successfully distilled. The result is that concepts subtending or generated by the corporeal facts of the matter—the corporeal fact of making a tool, of walking bipedally, of drawing, of speaking—are understood at their source.

Again, as with the thesis, readers curious or skeptical about the methodology or the successful resolution of methodological issues are invited to turn to the later chapters in Part III before proceeding to the paleoanthropological case studies of Part II.

RELATED MATTERS

PHILOSOPHICAL ANTHROPOLOGY

The thesis that thinking is modeled on the body provides in skeletal form the outlines of a bona fide philosophical anthropology. The corporeal analyses—the paleoanthropological case studies—provide its backbone.

A bona fide philosophical anthropology requires a study of the evolution of humans at the same time that it requires a sense of the body free of its typical Cartesian moorings. Why? Because to begin with, anything less than a global and historical understanding of human being falls short of a full understanding of what it is to be human. A *deus ex machina* notion of humans, for example, is patently creationistic. Although not recognized as such, the ontologies of many existential and analytic philosophers are ontologies in which, precisely, humans arrive on the scene as Special Creations.[19] In many of these instances language is something of a pied piper. It comes from nowhere and so charms those who hear it that they follow it anywhere, mesmerized. The followers are as unquestioning of where the lingual piper came from—how it could possibly have originated —as they are oblivious of the origins of other equally extraordinary dimensions of human life—art, for example, or the concept of death, a concept that names no-thing (a *dead person* is not the equivalent of *death*), and so cannot be pointed to or exemplified by something out there in the world, or indicate a first-person personal experience like pain. Scholars who have followed the piper and taken the linguistic turn would in fact have difficulty explaining the use of the word *death* since by their standard, public criteria validate the use of any word, and there is no behavior coincident with the concept of *death*. The concept entails something far more complex than any particular behavior. As Chapter 8 clearly shows, it entails certain compounded experiential understandings of the tactile–kinesthetic body.

For just such reasons, a bona fide philosophical anthropology demands a more equitable view of the body than that current in a Western Cartesian view. There is more to being a body than meets the eye. The living body is more than a thing extended in visual space. It is first and foremost the center of a tactile–kinesthetic world that, unlike the visual world, rubs up directly against things outside it and reverberates directly with their sense. The tactile–kinesthetic body is a body that is always in touch, always resounding with an intimate and immediate knowledge of the world about it. Reduced in status to a visual object, the body loses this quintessential sensorium. Stripped from the inside, it becomes an empty shell of "doings." Just as the scene in which humans arrive *deus ex machina* is not in the remotest sense a teeming, refulgent earthly one—it neither resounds with the history of ongoing creaturely life nor resonates with the sounds and smells of nature—so purely visual bodies are not either in the remotest sense earthly ones—they neither reflect the feel of things, nor radiate a sense of their own life.

In sum, the major forms of opposition to the thesis of this book— adherence to an all-pervasive and indiscriminate cultural relativism, and to a metaphysical dualism that diminishes the body and fails to give it its living due—also stand in the way of a bona fide philosophical anthropology. The latter is hardly conceivable apart from both an evolutionary history and a somatology that recognize tactility and movement not simply as sensorimotor pathways but as ways of knowing the world—as *gnostic* systems in the most fundamental (i.e., etymological) sense of that word. Because the beliefs and values that hold cultural relativism and metaphysical dualism in place also keep a bona fide philosophical anthropology at bay—or in positive terms, because the thesis of this book is so clearly tied to a philosophical anthropology in which humanness is unabridged, either historically or sensorily—it is appropriate to follow up the detailed discussions of cultural relativism and metaphysical dualism in Chapters 10 and 11 with a detailed consideration of philosophical anthropology. Accordingly, Chapter 12 presents a discussion of the properly interdisciplinary field of philosophical anthropology and sets forth in a concrete way the steps philosophers and anthropologists might take separately and jointly to cultivate such a field of study.

TACTILE–KINESTHETIC INVARIANTS

Just as the thesis and its oppositions are intimately connected to the possibility of a philosophical anthropology, so the two-stranded methodology is intimately connected to the identification of tactile–kinesthetic invariants. To see how this is so is to see how the question of sufficient similarity in point of view—between oneself and a creature other than oneself—is ultimately tied to the body, the tactile–kinesthetic body. If there are good grounds for saying that a methodology exists by which we may approximate to the world of our hominid ancestors, then there are good grounds for saying that there are fundamental pan-hominid tactile–kinesthetic invariants. The signal importance of these fundamental invariants is of course conceptual. The invariants are not only the evidential basis for affirming *fundamental* hominid concepts; they are the evidential basis for affirming *nonlinguistic* ones.

For readers interested in pursuing the case for nonlinguistic tactile–kinesthetic invariants, a detailed examination of the evidence is given in Chapter 15. It will suffice here to indicate in a brief way the nature of these concepts and something of the rationale substantiating their existence.

Present-day hominids have two legs of a certain form, teeth of a certain kind, tongues of a certain shape, all of which are, in *essential* respects, no different from those of ancestral hominids said to be capable respectively of bipedal locomotion, of chewing, of speaking. Just such corporeal uniformities are the foundation of fundamental tactile–kinesthetic invariants. The invariants transcend, or more precisely, underlie any and all individual diversity in tactile–kinesthetic experience—in the same way that human anatomical invariants underlie any and all individual diversity in human anatomy, and human physiological invariants underlie any and all individual diversity in human physiology. Otherwise stated, ancestral hominids and humans today share more than an essentially similar anatomy and corresponding functional abilities. They share certain fundamental sensory–kinetic experiences, and potentially certain concepts deriving from those fundamental experiences. The concepts arise in the simple act of noticing oneself; they are in other words latent in tactile–kinesthetic experiences. For example, the transfer of weight from one leg to the other in walking gives rise to a tactile–kinesthetic uniformity of felt impact and rhythm; the hardness of teeth to a tactile–kinesthetic uniformity of felt resistance; the mobility of tongue to a tactile–kinesthetic uniformity of possible patterns of articulation. Short of such tactile–kinesthetic uniformities, it could not justifiably be claimed that ancestral hominids and present-day humans belong to the same Family, Hominidae. To maintain that an essentially similar neuroanatomy and physiology and essentially similar behaviors (carrying, striking, pushing, pulling, chewing, biting, walking, throwing, and the like) give rise to essentially *dissimilar* tactile–kinesthetic experiences and potential conceptual meanings is unreasonable. Can a bipedal walk be the same bipedal walk and not be felt as binary, that is, first *one side*, then the *other*? Can the sound *m* still be the same sound and not be a touching of lips? A commonality of form and function across hominid history could not eventuate in fundamentally different tactile–kinesthetic experiences without dire consequences to evolutionary theory and to a good deal more besides. As Chapter 15 shows, what is at stake is not only biological classification but semantic truth, a logical ontology, and an intelligible regularity of corporeal experience.

What is additionally paramount to emphasize here is that concepts emanating from fundamental tactile–kinesthetic experiences are indeed *corporeal* concepts that are not in any way inferior to their linguistic relatives. It is relevant in this respect to point out that a very young child's concept of front and back has been shown *not* to hinge on linguistic designation.[20] Though not intended to support the thesis of fundamental tactile–kinesthetic invariants, such experimental findings nicely corroborate the existence of corporeal concepts and illustrate further how these concepts are intimately linked not to language but to the three-dimensional spatiality of the tactile–kinesthetic body.

Corporeal concepts that have their roots in interactive dimensions of animate form are similarly independent of language. The concept of hardness, for instance, is latent in the tactile–kinesthetic act of brushing the tongue across the teeth, just as the concept of softness is latent in the act of brushing the tongue across the lips. No words are necessary to the recognition of these pan-hominid tactile qualities. They are latent in corporeal experience. While such experiences are most often submerged in the course of everyday adult twentieth-century Western life, they cannot on that account be either denied or claimed to be a function of language.

THE COMMUNAL TASK

As preface to the paleoanthropological case studies that follow, this overview should finally call explicit attention to the nature of the presented analyses. The analyses describe corporeal experience—they are *phenomenological*, which means that they are empirically verifiable by the reader. If the descriptions are adequate to the task, they should meet with affirmation. The task, however, is actually a mutual task. As Husserl pointed out, "Obviously one cannot read and understand [a phenomenological account of experience] in the way one does a newspaper. One can understand descriptions only if he knows that which is described, and he can only know what is described if he has brought it into clear intuitive experience."[21] Taking time to *have* the experience is thus clearly a first step the reader must take.

There is perhaps even a prior necessary step. It is best formulated in a related remark by Husserl in which he specifies the proper reading analogy. "Let the reader try just once to read every assertion which I make in phenomenological contexts just as he reads a zoological or botanical description of an object—thus as an expression standing for something intuitively experienced or intuitively experienceable and as something that is really originally understandable only through direct intuitive experience."[22] By "intuitive experience," Husserl means an experience of simple perception, an experience that makes no appeal to inference or reasoning. The only way to have *that* experience is to have *that* experience. Thus the analyses that follow can be validated only on their own ground—by readers who allow their bodies to be heard. A just appraisal of the paleoanthropological case studies that follow hangs in the balance.

There is a further communal task beyond the descriptive/intuitive one. It is of the nature of phenomenological studies to be open-ended. One can always go back to experience, not only in order to validate empirically what is described, but to discover if there is more to be learned in the experience of the things themselves. In this sense, the substantive and methodological turn toward the body taken in this book is not to be conceived as a singular event producing a singular product. A *concerted* turn toward the body is long overdue. Clearly there is a vast field of corporeal understandings awaiting discovery and cultivation by many people. The field has in fact lain dormant for hundreds of years, being either preempted or covered over by many kinds of other concerns, the most recent predominant one being the concern with language. Heralded earlier this century by the work of Lévi-Strauss in anthropology and of Wittgenstein in philosophy, the linguistic turn produced extraordinary insights. A corporeal turn would assuredly do no less.

NOTES

1. Geza Teleki, "Chimpanzee Subsistence Technology: Materials and Skills," *Journal of Human Evolution* 3 (1974): 575–94.

2. M. Kawai, "Newly-Acquired Pre-cultural Behavior of the Natural Troop of Japanese Monkeys on Koshima Islet," *Primates* 6 (1965): 1–30.

3. Thomas S. Kuhn, *The Structure of Scientific Revolutions*, 2nd ed. (Chicago: University of Chicago Press, 1970).

4. Joseph Bleicher, *Contemporary Hermeneutics* (London: Routledge & Kegan Paul, 1980).

5. See, for example, Misia Landau, "Human Evolution as Narrative," *American Scientist* 72 (1984): 262–68.

6. Milford H. Wolpoff, "Discussion," in *Paleoanthropology: Morphology and Paleoecology*, ed. Russell H. Tuttle (The Hague: Mouton, 1975), p. 15.

7. Gunther Stent, "Hermeneutics and the Analysis of Complex Biological Systems" (Paper presented at the University of California at Davis, 14 November 1984); David Marr, *Vision* (New York: W. H. Freeman, 1982); Stent, "Hermeneutics," p. 17.

8. See Emilio Betti, "Hermeneutics as the General Methodology of the *Geisterwissenschaften*," in *Contemporary Hermeneutics*, pp. 51–94; and Erich Hirsch, *Validity in Interpretation* (New Haven: Yale University Press, 1967).

9. John Hall, "Comment II: Too Many Cooks Spoil the Broth," in *Theory and Explanation in Archaeology*, ed. Colin Renfrew, Michael J. Rolands, and Barbara Abbott Segraves (New York: Academic Press, 1982), p. 148.

10. See Paul Ricoeur, "Existence and Hermeneutics," in *The Conflict of Interpretations* (Evanston, Ill.: Northwestern University Press, 1974), pp. 11–24.

11. Cf. Paul Ricoeur, "The Model of the Text: Meaningful Action Considered as a Text," *Social Research* 38 (1971): 529–55.

12. See Mary LeCron Foster, "Meaning as Metaphor I," *Quaderni di semantica* 3, no. 1 (1982): 95–102.

13. Clifford J. Jolly, "The Seed-Eaters: A New Model of Hominid Differentiation Based on a Baboon Analogy," *Man*, n.s. 5 (1970): 5–26.

14. Lewis R. Binford, *Bones: Ancient Men and Modern Myths* (New York: Academic Press, 1981), and "Objectivity—Explanation—Archaeology 1981," in *Theory and Explanation*, pp. 125–38.

15. Binford, *Bones*, p. 25, and "Objectivity," p. 129.

16. For a brief and general statement of the aims of genetic phenomenology see Edmund Husserl's "The Origin of Geometry," trans. David Carr, in *Husserl: Shorter Works*, ed. Peter McCormick and Frederick Elliston (Notre Dame, Ind.: University of Notre Dame Press, 1981), pp. 255–70. It is of interest to note that Husserl actually received his doctorate in mathematics with a minor in philosophy, that his dissertation title was *Philosophie der Arithmetik* (published in 1891), and that his dissertation, like his consequent life's work in philosophy, was the result of his concern to *ground* everyday meanings.

Rather than simply taking over meanings as part of an already existing cultural tradition, Husserl wanted to know how we come to know the things we know (and take for granted), the question of origin being at the perennial center of his inquiries and analyses. Genetic phenomenology—the method he formulated to recover original meanings—is based upon a moment in Descartes's method (of doubting). See Husserl's *Ideas Pertaining to a Pure Phenomenology and to a Phenomenological Psychology, First Book*, trans. F. Kersten (The Hague: Martinus Nijhoff, 1983), in particular pp. 56–62.

17. It is appropriate to point out that misunderstandings and misrepresentations of phenomenology by anthropologists and psychologists—or by other scientists and even some philosophers—can easily distort its concerns and methodology, and that persons perhaps otherwise sympathetic to the aims of phenomenology inadvertently do it a disservice by characterizing it in rather odd ways. For example, the psychiatrist Anthony Stevens writes that Husserl adopted "a more introverted approach" than Kant: "He [Husserl] considered the shapes and colours that make up our visual percepts to stand as 'symbols' of the real objects perceived. . . . Thus, for Husserl, like Kant, it is our perceptions, rather than reality, that determine what we perceive." *Archetypes* (New York: William Morrow and Company, 1982), p. 55. Or again, Bruce Kapferer, an anthropologist, writes that "phenomenology, taking solitude as a fundamental basis of human existence, directs much of its analytic attention to the processes whereby individuals overcome or transcend their aloneness in the world and come to share their lived experience with others." "Performance and the Structuring of Meaning and Experience," in *The Anthropology of Experience*, ed. Victor W. Turner and Edward M. Bruner (Urbana: University of Illinois Press, 1986), p. 188. In his editorial introduction to the latter text, Bruner writes that "Kapferer, like Fernandez [another anthropologist], starts with the problematic of phenomenology: how individuals transcend their aloneness in the world and come to share lived experience. 'I do not experience your experience': he tells us, '. . . I experience my experience of you.' " Ibid., p. 21. Such characterizations of phenomenology are quite wide of the mark as almost any Husserlian text will show.

18. For example, Nicholas Toth, an archaeologist, has personally spoken to me of such a relationship. See also his article, "The First Technology," *Scientific American* 256 (April 1987): 112–21, in which the connection between dentition and tools, though implicit, is forcefully clear. See also Foster, "Meaning as Metaphor I," pp. 95–102; Milford H. Wolpoff, *Paleoanthropology* (New York: Knopf, 1980), pp. 92 and 168 for example; A. Mann, "Hominid and Cultural Origins," *Man* n.s. 7 (1972): 379–86.

19. Wilfred Sellars describes "the irreducible discontinuity" of "man" in just such capital terms. See "Philosophy and the Scientific Image of Man," in *Science, Perception and Reality* (London: Routledge & Kegan Paul, 1963), p. 6. See also Chapter 12, this book, for a brief discussion of his view.

20. Susan Cohen Leehey and Susan Carey, "Up Front: The Acquisition

of a Concept and a Word," in *Papers and Reports on Child Language Development* 15 (Stanford, Calif.: Stanford University, 1978).

21. Edmund Husserl, *Introduction to the Logical Investigations: A Draft of a Preface to the Logical Investigations (1913)*, ed. Eugen Fink and trans. Philip J. Bossert and Curtis H. Peters (The Hague: Martinus Nijhoff, 1975), p. 56.

22. Ibid., p. 57.

Part II

Paleoanthropological Case Studies

2

The Hermeneutics of Tool-Making: Corporeal and Topological Concepts

What is needed is a scientific study of tools, a science, as it may be called, of hoplonology (Gr. *Oplon*, a tool, implement). . . . Such a scientific study of tools could go a long way toward the reconstruction of something of the character and evolution of the behavioral characteristics of early man. As Sollas put it many years ago, "The works of man's hands are his embodied thought."

ASHLEY MONTAGU

INTRODUCTION

Early hominid tool-making originated and developed on the basis of concepts that were at once corporeal and topological. The concepts were full-blooded concepts, not *pre*-concepts (or pre-operational concepts) in the now popular Piagetian sense of that term among evolutionary anthropologists and archaeologists.[1] That this is so will be shown by a sensory–kinetic analysis of the concepts foundational to the act of making a tool, and by a corresponding critique of Piagetian accounts.

The tools will speak for themselves throughout and in so doing attest to the fact that they are the result of corporeal concepts in the sense in which turn-of-the-century anthropologist F. H. Cushing first applied the phrase *manual concepts* to distinguish using the hands from devising with the hands.[2] They will equally give evidence of their topological origins, not in those terms in which they are presently described—in the so-called topological *pre*-concepts of enclosure, proximity, separation, order, and so on—but in terms of the concepts with which topology deals directly and fundamentally: edges, sides, and dynamic transformations—or more generally, deformations and permanence through change.[3]

TACTILE–KINESTHETIC ANALOGY AND THE CORPOREAL CONCEPTS OF HARDNESS

The idea of a similarity between teeth and stones is not a new one but neither has it been analyzed to any depth. Anthropological linguist Mary LeCron Foster remarks that "early hominids obviously had discovered that a stone tool, whether for throwing or for cutting or bashing, was 'like' hand or teeth in efficiency for these tasks and also served to extend the power of the body beyond its own immediate orbit."[4] It is not merely efficiency, however, that marks the similarity between teeth and stone tools. While it is likely that the original use of a stone as a tool came about quite accidentally—perhaps one was picked up on a sudden whim and tried out in some way—the *making* of a tool out of stone involves conceptual thinking. At minimum it involves intention or purpose, and a conceptual knowledge of materials. Beyond these minima, it may also involve planning. From this perspective, a similarity in efficiency discovered between stones and teeth could not have been a *post hoc* similarity. The stone would have had to have been made into a tool and its efficacy anticipated *beforehand*. An analogy was thus perceived *before* stones were made into tools and their comparative efficiency tested. The analogy was the basis upon which the very idea of stones serving as tools arose.

The primary datum of stones and teeth alike is their resistant hardness. They are not squeezable; they do not bend. In contrast to other readily apparent bodily parts—whether arm or torso, hair or nails—and to other presumably ready-to-hand objects—leaves, bark, cakes of mud—they do not give way under easy or even moderate pressure. Moreover under extreme pressure, at its literal breaking point, neither gives way to a different material in the way that a shell when cracked yields some soft inner substance or that a living body when cut open yields an array of soft squeezable parts. Such finely detectable aspects as root canals aside, stones and teeth are to all untutored appearances stones and teeth all the way through. This quintessential resistant hardness of stones and teeth is a felt reality. It is a tactile–kinesthetic phenomenon. If one knew nothing of stones or teeth but merely saw them, there would be no reason to posit either as hard—or soft. The binary opposites are clearly tactile qualities.

The analogy first made between stones and teeth was thus one of structural correspondence. What was felt as hard by the tongue was analogous to what was felt as hard by the hand. Manual and lingual perception corresponded to one another and might even have been cross-collaborated from time to time, fingers feeling along teeth, tongue feeling along stones, the latter in a way similar to the way a chimpanzee runs its tongue over an object as a way of exploring it,[5] or to the way human infants take things into their mouths for the same purpose. The discovered fundamental structural analogy could thus have been borne out by further tactile–kinesthetic explorations and in turn reinforced.

Over and above the basal similarity in hardness, a textural similarity might have been equally apparent. The hardness of teeth and of cobblestones worked smooth by erosion is a texturally coincident hardness quite unlike the textural hardness of wood, for example, or other vegetable matter, and quite unlike the textural hardness of skin-covered bones. The textural quality has to do with the felt surface of the presenting hardness, which might best be described as having a certain *timbre*, textural hardness having as distinctive a character as the resonating quality of a sound. The textural similarity is undoubtedly connected with the fact that, like stone, the outer covering of teeth—the enamel—is practically devoid of organic material.[6]

That the hardness of teeth and stones is felt by tongue and hand respectively as a locus of resistance is unquestionable. This perception of resistant hardness is integral to the idea of *using* a stone as a tool. It is a necessary but not in itself sufficient awareness to call forth the idea of *making* stones into tools. Hence the question, In what else is the latter idea rooted?

There are two complementary ways of answering the question, the first corporeal, the second topological. The former is tethered to the idea of corporeal powers. It ultimately shows how the concept of a stone serving as an instrument for cutting, scraping, skinning, and other such actions—as an instrument capable of differentially transforming another object—is analogically latent in the everyday experience of eating, that is, in the tactile–kinesthetic experience of teeth as obdurate, differentially formed objects. The second is tethered to the answering of a further question: How is something which is hard but has no bite transformed into something which has?

The two complementary answers will be considered at length and in turn, in this and the following section.

THE CORPOREAL ANSWER

CORPOREAL POWERS AND MATERIAL TRANSFORMATION

Teeth bite through flesh and vegetable matter; they grind through sinewy material; they scrape off or strip surface layers of objects. They are multi-purpose tools for transforming an original material into something softer, smaller, and juicier. The transformation of the object is not a visual phenomenon but a tactile–kinesthetic one, a process that is felt rather than seen. In fact, the empirical reality of the felt experience is the basis of any visual assessment. If what is seen to enter whole into someone's mouth is fifteen seconds later spewn forth, it is assumed by the observer that the latter visually perceived objects are a transformation of the former visually perceived object. The observer's assumption is rooted in a belief in an invariant, pan-cultural tactile–kinesthetic causality. The powers of mastication are a pan-culturally empirically evident tactile–kinesthetic fact of which every hominid individual has personal knowledge. There is thus nothing magical-seeming about the two material appearances nor any puzzlement whatsoever about how the latter material appearance came to be. Given its empirical evidentiality, it is not absurd at all to speak of mastication as a corporeal power and corporeal powers in turn as comprising a global domain of *I can*'s, that is, a domain of corporeal possibilities that includes the power to effectuate change (to transform something by chewing it, for instance), to bring something to pass (by shaking a tree, for instance), and to initiate certain possible actions (walking, throwing, or striking, for instance, as well as chewing or biting).

Piaget's descriptions of infant/child behaviors in terms of *discovered powers* give brief but striking testimony to a developing domain of just such kinetic possibilities.[7] The latter are not a string of capacities. Indeed, the question is not of abilities per se but of *commanding* certain possibilities of action. Given the validity of evolutionary theory, it is incontestable that, *in a fundamental sense*, hominid infants across time have discovered the same powers of action—walking, throwing, chewing, kicking, running—and with them, certain tactile–kinesthetic invariants of their hominid existence.

As with self-awareness—moreover as a form of self-awareness—the awareness of corporeal powers does not (and could not) arise *ex nihilo*. It arises from tactile–kinesthetic activity: chewing, reaching, grasping, kicking, etc. The awareness of corporeal powers is thus not the result of reflective musings, whether with or without language. It is not a matter of wondering, What can I do? On the contrary, the sense of corporeal powers is the result either of moving or of already having moved—as Piaget's descriptions clearly show. The descriptions in fact validate the broader contention that a creature capable of heightened degrees of sensory differentiation discovers what it can do in the course of already doing it. Thus, in chewing, the creature catches itself in the act of *grinding something to pieces*. An "I move" clearly precedes an "I can."[8] In this sense, corporeal powers are the spawning ground of corporeal concepts. As the creature that is already chewing finds itself *grinding something to pieces*, so the creature that is *grinding something to pieces* is at the brink of conceptual awareness, namely the corporeal concept of transforming a material object.

Like the corporeal powers themselves, corporeal concepts stem not from a reflective musing about one's actions (again, whether with or without language), but from the very same original spontaneity of movement—the very same "original familiarity with kinesthetic abilities."[9] What must be emphasized in this regard is that such concepts are not idiosyncratic. Fundamental tactile–kinesthetic acts such as chewing give rise to a domain of fundamental *I can*'s (*ich kann*, a rich and seminal Husserlian concept; see note 8), which in turn engender potential tactile–kinesthetic conceptual invariants. Hence it can be said that chewing, biting, scraping, and the like potentially engender first the general concept of material transformation, and second, derivative concepts engendered by an awareness of differential transformations.

Sensory differentiation is commonly linked with intelligence.[10] But sensory differentiation can also be said to give rise to and enhance conceptual awarenesses. It could otherwise not be maintained that "the *contexts* in which intelligence is exhibited are limited in any given case by the animal's capabilities of perceptual differentiation."[11] A belief in the permanence of objects, for example, is rooted in the sensory differentiation of sameness and difference and in their ultimate *conceptual* differentiation. Were this not so, there would be nothing to prevent an infant or child from believing that the world is full of a never-ending procession of look-alike objects—the one just seen and having disappeared being replaced by an exact replica. Where recognition of sameness and of difference goes beyond a rote or conditioned awareness, its conceptual differentiation becomes a possibility—or an already established if taken-for-granted fact, as in Piaget's account of a human child's belief in the permanence of objects.[12]

The concepts of sameness and difference are basic to the concept of standardization, thus fundamental to the process of making a stone tool in accordance with a predetermined model, that is, from the same kind of material, using the same flaking procedure, striking with the same amount of force—in general, being vectorially worked in the same way. It should thus be clear why a creature capable of heightened sensory differentiation evinces not simply "intelligence," but burgeoning conceptual powers—in the case at hand, why early hominids became conceptually aware of their power not only to transform material in general, but to transform material differentially. On the one hand, they could chew; they could grind; they could bite; they could scrape; they could tear. On the other hand, they could flake stones in ways peculiar to the use(s) to which the stones would be put. In both cases, the potential to transform material differentially was clearly tied to certain corporeal powers and concepts. But it was also tied to teeth themselves.

TEETH, MATERIAL TRANSFORMATION, AND ANCESTRAL
HOMINID STONE TOOL-MAKING

The power of teeth to transform objects is clearly a differentially felt power. Depending on a hominid's diet, a particular transforming power might stand out more emphatically than others. In the most basic sense of transforming, however, what stands out is chewing itself, that is, the repetitive action through which the most radical transformation of an edible object occurs. It is relevant in this regard that dental analyses of fossil teeth show that ancestral hominids were originally adapted to prolonged and powerful chewing. It is thus likely that originally, prior to differentiating the powers of teeth, early hominids had an undifferentiated concept of teeth simply as battering tools, tools which were capable of hammering away, as it were, on the same object until it became smaller, juicier, softer.

The relationship between this primary use of teeth to impact over and over again upon the same object until it is reduced in size and consistency is similar to the use of a *hammerstone* (an archaeological designation) to batter a bone or nut until it opens. In each case, the action is repetitive, and in each case it is the repetitiveness of the action that brings results. Present-day chimpanzees who crack panda and coula nuts give evidence of precisely such a repetitive use of stones.[13] Whether with respect to early hominids or present-day chimpanzees, the repetitive action cannot be simply interpreted along Piagetian lines, that is, related simply to sensorimotor circular reactions or to the acquisition of the notion of causality.[14] In each of these serially defined Piagetian stages of development, infants and young children repeat an action over and over again to bring about "novel" results.[15] Quite apart from the debatable soundness of Piaget's stage model of behavioral development[16] (and quite apart too from the question of the soundness of phylogenetical extrapolations of his theory), Piagetian theory misses the critical and primary datum here together with its developmental counterpart; namely, the transformation of a material object as both experienced fact and corporeal concept. The functionality of a hammerstone in hammering—as of teeth in chewing—is not to produce "interesting" results but to transform an otherwise inedible object into an edible one. Repetitive action is in both instances pragmatic, not aesthetic. The analogical insight that links the two instances can indeed be considered a paradigm of *practical reasoning*.

While the act of chewing, perhaps like infant arm-waving as archaeologist Thomas Wynn has suggested,[17] requires no conceptual knowledge, the idea of using a hammerstone in a way similar to the way in which one uses one's teeth does require conceptual knowledge: it involves analogical insight. As with the awareness of corporeal powers, this conceptually based recognition of similarity is not a reflective manoeuvre. *Contra* Lévi-Strauss, it does not require a "bracketing of projects,"[18] that is, a *post hoc* drawing back from activity and a subsequent pondering of analogical possibilities on the order of "To what could my use of this stone be compared?" Analogical insight here is the result of a *prior* corporeally spawned awareness of the potential efficacy of the stone. It is on the basis of an original corporeal datum—the power of teeth to transform objects—that the similarity between the efficacy of the repetitive action of chewing and the possible efficacy of a repetitive striking of something with a stone is grasped. In default of the corporeal concept of material transformation, there would be no basis for seizing upon the potential utility of

a stone. Hence just as moving—"the original familiarity with kinesthetic abilities"—is the foundation of a global domain of *I can*'s, and
the domain of *I can*'s the foundation of corporeal concepts, so corporeal concepts are the foundation of analogical insights. Interlocking
levels of corporeal experience and understandings are clearly evident
in this hermeneutical schema. Equally in evidence is a credible foundation for positing analogical thinking at the origin of hominid stone
tool-making in the first place.

This latter point may be further elaborated and substantiated in
the following way. While a stone could have been picked up quite by
chance and subsequently used for the first time to hammer away at
a nut or a bone, its *actual* use, its *actual trial* against the nut or bone
comes from an insight that first disposes the creature toward the trial.
Why else would such an action be taken? The *chance* picking up of a
stone is not in itself a reason for doing anything in particular with it
—throwing it, putting it down again, rubbing it against another object, giving it to another individual, biting it, carrying it three feet and
dropping it, or whatever. What is definitive and cannot be ignored,
particularly with respect to *hominid* evolution, is the actual experience
of the chance event, namely, *the tactile–kinesthetic experience of the stone.*
What is manually felt in picking up the stone—and whether for the
first time or for the thousandth—is an obdurate hardness. That hardness, as described earlier, is strikingly similar to what is lingually felt
in running the tongue over the teeth or in feeling them with the fingers. Once basically launched in this way, the analogy of stones to
teeth is self-propelling. The experienced structural similarity triggers
the possibility of a functional similarity: Stones, like teeth, might have
the power to transform a material object. In this context, paleoanthropologist Milford Wolpoff's remarks can be recalled concerning both
the significance of the association between form and function in stone
tool-making and the apparently early appearance of their association
in the history of lithic tool production.[19]

Now even if, in addition to picking up the stone by chance, the
creature were to strike the stone against the nut or bone *by chance*, it is
not as if the hardness of the stone would not have been felt initially in
picking it up, or that its actual impact against the nut or bone would
not have been immediately related to a buccal happening. After all,
the ultimate concern of the creature at the moment is not to explore
the environment but to get something into its mouth. The stone is
struck against the nut or bone—not against another creature or a tree
trunk or the ground, for instance. Moreover even if the first strike
were entirely by chance—a distracted, inattentive gesture—it is not

as if the single strike would eventuate in an immediate fracture. The chance blow, if meaningful at all in terms of nut- or bone-cracking, would more than likely call forth concerted effort in the form of more precise and stronger blows, blows that were *intentional*—or in other words, conceptually associated with the possible extraction of something edible from within the ostensibly impervious covering in hand. In brief, if effective, the striking of the nut or bone with the stone is ultimately not a desultory action but *an anticipatory gesture aimed at eating*. Hence the chanciness of the initial blow (or even blows), as of the manual grasping of the stone, does not contravene corporeal concepts and analogical insight. Hence too, insistence upon a chance blow does not answer the question of the conceptual origin of stone tool-making. It only defers the answer toward a more thoughtful and penetrating analysis.

Just as the use of a hammerstone is analogically rooted in the undifferentiated corporeal concept of chewing, that is, in the concept of transformation through repetitive action, so the making of core and flake tools is analogically rooted in the differentiated corporeal concepts of grinding and biting, that is, in the concept of transformation through molar and incisor powers respectively. The difference between using something as a tool and making a tool is thus the difference between undifferentiated and differentiated experience. It is a matter of finer sensory discriminations together with their more refined corporeal concepts.

To show that the origin and evolution of hominid stone tool-making lies precisely in these finer bodily discriminations and concepts, a tactile–kinesthetic analysis will be made of the difference between molars and incisors—the major hominid tooth forms. Although not customarily spoken of as "major hominid tooth forms," there is no doubt that molars and incisors constitute fundamental hominid dental types, canines having become incisor-like, and premolars molar-like in the course of evolution.[20] The validity of the analysis is not contravened by differences among hominid teeth with respect to species variations in size, for in *essential* respects, hominid teeth are similar enough to each other to warrant hominid morphological classification.

A TACTILE–KINESTHETIC ANALYSIS OF TEETH AND A CORRELATIVE TACTILE–KINESTHETIC ACCOUNT OF STONE TOOL-MAKING

Hominid teeth that mash and grind food have a specific tactile character. Indeed, molars are complexly grooved objects. Declivities and ridges are not symmetrically aligned; occlusal (biting) surfaces are palpably uneven and thickly rather than pointedly edged. Even where worn flat their occlusal surface is palpably irregular. Labial and lingual surface features add to the irregular character. While round in a general sense, their roundedness is offset by clefts. The squatness and general thickness of molars are additional, palpably apparent features.

Scientific, visually based anatomical descriptions match the above tactile–kinesthetic account.[21] Topographical complexity and a comparatively low-profile roundedness are outstanding features in both descriptions.

Hominid incisors, in contrast, are rather simple tactile objects. They have a single, even, lingually traceable edge. They are thin rather than thick. Their slightly rounded labial surface is smooth and even. Their lingual surface, though palpably curved, presents an otherwise uncomplicated and smooth rather than irregular surface. Relative to the squatness of molars, incisors have a vertical and lengthier cast. Location adds to their spatial definition, that is, incisors are felt *in front*. They are exposed like the face itself. Partly in virtue of their thinness and relative evenness of surface, partly in virtue of their relative verticality and frontal exposure, incisors have more clearly pronounced *sides* than molars: They have a distinguishable corporeally related front and back side.

Again, scientific, visually based anatomical descriptions corroborate the tactile–kinesthetic account.[22]

The tactile properties of incisors make incisors as different from molars as the tactile properties of cobblestone core tools make cobblestone core tools different from flake tools—and in precisely the same respects. The basic differential anatomy of hominid teeth is in fact analogous to the basic differential anatomy of early stone tools. The analogy is not at all strange since (as is generally held) the processing of food by stone tools replaced the processing of food by teeth.[23] That wear analyses can be made on both,[24] and that complementary data is obtained attests to the strength of the analogy.

To demonstrate the relationship more precisely, the analogy must be spelled out more closely. It is not presumed in what follows that each Oldowan cobblestone core and flake tool—the oldest stone tools discovered to date—is analogous to its respective dental type in every single respect. As with many empirical generalizations, there are exceptions, but the exceptions do not nullify the preponderant number of cases in which the generalization—and analogy—is sustained.

A cobblestone core tool is first of all a relatively thick piece of stone. That it is normally held against the palm and not between fingers and thumb is an objective measure of its thickness. As a result of flaking, it has at least one but most usually several protruding edges. The latter most commonly stand out in relief in the same way that the edges of molars stand out in relief; a relative jaggedness in respect to functional surface is typical of each. This description does not ignore the fact that through use, core tool and molar alike wear down and surface features change. The similarity in structural change through use over time in tool and tooth alike strengthens the analogy. Functionally caused changes are thus not adversely significant to the present analysis since originally molars and core tools were *not* flat and thus could not be experienced as flat. Moreover structural alteration over time in both was likely to be noticed directly in terms of a gradual alteration in corporeal powers, that is, as a *diminished* sense of transforming abilities.

A flake tool, like an incisor, is relatively thin. The way in which it is normally gripped—pinched between finger(s) and thumb like a razor blade[25]—is again a measure of its comparative girth. A flake has a single manually traceable edge. In contrast to a cobblestone core tool, it has more readily distinguishable sides as well as a single pronounced edge. It is a lengthier, more vertically aligned object than the more squat and thick cobblestone core tool. Its surfaces are relatively flat like an incisor rather than rounded and irregular like molars.

The analogy between teeth and the earliest known stone tools is based not only on the tactile character of each major hominid tooth form, but on the distinctive tactile character of portions of the dental arcade as well. In fact, the analogy between early stone tools and teeth becomes all the more striking when the tooth row is taken into account and the differential tactile character of the occlusal surface as a whole is lingually examined. Starting at the molars and passing frontward to the anterior teeth, one finds that thickness, groovedness, and a discontinuous array of edges give way to thinness, evenness, and a single edge. The lingual passage is in essence a passage from *unevenness* to *evenness*. In functional, scientific terms, a "continuous anterior cutting blade" replaces a slicing and grinding instrument.[26] The two descriptions—functional and tactile—are qualitatively and conceptually congruent.

The character of edges can be differentiated in a further respect. Edges either stand out in relief or they define contour. As illustrated by the above-described lingual passage across the posterior teeth, the molar row is uneven, even bumpy; edges are palpably discontinuous and stand out in relief. The functional edges of core tools are discontinuous in a similar manner, their cutting surface showing irregularities, their edges standing out prominently. In contrast, the functional edges of incisors and flake tools alike do not stand out in relief but are definitive of contour. They mark a termination of magnitude, and one that is smooth rather than jagged. Differential structure is of course directly related to differential transforming powers; form and functions are clearly associated.

While the differential transforming power of edges is directly evident in both Oldowan tools and the act of eating, a more fundamental character of edges is equally apparent. From the perspective of sheer power, all edges are the same, that is, *whatever has an edge has power*. Common present-day metaphoric uses of the word *edge* in English bear out this recognition. That early hominid tool-makers were similarly aware of the fundamental power of an edge lends credence to the notion that originally, at the very beginning, rather than forging a specific tool, early hominids took whatever came their way. They used whatever pieces resulted from flaking.[27] The critical character of a tool was not that it be of a certain shape but that it "have an edge."

Short of acknowledging a perceptual/conceptual awareness of an edge as a locus of power, stone tool-making is inexplicable. Why would a creature chip away at a stone? Why would it not simply continue to use a hammerstone—an *unretouched* stone as it is described in the literature—in the manner of present-day chimpanzees to crack nuts? What, in short, is being accomplished, or more precisely, what is being *made* by fracturing or flaking if not an edge?

The fashioning of sides as distinctive features in their own right, though directly related to the creation of edges, is a further development in stone tool-making. Where edges are many and discontinuous, as with discoids, spheroids, and polyhedrons (archaeological names for specific Oldowan tools), a distinctive spatial relationship between surfaces—as frontside to backside—is tenuous. Where edges are not created as surface properties of the object but a single all-over edge dominates, thereby giving the object a simple definitive shape like the later Acheulian handaxes, surfaces are more likely to be perceived as sides: the same edge that defines simple contour *ipso facto* defines sides. Hands are a paradigmatic instance of this relationship. (So also, of course, is that renowned topological object, the Moebius strip.)

Now where sides are not accidents—mere by-products in the creation of edges as in the case of core tools known as choppers or even some flake tools—but are created in their own right, the stone has been shaped by turning it over, the knapper working the edge first from what will ultimately be one face, then from the other, then from the first, and so on. Rather than jagged edges, "evenly trimmed sides" result.[28] The act of turning over was thus ultimately a decisive turning point in the history of stone tool-making. The three-dimensional act eventuated in a two-sided object: the Acheulian handaxe, which, like the human hand,[29] can be turned over to reveal two distinct sides. With this tool, not only are contour and edge synonymous as they are not synonymous with cobblestone core tools, but *sides* are a prominent feature. The visual character of the tool is likewise prominent. Its visible contour is literally *out-standing* as the visible contour of a cobblestone core tool with its many facets is not. Both visual prominence and sides are the result of creating a new kind of edge, one that is relatively straight, smooth, and bounds the entire stone. With this new contouring edge, the *entire* stone was fashioned into a tool.

The elaboration of contour by hominid tool-makers is an emphatically visual change. Contour in Acheulian handaxes, for example, can be followed visually as *linear form*. The shift toward rectilinearity adds a new dimension to the tactile–kinesthetic foundations of tool-making. Several clarifications are pertinent in this regard.

To begin with, in the act of making a tool or in trying to create a certain surface or edge, it is axiomatic that the person so engaged feels the edge or surface as he or she goes along in order to test it. The eyes do not make such a test. They cannot ascertain objectively and conclusively in such matters. Feeling the edge or surface is the common gnostic gesture of anyone attempting to create an even edge or a smooth surface. The same is of course true of sharpness, jaggedness, roundedness, and so on. Though ultimately visually discernible and appreciated features, they are fundamentally tactile phenomena and are tested as such. The technical term *retouch* is clearly informative in this regard. A stone *made* into a tool is transformed by touch. It is given a new tactile character.

Insofar as visual shape came to play an increasingly dominant role in the creation of tools, the aesthetics of tool-making as well as its standardization become significant dimensions in an understanding of *Homo faber*. The designations "Acheulian Arts" and "The First Artists,"[30] and the designation of a particular handaxe as a *Michaelangelo*,[31] give evidence of a substantial visual artistry that cannot be ignored. What are to be emphasized in this regard are the essentially *tactile* values of aesthetic vision. "Correct drawing, fine modelling, subtle light and shade" are not themselves arbiters of the aesthetic.[32]

As with computer vision, mere contrasts in lighting are not in and of themselves sufficiently informative of the object's form. Artistic vision —like stereognostic vision—rests upon tangible foundations: "Tactile values and movement . . . are the essential qualities." So affirms the renowned American art critic Bernard Berenson.[33]

To understand the passage from an essentially tactile–kinesthetic object to a tactile–kinesthetic–visual one is to understand the way in which an edge, while losing nothing of its essential character, comes to be seen as a line. Where vision and tactility are confused rather than understood—where line and edge are used synonymously or otherwise confounded—as in Thomas Wynn's Piagetian analysis of Oldowan and Acheulian stone tools[34]—modal differences and related concepts are compromised. Lines are visual translations of tactile contour. They are a semantic advance, that is, an advance in meaning. The Acheulian tool culture is not simply the result of more refined hand–eye coordinations, as is claimed by Milford Wolpoff, for example; it is the result of a sensory–kinetic advance in perceptual meanings, a transfer of sense in the double sense of that term.

A consideration of straight edges is additionally instructive in this regard. Straightness is a visual datum, not a tactile one. Tactility determines the evenness of an edge, not its straightness—as any few moments with a blindfold will attest. The term "straight edge" is a case of synaesthesia: vision appropriates what is originally a tactile datum and makes it its own. In the process, a new meaning is forged. Straight edges produce straight lines, just as both Euclidean constructions and projective sightings presuppose.

Viewing the evolution of tools from a sensory–kinetic perspective means understanding the way in which a hominid sensorium functions, the how of the functioning being an experiential not physiological matter. The answer to the question of how tool-making arose lies in an analysis of interlocking levels of tactile–kinesthetic data: the hardness of teeth; their resistance in impacting upon another object; their instrumental power to transform another object; undifferentiated power in terms of repetitive action (chewing); differentiated powers in terms of edges (even or uneven, definitive of contour or in relief). The analysis has thus clarified how the idea of making tools in the image of teeth first arose, and how simple utilitarian praxis preceded fabrication, that is, how using tools (hammerstones as well as teeth) preceded the making of tools. In short, it has shown how, on the basis of a primary datum, an obdurate hardness, both the concept of a tool and the concept of making a tool originated.

A final word may be added that casts the fundamental relationship between tools and tactility in broad evolutionary perspective, a postscript in the nature of delineating ultimate as well as proximate aspects of hominid evolution.[35] Nonhuman primate grooming is a social act between two individuals serving to promote group solidarity.[36] It involves a good deal of time *and is a preeminently tactile act*.[37] The sociality of early hominid primates according to many paleoanthropologists centered on food sharing and possibly on related practices such as cooperative hunting and maintaining a home base,[38] all of the practices being group rather than dyadic activities. From an evolutionary perspective, it is reasonable to postulate the following changes in the process of hominidization. Group subsistence activities replaced grooming as a socially cohesive force. In so doing, they created a tactile void. The tactile void was filled by dyadic sexual relations. Direct bodily touchings replaced the vital primate tactile values of grooming.

The changes in social behavior serving to maintain group solidarity suggest a possible adaptationist answer to the perplexing question of "the naked ape."[39] With the above sequence of changes in social behavior, fur would no longer be a positive adaptation. Furry individuals elicit more grooming and need more grooming than nonfurry ones. They are unable to devote as much time to communal subsistence. Moreover fur is an impediment to direct bodily touchings and thus to the realization of maximum skin-to-skin contacts and tactile pleasure. It is pertinent to note in this regard that no more than other nonhuman primates do chimpanzees, for example, *stroke* each other. Stroking is a peculiarly *human* act, a distinctively gratifying one whether, as in grooming, one is stroking (grooming) or being stroked (groomed). In broader mammalian evolutionary perspective, what was originally done by the tongue came to be done by the hand: stroking replaced licking (as well as picking) as a mode of grooming.[40] Loss of fur was thus an adaptation both to a newly developing social structure and to a newly developing sexuality. Expressed in classic adaptationist evolutionary terms, selection favored those creatures with less fur both because of the decreasing social value of fur and because of its increasingly negative sexual value. A dyadically based sexuality and group-based sociality thus replaced a group-based sexuality and dyadically based sociality. In the process, the centrality of the tactile–kinesthetic body to primate individual and social well-being was preserved. The essentially tactile nature of human sexuality[41] may in this way be ultimately connected to the beginnings of hominid stone tool-making and the changing lifestyle it heralded.

THE TOPOLOGICAL ANSWER

AN INITIAL CRITICAL EXAMINATION OF PIAGETIAN TOPOLOGY

When stone tools speak for themselves as instruments that are *made*, they speak empirically and unequivocally of edges—of transformations by flakings—and indirectly of order. They speak a topological language, one in fact basic to the topology defined and investigated by Piaget and others following him.[42] The two topologies lead ultimately to two different assessments of early hominid intelligence. This is because the more elemental one is not derived from developmental organizational abilities (as Piagetian theory holds) but is implicit in corporeal life, thus implicit in sensory–kinetic acts such as making a tool. To show this will require an extended critical examination of Piaget's theories and experimental studies at several stages in the analysis. The end purpose is not to criticize Piaget per se, but to show how, through an uncritical appropriation and application of his topology, present-day archaeological and anthropological analyses of early hominid stone tool-making—and their related inferences concerning intelligence—are vitiated. The first step will be to show briefly how Piaget's topology is skewed toward metric geometries.

As a qualitative form of mathematics,[43] topology is misunderstood when put to quantitative test in the manner of Piaget's experimental studies of shape-recognition, linear order, and infinite divisibility. To consider the notion of a line, for example, as reducible to a series of infinite points in the name of topology (and absolute mathematical truth)[44] is misguided. Lines are topical in topology only insofar as they define regional spaces, hence Henri Poincaré's statement concerning topological propositions: "They would remain true if the figures were copied by an inexpert draftsman who should grossly change all the proportions and replace the straight lines by lines more or less sinuous."[45] In general, if what is being investigated are squares and rhomboids—as in Piaget's experimental studies—rather than bagels and pretzels, for example, or deflated and inflated basketballs, the research is not basically topological but Euclidean to begin with. Indeed, Piaget's investigation of what he identifies as basic topological concepts—proximity, separation, order, enclosure, and continuity—takes place from the viewpoint of an established Euclidean geometry: the concepts describe "pre-euclidean relationships."[46]

Piaget's estimation and conception of topological geometry as primitive and figure-bound in contrast to the comprehensive and

operational mathematical systems exemplified by Euclidean and projective geometries are perhaps at the root of his biased experimental
studies on behalf of topology. As he himself points out, "It is impossible for relationships of this type [of proximity, separation, order, enclosure, and continuity] to lead to comprehensive systems linking different figures together by means of perspective or axial co-ordinates,
and for this reason they are bound to remain psychologically primitive." [47] In a word, topology is at the nether end of the mathematical
stick because it literally and in turn metaphorically does not measure up. Even in his study of knots, Piaget investigates not so much
a topological object as "topological properties" (proximities, separations, etc.) of an essentially *linear form*—a one-dimensional object,
hence a Euclidean one. [48] It is precisely the static visual transformations of this linear form that his young subjects cannot fathom. (Piaget
has the young children visually inspect different knots fastened to a
piece of cardboard or lying on a table, or even has them attempt to
follow the knots' respective strings with the fingers.) Given the three
modes of transformation proper to topology (bending, stretching, and
twisting), it is perhaps not surprising that even those children who
know how to tie a simple knot have topological difficulties. Tying a
knot is a three-dimensional act involving bending, mock stretching
(pulling), and minimal twisting. Visual inspections and finger tracings
involve none of these actions. In this respect Poincaré's estimation of
the significance of three-dimensionality in topology is relevant: "Of
all the theorems of analysis situs [the name by which topology was
first known], the most important is that which we express by saying
that space has three dimensions." [49]

In brief, it is Piaget's approach itself, and not necessarily topological concepts at all, that presents *topological* difficulties for the children.
The point is further illustrated by the fact that, as Piaget describes it,
although children of three and four years of age "have a clear idea
of three dimensions," they have difficulty in tying a simple knot, and
even after mastering the task, they cannot appreciate the homeomorphic properties of various knots they are shown. [50] The difficulty is
attributed to their inability to pass from a one-dimensional system to
a three-dimensional one. In Piaget's own words, "It is not the three
dimensions as such which constitute the main obstacle . . . but the
transition from one dimension to another, within one and the same object." [51] If this is so, then what needs pointing out among other things
is that the transition demanded is not from the *known* to the *unknown*,
but from the *unknown* to the *known*—a difficult feat even for adults.

Recognition of this difficulty together with the validity of Poincaré's statement regarding the importance of three-dimensionality leads to the conclusion that a proper investigation of topology would start with the child's own "clear idea of three dimensions" (Where does it come from? How is it expressed?), and pass from there to a child's understanding of one-dimensional systems. Not only might actual bodily bending, stretching, and twisting be the only proper actions for assaying topological understandings in young children, but the most suitable testing materials outside of children's own bodies might be devised by keeping in mind the nickname given topology: rubber-sheet geometry. Moreover with respect to Piaget's experimental use of drawings, Poincaré's first-quoted statement is eminently suggestive in a further respect as to what might constitute both proper testing procedures and a proper evaluation of topological concepts in children. In sum, while metric relations are clearly those of interest to Piaget and best fit his conception of a logico-mathematical intelligence, and while his need to determine the origin of these relations can be appreciated in light of his ontogenetical program of study, Piaget does not properly investigate topological thought thoroughly or on its own ground.

Geometries are, by mathematicians' own evaluations, humanly made ways of spatially construing the world.[52] That there are alternative construals should already be instructive as concerns any axiological systematization that accords one form poor-cousin status in relation to others. Geometrical relativism and axiological equivalence notwithstanding, however, one absolute topology is possible: that qualitative one emanating from corporeal praxis with its entailed tactile–kinesthetic invariants, as lips enclosing a nipple, for example. Like the enclosive act of grasping with the hand, sucking is a topologically pregnant act. The most elemental topological language is indeed, and not surprisingly, a corporeal language. Given this fact, what must be examined first is how topology in both a Piagetian sense, that is, as represented by the concepts of enclosure, proximity, separation, and so on, and in a practicing topologist's sense, that is, as represented by the concept of qualitative invariance, is rooted in the body. Consequent to this examination, it will be possible to spell out the relationship of topology to stone tool-making in depth and with precision.

TOPOLOGICAL GEOMETRY AND CORPOREAL LIFE

In the sense of corporeal genesis, topology is indeed more primitive—more fundamental, not ruder or simpler—than Euclidean and projective geometries which operate at a visual remove from the body. The earlier development of notions identified by Piaget as topological actually accords well with experimental data showing the course of human sensory development to begin in tactility and end in vision.[53] The sensory progression does not of course support the notion that topological concepts are less sophisticated than those of other geometries but indicates only that topology might be less interesting and tractable vis-à-vis metrically oriented, visually anchored logico-mathematical theories of intelligence. Hence if distinctions are to be made in conceptual levels, it is first of all more apt (and more directly justifiable by querying mathematicians and letting them speak for themselves) to designate the mathematician's topological concepts *post*-concepts than the young infant's or child's topological concepts *pre*-concepts.[54]

The issue is not merely a semantic one. It is a far-reaching conceptual and theoretical one. What is granted to nonhuman primates and to human infants and children in the way of conceptual knowledge vouchsafes in a privileged way certain conceptual knowledge to human adults. Certainly an average human adult's topological knowledge is not on par with a topologist's. So far as proximity, separation, and the like are concerned, for example, the lay adult has no more than elementary notions learned in the course of infancy and childhood, beginning perhaps as far back as the initial act of nursing—or perhaps even earlier in the birth act itself—an occasion not commonly remembered but not on that account unexperienced. Clearly the concepts of proximity and separation are not originally mathematical ones but corporeal ones, a fact that Piaget overlooks completely even though describing the behavior of the nursling at length. The same is true of all concepts that Piaget invokes in the name of topology. Insofar as their origin lies in everyday corporeal experience, they are all part of a gnostic tactility and kinesthesia. The concept of enclosure, for instance, is elaborated, or generalized, by any normally developing infant and child who knows what it is to put or to have food (or any material substance) *in* its mouth; what it is to have a doubly open-ended body out of which materials *inside* pass *outside*; what it is to hurt on the *inside* (a stomachache) as opposed to the *outside* (a scraped knee); what it is to grasp something by enclosing it *within* the hand; and so on. Acknowledgment of these fundamental corporeal awarenesses of insides and outsides explains not only why a child's earliest prepositional understandings are of *in*, but why chimpanzees seem to have a similar behavioral preference for *insides* over topsides and undersides.[55] The motive powers of the felt body and the sensitivities that go with them need both recognition and examination.

In this context, it is apposite to recall the eighteenth-century origin of topology itself in the posing and solution of the Koenigsburg bridges problem, *viz*, Is it possible to cross each of the seven bridges in Koenigsburg in turn without recrossing any one of them? The problem is a spatio-kinetic problem. Indeed, it would not be amiss to speak of it as a choreographic problem insofar as, at its most pedestrian level, it involves moving bodies about in an exploratory way to the end that a certain form is realized within certain freedoms and constraints upon the spatiality of movement. The answer, like the question, has its origin in the tactile–kinesthetic possibilities of hominid experience, that is, in that original spontaneity of movement that gives rise to species-specific *I can*'s: walking, tracing, traversing, crossing and recrossing.

To speak of the tactile–kinetic character of topology in contrast to the visual character of Euclidean and projective geometries is not to say that the latter are exclusively visual and the former exclusively tactile–kinetic. Measuring, after all, is a tactile–kinetic act; assessing the traversability of a graph is a visual as well as tactile–kinetic undertaking, all the more so when translated into a symbolic notation. It is rather to call attention to the *predominant* sensory world in which the geometries originate. It can be shown, for example, that the reason young children do not easily master concepts pertinent to a projective geometry[56] is that the tactile–kinesthetic body is not a body for which any perspective exists. Whatever is corporeally felt—whether one's back in scratching it, one's leg in kicking it, or either part in repose—it is not felt from a particular point of view. While it has a definite spatial location, it is not at a certain *distance* from any *source* of awareness. Thus it is not surprising that Piaget finds *viewpoints* "difficult to come by": "The discovery that he [a child generally, up to seven years of age] has a particular viewpoint, even the child's becoming aware that he occupies one momentarily, is far more difficult to come by than might at first be supposed."[57] Projective geometry—as Piaget's experimental anchorage in "sightings" and "taking aim" clearly shows—is a visually oriented geometry.

Perhaps because of topology's origin in tactile–kinesthetic experience, concepts basic to topological thought appear to be modeled on the body and indeed to bear a striking similarity to basic corporeal concepts. Not only is a hominid body a richly movable body and therefore suggestive of a dynamic and malleable rather than static and rigid geometry, it has, in a combinatory sense, an unmatched range and subtlety of movement in precisely those three modes of transformation central to topology. Moreover, it is a body that remains "the same." Its sameness is coincident with the elemental topological principle of qualitative permanence through change. The principle in fact may be shown to be rooted in an awareness of basic bodily relationships and an awareness of self-identity over time, in other words, to be a corporeal concept. Just such a relationship between topological permanence and corporeal life was pointed out briefly by a mathematical physicist.[58] The connection is indeed remarkable and warrants precise clarification. It is the conceptual basis upon which any viable association between topology and early hominid stone tool-making necessarily and ultimately rests.

The topological concept of permanence across change entails a qualitative concept of conservation. There are two ways in which qualitative conservation is conceptually rooted in corporeal life: ontologically and structurally. Each is evident in an active and a passive sense. First, topological deformations do not violate the integrity of a person. No matter what is done in the way of active bendings, twistings, or stretchings, the individual remains the same individual; self-identity is not compromised. Second, even in passively undergone growth and aging, a human individual is not changed into another kind of creature, as a tadpole is changed into a frog or a caterpillar into a butterfly. Again, self-identity is sustained. The two kinds of corporeal changes describe a qualitative homeomorphism: the changes are lived-through transformations in which ontological identity is conserved.

In addition to ontological conservation, basic structural relationships are conserved. In crouching, for instance, shoulders and hips retain their topological positions relative to one another. In growing —topologically a form of stretching—corporeal relationships are similarly invariant. The concepts of proximity and separation are clearly rooted and elaborated in just such basic "facts" of hominid life. Whatever the behavior, action, movement, position, or stage of growth, the relationship of body parts is topologically invariant. What are proximal—a hand and wrist, for instance—and what are separated —a head and knee, for instance—remain so regardless of kinetic or passive maturational transformations.

Qualitative conservation is not reflectively *deduced* from experience (nor is it necessarily represented or articulated in any way of course). Whether structural or ontological in nature, it is a directly experienced and experienceable fact of corporeal life. What is to be shown in terms of hominid stone tool-making is how an analogous awareness of qualitative invariance across change—an awareness of qualitative conservation—informs the process of transforming a stone into a tool. Only by way of this analogous awareness can a basic relationship of topology to early hominid stone tool-making be sustained. To spell out the relationship is first of all to acknowledge the history of stone tool-making in the differentiated actions of *fracturing* and *flaking*, both of them common but undifferentiated archaeological descriptive terms.

TOPOLOGY AND EARLY STONE TOOL-MAKING

The acts of fracturing and of flaking produce qualitative change. They are both irreversible acts that transform an original object in an irreversible way. The concept of fracturing is implicit in the *use* of a hammerstone; that of flaking in the *making* of a chopper or handaxe. In line with their intuitive and linguistic differentiation, the implicit distinction between fracturing and flaking should be made explicit at this point. Flaking has its genesis in the earlier, simpler notion of fracturing and is a further refinement of it. Its aim is not simply to break something open or into pieces. As common usage suggests, it is a less haphazard activity and has more complex intentional overtones. Flaking means creating either edges in the form of multiple surface properties, or an edge in the form of a single contour. Fracturing and flaking are thus to be differentially understood in the sense of *using* a tool and *making* a tool. So distinguished, they can be understood in Cushing's terms: in the dual corporeal possibilities of *using the hands* and *devising with the hands*.

The two manual modes are not wholly separate realms of action. Using the hands is the basis for devising with them precisely in the sense that original kinesthetic abilities—chewing, walking, and the like—or in the case of hands, gripping, squeezing, pounding, striking, and so on—give rise to a domain of fundamental corporeal powers and ultimately to related fundamental corporeal concepts. It is these concepts that are the spawning ground of any and all devisings with the hands. The historical relationship of fracturing to flaking in the evolution of stone tool-using/tool-making is an example of this conceptual elaboration. Cushing acknowledges just such a corporeal relationship when he writes of "fossil concepts," of the fact that the actions of the hands and their ways of working—the striking of a nut with a hammerstone, for instance—"survive as impulses within them."[59] At the same time, however, devising clearly outstrips using, precisely as flaking outstrips fracturing. It does so by the cultivation of edges. Something that has no bite is transformed into something that has by giving it an edge. Modeled in the image of teeth, edges were the means whereby stones were transformed into tools. All creative activity and created attributes of a stone tool were in the service of its edges.

The implication of the conceptual priority of edges is that whatever geometric concepts can be said to be engendered in the manual act of making a tool, they originated in the awareness of teeth as tools. This means that if early hominids aimed at proximity or separation in their flakings, as Thomas Wynn claims,[60] it was because a particular proximity or separation of flakings was in the service of a particular edge. The concept of the particular edge determined the proximity and separation of impacts of stone on stone *and not the reverse*. Thus, if the stone knapper "[placed] successive flake removals in the same general area—that is, nearby one another," in making the *polyhedron*,[61] it was because the concept of *molar* edges dictated a discontinuous pattern of flakings; if the stone knapper "[placed] two flake removals, one right next to the other" in the creation of the *simple chopper*,[62] it was because the concept of an *incisor* edge dictated such coincident flakings; if the stone knapper "[placed] each successive flake removal . . . in relation to all of the preceding flake removals . . . by maintaining a constant direction of movement along the surface of the artifact,"[63] it was because the *scraper* was made in the image of a continuous blade, that is, in the image of the *anterior tooth row*, which indeed serves as a *scraping* instrument. The "spatial placement of elements" of which Wynn speaks over and over again was not a function of "topological concepts"—of the proximity, separation, and order of flake removals—but a function of an awareness of *edges* as entities having distinctive spatial attributes. In short, *proximate, separate,* or *ordered* flakings were the result of dontic concepts. To summarize the process of stone tool-making with the statement that "chipped stone artefacts are manufactured by organising the actions of flake removal,"[64] is to overlook completely the fundamental conceptual priority of edges and the tactile–kinesthetic sensorium from which it derives.

The progression from discoids to choppers to ever more refined cutting instruments is testimonial to the matrix idea of an edge cut in the image of teeth. How and where the hands came to devise was dictated by this matrix idea. There is in fact no way to explain the conceptual–historical progression from "using the hands" to "devising with hands," or from Oldowan choppers to the later Acheulian handaxes, by way of proximities, separations, and orderings. Moreover though originally corporeal concepts and though clearly entailed in the making of stone tools, proximity, separation, and order were not—now in this tool, now in that one—the controlling "geometric" principle. A more fundamental geometric concept was operative, an all-pervasive principle, which, in the passage from fracturing to flaking, and in the elaboration of flaking itself, lost none of its controlling power. This guiding concept was qualitative conservation.

Qualitative conservation was essential to the creation of edges— *functional* edges. In the creative labor of transforming a stone into a tool—in devising edges—hardness, resistance, and the latent transforming powers of the stone were conserved. Their conservation is what separated a usable tool from an unusable stone fragment. Whatever else an early hominid might have considered *débitage*—whether the same or different from present-day estimations[65]—it was precisely fragments esteemed to be lacking qualities essential to a tool. A shard too small to grasp effectively no longer had transformational powers; lithic material that crumbled would offer insufficient resistance or none at all. Archaeologist Nicholas Toth implies the reality of such judicative awarenesses when he argues that many stylistic norms associated with Oldowan tools were in fact "by-products of flake production."[66] To pick out functional by-products from nonfunctional ones in the course of flaking is to judge materials according to certain qualities that distinguish them as usable. These qualities could only be those mentioned above, that is, qualities having to do with the efficacy of a cutting edge. Moreover the idea that ancestral hominids "test[ed] out raw materials" in order to transport "the best pieces"[67] further validates a judicative awareness of qualitative conservation and its significance with respect to fracturing and flaking. Improvement in the creation of edges—evolution toward both more sophisticated and standardized tools—is further evidence of an ability to judge and insure qualitative conservation across transformations.

The second point to be made in support of the guiding concept of qualitative conservation turns on the fact that stone tools were *created*, and as such unequivocally reflect a creative intelligence at work.

Early hominid stone tool-making takes on a quite particular cast when viewed from the perspective of a creative intelligence. Making things —a boat, a piece of sculpture, or a cutting edge—means generally conserving the qualitative integrity of the materials being worked. Hence to understand the creative intelligence capable of devising stone tools is to understand an intelligence anchored in qualitative awarenesses —both structural and functional. Just as the efficacy of teeth as tools is proportional to the qualitative conservation of their hardness, resistance, and transforming powers, so the conservation of these same qualities is integral to the making of usable stone tools. In fact, the same question can be asked of their conservation as Piaget repeatedly asks of *quantitatively* conserved elements: is x the same before and after the transformation y? In the case of a resulting usable tool, the answer could only have been an unequivocal "yes."

The point in fact demands a broader look at the propriety of extrapolating Piaget's experimental studies and their theoretical underpinnings uncritically to early hominid stone tool-making. Not only were stone tools not ready-mades, in the beginning they were not objects that were copied. Spatial, that is, "topological," concepts pertinent to their manufacture must be understood in this context. More specifically, the application of Piaget's experimental research on the development of spatial concepts in children is not warranted because it does not properly investigate, nor does his gathered data properly substantiate, a *creative* intelligence. Piaget's declared aim, after all, is to chart stages of a *logico-mathematical* intelligence.[68] The two kinds are not the same.[69] A child's action in stringing beads or piling laundry items, for example[70]—actions investigated on behalf of the "topological" concept of *linear order*—is aimed at arranging or rearranging objects in accordance with a given model, not at creating an object itself. Early *Homo faber* was, *inter alia*, neither a model-copier nor a subject surrounded by already existing cultural items awaiting manipulation. Early hominid lithic industry was geared neither to play objects, to quantitative determinations, nor to mutable actions on an array of discrete objects with attention to their relative order. With respect to the latter, when making a tool, order once created was precisely *immutable*. Flaked edges and surfaces were *not* interchangeable like beads on a string or items in a pile of laundry.

The significance of this latter difference will become apparent presently in terms of another central Piagetian concept, the concept of irreversibility. For now, the remaining point to be emphasized concerns the fact that early stone tool-making testifies not simply to a decidedly *creative* intelligence at work, but to a comparatively *adult* creative maturity as well. While it is commonly remarked that early hominids are not little children, the reverse remark and its implications are not equally acknowledged. Yet clearly, little children are not early hominids. They are not out foraging for themselves every day, running from predators, defending young, and so on. They are not self-reliant, self-sustaining, mobile creatures, loose in a dog-eat-dog world. A small child hammering away at one block with another is in this sense not akin to an early hominid hammering away at another stone—much less at a nut in order to get something to eat. While the two behaviors might ostensibly be esteemed similarly "organized" by Piagetian scholars, their "contexts of utterance," to borrow a concept from linguistic philosophers, are consummately different. There is furthermore nothing within the small child's activities comparable to *making* a stone tool to begin with, that is, to creating a functional instrument where none existed before, and to using it for its very survival. Insofar as small children and early hominids lead radically different lives, there is every danger of omitting central aspects of the latter's intelligence by using the former's culturally groomed intelligence as a measuring rod.

In sum, the motivation of an early hominid in making a stone tool together with the latter's actual creation and use—its *total* context of utterance—is sufficient ground for questioning the notion that early hominid *intelligence* vis-à-vis stone tool-making is the same or even similar to the developing *logico-mathematical intelligence* of little twentieth-century human children. Perhaps most appropriate in this regard would be a study of intelligence in non-Western cultures to determine whether concepts and meanings other than those defined by a Piagetian logico-mathematical intelligence, particularly concepts and meanings related to characteristics identified in studies of *creative* intelligence,[71] are in evidence. (The most apt cultures to study might be those very hunter–gatherer societies to which comparison is consistently made in paleoanthropological reconstructions.) Until such alternative experimental studies are undertaken and other kinds of human intelligence examined with a comparative eye to Piaget's stage-development theory of intelligence, it would seem appropriate to temper judgment concerning the fit between Piagetian studies of intelligence and early hominid intelligence.

The centrality of the topological concept of qualitative conservation together with the recognition of a preeminently creative intelligence at work provide warrant for the analogical generalization that qualitative conservation is to creative intelligence as quantitative conservation is to logico-mathematical intelligence. The analogy might be considered a rule of thumb for assaying the lithic work of *Homo faber*, not that the two kinds of intelligence might never overlap but that a recognition of each in its own right is critical to a just assessment.[72]

A SUMMATION VIA THE CONCEPT OF ORDER

Now the legitimate question that has not been confronted in the foregoing analyses is how either a corporeal or a Piagetian topology is related to that of actually practicing topologists. When several were queried about the relationship of their work to Piagetian pre-concepts —proximity, separation, and the like—their response was unanimous: Piaget's topological investigations were deemed trivial. As one of them put it, "The [pre-]concepts have not really anything to do with my work."[73] When queried as to whether there was anything topological about stone tool-making, one topologist suggested several answers: stone flaking is a subject more proper to differential geometry than to topology insofar as the former treats hard objects; flaking does not violate the topological integrity of the stone since, for example, no hole has been cut into it; flaking simply produces two stones which are topologically homeomorphic; flaking can be understood topologically only by transposing the stone into rubber or clay. While it might not be altogether impossible to follow up each answer[74] and thereby possibly substantiate a relationship between topology—or some form of mathematics—and stone tool-making, any answer to the question seems to point in the same direction. Not only is there no topologist's topology in the order, proximity, or separation of flakings on a stone, there is no topological connection between the matrix idea of edges in stone tool-making and the topologist's consideration of edges. A topologist's concern with edges is indeed eons away from transformations having to do with functional edges. To put the matter in reverse, if queried about the traversability of a graph, the relevancy of the notion of sheer boundedness, or the topicality of Euler's theorem, an early hominid stone tool-maker would undoubtedly answer in the manner of the topologist: "The concepts have not really anything to do with my work."

The mutually expressed exclusivity of interests notwithstanding, a mutual concern with nonmetric properties is evident. Moreover the concept of qualitative conservation cannot be brushed aside with respect to stone tool-making nor can the matrix concept of an edge. Accordingly, the conclusion to be drawn from the investigation is not that there is *no* relationship between topology and early stone tool-making but that early hominid tool-makers were not *doing* topology or any other form of geometry—any more, it might be suggested, than bees and beavers are doing geometry in the course of their not un-impressive geometrically ordered constructions. The statement that "topological patterns are internal to stone artifacts" and that "the patterns resulted from some kind of intention,"[75] for example, can be interpreted in such a way as to lead to the erroneous conclusion that the stone artificer willfully put them there, that is, that *Homo faber* was *doing* topology. On the contrary, whatever topological patterns are there "internal to the artifact," are there by way of the body. In other words, ancestral stone tool-makers' concerns were topological only insofar as their working concepts share a certain sensory–kinetic origin with topology. The concepts of edges, of transformation, of invariance across transformations, and of qualitative conservation are in both instances grounded in the tactile–kinesthetic body.

Beyond this common grounding, like any concepts, topological concepts have a certain domain of intelligibility, that is, a variable range of possible applications. Yet however great the temptation to impute geometric practices to ancestral hominids on the basis of their conceptual applicability to tool-making, the more conservative interpretation would appear the wisest—and the best.[76] What early hominids were doing in making stone tools was creating edges. Their thinking was practical, not geometric as such. Whatever concepts came to the fore in the course of that reasoned labor that are similar today to geometric concepts in the name of a certain domain of intelligibility, they were present first of all in virtue of a certain gnostic tactility and kinesthesia. That gnostic system provided the basis for creative thinking—for "devising with the hands."

In short, the thinking that made possible the devising of stone tools *where none existed before* attests above all to a creative intelligence at work rather than to the presence of a practicing neophyte geometer —of whatever persuasion. The difference between interpreting stone tool-making in terms of doing topology (or any other kind of geometry) and of identifying and tracing out conceptual origins is an important distinction to make. The final consideration of this section, the concept of *order*, will illustrate the point.

The elaboration of edges in the history of stone tool-making is necessarily rooted in two corporeal concepts of order: causal order and sequential order. Since according to Piaget, "the notion of order cannot possibly be found in experience,"[77] the corporeal concepts are nowhere treated in his research. Piaget's non-experiential concept of order is tied to his epistemological distinction between knowledge rooted in action and knowledge rooted in objects: mathematical and physical knowledge respectively.[78] To this epistemological dichotomy should be added the related one Piaget makes between coordinated and individual actions. Only the former are esteemed conceptually potent; only they involve reflective abstraction. "Individual actions such as throwing, pushing, touching, rubbing" are aligned with *simple* abstraction, that is, with *mere* physical knowledge.[79] Neither coordinated nor individual action, it should be noted, is recognized as engendering a gnostic tactility or kinesthesia.

Piaget's first epistemological dichotomy is well illustrated in Thomas Wynn's discussion of *order* as a topological concept in the construction of a simple chopper. Wynn states that "the simplest kind of order is the 'pair,' one element placed immediately next to another."[80] He concludes his analysis by saying that while "it is quite possible that Oldowan knappers employed *a concept of ordered placement* in the manufacture of choppers . . . they need not have done so . . . and we cannot assume *a more complex coordination* than that of pairs" (italics added).[81]

Pairing is, in Wynn's analysis, a coordination at the level of physical knowledge. A conceptual muddle arises in the analysis, however, because the concept of order, and consequently of pairing, is taken for granted. As with all Piagetian spatial concepts, its *origin* is nowhere examined. In consequence, order—like other Piagetian spatial concepts —is at the same time conceived as the *source,* the *equivalent,* and the *result* of certain "co-ordinated actions." Wynn writes in one place that "the spatial concepts *required* to fracture stone can be relatively simple . . . or quite complex." He says at another point, "Such schemes [more complex actions resulting in a more complex end-product] *are* rudimentary spatial concepts." At a third place he states, "It is the placing of each flake removal that *reflects* spatial concepts" (italics added).[82]

Conceptual muddles aside, in such an analysis individual actions on the part of the stone knapper are not given their due. The oversight is critical in view of the fact that for there to have been an evolution of stone tool-making, an individual action must have been epistemologically significant from time to time, and not merely one in a series of coordinated actions, however simple or complex. Certainly to forge an effective if rudimentary biface, for example, the knapper would have had to have been aware of the qualitative character of each blow and its effect.[83] His attention in such instances would have had to have been directed toward a single action and its result rather than toward "a whole system of operations."[84] A knapper might even have tried out different kinds of flakings one by one and studied the result in each case. Precisely because stone tool-making was a creative enterprise and not a logico-mathematical sequence of operations, individual actions would have had to have counted for something in just this exploratory way. Insights would otherwise not have been had into improved modes of working and stone tool-making would never have become standardized. Even with standardization, its fundamental creative and explorative character were hardly lost.

There is an alternative interpretation of order that pays closer attention to just such aspects of the working body—*le corps engagé*—and to entailed modes of conceptual awareness.[85] With respect to flaking actions, there is first the conceptual awareness that *"if* I do *this* [e.g., a "random bash"[86] or a simple flaking], *then this* edge results"; or, *"if* I do *this, and then this, then this* edge results" (e.g., a simple chopper results). Corporeal concepts of just such *if/then* relationships were seminal to the evolution of stone tool-making. They were a causal dimension within an early hominid's global domain of *I can's*. Precisely *corporeal* concepts of causality allowed the possibility of an early hominid's random bashings, or proximate flakings, or paired flakings, or separated flakings on a piece of stone. In other words, whatever the spatial *placement* of flakings—the key concept in a Piagetian account—their actual creation was necessarily anchored in the corporeal concept of a particular if/then relationship.

Whether a tool was fashioned by trial and error or by (in Piagetian terms) "an operational intelligence," it would in either case have involved the corporeal concept of causal order. The fact that a tool was made by trial and error does not nullify the intention to *make* the tool. Insofar as *Homo faber* knew what he could do, or discovered what he could do in the course of doing it, he was at the same time aware of the results of his actions. In effect, the distinction to be drawn is not between tools made by trial-and-error and tools made by premeditated actions—the criterion for which is incidentally difficult if not impossible to specify—but between the complex of if-this/then-this relationships obtaining with respect to different kinds of tools. At the most rudimentary level, this means distinguishing between a generalized intentionality to make a tool—"If I bash the stone, then *an* edge will result"—and a more focused intentionality—"If I flake the stone thus, then *this* edge will result." The diversity, cultivation, and refinement of stone tools across time attests to an evolving awareness of more and more intricate causal relationships. The perfecting of simple flaking techniques at the earliest stages of stone knapping is a striking case in point. As Toth has pointed out, "Modern beginning knappers usually do not exhibit this ability [finding the proper angles on cores, striking the core with the proper amount of force and at the proper point of percussion] until they have several hours of flaking practice."[87] Clearly a range of if-this/then-this awarenesses develops in the course of *individual* acts of striking one stone with another.

If more and more refined tools appear in the evolutionary history of hominid stone tool-making, then direction, intensity, and placement were each a complex causal variable that came under intentional control in individual flaking actions. Wynn's statement that "Oldowan tools were the result of intention and intention implies the projection of action into the future,"[88] can thus be understood in two ways: in terms of a functional understanding of intentionality—the tool's use vis-à-vis what Wynn calls "an internally represented task"—and in terms of the *creation* of the tool, or the intentional labor of *Homo faber* him/herself in the act of transforming the stone into a tool. In fact, without this latter understanding of intentionality and consequent acknowledgment of the tactile–kinesthetic body, there is a conceptual hiatus between the action of the stone knapper and his/her "mental operations." As pointed out earlier, there is confusion as to whether Piagetian topological concepts are equivalent to, discovered, or embodied in the act of flaking. If the latter is the case—as Piagetian theory would undoubtedly want to hold in spite of the confusion—it is impossible to explain how the creation of order (pairing, proximity, or separation) could possibly be an intentional act. For it to be so, the concept would have to have been already *discovered*. The discovery is precisely a tactile–kinesthetic event: if I do thus and so, a certain order (pairing, proximity, or separation) results. In sum, there is no way the concept of order or any other Piagetian topological concept can work its way up to being a "mental operation" short of originating in a gnostic tactility and kinesthesia.

What is clear, then, is that tactile–kinesthetic experiences of ancestral stone tool-makers were, in the most basic sense, causally oriented. At the most fundamental level, there was an on-going, built-in structure of if/then relationships between perception and the tactile–kinesthetic body—precisely as Husserl's original investigations unequivocally show there to be.[89] To speak of hominid stone tool-making in terms of "coordinated actions" and omit reference to these bodily awarenesses is to ignore the necessity of corporeal concepts to the "mental operations" and reflective acts involved in stone tool-making.

In addition to engendering a concept of causal order, hominid stone tool-making necessarily came to engender a concept of sequential order: *first this* flake, *then this* flake; or *now this* flake, *now this* flake. A temporal as well as spatial dimension of order was integral to the evolution of stone tool-making. *Contra* Piaget's suggestion, ordinal sequencing is not a matter of "ordinatory activity" nor of neurophysiological functions; one need appeal neither to a "vitalistic" mechanism nor to reductionism.[90] An awareness of ordinal sequencing, like an awareness of causal order, arises from tactile–kinesthetic experience.[91] Within certain global behaviors, one movement brings forth a particular result that either precedes or follows another. Each movement is thus one in a temporal sequence, as in the binary experiences of walking, running, and breathing. As with an awareness of causal order, the stone knapper's awareness of temporal order put him less and less at the mercy of irreversibility and more and more in control of edges. Wynn's descriptive term "random bashings" is instructive in this regard. A sequentially imposed order is a conceptual step above a randomly imposed order—at least in the pre-quantum world of the early hominids.

In its most basic mathematical sense, order has to do with sequencing things in relation to a particular matrix: size, for example. But the idea of sequencing *tout court* is more primitive. It originates in bodily protentions and retentions, as Husserl would describe them[92]— in expectations and recollections of one thing following another, including at times a sense of their regularity. Thus a sense of invariant sequencings might arise, as lightning/*then* thunder, night/*then* day— or to bring the point directly home in corporeal terms—of one leg/ *then* the other, inhaling/*then* exhaling, chewing/*then* swallowing, and so on.

An awareness of sequential order in the form of corporeal regularities was the key to an awareness of the *irreversibility of action.* Just as an early hominid could not reverse the acts of chewing and swallowing, for example, so he or she could not go back to a previous time in which the flaked stone being worked was not so flaked. What was done could not be undone. The fact that once an action such as fracturing or flaking is carried out, it cannot be un–carried out, is a homely truth present-day hominids may take for granted, but one that earlier hominids must have literally hit upon in the process of working stone. The concept is a critical one. The much-used Piagetian notion of *pre-correcting errors*[93]—of mentally reversible operations—is parasitic on the concept of *irreversibility*. Like its conceptual predecessor, the concept of pre-correcting errors is a *temporal* concept.

The overall problem of interpreting order in stone tool-making in accordance with Piagetian topological theory is that it bypasses just such conceptual meanings originating in the experiencing and experienced tactile–kinesthetic body. The concept of order as "proximities . . . ordered by a constant direction of movement"[94] is a severely limited if not questionable concept with respect to stone tool-making. Even at a superficial level, it overlooks the ordering difference between the sequential *deconstruction* of a single three-dimensional mass, and the linear or circular *arrangement* (order) of an array of discrete items —clothes in a pile of laundry, beads along a string—as in Piaget's studies. For linear arrangement to be a proper conceptual standard for evaluating three-dimensional sequential deconstruction, certain items in the pile of laundry or certain beads along the string would have to be progressively *removed*. In this regard a further distinction is significant. Actions directed upon laundry items and beads are reversible because the objects can be—and are—picked up, exchanged, transposed, and so on—thus arranged and rearranged. There are no objects or actions comparable to these in stone tool-making. Flakings (considered as areas on a stone from which pieces have been removed) are not discrete manipulable objects but properties of an object. The properties are immutable. The flakings are not transposable, exchangeable, and so on; they are not reversible. While the *placing* of beads on a string or the *placing* of laundry items in a pile might on linguistic grounds seem the same as the "*placing* of elements" in stone tool-making, the two kinds of activity are demonstrably different in intention, action, and conceptual structure. Shaping a whole and lining up parts—"organizing physical phenomena" (to use Wynn's terms)[95] and creatively transforming them—are not the same.

In sum, the Piagetian topological concept of order is an improper standard for assaying order in ancestral hominid stone tool-making. The ruling concept in the creation of stone tools was that of an edge. Placement of flakings, both individually and with respect to one another, was determined with respect to that corporeal concept. Thus if actions such as "placings" engender a concept of order (pairing, proximity, or separation), it is because originally they entail not a burgeoning mathematical system of whatever persuasion, but a gnostic tactility and kinesthesia. It is this latter system that gives rise to concepts. Apart from the fact that conceptual origins are otherwise unaccounted for or at best vague outside of a corporeal anchorage, it furthermore does not make sense to insist that knowledge is rooted in bodily action—as Piagetian theory does—but that the body itself is corporeally deaf. It is not even ultimately parsimonious in the sense that the full potential explanatory scope of Piagetian theory is not utilized. Were it so utilized, it would obviate the need for *ad hoc* hypotheses to explain what the theory might explain but does not. The twofold concept of order—causal order and sequential order—was a working concept in the forging of stone tools. Like all such concepts, it was rooted in the working body itself.

AN AFTERWORD ON THE RELATIONSHIP BETWEEN TACTILITY–KINESTHESIA AND VISION AND ON ANALOGICAL THINKING

Tool-making is indisputably a tactile–kinesthetic activity. In the customary analysis of stone tools as visual objects,[96] not only is the tactile–kinesthetic nature of tool-making underestimated, but the tactile half of the dual modality gets the shorter of the already short shrift. Indeed, tactility is not commonly mentioned at all, or if mentioned, it is only indirectly or in passing. The oversight is critical. Insofar as a blind person is capable of making a tool and a sighted person deficient in tactile–kinesthetic functioning is not, a just appraisal of ancestral hominid stone tool-making clearly mandates recognition and analysis of a gnostic tactility–kinesthesia.

There are additional reasons for correcting the omission. Visual readings of behavior are different from the tactile–kinesthetic events themselves. As eighteenth-century British empiricist philosopher George Berkeley long ago pointed out, "There is no solidity, no resistance or protrusion, perceived by sight." Moreover as he also showed, only like qualities may be added together to constitute a sum. Thus just as mathematicians cannot add "a line to a solid, or conceive it as making one sum with a surface,"[97] so we cannot add a visual line to a tangible line to make one continuous sum or whole. In short, vision and touch are quite separate, epistemologically distinct modalities. In effect, a visual analysis cannot substitute for a tactile–kinesthetic one, nor can it make the latter analysis unnecessary. By the same token, an edge and a line are two quite distinctive sensorial entities, as the preceding analysis has shown.

As the analysis has also shown, epistemological differences notwithstanding, vision is impregnated with tactile values. Precisely because it is, the relationship of the one modality to the other cannot be treated simply under the rubric of coordination—of eye and hand, typically[98]—but rather must be more deeply understood as *a transposition of meanings* from an original datum to a second: as a transfer of *sense* in the double meaning of that word. Only through this transfer do what is seen and what is touched come to coincide in such a way that pointedness, for example, or smoothness, comes to be *visually* perceived.

Correction is furthermore called for in light of Piaget's analysis of haptic perception, and quite apart from the extensive analogical use made of his ontogenetical theory of the development of human intelligence on behalf of human evolution.[99] The most careful, non-partisan reading of Piaget's analysis shows clearly that a certain ratio among the senses is at all times enforced not in virtue of factual analysis but in virtue of theory. In other words, Piagetian theory subserves a certain sensorimotor model of intelligence decreed in advance, one in which, precisely visual knowledge predominates and a gnostic tactility has no place. Although Piaget consistently emphasizes how intelligence is grounded in action, and how action is rooted in tactile–kinesthetic behavior—in "perceptual activity"—the gnostic tactile and kinesthetic structures of that activity are not recorded. It is because they are overlooked that Piaget can express astonishment that topological relationships understood by young children (eleven or twelve years of age) can be "spatial whilst not as yet mathematical!";[100] and it is because they are not even conceived of in the first place that two-dimensional cardboard figures bearing no resemblance to objects in the "real" world can naively be esteemed legitimate test equipment for eighteen-month-old infants and very young children.[101] Only when it is recognized that tactility and movement are in themselves modes of knowing[102] and not merely "activities" in the service of the visual is it possible to gain insight into their conceptual structures.

This latter recognition is the spawning ground of other crucial insights that, similarly, can have considerable bearing on how ancestral hominids and their activities are conceived and analyzed. For example, recognition of a gnostic tactility and kinesthesia validates the suggestion that the root difficulty in building a hominid visual system into an artificial intelligence is not that of understanding an astoundingly complex visual neurophysiology but of understanding how, in default of a gnostic tactility that provides its normal undergirdings, vision is blind to everyday spatial meanings. In this sense, Berkeley may well be proved ultimately correct. What vision *knows* of objects in a spatial sense—their shape, size, remoteness or nearness—it learns from touch.

Precisely with respect to problems encountered in "computer vision" and artificial intelligence, it is of interest that without their tactile–kinesthetic basis in edges, the figural *lines* of any object would not typically be seen as such. The lines exist only in virtue of an edge along which sight travels. Lines of sight would otherwise not be conceived. Indeed, insofar as vision deals in color contrasts, in relative lightnesses and darknesses, it is already empirically apparent why sight cannot furnish such information by itself. The perception of a figure as a finite object hinges on the perception of terminated magnitude, a perception constituted originally not by sight but by touch. If it were otherwise, that is, a matter simply of intensity changes, edge detection by "computer vision," or artificially intelligent eyes, would not be difficult to achieve. Moreover although Molyneux's famous question regarding the priority of touch was never conclusively answered,[103] there is much more reason to affirm that vision does not in and of itself originally furnish definitive contours than that it does. The most recent evidence is to be found precisely in attempts to develop a visual artificial intelligence. Because object contour is not always straightforward, a computer faces the problem of separating one object from another when the boundary between them is fused— a horse from a rider, for instance—or of identifying an object when it is only partially in view. As David Marr noted in his book *Vision*,[104] in everyday visual discriminations and identifications, the most important *edges* are often nearly invisible.

While it might seem somewhat ironic that a logico-mathematical intelligence on the order of Piaget's determinations finds no anchor points in a gnostic tactility and kinesthesia (especially in light of both traditional accounts of the origin of numbers and corporeal modes of counting in non-Western civilizations),[105] it is not surprising that an intelligence incapable of generating tactile–kinesthetic concepts is artificial. In the one case a complete tactile–kinesthetic epistemology goes unheeded and in the other it is an impossibility. While tactile–kinesthetic discriminations might be built into a robot's repertoire of possible awarenesses (say, discriminations of roundedness and sharpness), the discriminations would not—and could not—lead the robot toward the resolution of novel appearances. Moreover a robot would never be impelled to sculpt a shoehorn[106] nor would it be capable of generating for itself basic notions of geometry. Lacking a full-fledged corporeal base, its intelligence is static—artificial in an added if not more fundamental sense.

Taken together, the above considerations show clearly that recognition of touch and movement as modes of knowing can generate insight into perception and perceptual relationships, into intelligence, and ultimately into thinking itself. In fact, the significance of the combined insights to a sound understanding of ancestral hominid stone tool-making becomes virtually transparent. If stone tools constitute the singular hard data by which the perceptual acuities and intelligence of ancestral hominids may be judged, then they provide the basis for a twofold interpretation. They attest not only to certain conceptual origins but to a certain mode of thinking: analogical thinking. This chapter has in fact shown the latter to be the fundamental *modus operandi* of early *Homo faber*. It has shown how thinking is modeled on the body, how the body functions as a semantic template in the development of fundamental new practices, how, in effect, analogical thinking is rooted in the body. Some final words may be said about the nature of this mode of thinking.

In analogical thinking, there is a transfer of meaning from one framework to another, or at the simplest level, from one thing to another. Two otherwise unrelated items or phenomena are perceptually conjoined—thus teeth and stones in the origin and development of stone tool-making. A hermeneutics of perception is thus evident, a hermeneutics complementary to that suggested by Marr's work on vision.[107] To perceive is not only to *extract* meaning but may involve a *transfer* of meaning. The transference is of critical significance. Just such transference is at the root of concepts. Without a relationship to like things perceived in the past, a thing presently perceived is devoid of *conceptual* significance. In reverse terms, were everything different from everything else, there would be no concepts. As concerns language, there would in fact be only proper names with which, incidentally, no sentences could possibly be formed. (The well-known linguist Ferdinand de Saussure remarked on this fact when he said that "the only [linguistic] forms left untouched by analogy are of course isolated words like proper nouns, especially place names which allow no analogies and consequently no interpretation of their elements.")[108]

Now while it might commonly be thought that the perception of similarity gives rise to analogical thinking, the former is not the point of departure for the latter. As suggested above, to perceive a similarity in an analogical sense is *already* to think; apprehension of the analogy occurs in the moment of perceptual experience itself. That it does testifies to the idea that perception is a form of thinking. Such an account of perception is Cartesian, but not on that account suspect. On the contrary, the more emaciated (and empirically unsubstantiated) notion of perception current today is the more apt candidate for suspicion. The current notion is more than likely the product of present-day Western academic specialization, that is, of an artificial separation of the "cognitive" from the "perceptual" sciences. With this separation, perception is typically reduced to hard-wiring—to neurophysiological mechanisms and brain events. It is stripped of its living character, which is to say it is stripped of any gnostic significance and relation to thinking.

Analogical thinking makes what is alien intelligible or what is insignificant significant, by bringing it within the sphere of the already known—as stones to teeth. Insofar as it brings what is not immediately or fully significant or intelligible into a prior framework of intelligibility, it is axiomatic that its roots are in bodily life. The tactile-kinesthetic body is *the known* par excellence. Indeed, it is difficult to conceive in what other consistent and always accessible terms thought could have been—and could be—originally formulated.

Mythological thinking corroborates the central role of the body in analogical thinking—at the same time that it corroborates the central role of analogical thinking in human thought. For ancestral hominids and present-day ones untouched by Western science, for example, there are no abstract forces that cause earthquakes, volcanoes, floods, rain, wind, or even sunrises and moonrises. Nothing happens except by concrete bodily agencies. In mythological thought, it is not a "how" but a "who" that is looked for with respect to causality.[109] Spirits, demiurges, or gods are modeled on the felt dimensions of corporeal life. They have *effectuating* powers; they *command* certain possibilities of action. Though not acknowledged as such, the "certain affinity with man" of which Lévi-Strauss speaks in explaining the supernatural beings with which Ojibwa peoples populate the world[110] is rooted precisely in a *bodily* affinity. How else explain the fact that these beings are either male or female? How else explain that they " 'move from place to place at will' "? Though hardly recognized as such, the science of the concrete—as Lévi-Strauss characterizes *"les pensées sauvages"*—is first of all a science of the body. Mythical thought is preferentially " 'attached to animals, celestial bodies, and other personified phenomena of nature' "[111] because all are subsumable within a personally understood corporeality.

In sum, analogical thinking is both basic to hominid thinking and basically corporeal. Its roots lie in a gnostic tactility–kinesthesia. Together the thinking and the gnostic system attest to the origin and elaboration of concepts. Together they inform the practice of ancestral hominid stone tool-making.

NOTES

1. See Jean Piaget, *La construction du réel chez l'enfant* (Neuchatel: Delachaux et Niestlé, 1967), *La psychologie de l'intelligence* (Paris: Librairie Armand Colin, 1967), *La naissance de l'intelligence chez l'infant*, 6th ed. (Neuchatel: Delachaux et Niestlé, 1968); Sue T. Parker and Kay R. Gibson, "Object Manipulation, Tool Use and Sensorimotor Intelligence as Feeding Adaptations in Cebus Monkeys and Great Apes," *Journal of Human Evolution* 6 (1977): 623–41, and "A Developmental Model for the Evolution of Language and Intelligence in Early Hominids," *Behavioral and Brain Sciences* 2 (1979): 367–408; and Thomas Wynn, "The Intelligence of Later Acheulian Hominids," *Man*, n.s. 14 (1979): 371–91, and "The Intelligence of Oldowan Hominids," *Journal of Human Evolution* 10 (1981): 529–41.

2. F. H. Cushing, "Manual Concepts: A Study of the Influence of Hand-Usage on Culture-Growth," *American Anthropologist*, o.s. 5 (1892): 289–317.

3. Edward Kasner and James R. Newman, *Mathematics and the Imagination* (New York: Simon and Schuster, 1940); and Michael Guillen, *Bridges to Infinity* (Los Angeles: Jeremy Tarcher, 1983).

4. Mary LeCron Foster, "Meaning as Metaphor I," *Quaderni di semantica* 3, no. 1 (1982): 97.

5. David Premack, "Symbols Inside and Outside of Language," in *The Role of Speech in Language*, ed. James F. Kavanagh and James E. Cutting (Cambridge: MIT Press, 1975), p. 49.

6. Alfred S. Romer and Thomas S. Parsons, *The Vertebrate Body*, 5th ed. (Philadelphia: W. B. Saunders, 1977), pp. 300–301.

7. Piaget, *La construction*. See in particular chapter 3 where Piaget describes an infant's discovery of both its *efficacy* vis-à-vis objects in the world about it, and the *power* of its hands.

8. The phrases "I can" and "I move" come from Edmund Husserl's insightful and seminal descriptive analyses of *"the kinestheses."* Ich kann (I can) in particular is a fundamental and eminently significant concept anchoring human experience. Its import will be made apparent many times over, implicitly as well as explicitly, in this book. See Edmund Husserl, *Ideen zu einer reinen Phänomenologie und phänomenologischen Philosophie, Zweites Buch*, ed. Marly Biemel (The Hague: Martinus Nijhoff, 1952); see also *The Crisis of European Sciences and Transcendental Phenomenology*, trans. David Carr (Evanston, Ill.: Northwestern University Press, 1970), particularly pp. 106–8, 161, 217, 331–32, *Cartesian*

Meditations, trans. Dorion Cairns (The Hague: Martinus Nijhoff, 1973), p. 97, and *Ideas Pertaining to a Pure Phenomenology and to a Phenomenological Philosophy*, trans. Ted E. Klein and William E. Pohl (The Hague: Martinus Nijhoff, 1980), pp. 106–12. For an elaboration of the relationship Husserl describes between "I move" and "I can," see Ludwig Landgrebe, "Phenomenology as Transcendental Theory of History," trans. J. Huertas-Jourda and R. Feige, in *Husserl: Expositions and Appraisals*, ed. Peter McCormick and Frederick Elliston (Notre Dame, Ind.: Notre Dame University Press, 1977), pp. 101–13.

9. Landgrebe, "Phenomenology as Transcendental Theory," p. 108.

10. Kay R. Gibson, "Brain Structure and Intelligence in Macaques and Human Infants from a Piagetian Perspective," in *Primate Biosocial Development*, ed. Suzanne Chevalier-Skolnikoff and Frank E. Poirier (New York: Garland Press, 1977).

11. Ibid., p. 114 (italics added).

12. Piaget, *La construction*.

13. T. Struhsaker and P. Hunkeler, "Evidence of Tool-Using by Chimpanzees in the Ivory Coast," *Folia primatologica* 15 (1971): 212–29; and C. Boesch, "Nouvelles observations: sur les chimpanzés de la forêt de Tai (Coté-d'Ivoire)," *La terre et la vie* 32 (1978): 195–201.

14. See Wynn, "Oldowan Hominids" and "Acheulian Hominids."

15. Piaget, *La construction* and *La naissance*.

16. See C. J. Brainerd, "The Stage Question in Cognitive–Developmental Theory," *Behavioral and Brain Sciences* 2 (1978): 172–213.

17. See Wynn, "Oldowan Hominids"; see also Piaget, *La naissance*.

18. Claude Lévi-Strauss, *The Savage Mind*, trans. George Weidenfeld and Nicolson Ltd. (London: Weidenfeld and Nicolson, 1972), p. 18.

19. Milford H. Wolpoff, *Paleoanthropology* (New York: Knopf, 1980).

20. See, for example, David R. Pilbeam, *The Ascent of Man* (New York: Macmillan, 1972); and Wolpoff, *Paleoanthropology*.

21. See, for example, Romer and Parsons, *Vertebrate Body*; and Pilbeam, *Ascent*.

22. Pilbeam, *Ascent*; see also Henry Gray, *Anatomy, Descriptive and Surgical*, ed. T. P. Pick and R. Howden (Philadelphia: Running Press, 1974).

23. Nicholas Toth, personal communication; see also Wolpoff, *Paleoanthropology*.

24. A. Walker and R. E. F. Leakey, "The Hominids of East Turkana," *Scientific American* 239 (August 1978): 54–66; Lawrence H. Keeley, "The Functions of Paleolithic Flint Tools, *Scientific American* 237 (November 1977): 108–26; Lawrence H. Keeley and Nicholas Toth, "Microwear Polishes on Early Stone Tools from Koobi Fora, Kenya," *Nature* 293 (1981): 464–65; and Donald C. Johanson and Maitland A. Edey, *Lucy* (New York: Simon and Schuster, 1981).

25. Both this description and the foregoing one regarding the manner in which a core tool is held are those of archaeologist Nicholas Toth (personal communication).

26. Pilbeam, *Ascent*, p. 59.

27. Nicholas Toth, "The Oldowan Reassessed: A Close Look at Early Stone Artefacts," *Journal of Archaeological Science* 12 (1985): 101–20.

28. André Leroi-Gourhan, *Prehistoric Man*, trans. W. Baskin (New York: Philosophical Library (1957), p. 66.

29. Kenneth P. Oakley, an archaeologist, has made this precise comparison in "Emergence of Higher Thought," *Philosophical Transactions of the Royal Society of London*, B Series, 292 (1981): 205–11.

30. Leroi-Gourhan, *Prehistoric Man*.

31. Nicholas Toth, personal communication.

32. Bernard Berenson, "The Central Italian Painters of the Renaissance," in *The Bernard Berenson Treasury*, ed. H. Kiel (New York: Simon and Schuster, 1962).

33. Ibid.

34. Wynn, "Oldowan Hominids" and "Acheulian Hominids."

35. For a discussion of the distinction between ultimate and proximate explanations, see E. O. Wilson, *Sociobiology* (Cambridge: Belknap Press, 1975).

36. See, for example, Jane van Lawick-Goodall, *In the Shadow of Man* (New York: Dell, 1971); Phyllis J. Dolhinow, "The North Indian Langur," in *Primate Patterns*, ed. Phyllis J. Dolhinow (New York: Holt, Rinehart, and Winston), pp. 181–238; K. R. L. Hall and I. De Vore, "Baboon Social Behavior," ibid., pp. 125–80; Alison Jolly, *Primate Behavior* (New York: Macmillan, 1971); and Jane B. Lancaster, *Primate Behavior and the Emergence of Human Culture* (New York: Holt, Rinehart, and Winston, 1975).

37. See, for example, van Lawick-Goodall, *In the Shadow*; Dolhinow, "North Indian Langur"; Lancaster, *Primate Behavior*; Harry F. Harlow, "Love," *American Psychologist* 13 (1958): 673–85; Harry F. Harlow and R. R. Zimmerman, "The Development of Affectional Responses in Infant Monkeys," *Proceedings of the American Philosophical Society* 102 (1958): 501–9; and Ashley Montagu, *Touching: The Human Significance of the Skin* (New York: Columbia University Press, 1971).

38. See, for example, Glynn L. Isaac, "The Food-Sharing Behavior of Protohuman Hominids," *Scientific American* 238 (April 1978): 90–108; Lancaster, *Primate Behavior*; Wolpoff, *Paleoanthropology*; Richard E. Leakey and Roger Lewin, *Origins* (New York: E. P. Dutton, 1977); and Sherwood L. Washburn and C. S. Lancaster, "The Evolution of Hunting," in *Perspectives on Human Evolution* 1, ed. Sherwood L. Washburn and P. C. Jay (New York: Holt, Rinehart, and Winston, 1968).

39. Desmond Morris, *The Naked Ape* (New York: Dell Publishing, 1967).

40. See Montagu, *Touching*.

41. Maxine Sheets-Johnstone, "Existential Fit and Evolutionary Continuities," *Synthèse* 66 (1986): 219–48.

42. Jean Piaget and Bärbel Inhelder, *The Child's Conception of Space*, trans. F. J. Langdon and J. L. Lunzer (New York: W. W. Norton, 1971); Parker and Gibson, "Object Manipulation" and "Developmental Model"; and Wynn, "Oldowan Hominids" and "Acheulian Hominids."

43. See, for example, Guillen, *Bridges*; and Kasner and Newman, *Mathematics and the Imagination*.

44. Piaget and Inhelder, *Child's Conception*.

45. Henri Poincaré, quoted in Kasner and Newman, *Mathematics and the Imagination*, p. 273.

46. Piaget and Inhelder, *Child's Conception*, p. 12.

47. Ibid., p. 153.

48. Ibid., pp. 104–24.

49. Quoted in W. Hurewicz and H. Wallman, *Dimension Theory* (Princeton: Princeton University Press, 1948), p. 3.

50. Piaget and Inhelder, *Child's Conception*, p. 110.

51. Ibid., p. 111.

52. See, for example, Morris Kline, *Mathematics in Western Culture* (New York: Oxford University Press, 1953).

53. G. Gottleib, "Ontogenesis of Sensory Function in Birds and Mammals," in *The Biopsychology of Development*, ed. E. Tobach, L. R. Aronson, and E. Shaw (New York: Academic Press, 1971), pp. 67–128.

54. The following mathematicians were in fact contacted: Paul Baum, Department of Mathematics, Brown University; Ron Kirby, Department of Mathematics, University of California at Berkeley; and John Paulos, Department of Mathematics, Temple University.

55. Premack, "Symbols."

56. Piaget and Inhelder, *Child's Conception*.

57. Ibid., p. 165.

58. Guillen, *Bridges*, pp. 158–59.

59. Cushing, "Manual Concepts," p. 309.

60. Wynn, "Acheulian Hominids" and "Oldowan Hominids."

61. "Oldowan Hominids," p. 533.

62. Ibid., p. 534.

63. Ibid.

64. Wynn, "Acheulian Hominids," p. 374.

65. Toth, "Oldowan Reassessed."

66. Ibid., p. 107.

67. Ibid., p. 115.

68. See, for example, *La psychologie de l'intelligence* (Paris: Armand Colin, 1967); *Genetic Epistemology*, trans. E. Duckworth (New York: Columbia University Press, 1970); and *Structuralism*, trans. C. Maschler (New York: Harper and Row, 1970).

69. Silvano Arieti, *Creativity* (New York: Basic Books, 1976).

70. Piaget and Inhelder, *Child's Conception*.

71. For studies of creative intelligence inside and outside of science, see, for example, J. P. Guilford, "Traits of Creativity," in *Creativity and Its Cultivation*, ed. H. H. Anderson (New York: Harper and Row, 1959), pp. 142–61; Frank Barron, "The Needs for Order and Disorder as Motive in Creative Activity," in *Scientific Creativity: Its Recognition and Development*, ed. C. W. Taylor

and Frank Barron (New York: Wiley and Sons, 1963), pp. 153–61; E. P. Torrance, "Scientific Views of Creativity and Factors Affecting Its Growth," *Daedalus* 94 (1965): 663–81; Albert Einstein, "Letter to Jacques Hadamard," in *The Creative Process*, ed. B. Ghiselin (New York: New American Library, 1952), pp. 43–44; Henri Poincaré, "Mathematical Creation," trans. G. B. Halsted, ibid., pp. 33–42.

72. The analogy can be validated in further ways. While it is recognized that Euclidean and projective geometries are concerned with quantitative determinations and topological geometry with qualitative ones, the difference between a concern with rigid bodies and changeable ones vis-à-vis creative praxis is not immediately obvious. Early hominid tool-makers dealt quite literally with *changing* bodies. Making a tool meant initiating and carrying through a program of transformations upon a stone. The creative enterprise that marks the fabrication of stone tools is thus inherently coincident with basic topological concerns, namely, the conservation of invariant qualities across *created* changes in an object.

The aptness of the analogy can be extended anthropologically, and in a way that further concretizes the distinction. The first early hominid toolmaker could well be defined as the first *bricoleur:* "someone who works with his hands and uses devious means compared to those of a craftsman" (Lévi-Strauss, *Savage Mind*, pp. 16–17). *Bricolage* is a creative putting together of "whatever is at hand" (p. 17). Lévi-Strauss's original formulation of the bricoleur/engineer relationship is thus in broad outline akin to the relationships specified in the analogy: a bricoleur's work is to qualitative conservation and a creative intelligence as an engineer's is to quantitative conservation and a logico-mathematical intelligence. Whatever the engineer's project, it constrains him to a rigorous approach to its solution, that is, a working from hypothesis or theory to definitive end (or *event*, to use Lévi-Strauss's term). It is essentially a logico-mathematical enterprise. The bricoleur is not so constrained. His work is open-ended in the sense that "he interrogates all the heterogeneous objects of which his treasury is composed to discover what each of them could 'signify' and so contribute to the definition of a set which has yet to materialize" (p. 18). The open-endedness has to do with the possible use of materials, not with possible results that are indeed constrained by the choice of materials. While "the engineer questions the universe" in cross-examining his resources, the " 'bricoleur' addresses himself to a collection of oddments" (p. 19).

Lévi-Strauss's suggestion that unlike the engineer's, the bricoleur's concern is with secondary qualities rather than Galilean primary ones provides even further justification for the analogy and its distinctions. Even if amenable to mathematization in the twentieth-century, dontic and lithic hardness, resistance, and transformational powers known to early hominid stone toolmakers could hardly be subsumed in the latter Galilean category. And of course the essentially qualitative conservation of these properties could not be so subsumed either.

73. Ron Kirby. See note 68 above.

74. For instance, the notion that flaking does not violate the topological integrity of the stone is borne out by the topologist's estimation of polyhedra as the simplest topological objects (P. J. Hilton and S. Wylie, *Homology Theory* [London: Cambridge University Press, 1960]), and the coincident general estimation of polyhedra as the simplest of early fabricated stone tools by paleoanthropologists and archaeologists. In neither evaluation is the number of sides—or edges—a measure of the object's complexity, which is why it can remain the same object topologically whether it has four or twenty-four sides, and why, in addition, all polyhedra are essentially homeomorphic. For the topologist, edges and sides have to do not with *how*, but with *that* a figure is bounded. In other words, as Ron Kirby put it, "dents don't matter." The classical four-color map problem is an expression of the topologist's concern with sheer boundedness unqualified by absolute shape.

A further example might center on the fact that stone tools are simply connected solids. As such, the spatial relationship between their sides and vertices on the one hand, and their edges on the other, is formalizable in "the simplest universal statement about solids" (Kasner and Newman, *Mathematics and the Imagination*, p. 290): Euler's theorem would apply even if a stone tool were transformed into rubber and then inflated into a sphere. Its topological integrity would not be violated. Its sides would simply become regions on the sphere, its edges boundaries of the regions, and its vertices common regional meeting points.

75. Wynn, "Oldowan Hominids," p. 529.

76. The issue is not unrelated to the broader one of "conceptual assignments" in the writing of history. When it is said of a certain period, for example, that "ideas were in the air," were they there ready to be picked off like flies, or were they rather diffused and impalpably present like pollen dust? For a discussion of the issue in relation to the idea of evolution and Lamarck's and Darwin's historical relationship, see Maxine Sheets-Johnstone, "Why Lamarck Did Not Discover the Principle of Natural Selection?" *Journal of the History of Biology* 15 (1982): 443–65.

77. Jean Piaget, *Biology and Knowledge*, trans. B. Walsh (Chicago: University of Chicago Press, 1971), p. 164.

78. Piaget, *Genetic Epistemology*.

79. Ibid., p. 18.

80. Wynn, "Oldowan Hominids," p. 533.

81. Ibid., p. 535.

82. Ibid., pp. 532, 533, and 534 respectively.

83. See, for example, Leroi-Gourhan's *Prehistoric Man* on this point.

84. Piaget and Inhelder, *Child's Conception*. See, for example, pp. 153, 149–51.

85. Compare *the labor process* in V. P. Yakimov's article, "Traits of Discontinuity in Human Evolution," in *Paleoanthropology: Morphology and Paleoecology*, ed. Russell H. Tuttle (The Hague: Mouton, 1975), pp. 163–72.

86. Wynn, "Oldowan Hominids."

87. Toth, "Oldowan Reassessed," p. 113.

88. Wynn, "Oldowan Hominids," p. 535.

89. Husserl, *Ideen, Zweites Buch*, and *Crisis*.

90. Piaget, *Biology and Knowledge*, p. 165.

91. Maxine Sheets-Johnstone, "On the Origin of Counting: A Re-Thinking of Upright Posture" (Paper presented at the 65th annual meeting of the American Association for the Advancement of Science, San Francisco, June 1984). An expanded version of the paper is forthcoming in *The Life of Symbols*, ed. Mary LeCron Foster and Jayne Botscharow (Boulder, Colo.: Westview Press, 1990) and is included as Chapter 3 of this book.

92. Edmund Husserl, *The Phenomenology of Internal Time-Consciousness*, trans. J. S. Churchill (Bloomington: Indiana University Press, 1964).

93. See, for example, Piaget, *La psychologie de l'intelligence* and *Genetic Epistemology*; Piaget and Inhelder, *Child's Conception*; Parker and Gibson, "Object Manipulation" and "Developmental Model"; and Wynn, "Acheulian Hominids" and "Oldowan Hominids."

94. Wynn, "Oldowan Hominids," p. 533.

95. Wynn, "Acheulian Hominids," p. 385.

96. See, for example, Kenneth P. Oakley, *Man the Tool-Maker* (Chicago: University of Chicago Press, 1949); Keeley, "Functions of Paleolithic Flint Tools," pp. 108–26; and Wynn, "Acheulian Hominids" and "Oldowan Hominids."

97. George Berkeley, *Essay Toward a New Theory of Vision* (1709), in *Berkeley Selections*, ed. Mary W. Calkins (New York: Charles Scribner's Sons, 1929), p. 86; ibid., p. 83.

98. See, for example, Piaget, *La naissance*.

99. Piaget and Inhelder, *Child's Conception*. Regarding extensive analogical use, see references in note 1 and Gibson, "Brain Structure," pp. 113–57; Sue T. Parker, "Piaget's Sensorimotor Series in an Infant Macaque: A Model for Comparing Unstereotyped Behavior and Intelligence in Human and Non-Human Primates," in *Primate Biosocial Development*, pp. 43–112; and Suzanne Chevalier-Skolnikoff, "The Ontogeny of Primate Intelligence and Its Implications for Communicative Potential," in *Origins and Evolution of Language and Speech*, ed. Stevan R. Harnad, Horst D. Steklis, and Jane B. Lancaster, *Annals of the New York Academy of Sciences* 280 (1976): 173–211.

100. Piaget and Inhelder, *Child's Conception*, p. 460.

101. Ibid., pp. 18–20.

102. See Maxine Sheets-Johnstone, "Thinking in Movement," *Journal of Aesthetics and Art Criticism* 39 (1981): 399–407.

103. See John Locke, *An Essay Concerning Human Understanding* (1689), ed. M. Cranston (New York: Collier Books, 1965); Berkeley, *Essay*; and M. von Senden, *Space and Sight*, trans. P. Heath (London: Methuen, 1960).

104. David Marr, *Vision* (New York: W. H. Freeman, 1982).

105. See, for example, Aaron Bakst, *Mathematics*, 3rd ed. (Princeton:

D. Van Nostrand, 1967) for an account of the origin of numbers; see Lucien Lévy-Bruhl, *How Natives Think*, trans. Lilian A. Clare (New York: Washington Square Press, 1966); and see Ernst Cassirer, *The Philosophy of Symbolic Forms*, vols. 1–3, trans. R. Mannheim (New Haven: Yale University Press, 1957), vol. 3, for an account of corporeal modes of counting in non-Western civilizations. See also this book's Chapter 3.

106. See Oliver Sacks, "Hands," *New York Review of Books*, 8 November 1984, p. 15.

107. Marr, *Vision*; see also Gunther Stent, "Hermeneutics and the Analysis of Complex Biological Systems" (Paper presented at the University of California at Davis, 14 November 1984).

108. Ferdinand de Saussure, *Course in General Linguistics*, ed. C. Bally and A. Sechehaye, trans. W. Baskin (New York: Philosophical Library, 1959), p. 173.

109. F. Frankfort and H. A. Frankfort, *Before Philosophy* (London: Penguin, 1949).

110. Lévi-Strauss, *Savage Mind*, p. 37.

111. Ibid., p. 135. Lévi-Strauss is quoting Franz Boas.

3

On the Origin of Counting:
A Re-Thinking of Upright Posture

It must have required many ages to discover that a brace of pheasants and a couple of days were both instances of the number 2; the degree of abstraction is far from easy.

BERTRAND RUSSELL

Somewhere back in the early days of humankind a hairy hand hesitatingly notched a tree to record a kill, or the suns of his journeying. . . . In some such unprofessional way man took his first plunge into the mathematical world and came up with a revolutionary concept—how to count.

AARON BAKST

A BRIEF OVERVIEW OF THE TERRAIN

The starkly contrasting views of Russell and Bakst cited above on the origin of counting call for clarification—and not simply from the viewpoint that a philosopher and a mathematician inhabit two different academic worlds. What is at issue is not a question of philosophy or mathematics; it is a question of the scientific validity of a certain rendering of the origin of counting.

There are undoubtedly many favored versions of the traditional story of how counting originated. Credibility in each case, however, rests upon the acceptance of a rather queer scenario, queer in the sense of being almost biblical, or creationist, in character. In the same way that Yahweh said, "Let there be light," and there was light, so, as Bakst's version would have it, our hominid ancestors said, "Let me count," and there was counting. Of course it is also possible for a traditional scenario to be straightforwardly creationist, but that would be to disavow the facts of evolution and the theory that follows in their wake. The problem is, How did arithmetic counting originate if not by decree—or by divine intervention?

The classic five-finger version of the origin of counting might appear more credible than Bakst's version at first glance since it ostensibly replaces decree by discovery. But arithmetic counting was not instituted as a result of some creature's eureka moment: An ancestral hominid did not look at his or her hand one day, discover protuberances at the end of each, decide to count them in turn, and thereby determine how many there were. Like spontaneous generation, spontaneous enumeration explains nothing. It furthermore assumes as given the very thing that needs to be explained. Although the classic five-finger account points in the right direction in seeking empirical data through corporeal analyses, it stays on the visual surface of the body and stops far short of a substantive derivation of numbers.

In brief, the classic five-finger version of the story fails, as other traditional versions fail, to answer the question, Where did numbers come from? A credible account of the origin of counting must begin with that question. Unless the origin of *numbers* is determined, an explanation of the history of *counting* will remain not only oversimplified, but wholly speculative—as Bakst's account well illustrates. Perhaps if numbers were not considered subaltern to language,[1] more might be known of their origin. Such is at least suggested by anthropologist C. R. Hallpike's comment in *The Foundations of Primitive Thought*: "The study of primitive conceptions of number has been much neglected in this century."[2] But it may be too, following Franz Boas's characterization of the concerns of primitive peoples,[3] that the neglect is a function of twentieth-century Western interest in abstract over mundane ideas, in effect with arithmetic numbers themselves, and not with their antecedent or rudimentary forms. Whatever the reason for neglect might be, insofar as numbers have long been woven into the texture of Western culture, and at times with overwhelming cosmological significance,[4] it is more than timely to consider where they came from. How *did* we, a hominid species, come to count? What is to be sought is corporeal data that, in addition to being internally consistent in their own right, support and are supported on the one hand by anthropological data on primitive modes of counting, and on the other by accepted linguistic theory, which holds that "man's first precise counting went only from one to two."[5]

NUMBERS AS SUCH ARE NOT ESSENTIAL TO COUNTING

To reckon the number of something—apples, buttons, bones, children —it is not essential to name each individual numerically and in turn. Wittgenstein put the fact of the matter several times over. In his lectures on the foundations of mathematics, for example, he states that by physical manipulation, or by devising a "counting-pattern," or by looking, "we may have 'the same number in different senses.'"[6] In a later lecture, he takes up the notion again: "There are many different ways of finding and comparing numbers. We can, for example, compare numbers by the eye. . . . That there are the same number of dashes there [on the page] and here [on the same page], nobody gets by counting."[7] Echoing this last observation in his *Remarks on the Foundation of Mathematics*, he points out, "It is superfluous to count two apples which are before my eyes."[8]

Mathematicians have similarly pointed out that numbers as such are not essential to counting. One can determine the number of chairs and people in a room in the same way one can determine that there are the same number of fingers on each hand—by matching: "Without knowing anything about numbers, one may ascertain whether two classes have the same number of elements."[9] Clearly, one can have a certain numerical concept, that is, a concept based on one-to-one correspondence, and utilize that concept in the course of daily activities without ever having a notion of number in an abstract sense.

Whether a matter of comparing one group to another physically— for example, the fingers of each hand—or by merely looking—for example, at the number of dashes in two separate clusters on a page—or whether a matter of perceiving straightaway the number of a particular group—for example, the *twoness* of two apples—an awareness of a one-to-one correspondence among the things compared or between the things perceived is central. But in contrast to actual arithmetic counting, at this inchoate stage of counting, the one-to-one correspondence is not upheld by a standard. In the matching of fingers of both hands, for instance, one set of fingers is not the standard of measurement of the other. If it is taken to be so, the chosen standard is arbitrary. The same is true of two apples or two hands. But the notion of a one-to-one correspondence between two apples or two hands needs clarification to begin with, not simply because it might at first seem farfetched to speak of such a thing in this instance—it might be thought that the perception of *twoness* involves no matching—but because the experience of a one-to-one correspondence can actually be seen there in its most primitive form.

In the seeing of two apples or two hands, matching is not a numerical comparing per se—as in the case of the five fingers of each hand where individuals of one group are explicitly matched one by one with individuals of another group—but a noticing of similarity. A plum and a balloon, for instance, are not *two* in the same rudimentary sense that two apples are *two*. The difference is akin to the difference Russell noted between a couple of days and a brace of pheasants: immediately apparent perceptual similarity precedes latent or less immediately apparent perceptual likeness. The *twoness* of two hands or of two apples is an immediate numerical awareness contemporaneous with the seeing of their similarity. One-to-one correspondences here are not a matter of *comparing*, but of perceiving a numerical relationship straightaway.

Where there is no numerical standard, or where a numerical standard is arbitrary, the same rudimentary numerical sense grounds numerical comparisons. In other words, just as immediately apparent perceptual similarity precedes latent or less directly grasped perceptual similarity, so it also constitutes the basis for that elementary matching procedure in which several items of one group are numerically compared to several items of another group. Were they not first seen as similar, the fingers on each hand would not be compared initially one by one with each other. At this rudimentary stage of counting, fingers are not numerically compared to jointed segments of the body, for example, or to facial features, nor are they paired in one-to-one correspondence with each other, and this on the basis of their likeness to each other. It is the likeness of fingers on one hand to fingers on the other hand that precipitates the explicit matching. The same is true of two sets of dashes on a page. Matching by comparison and matching by a noticing of similarity are thus distinctive experiences, even at this elementary level, but the former is rooted in the sense of likeness implicit in the latter.

At the most rudimentary stage of counting, then, matching is equivalent to the noticing of similarities—simple, qualitative, immediately apparent likenesses. Numerical awareness is thus in these cases adumbrated in the very act of perception. Given this perceptual base, the capacity to ascertain numerical relationships, or to perceive "how many" without giving a number to each individual in turn, may broadly be characterized as "recognition-counting." It is just this kind of rudimentary counting philosopher–anthropologist Lucien Lévy-Bruhl[10] was at pains to describe in his study of "how natives think." Following a detailed description of counting practices in a variety of non-Western cultures, all of which practices show that numbers are "felt and perceived . . . not conceived in the abstract," he goes on to point out how erroneous it is to propose twentieth-century reasons to explain the basis (for instance, quaternary or quinary) of any one of these preliterate counting systems. From the evidence, he concludes that "numbers . . . had a pre-existence, in that long period when they were as yet undifferentiated"; in other words, when, as in recognition-counting, the number of something was reckoned without enumerating each individual in turn. He ends the passage with the following admonishment and summary judgment: "It is a mistake to picture the human mind making numbers for itself in order to count, for on the contrary men first of all counted, with much effort and toil, before they conceived of numbers as such."[11]

The ability to count without numbers is both a strange and altogether impressive capacity. It is not just that ordinarily one would think it impossible to have any numerical awareness short of knowledge of what it is to number things in turn, but that at a pristine level, this awareness is apparently there for the noticing of similarities in the world—in the seemingly simple perceptual insight that one thing matches another thing in some aspect or other. What is the basis of this noticing of simple one-to-one correspondences and what would have disposed our hominid ancestors ultimately toward such a numerical awareness?

The corporeal analysis that follows proposes answers to these questions. It thus provides the backbone for a theory about the origin of counting. Should the answers prove valid and the theory tenable, they would provide the basis for inquiry into the evolution of counting —into the evolution of numbers as such, that is, as arithmetic entities, and into the actual use of numbers to count. They would furthermore provide an empirical basis for explaining how primitive two-count systems of counting gave rise to the decimal system—"by far the most widespread system in the world today"[12]—and thus for explaining how fingers came to set the standard for enumerative counting. Moreover valid answers and a tenable theory would have considerable evolutionary import with respect to a fuller understanding of human/

nonhuman continuities as well as of early hominid thinking and its evolutionary antecedents. For example, given the numerical matching ability of some nonhuman animals,[13] matching is clearly a biological evolutionary possibility rather than a purely cultural one. What is the basis of a nonhuman animal's "number sense"?[14] Is recognition-counting in hominids a species of quantitative recognition in non-human animals? If so, how many ways are there of counting without numbers, how can they be identified, and how are they related? Furthermore, would an understanding of the passage from nonverbal counting to verbal counting provide clues to an understanding of evolutionary connections between nonverbal and verbal thinking, and thus between nonhuman and human intelligence? So long as there is evidence of nonverbal thinking—evidence of counting without numbers—there is an empirical starting point for assaying the difference between thinking with and without language.

Pursuit of any of the above lines of inquiry clearly requires a prior elucidation of how hominid counting originated. Thus the seminal importance of the question, How did ancestral hominids come to an awareness of "how many" without giving a number to each item in turn?

BINARY PERIODICITIES AND ANIMATE FORM: QUINTESSENTIAL MEANINGS OF UPRIGHT POSTURE

Upright posture is pictured by paleoanthropologists as one of the dominant themes, if not *the* dominant theme of early hominid existence. It is customarily spoken of in terms of freeing the hands and of seeing to greater distances; that is, the emphasis is invariably on certain manual and visual changes, notably on the ability to carry objects about—especially food, children, and implements—and on the making and using of tools, and on the capacity to extend the range of visual perception. Now certainly it appears possible to relate both kinds of empowering changes straightaway to rationality, the latter being presumably integral to the ability to count. The making of tools, for example, would seem to require a certain kind of intelligence, one capable of entertaining and planning for a future, just as the carrying of tools from one place to another would seem to bespeak a certain kind of efficiency and strategy. The enhancement of visual perception would seem equally bound up with an intelligence capable of distinguishing and discriminating among things not immediately at hand. In both cases, however, the connection is extrinsically forged.

It is a matter of putting two things together rather than showing an intrinsic connection between them. Moreover to show an exclusively hominid relationship between rationality and upright posture by such examples would be extremely tenuous. A chimpanzee who fashions a stick in a certain way for probing termite mounds, for example, and who, on another occasion, walks upright, its arms and hands laden with fruit, would seem somewhat difficult to distinguish *qua* erect-walking, rationally behaving creature from an ancient hominid.

The thrust of the above observations might lead one to think an elucidation of the origin of counting is no more than a matter of showing that *consistent* upright posture facilitated a noticing of fingers and in turn a counting of them so that, in effect, the story of the origin of counting—told in terms of the marriage of rationality and upright posture—is a short and simple tale to tell. Corporeal analyses, however, thicken the plot considerably. To begin with, upright posture did not simply free the hands, it freed the whole body. More than this, the entire grid of spatial orientations of an upright hominid creature became fundamentally distinguished from that of a quadruped. Further still, a wholly different tactile–kinesthetic domain of powers and sensitivities emerged with consistent upright posture—a wholly different domain of "*I can*'s"—and with it a host of radically different meanings. Let us back up these claims of a corporeal revolution by a fresh analysis of upright posture.

In corporeal terms—and perhaps first and foremost in these terms —upright posture meant that a quadrupedal rhythmic complexity was reduced to *a simple binary periodicity*. Though consistently regarded as more complex because of the challenge to balance, the stress on supporting anatomical segments, and the like, upright posture was in another, concept-enhancing sense a radical simplification. Instead of four footfalls there were two, and instead of a variety of possible patternings of footfalls—trotting, galloping, and pacing, for example— there was basically one pattern variable only in terms of speed: walking and running. Hopping and jumping were possibilities as well of course, but these forms, although useful at times, perhaps to reach something or to move out of the way quickly, were undoubtedly not customary or consistent ways of getting about in the world, any more than they are for hominids today. Moreover it is the binary periodicity of stride and arm swing as well as footfalls that is remarkable in bipedal as opposed to quadrupedal locomotion. The emphatically binate nature of hominid walking in actuality comprises a number of mutually reinforcing binary periodicities.

Binary periodicities are felt realities. They are not visual noticings but tactile–kinesthetic ones. To speak of a binary periodicity of the legs in walking or running, for example, is not to speak of legs as visual things, much less of the word *legs*. It is to speak of alternating, tactile–kinesthetically experienced weights, bulk, heft, or mass. Walking or running legs are *felt magnitudes in motion*. What is noticed in each case are tactile–kinesthetic apparencies and patternings. Footfalls, strides, arm swings, all are processually intuited in the sense of being dynamically felt-through happenings. One might say that it is superfluous to count two footfalls or two strides or two arm swings. Each of these binary periodicities is a dynamically lived-through event; each is transparent in the very act of walking and running bipedally—just as the number of apples is transparent in the very act of seeing two apples. That Westerners today are more accustomed to think and speak of the matching of *visual* objects does not diminish, much less nullify, the ever-present possibility of tactile–kinesthetic matching. Given the requisite attentiveness, the matching of tactile–kinesthetic elements is immediate. A one-to-one correspondence is noticed. A perfect *ratio* is found to exist between one felt thing and another—just as it is between one visual thing and another.

It would seem rather queer to ask how the requisite attentiveness came to be. After all, it was a question of noticing one's very self. Short of a lapse in tactile–kinesthetic functioning, in which case survival would have been seriously jeopardized if not impossible, there is no way ancestral hominids could be said to have lived in a tactile–kinesthetic void. A felt awareness of the binary nature of locomotion was something not likely to have escaped the notice of creatures whose very survival depended upon moving themselves about continuously and exclusively on their own two feet. What an ancestral hominid would have been attentive to in noticing the binary periodicities of walking and running were aspects of him- or herself in motion, aspects that were there continuously: any time he or she happened to notice, there they were. In effect, an awareness of a certain numerical reciprocity in the acts of walking and running would seem hard to miss rather than difficult to achieve. The same observations could of course be made by hominids today.

Let us consider briefly how an upright spatial orientation would have reinforced an awareness of the fundamental locomotor binary periodicities, that is, how an awareness of certain dimensional correspondences arose with the evolution of upright hominid posture and locomotion. Up/down, side/side, and front/back are binary spatial correspondences. A quadrupedal animal can turn to this side and that, and some, though not cows or turtles, are capable of a variety of movements and postures along a vertical axis—of sitting down, for instance. It might be said that all terrestrial animals can turn from side to side and thus have a lateral oppositionality; that some terrestrial animals can leap and crouch or sit and thus have a vertical oppositionality; but that only those terrestrial creatures capable of upright posture have the potential dimensions of front and back as *binary oppositional surfaces*. Dogs and cats, for example, do not have a frontside and backside. Baboons and chimpanzees do. Of course dogs and cats have a bottomside and a topside that are the anatomical equivalent of a hominid frontside and backside, but that bottomside and topside are not existentially equivalent to the latter any more than their actual front and back *ends* are.

The possibility of a frontside and a backside is a possibility only for an upright creature. But it is one thing to *have* a frontside and backside and another to have a *felt*, tactile–kinesthetic frontside and backside as consistent and permanent binary spatial dimensions of animate form. If a comparison were made of front/backness in the upright locomotion of a gibbon and of a human, for example, it would likely be judged that the torque action apparent in brachiation precludes a strong and precise feeling of frontness and backness. In this observer-based appraisal, the visual is taken as a clue to the non-presence of a highly defined tactile–kinesthetic reality. Even were one to imagine oneself brachiating all of one's life through the middle story of a tropical rain forest, one would likely judge that those continued twistings and sideward openings of the body do not support a consistent and permanent felt oppositionality of front and back surfaces of the body. Of course in actually observing a gibbon, one might notice too that its legs do not swing in contralateral alternation with its arms. The consequent judgment would likely be that brachiatory periodicities aside, a sense of binariness would be difficult to come by: an overall binary kinetic patterning is not corporeally evident. Neither judgment carries with it of course the notion that gibbons have *no* felt awareness of a frontside and backside. The judgments suggest only that the gibbon's upright binary form of locomotion is not the spawning ground of correlative and mutually reinforcing binary spatial correspondences. Indeed, its world appears less anchored to a dominant front/back planar orientation than to a *non*-planar, all-enveloping curved space. Were an analysis of its spatial relationships undertaken in depth, it might even be shown that the gibbon's brachial form of locomotion is not fundamentally compatible with a sense of bodily periodicities at all.

In brachiating through a rain forest, a gibbon swings from one arm to the other, but in surroundings that make the alternation uneven. In effect, not only the spatial, but the temporal aspects of its motion are decisive. Since alternation in arm swing is a function of wherever the next tree branch happens to be, a sense of temporally symmetrical phases of movement—regular periodicities—would appear unlikely to develop. The earth is in contrast ever ready to terrestrially locomoting hands and feet. Hominid footfalls are in turn even. Hence the potentially felt binary periodicity.

With the possibility of hominid upright posture, comes the possibility of precisely felt three-dimensional binary correspondences. Front/back, side/side, up/down are in each case perceived as correlative dimensions. *Up* is not matched to *front*, for example, or *side* to *down*. The tactile–kinesthetic binary relationship is in each case distinct; that is, the sensed corporeal form of the matched items is unique, and fundamental meanings of each correspondence are in consequence different. In present-day humans, for example, the permanent and consistently felt oppositionality of front and back surfaces is perhaps best epitomized in the feeling of the backside as vulnerable, a feeling one would have little reason to suppose is peculiar to contemporary hominid life. In fact, quite the contrary if we are to believe evolutionary theory, which pictures ancestral hominid existence as one of perpetual vulnerability, thus an existence requiring constant vigilance. A felt awareness of one's backside would likely have been tied to an attentiveness to possible attack from the direction one felt least capable of defending.

Each of the three binary spatial correspondences is a tactile–kinesthetic phenomenon, a sensed structure of the upright body. As the previous example suggests, the oppositionality of surfaces is not an inert, static relation, but one charged through and through with possible tactile–kinesthetic meanings rooted in the fundamental creaturely possibilities of *approach* and *avoidance*. In the world of the ancestral hominids it is likely that a sense of safety and danger were commonly felt meanings of frontness and backness, not of course in an absolute sense—a creature can feel as vulnerable from the front as from behind—but in the sense that upright as opposed to quadrupedal posture is an on-going ever-present *exposure* of the body. Simply from the viewpoint of survival—in sociobiological terms, of passing on one's genes—tactile–kinesthetic meanings were necessarily engrained in this exposed body, meanings running all the way from caring and security, as in mother/child corporeal relationships, to aggression and avoidance or defense, as in hunter/hunted ones. Side/side and up/down were no doubt similarly permeated with tactile–kinesthetic meanings tied to survival. They too were implicated in the binary powers of an upright body, one that reaches, crouches, ducks, jumps, compacts itself in hiding, alternates moments of impact and suspension in running and leaping, sidesteps, and perhaps even tiptoes. That the reality of these binary powers in the lives of ancestral hominids cannot be doubted emphasizes the strong and crucial evolutionary role felt binary spatial correspondences of the body would likely have played. In virtue of their own considerable import to ongoing survival, it is reasonable to think they would have strongly reinforced an awareness of the fundamental binary periodicities engendered in upright hominid walking and running. Indeed, perhaps the most vivid—and obvious—example of this intimate reinforcement is in the laterality of the locomotor periodicities themselves: footfalls, strides, and arm swings are felt to alternate not just over and over again, but over and over again in a particular tactile–kinesthetic space each time. An association of these binary periodicities with particular sides of the body would seem transparent—especially as compared to the relative complexity of the equivalent possible numeric–lateral relationships in quadrupeds. Anthropologist Milton Hildebrand, for example, lists eighteen possible support sequences in the symmetrical gaits of primates alone.[15]

Still other aspects of upright hominid life, functional as well as structural, would have reinforced an awareness of the fundamental locomotor binary periodicities. There is first of all the felt—and at times audible—binary periodicity of breathing. In a creature for whom the consistent and ever-present binary rhythms of walking and running do not exist, there is no reason to think that the two-phased cadence of breathing would stand out. It does not match any dominant and repetitive tactile–kinesthetic event. The dual nature of everyday excretory acts and of everyday bodily excretions might have been similarly reinforcing. Urinating and defecating are corporeally located in different but related tactile–kinesthetic spaces. Front and back are not oppositional surfaces here but oppositional loci. They mark correspondent openings and ones from which two corresponding kind of materials pass out of the body. There are not three such places, for instance, or three different kinds of materials. Neither are the two orifices spatially disjoint—they are not both in back nor is one on the side, for instance. Like the tactile–kinesthetic periodicity of respiration, everyday excretory acts and their respective bodily excretions have a binary character.

Mention might be made too of the fact that hominids, like higher primates generally, do not have litters but usually produce one offspring at a time. That single offspring receives considerable attention and care, and for a relatively long period of time before it walks, let alone runs on its own. An intimate and extended mother/child relationship would have been a further expression and reinforcement of the preeminently binate theme of hominid life. It might in fact have been the primordial experiential source of a fundamental numerical concept: pairing—a concept too dense to broach even briefly here, but certainly one that is immediately suggestive of such basic and potentially critical binary awarenesses as large and small, wet and dry, smooth and rough, sharp and blunt, paired meanings an evolving hominid would certainly have come to distinguish as such, particularly since some of them are central to the making and using of tools.

There is, in fact, an already evident and quite striking binary motif in the earliest known hominid stone tools, and this quite apart from paired meanings such as blunt and pointed, rough and smooth. Although there are many different types of Oldowan tools, a common form is the bifacial chopper, a tool that is flaked precisely twice to make a cutting edge. Moreover in the fabrication of later tools, stones were flaked along two sides to produce an all-over cutting edge and a pointed end as well. In order to make these later bifacial tools, the maker was required to flake one side, then turn the stone over and flake the opposite side.[16] These tools, in other words, required that the maker distinguish between one side of a stone and the other; they required a sense of oppositional surfaces, an awareness of a binary relationship. The order and progression of movement necessary to the making of the tool—first *this* (flake and side), then *this* (flake and side)—is a testimonial to this awareness. Indeed, considerable long-range significance attaches to the binary awareness. To make a bifacial tool in any standardized way would have required a distinct sense of paired movements. Haphazard flaking would hardly produce consistent tools, let alone consistently usable ones. It is interesting in this regard to note Ashley Montagu's comments concerning the later and more complicated two-sided Acheulian handaxes: "It is clear that each flake has been removed in order to produce the cutting edges and point of the tool with the minimum number of strokes; for if one examines this tool carefully, one may readily perceive that no more flakes have been removed than were minimally necessary to produce the desired result." [17] Given this degree of refined tool-making and the awareness of "how many" it reflects, there is every reason to believe that a binary theme was central in much of the developing hominid tool technology and that it grew out of, and at the same time re-inforced, binary awarenesses of the body itself, that is, the body's own oppositional surfaces and its very movement in forging the tool. In the numerical sense of stone tool-making, body and tool went hand in hand.

Given the whole of the preceding corporeal analysis, it is possible to conceive hominid upright posture in a new and fundamental evo-lutionary sense, that is, as the primate evolutionary culmination of an already existing and emphatically binary mode of being present in the world: two eyes, two ears, two nostrils, two arms, two legs, two hands, two feet, two buttocks, two testicles, two breasts, in addition, of course, to the twofold nature of the very basic creaturely functions of breathing and excreting, and to the dyadic nature of the mother/child relationship. With the evolution of hominid upright posture, the numerical aspect of these binary forms was liberated, or better, the essentially binary meanings of these *already* binary forms were awak-ened. Arms did not just become functionally separated from legs. Arms and legs were existentially transformed. Rather than compris-ing a fourfold phenomenon, appendages were now paired, arm with arm, leg with leg. What was potentially binary *became* binary. Clearly, upright posture did not just "free the hands." It freed the legs as well. *It in fact freed the whole body to become a binary subject.*

A certain commensurability is thus evident between what was and what came to be, between a quadrupedal lifestyle in which binary motifs and structures remained virtually submerged, and a newly developing upright style in which they ultimately surfaced to aware-ness. The new lifestyle appropriated already existing binary corre-spondences, unified them under one dominant theme, and thus gave them proto-numerical meanings. This dominant theme sounded over and over again in the tactile–kinesthetic life of ancestral hominids. With consistent upright posture and locomotion, corporeal ratios were born; qualitative reciprocities were experienced. Two continuously alternating magnitudes in motion, two continuously alternating im-pacts of feet on ground, gave rise to a binate subject and world, one in which multiple similarities came to be noticed—similarities between something felt *here* and something felt *here,* and between something felt *now* and something felt *now.*

RECOGNITION-COUNTING AND
THE EVOLUTION OF NUMERICAL THINKING

In the numerical awareness of corporeal similarities, namely, *in recognition-counting,* the thing experienced as a numerical entity was not distinguished from the thing itself. Indeed, recognition-counting could not otherwise have arisen. Two striding legs, two swinging arms, front and back, inhaling and exhaling, all were originally intuited as felt qualitative magnitudes—binary correspondences analogous to the intuition of two visible apples. In the beginning, number was just such an aspect of the perceived object, or, to cite a passage from Lévy-Bruhl's description of counting in extant non-Western cultures, "Prelogical mentality . . . does not distinctly separate the number from the objects numbered. That which it expresses by speech is not really numbers, but 'number totals'"; it expresses qualitatively perceived, or "felt," [18] collections of familiar objects. There is no reason to think an analogy could not be made to these non-Western cultures in reconstructing the origin of numerical thinking in hominids, particularly since people in these cultures would seem to be the very hunter–gatherer people to whom analogy is made in support of paleoanthropological reconstructions of ancestral hominid hunting. [19] Moreover, and interestingly enough, the well-known mathematician Morris Kline has pointed out that "the appreciation of number as an abstract idea, abstract in the sense that it does not have to relate to particular objects, was one of the major advances in the history of thought. *Each of us in his own schooling goes through a similar intellectual process of divorcing numbers from physical objects*" (italics added). [20] It is worth noting that Kline's generalization regarding the ontogenetic development of numerical thought is backed up by Piaget's findings from experimental studies of numerical thinking in children:

We can watch how the child starts from a level of utter confusion, without a notion of what number really means . . . a level where number is completely mixed up with size, shape and arrangement, or constantly shifts according to the way it is subdivided or added up. And we can see how, on an average two years later, children declare of their own accord that a number must stay the same, whatever you do with it; so long as you do not actually add to it or take away from it.[21]

Where the evolution of numerical thinking in children differs from its evolution in ancestral hominids is in the fact that numbers as such are already part of the culture in which the child grows up, whereas our hominid ancestors forged them *originally*, an achievement that, as suggested above, could not have been easy. The difficult problem for future inquiry concerns precisely the latter evolution. How is it that collections of familiar objects, qualitatively recognized quantities, gave way to quantitative concepts as such? or, in other terms, How did felt correspondences—*tactile–kinesthetic ratios*—give rise to visual correspondences perceived on one's own body and in the world? It would seem likely indeed that while at the rudimentary stages of counting described here, there was no standard, one was nonetheless slowly to evolve. The tactile–kinesthetic body came to be the standard against which the numerical measure of the world was initially taken. Such an evolution of counting appears implicit in linguistic estimations of the primitiveness of one–two counting systems over the decimal system, and in the accounts cited by Lévy-Bruhl of practices of non-Western peoples in counting beyond *two*. According to many of these accounts, counting cannot proceed without the person's actually touching the body part signifying the intended number. In other words, enumeration takes place only on and with the tactile–kinesthetic body. In one such system of counting on the body, the person commences

at the little finger of the left hand: 1. *kutadimur* (end finger); 2. *kutadimur gurun-guzinga* = a thing following the end finger (fourth finger); 3. *il get* = middle finger; 4. *klak nitui get* (index finger) = spear-throwing finger; 5. *kagabet* = paddle finger (thumb); 6. *perta or tiap* = wrist; 7. *kudu* = elbow joint; 8. *zugu kwuick* = shoulder; 9. *susu madu* = breast flesh, sternum; 10. *kosa dadir* = right nipple; 11. *wadogam susu madu* = other side breast flesh; and so on, in reverse order, preceded by *wadogam* (other side); the series ending with the little finger of the right hand.[22]

A similar practice is recorded among the Maipua and Namau peoples in British New Guinea. They in fact use the same word—*ano*, meaning *neck*—for the numbers *ten* and *fourteen*, *ten* being the left side of the neck touched, *fourteen* being the right side of the neck touched. As Lévy-Bruhl notes, the practice "would be quite impossible if it were a question of numbers and numerals."[23]

Furthermore a preponderantly kinesthetic rather than tactile system of counting is cited and discussed by Lévy-Bruhl. The system offers particularly strong evidence against an easy conceptual privileging of a quinary (or decimal) base. In so doing it underscores the error of assuming five fingers to be "the most evident objective [realities]."[24] At the same time it illustrates the astounding degree of complexity possible in the relationship between counting and the body. An extended quotation is warranted:

> Here is the method of counting by a Dènè Dindjié in Canada. . . . "Extending the left hand, the palm turned towards his face, he bends his little finger, saying 1; then he bends the ring finger, saying 2, and bends the end again. The middle finger is bent for 3. He bends the index and says, showing the thumb, 4; there are no more but this. Then he opens the hand and says 5; it is finished with my (or one, or the) hand. The Indian, holding his left hand stretched out, three fingers of it fastened together, separates the thumb and index, which he brings near to the thumb of the right hand and says 6; i.e., there are three on each side, three by three. He joins four fingers of the left hand, brings the left thumb near the thumb and index finger of the right hand, and says 7; (one side there are four, or else, there are still three folded, or again, three on each side and the point in the middle). He brings the three fingers of the right hand to touch the left thumb, and thus obtaining two sections of four fingers, he says 8; (four on four, or four on each side). Then showing the little finger of the right hand, which alone remains folded, he says 9; (there is still one below, or—one is still wanting, or—the little finger is lying down). Finally, clapping the hands in joining them, the Indian says 10: i.e., each side is finished or, it is counted, reckoned, it is a count. Then he begins the same manoeuvre once more, saying: one filled plus one, one counted plus one, etc."[25]

CONCLUSION

If the origin of arithmetic counting lies in an upright hominid posture, then there are empirical grounds for explaining why numbers as such are not essential to counting, but why perceptual, that is, *felt*, correspondences are. One-to-one corporeal ratios were the conceptual ground of numerical thinking. This preverbal mode of thinking was attuned in the beginning to a qualitative world of perceived correspondences—a world of felt magnitudes in motion, of dimensional vulnerabilities, of impacts and suspension, and so on. The strength and consistency of these binary corporeal events are attested to by the widely acknowledged linguistic theory that a one–two counting system predated the use of the fingers to count, that is, predated the decimal system. Being anchored for the most part in fingers and toes as visual entities, traditional accounts of the origin of counting are at a loss to explain the primitiveness of the one–two system, and to accord with anthropological data on corporeal counting practices in non-Western cultures. The corporeal analysis given here provides firm empirical grounds to support both anthropological data and linguistic theory.

NOTES

1. Susanne K. Langer, *Mind: An Essay on Human Feeling*, 3 vols. (Baltimore: Johns Hopkins University Press, 1972), 2: 349–50.

2. C. R. Hallpike, *The Foundations of Primitive Thought* (Oxford: Clarendon Press, 1979), p. 238.

3. Franz Boas, *The Mind of Primitive Man* (New York: Macmillan, 1938).

4. G. S. Kirk and J. E. Raven, *The Presocratic Philosophers* (Cambridge: Cambridge University Press, 1962); and Aristotle, *Metaphysics*, trans. W. D. Ross, in *The Basic Works of Aristotle*, ed. R. McKeon (New York: Random House, 1968).

5. Morris Swadesh, *The Origin and Diversification of Language* (Chicago: Aldine-Atherton, 1971), p. 183.

6. Ludwig Wittgenstein, *Lectures on the Foundation of Mathematics*, ed. Cora Diamond (Ithaca, N.Y.: Cornell University Press, 1976), p. 157.

7. Ibid., p. 257.

8. Ludwig Wittgenstein, *Remarks on the Foundation of Mathematics*, trans. G. E. M. Anscombe (Oxford: Basil Blackwell, 1967), p. 24.

9. Edward Kasner and James R. Newman, *Mathematics and the Imagination* (New York: Simon and Schuster, 1940), pp. 28–29.

10. Recognition of leading figures of the past clearly waxes and wanes according to currently popular perspectives and methodological practices. Apart from earlier criticism, Lévy-Bruhl's scholarly contributions to anthropology were in recent times severely negated by Lévi-Strauss and the advent of structuralism. To judge from evaluations by well-known authorities outside anthropology, however, they need more just appraisal. Arieti and Piaget, for example, both pointedly speak out against wholesale condemnation of Lévy-Bruhl's work, Arieti in discussing his own concept of *paleologic* thinking (see Silvano Arieti, *Creativity* [New York: Basic Books, 1976], pp. 72–73), Piaget in discussing his own concept of "pre-logical" or *pre-operational* intelligence (see Jean Piaget, *Structuralism* [New York: Harper Colophon Books, 1970], p. 116). The problem is one of throwing out the baby with the bath water:

while Lévy-Bruhl's estimation of primitive people's mentality as *inferior* can be justly criticized, the whole of his work cannot be. In the present case, his recognition of a common thread in field studies of primitive counting techniques deserves acknowledgment. Specifically, his identification and analysis of the way in which the body is implicated in the practice of counting in various non-Western cultures makes clear both that the Bakst—indeed, popular —version of the origin of counting is *not* credible and that a deeper understanding of "the felt" body is needed. It should be noted too that the deserved and desirable reevaluation appears to be well launched in the new edition of *How Natives Think* (Princeton: Princeton University Press, 1985), with its sympathetic and provocative introduction, "Lucien Lévy-Bruhl and the Concept of Cognitive Relativity," by C. Scott Littleton.

11. Lucien Lévy-Bruhl, *How Natives Think*, trans. Lilian A. Clare (New York: Washington Square Press, 1966), p. 180.

12. Swadesh, *Origin and Diversification of Language*, p. 183.

13. See, for example, Otto Koehler, "The Ability of Birds to 'Count,'" *Bulletin of Animal Behavior* 9 (1952): 41–45; W. H. Thorpe, *Learning and Instinct in Animals*, rev. ed. (London: Methuen, 1963), and *Animal and Human Nature* (London: Methuen, 1974); John C. Lilly, "Vocal Mimicry in Tursiops: Ability to Match Numbers and Durations of Human Vocal Bursts," *Science* 147 (1965): 300–301, and *The Mind of the Dolphin* (New York: Avon, 1967); Duane M. Rumbaugh, "Learning Skills of Anthropoids," in *Primate Behavior: Developments in Field and Laboratory Research*, vols. 1–4, ed. L. A. Rosenblum (New York: Academic Press, 1970), vol. 1; Keith J. Hayes and Catherine H. Nissen, "Higher Mental Functions of a Home-Raised Chimpanzee," in *Behavior of Nonhuman Primates: Modern Research Trends*, ed. A. M. Schrier and F. Stollnitz (New York: Academic Press, 1971); Bernard Rensch, *Biophilosophy*, trans. C. A. M. Sym (New York: Columbia University Press, 1971); and David Premack and Ann James Premack, *The Mind of an Ape* (New York: W. W. Norton, 1983).

14. Thorpe, *Learning and Instinct*, pp. 132, 464; and Karl Menninger, *Number Words and Number Symbols*, trans. Paul Broneer (Cambridge: MIT Press, 1969), p. 11.

15. Milton Hildebrand, "Symmetrical Gaits of Primates," *American Journal of Physical Anthropology*, n.s., 26 (1967): 119–30.

16. André Leroi-Gourhan, *Prehistoric Man*, trans. W. Baskin (New York: Philosophical Library, 1957).

17. Ashley Montagu, "Toolmaking, Hunting, and the Origin of Language," in *Origins and Evolution of Language and Speech*, ed. Stevan R. Harnad, Horst D. Steklis, and Jane B. Lancaster, *Annals of the New York Academy of Sciences* 280 (1976), p. 271.

18. Lévy-Bruhl, *How Natives Think* (1966), pp. 169 and 160 respectively.

19. See, for example, Jane B. Lancaster, *Primate Behavior and the Emergence of Human Culture* (New York: Holt, Rinehart, and Winston, 1975); and Richard E. Leakey and Roger Lewin, *Origins* (New York: E. P. Dutton, 1977).

20. Morris Kline, *Mathematics in Western Culture* (New York: Oxford University Press, 1953), p. 14.

21. Nathan Isaacs, *A Brief Introduction to Piaget: The Growth of Understanding in the Young Child and New Light on Children's Ideas of Numbers* (New York: Agathon Press, 1972), p. 25.

22. Lévy-Bruhl, *How Natives Think* (1966), p. 163.

23. Ibid.

24. Ibid., p. 180.

25. Ibid.

4

Hominid Bipedality and Primate Sexuality: A Further Re-Thinking of Upright Posture

We ought to be cautious in assuming that knobs and various fleshy appendages cannot be attractive to the female.

CHARLES DARWIN

But the evidence is rendered as complete as it can ever be, only when the more
ornamented individuals, almost always the males, voluntarily display their
attractions before the other sex; for we cannot believe such display is useless,
and if it be advantageous, sexual selection will almost inevitably follow.

MICHAEL T. GHISELIN

INTRODUCTION

The purpose of this case study is to launch an examination of a posturally significant and behaviorally critical aspect of hominid bipedality
that is consistently overlooked in assessments of its evolutionary impact. Hominid bipedality eventuated in a radically different primate
bodily appearance: male sexual characters relatively hidden in quadrupedal primates are visibly exposed in bipedal ones. Conversely,
female sexual characters normally visible in quadrupedal primates are

relatively hidden in bipedal ones. Loss of estrus—physiological and behavioral—can be explained in the light of continuous and direct male genital exposure. Typical primate estrus cycling was replaced not by year-round female receptivity, as is so commonly claimed,[1] but by year-round penile display. The phenomenon of sexual signaling in primates, early hominids in particular, thus requires new analysis. This is the first requisite. Early hominid sexual signaling behavior needs furthermore to be situated within the context of hominid communication: specifically, it can be shown that bipedal penile display is exemplary of a fundamental biological matrix, *corporeal representation*, and is thus on a semantic continuum with primordial language. Moreover since the radical reversal in visible male/female sexual morphology that originated with consistent upright posture has substantial implications for sexual selection in hominids, penile display needs to be examined within the purview of Darwin's original theory of sexual selection.

In keeping with these three requisites, the present chapter addresses itself to a fundamental reconceptualization of upright posture with respect to display behavior, Chapter 5 to an analysis of male hominid sexual display within the larger perspective of an evolutionary semantics, and Chapter 7 to the specifics of early hominid sexuality in light of sexual selection theory. (Chapter 6 critically examines entrenched beliefs about primordial language and is thus relevant to the investigation of an evolutionary semantics in Chapter 5.)

PRIMATE POSTURE AND SEXUAL SIGNALING BEHAVIOR: THEORETICAL CONSIDERATIONS

Because consistent bipedality radically changed the visible primate body, paleoanthropological reconstructions of the sexual life and practices of early hominids can be neither conclusively nor exclusively anchored in analogies to nonhuman primate sexuality.[2] To anchor them thus is to overlook precisely both the decisive shift in spatiokinetic possibilities of an upright as opposed to quadrupedal body, and the decisively different, immediately visible genital features that distinguish present-day upright male hominids from present-day quadrupedal male chimpanzees (and other primates),[3] and by inference early hominids from both early chimpanzees and the common ancestor from which each is thought to have emerged.[4] Accordingly, what is wanted is a tracing out of disanalogies as well as analogies between hominid and nonhominid sexuality.[5]

Bipedality is consistently taken as a prime diagnostic feature of hominids if not *the* prime feature.[6] It is traditionally connected with enhancing carrying capacities—transporting food, tools, or infants—and visual range.[7] Its origin, or motivating cause, is thus traditionally pinpointed in identifiable pragmatic acts: in the advantages and relative efficiency of transporting something from one place to another with two free hands, or of standing up to survey a locale for possible danger. Bipedality has not been tied to sexual selection as an enhancement of the body itself. More broadly, it has not been seriously considered and analyzed as a form of *display behavior*, either in its own right or as a critical feature of other displays, and this in spite of nonhuman primate display behaviors in which bipedality is central—for instance, in bipedal swaggering in chimpanzees,[8] or where short of an elevated posture, the particular display behavior in question would be significantly less impressive as in the chest-beating of a male gorilla.[9]

Given the traditional focus on primate *female* genitalia and behavior, it might appear reasonable to dismiss the possibility of sexual bodily enhancement via bipedality. On the one hand, cyclical genital swellings and colorations would no longer be immediately visible advertisements of sexual readiness were quadrupedal females to present (i.e., turn their backsides toward a fellow creature) bipedally. Conversely, genital swellings and colorations, if they existed in already bipedal females, would not be easily visible but would indeed require a shift to a quadrupedal posture every time the females wanted to approach a male sexually, a behavioral shift that, quite apart from considerations of economy of effort, negates any claim of bipedality to be either a form of sexual display behavior or a sexual enhancement of the body. In short, if bipedality works against typical primate *female* sexual signaling, how can it possibly be an enhancement?

Such reasoning breaks down with respect to primate males, specifically male chimpanzees and, to a significantly greater extent, male hominids.[10] It in fact collapses straightaway. Bipedality affords the opportunity of direct and continuous male sexual signaling. Just as significantly, consistent male bipedality allows a mobilized, that is, *ambulatory*, rather than static, sexual signaling, in the same way, interestingly enough, that a quadrupedal posture allows nonhominid female primates to signal sexual readiness and potency continuously while moving about; and correlatively, consistent male bipedality allows females to monitor bipedal male sexual readiness and potency continuously in the same way that a quadrupedal position allows nonhominid male primates to monitor female sexual readiness and potency continuously.

That penile display has not been seriously considered before with respect to bipedality is due to the practice of anchoring and evaluating primate sexual behavior primarily in female rather than male genitalia or in the genitalic changes and behaviors of both sexes equally. The effect of the practice—an under-reporting and under-analysis of the fact, dynamics, and significance of penile erection—will be discussed in several contexts below. The point here is twofold: first, the "theory of receptivity" (estrus) is to a considerable extent the generative conceptual force behind the practice; and second, the motivating factors underlying the practice—a greater readiness on the part of researchers to focus on female genitalia in their descriptive studies of primate sexual behavior,[11] and a general reluctance to focus on penile erection —may well be a reflection of the fact that penile display in Western society is classified as perverted and is legally punishable.[12] Each point merits brief discussion.

The concept of receptivity (or estrus, that is, "loss of estrus" being consistently equated with "year-round receptivity") is a concept in need of examination, both in terms of a straightforward clarification of meaning, and in terms of its implicit (and attitudinally powerful) connotations—for example that males are "more or less constantly potent"[13] but are restrained by "female receptivity," hence that, but for the fact that females hold the sexual strings, males would engage in sexual activity all the time.[14] Receptivity is used as a synonym for *responsiveness* (e.g., "a circumscribed period of time in mammals during which the female is responsive to courtship and mating");[15] as a sign of *willingness* (e.g., "oestrus should be a strictly behavioral term signifying willingness to mate");[16] as closely synonymous with the *openness* or *closedness* of a receptacle for males (e.g., an estrus female is one who is not "continuously copulable," hence who cannot provide continuous service, hence whose receptacle is not perpetually open hormonally and theoretically for male use);[17] and as synonymous with being on the *receiving* end of copulatory transactions (e.g., "In most [mammalian species,] these simple activities ["assumption of the mating posture which facilitates the male's achievement of intromission, plus maintenance of this position until intravaginal ejaculation has occurred"] comprise all of the female's receptive behavior").[18]

Given the central emphasis on female receptive behavior and its implicit attitudinal connotations, it is not surprising that the dominant picture to emerge is of a male being "serviced."[19] Receptivity is an essentially male concept. Insofar as females invite copulation, however, male as well as female behaviors are describable as receptive. When a female primate *invites* copulation by presenting, for example, and when the male accepts the invitation by mounting, the male is clearly (1) *responsive* (to courtship and mating) and (2) *willing* to mate. Moreover he might be said to be (3) *providing a service* to the female in the sense that (a) she is soliciting something from him—an erect, sexually potent penis—and (b) he is acceding to her solicitations. (In finer proximate terms,[20] he is providing a service in the form of tactile stimulation: see Chapter 7 and the elaboration of Eberhard's thesis of male genitalia as tactile stimulators.) Only in the literal sense—the female is receiving something from the male (penis and sperm) in copulatory transactions—is receptivity a concept applying exclusively to females.

The central emphasis on female receptivity and its connotations explains a further curious fact about the way in which male and female sexual behavior is (or is not) investigated. Mountings, intromissions, and ejaculations are uniformly reported and analyzed in accounts of primate sexual behavior.[21] More often than not, however, if one did not know that a penis was present and dynamically instrumental in these various male acts, there would be no reason to suspect its existence. Like male receptivity, male genitalia are seldom remarked upon as a separate topic on par with female genitalia.[22] In contrast to sexual swellings in females, virtually nothing is said of sexual swellings in males. Once the notion of year-round receptivity in hominid females is reconceptualized, that is, once penile display is recognized as a necessary entailment of hominid bipedality, male genitalic changes and their socio-sexual behavioral effects can be recognized and investigated.

Current cultural strictures should not prohibit such investigations. Whatever the unspoken mores and legal sanctions against certain present-day male sexual behaviors, they should not rule out a dispassionate examination of past male sexual behaviors, ones against which legal sanctions were not imposed and clothes were not mandated. While the danger of imputing too much to early hominids by failing "to distinguish current utility from reasons for origin" has been recognized,[23] the correlative and equal danger of admitting too little by failing to throw off cultural blinders has not been. Moreover while it may be more appealing to be linked to tool-transporting, food-provisioning, or infant-carrying ancestors *pace* current pragmatic Western attitudes and orientations, the objective facts of consistent bipedality make linkage with penis-displaying ancestors an empirical necessity.

The necessity can in fact be spelled out in terms of an overarching architectural constraint similar to the paradigmatic one described by biologists Stephen J. Gould and R. C. Lewontin.[24] Consistent bipedality imposes as specific and rigorous a *Bauplan* vis-à-vis visible male hominid genitalic features as does the fan-vaulted ceiling of St. Mark's Cathedral vis-à-vis structural design features. The architectural entailment imposes a further entailment. Penile exposure necessarily entails both continuous sexual display and continuous sexual signaling, not of course in the form of a continuous erection, but in the form of a potential and graded sexual readiness and power that can be continuously monitored. Bipedality is thus an architectural constraint that eventuates in a behavioral constraint: short of masking penile exposure, there is no way of shutting off the continuous visual signal.

Virtually no description of nonhuman primate social life is without reference to display behavior. On the contrary, displays are at the center of studies of primate social life and interanimate communications.[25] As Darwin's and present-day ethologists' research has shown, they are at the center of avian life as well.[26] It is surprising, then, that in scenarios of early hominid life, no mention is typically made of displays at all. With hominids, display behavior suddenly drops out of the primate evolutionary picture. It is as if, from the very beginnings of hominid life, this "archaic" form of communicating disappeared; even as if *hominid* bipedality and display are mutually exclusive. The omission is all the more surprising, indeed puzzling, given not only the implicit conjunction of bipedality and display behaviors in descriptive accounts of nonhuman primate life, but explicit if in-passing acknowledgment of the conjunction by David Pilbeam, a well-known primatologist.[27]

What is the explanation for the disappearance—or rather nonappearance—of this major form of primate communication? Were early hominids *without* sexual signals? Were the communicating powers of these consistently upright creatures from the very beginning *above* such behaviors? Clearly the relatively late evolutionary development of a verbal language militates against the possibility of hominid speech behavior replacing nonhominid display behaviors straight off. Furthermore, while display behaviors might be semantically linked with an early-developing gestural language, the vocabulary of the latter possibly evolving out of the vocabulary of the former, the semantics of the display behaviors would have had to have been already thoroughly inscribed on the hominid body to serve as a template for the newly emerging gestural language. In short, visual displays in general and sexual displays in particular cannot reasonably be assumed to have been absent in newly consistent bipedal primates —unless, of course, currently accepted evolutionary assessments of primate relationships are in error. If early hominid society was more like that of present-day orang-utan than chimpanzee society, then sexual displays might well have been absent since "no male courtship displays as such" are evident in orang-utan "society." [28]

A more compelling explanation for the peculiar absence of sexual display behavior in paleoanthropological reconstructions of hominid life lies rather in the emphasis on female receptive behavior and on the twentieth-century cultural biases noted above. The result is that a decisively pragmatic *doing*, especially manual, and predominantly male, is regularly envisioned at the heart of early hominid life and as at the origin of bipedality.[29] It is thus on an exalted model of *Homo faber* and all the related activities that exalted model suggests that early hominid life is patterned. Sexual behavior on this model is described in terms of economics and politics—sexual roles, division of labor, and the like.[30] Hardly a word is offered as to how the sexual bonding was concretely negotiated and secured to begin with. Moreover if australopithecines were indeed *swingers*, as one anthropologist has suggested, how their "copulatory bouts" came about remains a mystery.[31] In short, the whole question of hominid communication is nowhere broached.

No doubt twentieth-century Westerners relate much more sympathetically to an ancestral *Homo faber* than to an ancestral *Homo exhibere*. (Note however that it should not at all be a matter of choosing but of proper recognition.) In addition, evolutionary science provides far more in the way of hard inferred data when concrete products—be they tools, food, or infants—are involved in the reconstruction of the hominid past. Anthropologist Tim White's skeptical remark is apposite in this regard: "I've never seen an estrus fossil." Yet creatures who reproduce through internal fertilization engage in some form of sexual signaling. In effect, without a communicative system by which to signal sexual readiness and potency, how could male and female early hominids have come together to reproduce in the first place? Short of a model of early hominid sexual signaling behavior, present-day analyses of ancestral hominid reproductive effort and success, and of parental investment[32]—or appropriation of related, sophisticated human concepts such as cuckoldry, cruel binds, desertion, war propagandists, and the like[33]—appear premature. The actual sexual behavior by which one sex advertises readiness and solicits copulation with another is a prime reproductive variable that is unaccounted for. Reproductive effort begins with the male or female who initiates copulation through some form of display, as Darwin first showed. Measurement of reproductive success necessarily begins with that same act.

The same point can be put in the broader perspective of primate intelligence. Relative to hominid evolution, nonhuman primate display behavior is not treated with the same *intellectual* interest as hominid pragmatic behaviors on the order of tool-making or carrying objects about. Nonhuman primate display behaviors fail to come up to or even suggest the enterprising stature and innovating strategies and practices that are consistently thought to define early hominids, that are consistently attributed to them, and that are ultimately tied to bigger brains. In brief, nonhuman primate display behavior has no intellectual status and thus no long-term evolutionary hominid significance. To reinstate display behavior, specifically sexual display, into the hominid evolutionary picture, it is therefore necessary to flesh out the model of *Homo exhibere* and demonstrate its long-term evolutionary implications. The procedure will be to review briefly Darwin's original evidence for sexual displays in nonhominid species, thereby demonstrating a basic pattern in male sexual display, and then, by showing the connection between primate bipedality and penile erection in greater detail, demonstrate a new and profound evolutionary dimension of erect posture. The results of this analysis will lead directly to the consideration of an evolutionary semantics, the subject of Chapter 5. It will be shown there how early hominid sexual display is on a semantic continuum with primordial language—how communicated meaning is mediated by iconic corporeal representation in both cases. Early hominid bipedal sexual display behavior will thus ultimately be shown to be part of those innovative practices that are consistently thought to define early hominids, that are consistently attributed to them, and that ultimately culminate in bigger brains.

BASIC PATTERN IN MALE SEXUAL DISPLAYS

Darwin speaks repeatedly of erections and expansions in his descriptions of male courtship displays in birds—all quite apart, of course, from male genitalia. For example (italics added in each case), "the gold-pheasant (*Thaumalea picta*) during his courtship *expands* and *raises* his splendid frill"; "Birds of Paradise . . . *raising* their wings, *elevating* their exquisite plumes, and making them vibrate," display before the females; when the Argus pheasant displays himself, "both wings are *vertically erected* and *expanded*"; "the wild turkey-cock *erects* his glittering plumage, *expands* his finely-zoned tail and barred wing-feathers." Even in modestly ornamented birds, erection and expansion are common—as in the reed-bunting.[34]

Making some part stand up or inflating it are fundamental biological means of calling attention to it (as further examples, dewlaps are extended by reptiles in courtship displays, pilo-erection is common in chimpanzees, and gular pouches are extended by orang-utans).[35] But ultimately, of course, erection and expansion are the means whereby the displaying animal calls attention *to itself* and gets a certain message across: "displays serve to focus the attention, and complete displays are most often followed by . . . acts performed toward the displayer."[36]

Penile erection is an evolutionary elaboration of the basic male pattern of erection/expansion. In male primates—and male mammals generally—an external fleshy bodily organ rather than feathers and wings (or dewlaps, or in addition to hair or pouches) undergoes spatio-kinetic transformation in courtship and copulatory behaviors. The conformance of primate penile erection to basic male sexual display behavior is indeed further reason for calling the fact, dynamics, and significance of penile erection to attention. If Martian scientists were attempting to understand male primate sexual behavior on the basis of the literature alone, not only would they not necessarily even conceive of a penis—a fact intimated earlier—but they would certainly not conceive of its spatio-kinetic transformational powers or its dynamic conformance to basic male sexual display behavior. Thus to assume that the penis and penile erection can go without saying in accounts of primate sexual interactions on the grounds that explicit attention and description belabor the obvious skirts the point at issue. The following example will show that the omission constitutes a critical oversight with respect to primate sexual behavior generally and to veridical reconstructions of early hominid sexual behavior in particular.

The pygmy chimpanzee is regarded by many as the living ape closest to humans.[37] Consider then the following recent description of a male's typical courtship behavior:

Most frequently, a male approached within 15 feet of a female and sat leaning back and displaying his erect pink penis while gazing intently in the female's direction. This period of penile erection and gazing was sometimes prolonged: one male was recorded in courtship posture for 18 minutes.[38]

Even if penile erection is regarded a quasi-voluntary act (van Lawick-Goodall classifies it as "autonomic behavior")[39] and thus not wholly intentional, it is nonetheless clearly apparent from the description that the pygmy chimpanzee is engaged in display behavior— not merely because the word *display* is used to describe his behavior but because *display* effectively describes and classifies his behavior: the male *leans back* and thereby calls attention specifically to his erect penis. He makes his penis as starkly and directly visible as possible by assuming a posture coincident with that end. In short, the male pygmy chimpanzee actively focuses attention on his "sexual desire and readiness for copulation."[40]

CONSISTENT BIPEDALITY AND PENILE ERECTION: BASIC PRIMATE BEHAVIORAL ANALOGIES AND DISANALOGIES

Consistent bipedality exposes the penis and facilitates a focusing of attention on it in a manner not equal to, but greater than the diagonally recumbent sitting posture of the male pygmy chimpanzee. These entailments of consistent bipedality are to some degree already apparent in other chimpanzee behaviors—in one instance (documented below), the mere assumption of an erect posture constitutes and/or enhances male sexual display. Itemized identification of these other behaviors will suggest specific hominid/nonhominid evolutionary continuities and discontinuities. It will thus lay the groundwork for distinguishing those analogies and disanalogies that together shed light on early hominid bipedality and sexual display behavior. The general and the specifically sexual behaviors will be taken up in turn, the former in a brief survey, the latter in greater detail.

Examination of the descriptive literature shows that, in addition to being functional in circumstances all the way from jump fights[41] to situations where upright posture affords a pragmatic solution to a difficult problem,[42] bipedality functions regularly in at least four major types of nonhuman primate display. It occurs in straightforward aggressive or threat displays—in charges or chases, for example; in self-assertive or conflict displays—where an animal brandishes some object, rocks from side to side, or beats its chest, for instance; in declarative displays—as when a male makes his sexual inclinations known to a female by swaggering; and in displays associated with excitement—in "carnival" situations or situations of plenteous food.[43] In all these instances upright posture and locomotion are not simply an epiphenomenon of the behavior but enhance stature (size) and full-body exposure. The effectiveness of the display hinges upon the animal's being bipedal.

Primate penile erection functions in the same type of circumstances as bipedal posture/locomotion (and often accompanies the latter behaviors in chimpanzee societies). Primatologist K. R. L. Hall and ethologist Wolfgang Wickler separately report on conspecific-oriented warning behavior by male savanna baboons, behavior in which the animal sits facing away from its own group and displays its genitals toward a neighboring group. Detlev Ploog and other ethologists give accounts of penile erection in the thigh-spreading greeting and dominance behavior of male squirrel monkeys, the behavior occurring in both agonistic and sexual encounters. Jane van Lawick-Goodall reports penile erection (chimpanzee) in bipedal swaggering, in situations of heightened excitement over food, and in greeting situations. Penile erection is also reported in the infant and juvenile play of Japanese monkeys and in intertroop encounters of colobine monkeys. In short, although references are few and scattered—the result perhaps of under-reporting—it is clear that as with bipedality, penile erection occurs in both sexual and nonsexual contexts.[44]

The erection of a body part—plumage or penis—and the assumption of an erect posture afford an increase in both general body size and member size. Apparent size has been recognized as a prime factor in both natural and sexual selection from the time Darwin first wrote about it.[45] If an animal looks large by virtue of its build or posture, or becomes larger by spatially extending itself in some way, whether naturally or by brandishing something, its possibilities for avoiding predation, for successful combat, for obtaining a favored food before others, and for procurement of a mate are all proportionately enhanced. Bipedality and penile erection effectively capitalize on this spatio-morphological fact of life. Moreover behavioral convergence augments behavioral effect. Standing up both in part and in whole—double erection—has increased signaling power and is ultimately of increased selective advantage. It is similar to the graduated threat-display through additive signaling in baboons.[46]

The most apt prototypical model of hominid double erection is the bipedal swagger of the common chimpanzee *Pan troglodytes*. The swagger was first reported in 1928 by Bingham as a "waddle."[47] It has probably not been intensively studied as a male sexual display for the same reasons that penile display has not been postulated for early hominids. Van Lawick-Goodall's general description of male chimpanzee courtship behaviors is instructive on several points in this regard.

When males took the initiative in 176 out of 213 witnessed matings (a proportion already indicative of the attention properly due male sexual display), van Lawick-Goodall reports that "in 50% of these occasions they merely approached the female with both hair and penis erect; or on other occasions they gave 'courtship displays.'"[48] She offers no further comment on combined pilo/penile erection, nor does she specify whether a quadrupedal or bipedal approach was typically used in conjunction with the double erection. The brevity of the description notwithstanding, its wording strongly suggests (rightly or wrongly) that double erection of hair and penis is an astoundingly potent signal ("they merely approached"), one that prompts immediate female response.

With respect to "courtship displays," van Lawick-Goodall first qualifies the term by stating, "It is used here simply as a means of describing postures and gestures commonly directed towards a receptive female prior to copulation"; she then notes that several of the "displays" occur frequently in nonsexual contexts. The implications are (1) that the male "courtship displays" are not real displays, but (2) are merely a passing stage in (3) the progression, receptive female > copulation; and that their more proper classification is under nonsexual behavior. Bipedal swagger, the first male display mentioned, is briefly described: "the male may swagger in one spot or advance towards the female in this manner." Under the heading of aggressive behavior, van Lawick-Goodall gives a remarkably fuller description:

THE BIPEDAL SWAGGER is typically *a male posture* and occurs only rarely in females. The chimpanzee stands upright and sways rhythmically from foot to foot, his shoulders slightly hunched and his arms held out and away from the body, usually to the side. He may swagger in one spot or he may move forward in this manner. *This posture occurs most commonly as a courtship display,* but it also occurs when one male threatens another of similar social status (italics added).[49]

Several aspects of the account warrant comment. To begin with, there is no mention of penile erection coinciding with (sexually oriented) bipedal swaggering, yet it seems highly likely that the two occur simultaneously. Consider the following description by primatologist C. M. Rogers:

Soliciting by the normal male [chimpanzee] is highly stylized and involves squatting with knees spread wide to display an erect penis; most wildborn males accompany this by slapping the ground with open palms. If a female does not present to him, he may after several seconds rise to an erect posture and execute a short dance in some respect similar to a threat display. He will then frequently alternate from one pattern to the other if not interrupted by a sexually-presenting female.[50]

What Rogers identifies as a "short dance," particularly in its similarity to threat display, appears to be what van Lawick-Goodall identifies as *bipedal swagger*. Thus penile display and bipedal swagger are behaviorally convergent. Although Rogers does not explicitly state that the male's penis remains erect while alternating between the two displays, it is reasonable to assume—on the grounds of behavioral economics and effective sexual communication—that the penis does not undergo tumescence and detumescence with each shift from one display to the other.

A second point concerns male initiative. If males habitually approach females, and as much as 83 percent of the time as van Lawick-Goodall reports, then male initiatory behavior, *male* sexual signaling, merits as precise and explicit description as the fully researched and consistently prominent topic of *female presenting*. Lack of due attention to male display behavior—whether the latter is prompted by female genital signals or not—skews understanding of chimpanzee sexual communication. The skewed picture constitutes an even greater liability when chimpanzee sexual behavior is taken as a model (or counter-model) of early hominid sexual behavior.

A third point turns on the fact that bipedal swaggering in the interest of copulation is a male display. This fact would, in itself, seem to secure its alliance with penile display, for, with the assumption of an erect posture, the chimpanzee's erect penis is automatically exposed. Bipedality is thus an essentially male option with respect to sexual signaling and choice of partner. An erect and ambulatory male can direct his penile display toward one female rather than another and approach the desired female directly. (This point is discussed in greater detail in Chapter 7 with respect both to male choice and to differential hominid/chimpanzee hip-joint anatomy.)

A fourth point argues persuasively for penile display and bipedal swaggering's being considered seminal male chimpanzee behaviors in an extended sense. Like female presenting, penile display and bipedal swaggering have meanings in nonsexual contexts. These nonsexual meanings are in general the inverse of those of presenting. In finer terms, when male and female chimpanzee sexual signaling behaviors are employed in other than sexual situations, the meaning of the male behavior—bipedal stance and swagger—is generally assertive or agonistic; the meaning of the female behavior—presenting—is generally appeasing. Corporeal evidence shows that the oppositional meanings are not accidental, that is, that the behaviors are inherently significant *as postures*. As primatologist Alison Jolly has remarked, "Bodily posture is one of the most consistent communicative gestures throughout mammals as a whole."[51] To turn one's back on a conspecific in the manner of a chimpanzee in the act of presenting is to assume a posture that is inherently vulnerable. It would otherwise not be observed that "presenting [in non-sexual contexts] is often accompanied by nervous, even fearful behavior on the part of the presenting animal."[52] The posture cannot be considered aggressive on any count. By the same token, an upright posture which highlights size and in which the full frontal expanse of the body is presented to another, is an assertive posture that cannot be taken as appeasing or submissive. (Consider the present-day human necessity of a white flag to dampen and refocus the typical meaning of upright posture and approach.) Although no such studies have been undertaken, it is probable that these postures constitute primate postural archetypes.

A *consistently* upright posture tightens the association between bipedality and penile erection. It does this on three counts. Two of these emanate from the architectural constraint indicated earlier: consistent bipedality is a postural constraint in automatically exposing the penis; it is a behavioral constraint (more positively, a built-in behavioral advantage) in heightening male sexual signaling power. The constraints make consistent bipedality equivalent to year-round sexual advertisement—to *receptivity* in the sense that at any time he feels himself so motivated, the male's willingness to copulate is straightaway signaled to all females in visual range. In other words, his erection is a sign of his receptivity.

Year-round sexual advertisement is what in part necessarily distinguished nonhominid primate males from early hominid males. This means that disanalogies between the sexual behavior of present-day chimpanzees and the sexual behavior of early hominids begin with a recognition of the two constraints identified above. The disanalogies do not, however, end with year-round male sexual advertisement. A third factor operates to strengthen even further the association between consistent bipedality and penile erection. This third factor is the result of semantic reinforcement through corporeal representation.

The assumption and maintenance of an erect posture dynamically mirror the assumption and maintenance of an erect penis.

The semantic impact of corporeal representation is aptly captured in bio-sociologist B. S. Low's statement that "[with respect to sexual selection] the use of symbols can augment the display of conspicuousness."[53] The statement was made with reference to the use of selected decorations by humans in various cultures, but clearly such symbolic enhancement is not limited to cultural embellishments—clothes and ornamentations, for example. In the process of achieving both an erect posture and an erect penis, a fourfold dynamic congruency is evident, erect posture augmenting the display of the already conspicuous erect penis in (a) upward direction of movement; (b) increase in apparent size; (c) altered and more visibly distinctive shape; and (d) degree of tautness (with respect to bipedality, greater tautness relative to a sitting, not a quadrupedal, posture). In effect, the same kind of *spatial and tactile–kinetic transformations* take place in the achievement of an erect posture as in the achievement of an erect penis. A quasi-voluntary gesture has its spatial tactile–kinetic analogue in a fully voluntary corporeal act. It is this analogical dimension of the association that situates penile/bipedal display within an evolutionary semantics. Before pursuing a detailed investigation of the latter, a brief summary of the impact of consistent bipedality on early hominid sexual behavior is in order.

SUMMARY

Given its architectural constraints and analogical correspondence to penile erection, it is clear why consistent bipedality heightens a male hominid's stature in more than the literal elevating sense: it heightens his stature *as a male*. This heightening can be seen most clearly in the perspective of the behavior of the male pygmy chimpanzee cited above. First, since erect posture automatically exposes the penis and keeps it on perpetual display, no postural adjustment like the chimpanzee's is necessary to make it starkly visible. Sociobiologist Donald Symons's observation concerning the most effective male sexual advertisement for women is of interest in this regard. In his analysis of the evolution of human sexuality, he states, "Photographs of men with erect penises will be far more effective than photographs of men with flaccid penises in sexually arousing women. The former suggest an actual sexual interaction, not just the possibility of a future interaction."[54] If indeed it is actual interaction and not just the possibility of same that arouses women (and presumably Symons's *evolutionary* analysis pertains to ancestral as well as present-day females), then not only will an erect penis be a more effective advertisement than a flaccid one but any penis will be more effective than no visible penis at all (that is, a penis hidden in quadrupedal posture). On Symons's account, the advent of consistent bipedality would have had to have been the most powerful reinforcement possible of male sexual display, that is, of sexual desire and copulatory readiness.

Second, since the male can keep his erect penis in view while moving toward the female, he can do more than gaze intently at her; he can approach her intently. That an approach by a consistently bipedal, sexually motivated male carries a far stronger visual signal than that of a quadrupedally approaching male is further evidence of the increased impact of maleness through consistent bipedality. Penile exposure plus *continuous* signaling in movement toward a female constitutes a doubly potent advertisement of male presence.

Third, since in assuming an erect posture the male semantically reinforces the meaning of penile erection, the postural force of his display is greater than the postural force display of the chimpanzee whose diagonally recumbent sitting posture has no similarly dynamic sexual features. Analogical transformations in upward movement, in size, in shape, and in tautness together constitute not only a decisively power-packed male display, but one which is decisively different from the pygmy chimpanzee's "courtship posture" described earlier.

In sum, there are marked contrasts between consistently bipedal primates and essentially quadrupedal ones in sexual penile display. They can be summarily specified in nonhominid terms as follows: (1) a particular sitting posture is the preferential mode of penile display in chimpanzees;[55] and (2) bipedal swaggering is a secondary form of penile display. As a secondary form, bipedal swaggering is partially congruent to penile erection, but the bipedal stance is not thoroughly utilized. Indeed, the stance appears to be more a tableau-like display than an ambulatory one. The spreading of the arms away from the body—presumably so that the view of the penis is as visually uncluttered as possible—and the fact that the chimpanzee does not necessarily move forward, suggest greater emphasis on optimal *visual* presentation of the body alone rather than on optimal visual presentation *plus* optimization of the possibilities of movement opened up by a bipedal stance. The fact that the chimpanzee penis is bright pink strongly suggests further that *color* rather than *size*—or dynamic transformations generally—is the key visual sexual signal. It is of interest to note in this regard that "red is a very conspicuous colour commonly found in the pigmentation of the penis in Old World monkeys."[56] Indeed, color is not a strong visual character of the human penis, which typically is not described as bright or pink—or red—but as *large*.[57] A dynamic visual character, not a static visual property, distinguishes its signaling potency.

NOTES

1. See, for example, Donald Symons, *The Evolution of Human Sexuality* (Oxford: Oxford University Press, 1979); Milford H. Wolpoff, *Paleoanthropology* (New York: Knopf, 1980); Sarah B. Hrdy, *The Woman That Never Evolved* (Cambridge: Harvard University Press, 1981); Jane B. Lancaster, *Primate Behavior and the Emergence of Human Culture* (New York: Holt, Rinehart, and Winston, 1975); Desmond Morris, *The Naked Ape* (New York: Dell, 1967); C. Owen Lovejoy, "The Origin of Man," *Science* 211 (1981): 340–450; and David R. Pilbeam, *The Ascent of Man* (New York: Macmillan, 1972).

2. See, for example, Wolfgang Wickler, "Socio-Sexual Signals and Their Intraspecific Imitation among Primates," in *Primate Ethology*, ed. Desmond Morris (Garden City, N.Y.: Anchor, 1969), pp. 89–189; Lancaster, *Primate Behavior*; and Hrdy, *Woman*.

3. See R. V. Short, "Sexual Selection and Its Component Parts, Somatic and Genital Selection, as Illustrated by Man and the Great Apes," in *Advances in the Study of Behavior* 9, ed. J. S. Rosenblatt, R. A. Hinde, C. Beer, and M-C. Busnel (New York: Academic Press, 1979).

4. See, for example, Vincent M. Sarich, "Human Origins: An Immunological View," in *Perspectives on Human Evolution* 1, ed. Sherwood L. Washburn and P. C. Jay (New York: Holt, Rinehart, and Winston, 1968), pp. 94–121, and "Pygmy Chimpanzee Systematics: A Molecular Perspective," in *The Pygmy Chimpanzee*, ed. R. L. Susman (New York: Plenum Press, 1984), pp. 43–48; Morris Goodman and Gabriel Ward Lasker, "Molecular Evidence as to Man's Place in Nature," in *Primate Functional Morphology and Evolution*, ed. Russell H. Tuttle (The Hague: Mouton, 1975), pp. 71–101; Colin Patterson, *Evolution* (London: British Museum, 1978); Sherwood L. Washburn, "The Analysis of Primate Evolution with Particular Reference to the Origin of Man," *Cold Spring Harbor Symposia on Quantitative Biology* 15 (1950): 57–78; and Bernard G. Campbell, *Human Evolution* (Chicago: Aldine, 1966); see also Morris Goodman, "The Chronicle of Primate Phylogeny Contained in Proteins," *Symposia of the Zoological Society of London* 33 (1973): 339–75, for a general background on assessments of hominoid relationships through protein analysis.

5. Compare J. N. Spuhler, "Continuities and Discontinuities in

Anthropoid–Hominid Behavioral Evolution: Bipedal Locomotion and Sexual Receptivity," in *Evolutionary Biology and Human Social Behavior*, ed. N. A. Chagnon and W. Irons (North Scituate, Mass.: Duxbury Press, 1979), pp. 454–61.

6. Charles Darwin, *The Descent of Man and Selection in Relation to Sex* (Princeton: Princeton University Press, 1981 [1871]); Sarich, "Pygmy Chimpanzee Systematics"; John E. Pfeiffer, *The Emergence of Man* (New York: Harper & Row, 1969); W. E. Le Gros Clark, *The Fossil Evidence for Human Evolution* (Chicago: Chicago University Press, 1978); Washburn, "Analysis of Primate Evolution"; Gabriel Ward Lasker, *Physical Anthropology* (New York: Holt, Rinehart, and Winston, 1973); David R. Pilbeam, "Distinguished Lecture: Hominoid Evolution and Hominoid Origins," *American Anthropologist*, n.s. 88 (1986): 295–312; W. Howells, *Back of History*, rev. ed. (Garden City, N.Y.: Doubleday, 1963); Richard E. Leakey and Roger Lewin, *Origins* (New York: E. P. Dutton, 1977); F. C. Howell, "The Hominization Process," in *Human Evolution*, ed. N. Korn and F. Thompson (New York: Holt, Rinehart, and Winston, 1967), pp. 84–92; John T. Robinson, *Early Hominid Posture and Locomotion* (Chicago: University of Chicago Press, 1972); Lancaster, *Primate Behavior*; C. Loring Brace and Ashley Montagu, *Man's Evolution* (New York: Macmillan, 1965); and George G. Simpson, "The Biological Nature of Man," in *Perspectives on Human Evolution* 1, pp. 1–17.

7. See, for example, Stephen J. Gould, *Ontogeny and Phylogeny* (Cambridge: Belknap Press, 1977); Lovejoy, "Origin of Man"; and Robinson, *Early Hominid Posture*.

8. Jane van Lawick-Goodall, "The Behaviour of Free-Living Chimpanzees in the Gombe Stream Reserve," in *Animal Behaviour Monographs*, vol. 1, pt. 3 (1968): 165–311, and "A Preliminary Report on Expressive Movements and Communication in the Gombe Stream Chimpanzees," in *Primate Patterns*, ed. Phyllis J. Dolhinow (New York: Holt, Rinehart, and Winston, 1972), pp. 25–84.

9. See George B. Schaller, *The Mountain Gorilla* (Chicago: University of Chicago Press, 1963), and "The Behavior of the Mountain Gorilla," in *Primate Patterns*, pp. 85–124.

10. See Short, "Sexual Selection," on the difference in visibility of male genitalia in higher primates.

11. See, for example, J. H. Crook, "Sexual Selection, Dimorphism, and Social Organization in the Primates," in *Sexual Selection and the Descent of Man, 1871–1971*, ed. B. Campbell (Chicago: Aldine, 1972), pp. 231–81.

12. See R. V. Short, "The Origins of Human Sexuality," in *Reproduction in Mammals* 8, ed. C. R. Austin and R. V. Short (Cambridge: Cambridge University Press, 1980), pp. 1–33, on the legal double standard: females "have nothing indecent to expose."

13. Symons, *Evolution of Human Sexuality*, p. 122.

14. For an alternative view with interesting implications, see J. Hanby on the sexual behavior of adult Guinea baboons: "The maturing male in all these

groups seems to be concerned more with status, control, and courtship than with copulation, an activity he would have perfected in early adolescence." "Sociosexual Development in Primates," in *Perspectives in Ethology*, ed. P. P. G. Bateson and P. H. Klopfer (New York: Plenum Press, 1976), 2: 37.

15. N. Thompson-Handler, R. K. Malenky, and N. Badrian, "Sexual Behavior of *Pan paniscus* under Natural Conditions in the Lomako Forest, Equateur, Aire," in *Pygmy Chimpanzee*, p. 362.

16. Thelma Rowell, *The Social Behaviour of Monkeys* (Middlesex: Penguin, 1972), p. 123.

17. Symons, *Evolution of Human Sexuality*, p. 106. The phrase "continuously copulable" is one Symons borrows from Frank A. Beach. See the latter's "Human Sexuality and Evolution," in *Reproductive Behavior*, ed. W. Montagna and W. A. Sadler (New York: Plenum Press, 1973), p. 357.

18. Frank A. Beach, "Cross-Species Comparisons and Human Heritage," in *Human Sexuality in Four Perspectives*, ed. Frank A. Beach (Baltimore: Johns Hopkins, 1976), p. 303.

19. Symons, *Evolution of Human Sexuality*.

20. For a distinction between ultimate and proximate biological explanations, see E. O. Wilson, *Sociobiology* (Cambridge: Belknap Press, 1975).

21. See, for example, H. C. Kraemer, J. R. Horvat, C. Doering, and P. R. McGinnis, "Male Chimpanzee Development Focusing on Adolescence: Integration of Behavioral with Physiological Changes," *Primates* 23 (1982): 393–405; N. Itoigawa, K. Negayama, and K. Kondo, "Experimental Study on Japanese Monkeys (*Macaca fuscata*)," *Primates* 22 (1981): 494–502; R. P. Michael, M. Wilson, and T. M. Plant, "Sexual Behavior of Male Primates and the Role of Testosterone," in *Comparative Ecology and Behavior of Primates*, ed. R. P. Michael and J. H. Crook (London: Academic Press, 1973), pp. 263–313; Suzanne Chevalier-Skolnikoff, "Heterosexual Copulatory Patterns in Stumptail Macaques (*Macaca arctoides*) and in Other Macaque Species," *Archives of Sexual Behavior* 4 (1975): 199–220; and Symons, *Evolution of Human Sexuality*.

22. For an exception, see Short, "Sexual Selection"; for an inverse criticism on this same point, see Hrdy, *Woman*.

23. Stephen J. Gould and R. C. Lewontin, "The Spandrels of San Marco and the Panglossian Paradigm: A Critique of the Adaptationist Programme," *Proceedings of the Royal Society of London*, Series B, Biological Science, 205 (1979): 581–98; see also M. E. Hamilton, "Revising Evolutionary Narratives: A Consideration of Alternative Assumptions about Sexual Selection and Competition for Mates," *American Anthropologist*, n.s. 86 (1984): 651–62.

24. Gould and Lewontin, "Spandrels."

25. See, for example, C. A. Bramblett, *Patterns of Primate Behavior* (Palo Alto, Calif.: Mayfield, 1976); Franz De Waal, *Chimpanzee Politics* (New York: Harper Colophon, 1982); R. W. Sussman and I. Tattersall, "Behavior and Ecology of *Macaca fascicularis* in Mauritius: A Preliminary Study," *Primates* 22 (1981): 192–205; F. Pelaez, "Greeting Movements among Adult Males in

a Colony of Baboons: *Papio hamadryas, P. cynocephalus* and Their Hybrids," *Primates* 23 (1982): 233–44; Yukimaru Sugiyama, "Social Behavior of Chimpanzees in the Budongo Forest, Uganda," *Primates* 10 (1969): 197–225; K. R. L. Hall and I. De Vore, "Baboon Social Behavior," in *Primate Patterns*, pp. 125–80; Phyllis J. Dolhinow, "The North Indian Langur," ibid., pp. 85–124; H. Kummer, *Primate Societies* (Chicago: Aldine, 1971); Schaller, "Behavior of the Mountain Gorilla," pp. 85–124; van Lawick-Goodall, "Free-Living Chimpanzees"; R. Dawkins and J. R. Krebs, "Animal Signals: Information or Manipulation?" in *Behavioral Ecology*, ed. J. R. Krebs and N. B. Davies (London: Basil Blackwell, 1978), pp. 282–309; and T. K. Pitcairn, "Aggression in Natural Groups of Pongids," in *Primate Aggression, Territoriality, and Xenophobia*, ed. Ralph L. Holloway (New York: Academic Press, 1974), pp. 241–72.

26. Darwin, *Descent*. See also, for example, A. Daanje, "On Locomotory Movements in Birds and the Intention Movements Derived from Them," in *Function and Evolution of Behavior*, ed. P. H. Klopfer and J. P. Hailman (Reading: Addison Wesley, 1972), pp. 259–96; Desmond Morris, "The Feather Postures of Birds and the Problem of the Origin of Social Signals," *Behavior* 9 (1956): 75–113; N. Tinbergen, " 'Derived' Activities: Their Causation, Biological Significance, Origin, and Emancipation during Evolution," *Quarterly Review of Biology* 27 (1952): 1–32; and Konrad Lorenz, "Comparative Studies on the Behaviour of *Anatinae*," in *Function and Evolution of Behavior*, pp. 231–59.

27. See, for example, van Lawick-Goodall, "Free-Living Chimpanzees." David R. Pilbeam, *The Evolution of Man* (New York: Funk & Wagnalls, 1970), p. 95, and *Ascent*, pp. 71, 152; see further in the text for a detailed elaboration of Pilbeam's passing acknowledgments.

28. B. M. F. Galdikas, "Orangutan Reproduction in the Wild," in *Reproductive Biology of the Great Apes*, ed. C. E. Graham (New York: Academic Press, 1981), p. 290; see also R. V. Short, "Human Sexuality."

29. For exceptions to the hunter image and/or to the predominant male focus, see Sue T. Parker and Kay R. Gibson, "A Developmental Model for the Evolution of Language and Intelligence in Early Hominids," *Behavioral and Brain Sciences* 2 (1979): 367–408; Lewis R. Binford, *Bones: Ancient Man and Modern Myths* (New York: Academic Press, 1981), and *In Pursuit of the Past* (New York: Thames and Hudson, 1983); Pat Shipman, "Scavenging or Hunting in Early Hominids: Theoretical Frameworks and Tests," *American Anthropologist*, n.s. 88 (1986): 27–43; and Lovejoy, "Origin of Man," pp. 340–50.

30. See especially Lancaster, *Primate Behavior*, and "Carrying and Sharing in Human Evolution," *Human Nature* 1 (1978): 82–89; Jane B. Lancaster and C. S. Lancaster, "Parental Investment: The Hominid Adaptation," in *How Humans Adapt*, ed. D. J. Ortner (Washington, D.C.: Smithsonian Institute, 1983), pp. 33–56; see also, for example, Wolpoff, *Paleoanthropology*; Pilbeam, *Ascent*; and Sherwood L. Washburn and C. S. Lancaster, "The Evolution of Hunting," in *Perspectives on Human Evolution* 1, pp. 213–29.

31. R. G. Whitten, "Hominid Promiscuity and the Sexual Life of Proto-

Savages: Did *Australopithecus* Swing?" *Current Anthropology* 23 (1982): 99–101. The phrase "copulatory bout" is from E. Sue Savage-Rumbaugh and B. J. Wilkerson, "Socio-sexual Behavior in *Pan paniscus* and *Pan troglodyte: A Com-parative Study," *Human Evolution* 7 (1978): 327–44.

32. See, for example, Sue T. Parker, "A Sexual Selection Model for Homi-nid Evolution," *Human Evolution* 2 (1987): 235–53.

33. See R. L. Trivers, "Parental Investment and Sexual Selection," in *Sexual Selection and The Descent of Man*, pp. 136–79; and Gerald Borgia, "Sexual Selection and the Evolution of Mating Systems," in *Sexual Selection and Reproductive Competition in Insects*, ed. M. S. Blum and N. A. Blum (New York: Academic Press, 1979), pp. 19–73.

34. Darwin, *Descent*, pp. 89, 88, 91, 87, and 95 respectively.

35. R. L. Trivers, "Sexual Selection and Resource-Accruing Abilities in *Anolis garmani*," *Evolution* 30 (1976): 253–69; van Lawick-Goodall, "Free-Living Chimpanzees"; A. H. Schultz, "The Recent Hominoid Primates," in *Perspectives on Human Evolution* 1, pp. 122–95.

36. Pitcairn, "Aggression in Natural Groups," pp. 243–44.

37. H. J. Coolidge, "*Pan paniscus:* Pygmy Chimpanzee from South of the Congo River," *American Journal of Physical Anthropology*, o.s. 18 (1933): 1–57, and "Foreword," in *Pygmy Chimpanzee*; Adrienne L. Zhilman, "Body Build and Tissue Composition in *Pan paniscus* and *Pan troglodytes* with Comparison to Other Hominoids," ibid., pp. 179–200; Adrienne L. Zhilman, J. E. Cronin, D. L. Cramer, and Vincent M. Sarich, "Pygmy Chimpanzee as a Possible Prototype for the Common Ancestor of Humans, Chimpanzees and Gorillas," *Nature* 275 (1978): 744–46; and Sarich, "Pygmy Chimpanzee Systematics"; but see also H. M. McHenry's counterclaim in "The Common Ancestor: A Study of the Postcranium of *Pan paniscus*, *Australopithecus*, and Other Hominoids," in *Pygmy Chimpanzee*, pp. 201–30.

38. Thompson-Handler, Malenky, and Badrian, "Sexual Behavior," p. 353.

39. Van Lawick-Goodall, "Free-Living Chimpanzees."

40. C. R. Carpenter, "Societies of Monkeys and Apes," in *Primate Social Behavior*, ed. Charles H. Southwick (New York: Van Nostrand Reinhold, 1963), pp. 49–50. The quotation is given in full and discussed in detail in Chapter 5.

41. Alison Jolly, *Lemur Behavior* (Chicago: University of Chicago Press, 1966).

42. H. R. Bauer, "Chimpanzee Bipedal Locomotion in the Gombe Na-tional Park, East Africa," *Primates* 18 (1977): 913–21; and Duane M. Rumbaugh, "Discussion," in *Socioecology and Psychology of Primates*, ed. Russell H. Tuttle (The Hague: Mouton, 1968), pp. 367–68.

43. See, for example, van Lawick-Goodall, "Free-Living Chimpanzees"; Sugiyama, "Chimpanzees of the Budongo Forest," pp. 197–225; David A. Hamburg, "Aggressive Behaviour of Chimpanzees and Baboons in Natu-ral Habitats," *Psychiatric Research* 8 (1971): 385–98; Schaller, "Behavior of the

Mountain Gorilla"; H. C. Bingham, "Sex Development in Apes," *Comparative Psychological Monographs* 5 (1928): 1–161; T. Patterson, "The Behavior of a Group of Captive Pygmy Chimpanzees (*Pan paniscus*)," *Primates* 20 (1979): 341–54.

44. K. R. L. Hall, "Social Vigilance Behaviour of the Chacma Baboon (*Papio ursinus*)," *Behavior* 16 (1960): 261–94; Wickler, "Socio-Sexual Signals;" Detlev W. Ploog, J. Blitz, and F. Ploog, "Studies on Social and Sexual Behavior of the Squirrel Monkey (*Saimiri sciureus*)," *Folia primatologica* 1 (1963): 29–66; Van Lawick-Goodall, "Free-Living Chimpanzees;" T. Enomoto, "The Sexual Behavior of Japanese Monkeys," *Human Evolution* 3 (1974): 351–72; Frank E. Poirier, "Colobine Aggression: A Review," in *Primate Aggression*, pp. 123–57; C. E. G. Tutin and P. R. McGinnis, "Chimpanzee Reproduction in the Wild," in *Reproductive Biology of the Great Apes*, pp. 239–64; and Irenaus Eibl-Eibesfeldt, *Ethology*, 2nd ed. (New York: Holt, Rinehart, and Winston, 1975).

45. Charles Darwin, *Descent* and *The Origin of Species* (Middlesex: Penguin, 1968 [1859]).

46. For a finely detailed if popular account of the graduated display see S. Eimerl and I. De Vore, *The Primates* (New York: Time, 1975).

47. Bingham, "Sex Development."

48. Van Lawick-Goodall, "Free-Living Chimpanzees," p. 217.

49. Ibid., p. 276.

50. C. M. Rogers, "Implications of a Primate Early Rearing Experiment for the Concept of Culture," in *Precultural Primate Behavior*, ed. Emil W. Menzel (Basel: Karger, 1973), p. 188.

51. Alison Jolly, *The Evolution of Primate Behavior* (New York: Macmillan, 1985), p. 208.

52. Hall and De Vore, "Baboon Social Behavior," p. 174.

53. B. S. Low, "Sexual Selection and Human Ornamentation," in *Evolutionary Biology and Human Social Behavior*, p. 467.

54. Symons, *Evolution of Human Sexuality*, p. 183.

55. In addition to the description of *Pan paniscus* by Thompson-Handler et al. in "Sexual Behavior," see De Waal, *Chimpanzee Politics*, for descriptions and pictorial data on the sexual behavior of male chimpanzees, *Pan troglodytes*.

56. Wickler, "Socio-Sexual Signals," p. 151.

57. See, for example, Short, "Sexual Selection" and "Human Sexuality"; Crook, "Sexual Selection"; Morris, *Naked Ape*; and William G. Eberhard, *Sexual Selection and Animal Genitalia* (Cambridge: Harvard University Press, 1985).

5

Corporeal Representation

The rudiments of every human behavioral mechanism will be found far down in the evolutionary scale and also represented even in primitive activities of the nervous system.

KARL S. LASHLEY

SIMILARITIES IN PRIMATE SEXUAL SIGNALING BEHAVIOR AND AN EVOLUTIONARY SEMANTICS

To place early hominid sexual signaling behavior in the broader context of communication, and in fact in the broader context of an evolutionary semantics, necessitates first of all an examination of similarities—and thus ultimately continuities—in primate sexual signaling behaviors. It furthermore requires an extensive critical analysis of the privileging of human language since preferential treatment of the latter precludes not only an unbiased investigation of the root of the similarities (and continuities) but acknowledgment and analyses of the body which is the dynamic locus of communicative acts. In the course of meeting both requirements, this chapter will show how corporeal representation runs the communicational gamut from primate sexual display to primate gestural language to hominid primordial language, and how it is, in fact, a fundamental biological matrix.

To begin with, the disanalogies in penile display between a diagonally recumbent chimpanzee and an upright hominid discussed in

the last chapter contrast with another type of chimpanzee sexual behavior analogous to bipedal penile display. The analogy rests not on
content but on form. In their gestural communications, male pygmy
chimpanzees use a mode of corporeal representation to request sexual
compliance.[1] The spatio-kinetic iconicity of these representational gestures is on a formal continuum with the spatio-kinetic iconicity of
representational sexual display behavior, for example, the dynamic
mirroring of erect penis by erect posture. The specific gestural data
will make this formal semantic analogy clear.

In the study cited above, it is reported that "pygmy chimpanzees
regularly employ a form of simple gestural communication to reach
agreement regarding copulatory position prior to actual copulation."[2]
In each of the three types of gesture identified by the researchers,
either a desired bodily position, or a desired spatial placement, or a
desired motion is indicated iconically by the male. That is, the male indicates either the bodily position he would like the female to assume,
or the place he would like her to go, or the direction in which he would
like her to move—in each case by corporeally representing it to her.
For example, in *positioning movements*—the first of the three gestural
types—he gently pushes a limb and starts it moving in the direction
in which he would like the female to move it; in *iconic hand motion*, he
moves his hand toward a particular place to request that the female go
there; in *touch plus iconic hand motions*, he touches the female's shoulder, then gestures across his body to request that the female move
past him and turn around. In all these instances, the male is representing a particular spatio-kinetic act by certain spatio-kinetic or spatial/
tactile–kinetic actions of his own body. The representation is iconic:
the desired spatio-kinetic transformations of the female are spatio-
kinetically mirrored by the male chimpanzee's gestures. In brief, the
male uses his body as a semantic template.

The same kind of spatio-kinetic representational congruency is
evident not only in bipedal penile display but in the display behavior
of female howler monkeys in estrus: "When approaching a male, [the
female] will form an oval opening with her lips and her protruding
tongue will rapidly oscillate in and out and up and down. It is clear to
an observer . . . that the function of this gesture is to invite copulation.
. . . In a real sense the act is symbolic of sexual desire and readiness
for copulation in the female and it stimulates appropriate responses
in the male."[3]

The above descriptive report was written by primatologist C. R.
Carpenter, whose worldwide, world-renowned field studies in the

1930s "established many of the motivations, goals, methodologies, and basic concepts of the subsequent work in this field [of non-human primate social behavior]."[4] The description implicitly affirms the tongue to be a readily available spatio-kinetic analogue of the penis and the mouth a readily available spatio-kinetic analogue of the vagina in the sexual communication of howler females. Tongue and mouth are in fact sexual analogues in the behavior of other primates as well. Female langurs use tongue movements in and out of the mouth as a submissive gesture—a lingual/buccal usage akin to the usage of the genitals (in the act of presenting) to signal submissiveness.[5] The tongue-smacking face of some monkey species, especially *Macaca nemestrina* in mating situations, is equally indicative of the genital/oral relationship.[6] In present-day hominids there is evidence of genital symbolization in the sexual tongue-flicking behavior of the !Ko Bushmen.[7] Even a ram, in his attempts to interest a ewe in being mounted, flicks his tongue in and out of his mouth as he thrusts his head forward, sidles up to, and nudges the ewe—as any sheep farmer will attest.

The basic difference in corporeal representation between the above display behaviors and the male pygmy chimpanzee's gestural behavior turns on the nature of the representative act—in other words, on how the body functions as a semantic template. In the male pygmy chimpanzee's gestural behavior, representation is strictly *inter*corporeal, the male's body being the model for the female's body. In the display behaviors cited above, representation is *intra*corporeal and/or *inter*corporeal, one body part being the model for another body part of the same individual and/or of another's body. The same corporeal distinctions are implicit in ethological studies of mimicry and in studies of mimicry generally. One of the most commonly discussed types of mimicry, for example—what can be termed behavioral/morphological mimicry—is based on intercorporeal representation. The bodily form and comportment of one organism are finely replicated by a second—as with the bodily form and comportment of the true cleaner fish and its mimic.[8] In these cases, formal similarity—iconicity—is at its most extreme. The benefits to the mimic would otherwise be compromised. Those benefits aside, *inter*corporeal representation is also the basis of primatologist Wolfgang Wickler's hypothesis concerning the mimetic similarity between Old World male and female monkeys' ano-genital coloration.[9] Indeed, although he confuses the order of representation by melding template and template product (he speaks of the *model* for the conspicuous colorations in the male being *represented* by the female's colorations), he clearly sets forth the formal representational correspondence between the male and female bodies. As for *intra*corporeal mimetic representation, it is exemplified by both Wickler's and Desmond Morris's respective hypotheses concerning the male mandrill's representation (literally, re-presentation) of his penis by his facial coloring, and the human female's frontal representation of her posterior buttocks by her anterior enlarged breasts.[10]

It is important to identify mimicry as a form of iconic corporeal representation and at the same time to distinguish it from the kind of iconic corporeal representation of concern here. With respect to the latter, representation is not the mimetic result of a natural morphology and behavior but the symbolic result of active, deliberate display, specifically sexual display. Furthermore, the aim of the display is not perceptual deception but straightforward communication, specifically sexual communication. In active, communicative corporeal representation, a certain display behavior is purposefully enacted in virtue of its meaning. The analogical transfer of sense from one bodily part and behavior to another is in other words produced in order to mean. Thus with respect to what is at once both intracorporeal and intercorporeal representation, the form and dynamics of a protruding tongue rapidly oscillating in and out and up and down semantically mirror the form and dynamics of actual copulation. With respect to intracorporeal representation, the form and dynamics of a body in the act of standing —of assuming an erect posture—semantically mirror the form and dynamics of penile erection. Representation in both these displays is in consequence rightly defined as *symbolic* rather than *existential*, the latter most simply exemplified by mimetic corporeal representation in which form and/or behavior is what it is and does not stand for another thing or refer beyond itself.[11] As Carpenter clearly indicates in his description of a female howler monkey's behavior and its immediate effect upon the male, in *symbolic* corporeal representation certain past experiences and present actions are iconically and semantically associated by both displaying and displayed-to animal. Semanticity is thereby an intrinsic dimension of these kinds of sexual displays.

In the gestural language of the pygmy chimpanzee, an analogical transfer of sense is equally evident, and the behavior is again clearly enacted in order to mean. Here, however, iconicity functions in a purely intercorporeal semantics. Corporeal representation is not in any way self-reflexive. The spatio-kinetic actions of the male mirror not the spatio-kinetic actions of his own body but the desired spatio-kinetic actions of the female. Similar distinctions thus again obtain with respect to mimicry; the male actively shapes the iconic spatio-kinetic components of meaning—they are not morphological or behavioral givens—and his gestures are symbolically rather than existentially meaningful.

With its relationship to mimicry sketched out, it is pertinent at this point to cast the practice of corporeal representation in still broader perspective in order to bring its semantic values into finer focus and place them in a specifically evolutionary context. In primordial language (to be more fully treated below), corporeal representation is yet again produced in order to mean, but the analogical transfer of sense is *meta*corporeal: iconicity is between the articulatory (tactile–kinesthetic) gestures of speech and the spatio-kinetic character of the worldly processes or events referred to.[12] Iconic spatio-kinetic corporeal representation is thus evident all the way from mimicry through display and gestural language to hominid primordial language. At the level of *symbolic* corporeal representation it defines an evolutionary semantics and places animal communicative systems within a conceptually analyzable and appropriately broad spectrum: biological modes of meaning. It suggests *contra* Noam Chomsky[13] that human and non-human forms of communication can be understood within a common, *non-abstract* frame of reference, and one that is not either *ahistorical* (see below: the Athena paradigm of human language). The two basic features of this evolutionary semantics are semanticity and iconicity, both of them clearly the work of symbolic corporeal representation.

Primary modes of human symbolization substantiate the seminal importance of semanticity and iconicity in the evolution of hominid communication systems including human language, and in consequence underscore the significance of these features to bipedal penile display in the evolution of human sexuality. In particular, in diverse analyses of primary human symbolization—Freud's psychology of dreams, Susanne Langer's aesthetics of art objects, André Leroi-Gourhan's archaeology of prehistoric artifacts, Mary LeCron Foster's linguistics of primordial language[14]—great emphasis is placed on both the semanticity and the iconicity of the symbolizing behavior. The emphasis merits particular attention in light of the comparatively great corporeal investment (and "primitiveness") common to these areas relative to analytical pursuits, for example, or to mathematical formalizations, and in light of the fact that dreams, art objects, archaeological artifacts, and primordial language are all the result of essentially creative behaviors. In each case something is produced out of nothing, as it were; what is produced is in each case an original embodiment of an original thought.

The conjoined emphasis on semanticity and iconicity together with the strongly corporeal and creative character of these symbolizing behaviors suggests that semanticity and iconicity are intimately linked and mutually reinforcing; and further, that they are, and have been from the beginning, fundamental rather than adjunctive or secondary characters of hominid communication. To show convincingly that this is so requires first a critical examination of how an abstract, ahistorical view of human language effectively ignores the fundamentally corporeal nature of communication and in so doing overlooks the biological pervasiveness of corporeal representation and the two basic features that define it; and second, an identification and analysis of the behavioral dispositions underlying the pervasive biological practice of corporeal representation.

SEMANTICITY AND ICONICITY

THE PRIVILEGING OF HUMAN LANGUAGE

The psychologist's, aesthetician's, archaeologist's, and linguist's emphasis on semanticity and iconicity does not coincide with the current general favoring of pragmatics over semantics. Many recent theories of animal communication—Richard Dawkins and J. R. Krebs's being the most extreme example[15]—interpret communicative behavior in terms of self-interest, manipulation, and the like, rather than in terms of signification or meaning. The same pragmatic concern generates the not uncommon adaptationist explanation of why a *verbal* language arose: "It leaves much of the body free for other activities that can be carried on at the same time."[16] In such a perspective, the origin and evolution of concrete bodily acts productive at once of both sound and meaning remain unexamined.

Pragmatic favoring is directly related to the privileging of human language through a depreciation of iconicity—a feature putatively characteristic of nonhuman communication systems only. The two-step reasoning upholding the depreciation is as follows: (1) "The most instructive way to view the communication systems of animals is to compare these systems first with human language,"[17] that is, human language is *the* standard against which all nonhuman animal communication systems are to be measured and evaluated; (2) the linguistic elements of human language are deemed arbitrary, not iconic.[18] A critical look at linguist Charles Hockett's model of "communication systems"—the most widely accepted and utilized model[19]—will show that the privileging of human language results ultimately not in an evolutionary schema of hominid communication but only in an uncovering of certain abstract, that is, essentially noncorporeal, features ostensibly common to the speech of all present-day human speakers. It will show further that evolutionary estimations of nonhuman animal communication based on the privileging of human language (and note that the estimations necessarily include the communication of *nonverbal* and *inchoately verbal* ancestral hominids) are actually based on an ahistorical model: human language—whenever it is deemed to have arisen—arose full-blown from the mouths of hominids like the goddess Athena arose full-blown from the head of Zeus.

An Athena-like paradigm prevails first of all because those design features of human language identified by Hockett that are found below the human stage, that is, in the communication systems of nonhuman animals as well, do not have any status as speech (*pro forma* designations "pre-speech," "Protospeech," "Prelanguage," and the like, to the contrary). Otherwise stated, it is only the final confluence of *all* of the design features under one cortical roof that constitutes speech and thus differentiates *language* from mere earlier hominid and other animal sounds. For example, Hockett has stated both that "no known system of nonhuman animal communication has duality of patterning"; and that "the crucial feature shared by all languages in the ethnographic present, but which we assume was missing from prelanguage, is duality of patterning."[20]

Correlatively, it is because the beginning of language is fixed at the start by definition that the paradigm prevails. Only humans have language; therefore language arose (and can only have arisen) "with their kind." Exclusive privileging explains why no data can be adduced that convincingly show how linguistic behavior arose from nonlinguistic behavior, for example, how the design feature *discreteness* ("the elementary signaling units of a language [in contrast] with the use of sound effect") is functionally or causally connected to the "related characteristic" Hockett identifies as "bipedal locomotion, not upright."[21] In contrast, physio-anatomical changes—those of the larynx and tongue (the latter organ is not mentioned in Hockett's model), for example, or modifications in the degree of basicranial flexion[22]— approximate to necessary, though not of course sufficient, conditions for the passage from nonspeech to speech and thereby possess the explanatory power credited to them. The behavioral motivations proposed by Hockett for the various design features are imaginative but lack equivalent explanatory power. This is in fact linguist Edwin

Pulleyblank's criticism with respect to the all-important design feature, *duality of patterning*. Precisely how could it have originated? It is purportedly based on the arbitrariness of linguistic symbols, yet Hockett gives no plausible explanation of how arbitrary symbols could possibly have been coined in the first place, that is, how the concept of "meaningless message elements" arose and anchored duality of patterning. (Anthropologist Gordon Hewes has remarked that "the greatest obstacle in any glottogonic theory is not that vocal sounds, or manual gestures, or whatever, could not be used as linguistic signs, but how any system based on seemingly arbitrary signs would have got started."[23] The difficult question posed by arbitrary symbols is taken up in detail in Chapter 6.) Pulleyblank has pointed out that what is wanted are not speculative scenarios of the beginnings of verbal language but a logical sequence of "what may actually have happened."[24] He finds this logical sequence by hypothesizing and demonstrating iconic rather than arbitrary initial verbal sounds.

The Athena paradigm effectively masks further deficiencies. With the failure to distinguish current appearances from formal origins[25]— a failure succinctly illustrated above in Hockett's characterization of the linguistic past on the basis of the linguistic "ethnographic present" —not only is the study of root forms neglected,[26] but no rigorously detailed analysis is offered showing what "language" would actually have been like with progressively fewer than all of its present-day features. A step-by-step temporally reversed model of the origin and evolution of language by a process of feature elimination is not given. While theoretically an account *could* be given, it would likely result in the kind of problematic reasonableness identified by Pulleyblank with respect to duality of patterning. Pulleyblank is rightly skeptical of the "brilliantly successful mutation" Hockett posits—the phrase is Hockett's own[27]—to explain how duality of patterning arose. The end result is that what was and what was not possible to communicate verbally at designated stages of linguistic sophistication is nowhere spelled out. In broader terms, evolutionary–semantic relationships among different forms of hominid communication—displays, gestures, vocalizations, rudimentary verbalizations, and finally speech—are nowhere conceived much less hypothesized. A *bona fide* evolutionary schema of hominid communication is sacrificed to the privileging of human language.

The broader point is aptly illustrated by primatologist Emil Menzel's observations and experimental research on chimpanzee communication. Menzel emphasizes that the most important questions about animal communication are, What is communicated? and How is it communicated?, in other words, questions of semantics.[28] A significant finding in his research is that chimpanzees—unrepresented in Hockett's 1960 model—are capable of lying (*prevarication* is a design feature in Hockett's 1964 model). They do this not through the "vocal–auditory channel" (Hockett's *primary* design feature) but through *bodily comportment, orientation*, and *movement*—what linguist Philip Lieberman in referring to Menzel's work has aptly termed "a whole body gestural system."[29] Given the close evolutionary ties between humans and chimpanzees,[30] and the consistent analogical ties regularly predicated between early hominids and present-day chimpanzees in paleoanthropological reconstructions,[31] a proper and thorough evolutionary approach to hominid communication would necessarily acknowledge and take into close account "the whole body gestural system" of chimpanzees and spell out its semantic components in detail. In fact it might perhaps ultimately specify how, and on what basis, the same design feature—for instance, prevarication—is differentially encoded by animate bodies. To put the point in concrete corporeal–semantic focus, *What sexual behavior, after all, brought early hominid male and female together?* Like other forms of primate sexual behavior discussed above, bipedal penile display is a phenomenon analyzable within a corporeal system of comportments, orientation, and movement. At the same time, *how* it communicates the meaning it does ties it to primordial language: Corporeal representation anchors meaning in both cases.

The overall effect of the paradigm on evolutionary estimations of nonhuman animal communicative systems is to do less than full justice to the systems represented in the model—those that happen to share features with human language—and of course no justice at all to those that are not represented. Of prime significance in this regard is the fact that other channels of communication—particularly tactile, kinetic, and visual modalities, given their seminal role in primate communication[32]—are totally overridden by Hockett's exclusively featured vocal–auditory channel. Peter Marler, an ethologist, makes this point unequivocally when he declares that, "to force systems of animal communication into functional categories designed for human language detracts from the subtlety of the relationships between structure and function in animal signals."[33] Marler's criticism can be stated in the form of a general biological maxim: no animal can communicate in ways for which it is corporeally unprepared, not just in the sense of a facilitating anatomy (including a brain of a certain size and complexity), but in the sense of an experiential capacity for certain sensory–kinetic awarenesses and powers (or of comparable reflexive mechanisms).

The pragmatic privileging of the vocal–auditory channel, a privileging psychologist Ernst von Glaserfield understatedly terms a "somewhat anthropocentric restriction,"[34] is symptomatic of the tendency to tie verbal language to tool-making[35] and in so doing, to bypass both an examination of those sensory–kinetic modes by which early hominids—nonhuman animals—communicated *before* the dawn of a verbal language and an examination of the nature of primordial language itself.[36] A reinstatement of semantics at the heart of communication not only palliates pragmatic "anthropocentric restrictions," but itself suggests a more propitious evolutionary model, one directly tied to corporeal representation and an evolutionary semantics, and in fact one actually acknowledged by Hockett from the very beginning as primary. If as Hockett avers, "a [communicative] system cannot be either arbitrary or nonarbitrary unless it is semantic, and it cannot have duality of patterning unless it is semantic,"[37] then clearly, semanticity is not simply another design feature of language. It has fundamental import in the origin and evolution of the system itself. As Menzel suggests, an examination of semanticity is quite plainly the proper point of departure for the study of communicative systems. The theoretical basis for this alternative model warrants brief comment.

A focus of attention on the semantics of communication restores a focus of attention on the body. The seemingly trivial truism that whatever the form of animal communication, it is always the result of a living body, expresses an axiomatic biological truth. Meanings are not free-floating entities; meanings are incarnated, anchored in living bodies. It is thus clear why corporeal representation is a fundamental biological matrix. It is a primary mode of symbolization and communication. Where meanings are *represented*, animate bodies represent them corporeally. In their form and behavior animate bodies are potential semantic templates. This is why a psychology, aesthetics, archaeology, and linguistics of symbolizing behaviors is possible —why pears and mountains can represent female breasts and umbrellas and tree trunks can represent penes;[38] why traditional works of art can be understood as symbols, their dynamic forms being logically congruent to the dynamic form of human feeling;[39] why archaeological artifacts in their design features can be interpreted as representations of female and male genitalia;[40] why the articulatory gestures of primordial language can be shown to be tactile–kinesthetic analogues of their referents.[41] Analyzed at molecular and physiological levels, living intact organisms can themselves be regarded as the ultimate result of meanings mediated by a form of corporeal representation. In these instances representation is not synonymous with certain iconic spatio-kinetic (or spatial/tactile–kinetic) actions or behaviors of an agent, an individual who by choice or design represents in order to mean. It is the result of natural meaning, akin to the discovered causal–semantic connection between smoke and fire. The causal–semantic association that obtains in the latter case obtains, for example, between UUU and phenylalanine and between certain cellular behaviors and certain concentrations of salt in the blood. The well-known British biologist J. Z. Young specifically identifies hypothalamic cells' shrinking and swelling behaviors as "physical symbols 'representing' the required water content."[42] The single quotation marks presumably denote a metaphorical truth, a kind of truth no less exacting than the literal kind, as natural selection *selecting* so forcefully shows. That living bodies should represent in some corporeal manner—a blueprint at the molecular level, a state of affairs at the physiological level, or a sexual desire at the living organism level—is not surprising. Only in a world of disembodied spirits or extrasensory forms of life would a different biological semantic matrix for representation obtain.

BEHAVIORAL DISPOSITIONS

The biological pervasiveness of corporeal representation itself suggests the disposition toward semanticity and iconicity at the base of both hominid and nonhominid symbolizing behaviors. Animate bodies are already a system of meanings, and not only at the molecular and physiological levels. The meanings in part coincide with what the German biologist Adolph Portmann calls *form value:*[43] those visible patterns—colorations and designs—that distinguish animals of a given species not only as to age and sex, for example, but morphologically—as head end from anal–sexual end—and behaviorally—by "semantic patterns designed for their signaling effect."[44] In addition to these form values are meanings generated by an animal's bodily comportment, movement, and orientation, as Menzel's work has shown.[45] For example, an animal's movement (or lack of movement) is meaningful as when it flees or freezes, erects its ears, or paws the ground. Other animals, including human ones, regulate their behavior according to these movements. Bodily orientation is equally significant: a creature's primary spatiality as a body is a further dimension of its ready-made system of meanings. Primary spatiality is precisely the focus of Menzel's neglected insight that "one good reason that chimpanzees very seldom point manually is that they do not have to; rising to a quadrupedal position, glancing at a follower, and orienting 'out there' conveys all the directional information one could ask for."[46]

Rising to a bipedal position engenders radically different but equally significant spatial meanings. Frontal exposure, verticality, and increased size as discussed earlier are primary among these. Moreover as pointed out in Chapter 4, apart from all other considerations, an animal's posture is significant *tout court*. Gordon Hewes's pictorial data on the difference between present-day human male and female sitting positions with respect to their typical leg placements give striking evidence of this fact.[47] In sum, form values, posture, comportment, movement, and orientation, both singly and together, demonstrate that semanticity is a built-in of bodily life, literally a built-in of being a body. Further, all enter into the global archetypal profile of a species.

Corporeal representation is based upon a natural disposition toward iconicity as well as semanticity. Avian ritualized displays that have evolved from intention movements bear out this relationship of similarity, even when the original movement pattern is radically transformed by the process of "symbolic formalization," the latter process being analytically teased out by species comparisons.[48] Whether ritualized or original movement patterns, symbolic behaviors of nonhumans and humans alike are basically iconic, not arbitrary. There are exceptions to this basic iconicity. The eye spot flash of a threatening/warning baboon is akin to the wagging finger of a threatening/warning mother. In traditional semantic terms, similarity between signified and signifier appears non-existent in these instances. In general, however, animate bodies represent by symbolizing the spatio-kinetic dynamics of their own experiences (or spatio-kinetic reflexive corollaries thereof). In this respect, the Tanzsprache of the honeybees—their repertoire of dances relating information regarding honey sources—is no different from hominid primordial language, and both the Tanzsprache and primordial language are no different from the tongue-flicking sexual display of female howler monkeys or from the bipedal sexual display of male early hominids. In each case, tactile–kinesthetic experience and its spatio-relational correlates are iconically linked. A brief examination of the Tanzsprache is especially edifying in demonstrating these relationships both because its status as a symbolic communicative system has been contested and the subject of investigation for many years,[49] and because in the long contentious debate, a basic corporeal dimension shared not only by human language but by the above-discussed sexual displays has been overlooked.

What has not been explicitly recognized is the fact that information gathered and conveyed by the dancing bee is rooted in tactile–kinesthetic experience—or its reflexive (robotic) corollary. Whether a humanlike equivalent of experience is granted to the bee or not is beside the point. There is a *meta*corporeal similarity, a body/world iconicity, between the actual flight of the bee and the dance by which she represents her flight. This is true not only with respect to her bodily orientation to the sun in her actual flight and her correlative orientation to gravity in her symbolic rendition of the flight, for example, but with respect to other behaviors that strikingly point up the role of tactile–kinesthetic elements even further. For example, if the honeybee's flight is experimentally made more arduous, the Tanzsprache reflects the greater effort; if the sugar concentration is high—basically a tactile datum—the vigorousness of the dance is greater.[50] An iconic relationship clearly exists between tactile–kinesthetically *experienced*—or "recorded"—meanings and tactile–kinesthetically *represented* meanings. The spatio-kinetic dynamics of actual corporeal activity serve as a semantic template for the spatio-kinetic representations that constitute the dance—in the same way that the male pygmy chimpanzee's body functions as a semantic template in his gestural language, and in the same way that the act of copulation and of penile erection function as semantic templates for the tongue-flicking behavior of a female howler monkey and the upright posture of a sexually motivated male early hominid respectively.

Primordial language is similarly rooted in tactile–kinesthetic experience. Reconstructions of root forms have demonstrated that articulatory (tactile–kinesthetic) gestures are iconic with respect to their referents. For example, all root forms with *m* refer to some kind of bilateral relationship—"the fingers or hands in taking or grasping," for instance, or "two opposed surfaces in tapering, pressing together, holding together, crushing, or resting against."[51] The relationship is in each case isomorphic with the bilateral articulatory gesture that produces the sound *m*. Moreover as the examples suggest, meanings in primordial language tend to focus on "motional–relational complexes" rather than discrete objects,[52] in the same way that the Tanzsprache represents not an objectified geographical location, but *how far* and *in what direction* a sugar source is in relation to "home." Furthermore representation in primordial language as well as in the Tanzsprache is *meta*corporeal. The iconic articulatory gestures are in each case a spatial/tactile–kinetic transcription of worldly experience or activity. They specify something out in the world apart from the body yet iconically related to corporeal experience or activity. This is of course immediately apparent in the case of the Tanzsprache. But it is also clear in the case of primordial language. The bilateral relationships *resting against, pressing together,* or *crushing,* for example, are primordial perceptual meanings—"motional–relational complexes"— anchored in what might aptly be termed *primordial bodily experiences,* that is, in correlative "root" behaviors: *resting against* nest materials in sleeping or the earth in standing, for example; *pressing together* in copulating or in producing the sound *m; crushing* in chewing food or pounding one thing with another.

Where the Tanzsprache and primordial language differ is in both mode of articulation and mode of communication. In the Tanzsprache, articulation is of the whole body—in effect, a "whole body gestural system." Communication is likewise a "whole body gestural system": information is transmitted tactile–kinetically from dancer to potential recruit. In primordial language, articulation is of the supralaryngeal parts of the body.[53] Communication here takes place not through intimate body-to-body contact of articulatory parts, but aurally, through a *second* sensory medium. Communication in the one instance is thus directly by way of the tactile–kinetic gestures themselves; in the other by way of the sounds the gestures create. Thus articulatory gestures constitute the language in the Tanzsprache; in primordial language, articulatory gestures are the means whereby the language is constituted. What is both interesting and significant, however, is that studies of human speech show that speech perception is actually speech *apperception.* The listener makes co-present with actual perception something that is not actually given in the perception: "the listener responds as though he is interpreting the acoustic signal in terms of the articulatory gestures that a speaker would employ to generate the word."[54] This *tactile–kinesthetic decoding of speech*[55] is not random or accidental: "The human brain decodes . . . the acoustic signal in terms of the articulatory maneuvers that were put together to generate the syllable. . . . The process of human speech *inherently requires* 'knowledge' of the acoustic consequences of the possible range of human supralaryngeal (tongue, lips, and so on) vocal tract speech articulation" (italics added).[56] There is no reason not to assume that in primordial speech, tactile–kinesthetic empathy with the articulatory gestures of the speaker was similarly inherently required. From this perspective, the ultimate difference in mode of sensory communication between the Tanzsprache and primordial/present-day human language is the difference between *actual* tactile–kinetic experience (or "recording") of dance by recruit, and tactile–kinesthetic *empathy* of listener with speaker.

The sexual displays of a female howler monkey and of a male early hominid stand in the same relation to the tactile–kinesthetic body as primordial and present-day human language stand to the articulatory gestures of speech, and the Tanzsprache stands to the articulatory gestures of the dancer. In each case the body is iconically representing its own experiences (or activity) and is thereby communicating either its bodily dispositions of the moment, or information about a "motional–relational complex" in the world. The fact that such experiences are communicated attests to species-specific tactile–kinesthetic invariants. Indeed, Hockett's design feature *interchangeability* ("a speaker of a language can reproduce any linguistic message he can understand"),[57] is dependent upon just such invariants, a fact implicitly apparent in the research on speech (ap)perception cited above. Short of tactile–kinesthetic invariants, neither primordial language, present-day human language, the Tanzsprache, nor sexual displays would be possible—not that the performing individual could not continue speaking, dancing, or displaying, but that the action would be meaningless to the individual to whom it was addressed. What is represented visually, auditorily, or tactile–kinetically is in each case related to the addressed animal's own body of prior tactile–kinesthetic experiences (or activities). This is precisely the concept primatologist Stuart Altmann tries to capture by his term *comsign*.[58] The term refers to one of the two prime factors making primate interchangeability possible, *viz.*, most primate signals are part of the repertoire of *all* of the members of the species (or of a particular group in question), at the very least for some period in the animals' lives. What is true of primates is in this instance also true of bees. Potential recruits are potential dancers because tactile–kinesthetic invariants anchor interchangeability.

At minimum, tactile–kinesthetic invariants predispose organisms toward iconicity since the most easily formulated, consistently utilizable, and readily understood signals are those that are similar to bodily behaviors and experiences shared by all of the members of the species—like the pressing together of the lips to produce the sound *m*, or the pelvic thrusting, in and out movements typical of copulation, or the upward direction, increasing size, and progressive frontal exposure of the body in assuming an erect posture. That female primates, early hominid ones in particular, while capable of assuming an erect posture are not capable of penile erection or display—or of intromission as Altmann specifically points out[59]—does not mean that they do not have direct and highly discriminatory tactile–kinesthetic or visual experiences of these male behaviors, hence that the behaviors are not comsigns. Dawkins and Krebs's observations on built-in template learning and template formation through past experience of conspecifics' behaviors offer additional confirmation of the tactile–kinesthetic basis of iconic signaling behaviors.[60]

It is important to emphasize that the behavioral disposition toward iconicity, as toward corporeal representation itself, is not a conscious one (or *necessarily* a conscious one), nor are any of the associated communicative behaviors discussed above (necessarily) consciously planned and executed. The tactile–kinesthetic symbols are structured not in reflective acts but in prereflective corporeal experience (or correlative reflexively activated mechanisms), that is, they are the spontaneous product of certain species-specific bodily experiences. What Freud said of the dreamer is thus true of the symbolizing animal: "The dreamer's knowledge of symbolism is unconscious."[61] But while the symbolizing animal is, like the dreamer, unconscious of its symbolizing behavior as such, *unlike the dreamer*, it is not unconscious of its behavior. It is aware of its own actions in a way gradient to that in which a bird, a song sparrow, for instance, is fully and directly aware of its own song in the process of singing it. Both ethologists and sociobiologists have documented this awareness.[62] Although not specifically identifying the described behavior as symbolic, an example from Darwin is instructive. Speaking of "two males fighting for the possession of the female, or several male birds displaying their gorgeous plumage, and performing the strangest antics before an assembled body of females," Darwin states that "they . . . know what they are about, and consciously exert their mental and bodily powers."[63] In brief, awareness proceeds along a gradient, and while dreaming exceeds the limit case for self-experience at one extreme, a bird's experience of its own song—or of its own courtship behavior, as Darwin affirms—defines optimum self-experience at the other extreme. Prereflective corporeal experience defines a variable degree of awareness between the two limits. It is not at the forefront of awareness—attention is directed outward toward something in the world—but is to varying degrees in relief with respect to a particular focal point of attention.

Piaget's description of the buccal behavior of an infant is an apt —even strikingly pictorial—confirmation of this fact.[64] The infant's progressive opening of its mouth coincident with its focal attempt to open a matchbox is a prereflective gesture symbolic of the dynamics and anticipated result of its manual activity. The oral gesture is a spontaneous tactile–kinesthetic symbol, a spatio-kinetic analogue of the behavior: opening a matchbox. The infant is unaware of the symbolism as such, but clearly knows corporeally, in a tactile–kinesthetic sense, the meanings: *open* and *opening*. The inherent epistemological requirement of speech perception discussed above—the listener must know corporeally, that is, "inherently" or prereflectively, the articulatory gestures of the speaker—is again corroborative of the same fact. Equally, the sexual display embodied by the protruding and moving tongue of a female howler monkey or by the erect posture of a sexually aroused and motivated early male hominid is not the result of thought exercises in corporeal representation or in the semantics and iconicity of symbols, but is a spontaneous (species-specific) symbolic behavior rooted in prereflective tactile–kinesthetic corporeal experience.

In sum, whatever their particular context, tactile–kinetic symbols are spontaneously formed behavioral analogues anchored in the tactile–kinesthetic perceptual lives of the creatures (and species) concerned. That they are structured in prereflective corporeal experience is substantiated not only by speech perception and infant behavioral data, and by analogy to the dreamer in relation to the symbols of the dream, but by Carpenter's untroubled interpretation of the female howler's tongue-flicking behavior: "It is clear to an observer who has seen this series of events . . . that the function of this gesture is to invite copulation."[65] Carpenter was not puzzled by the behavior nor did he have to analyze it painstakingly either to determine its meaning or to justify that meaning to his readers. On the contrary, his brief verbal description suffices to convey immediately to the reader the same unequivocal meaning the actual behavior embodied for him in the flesh. By the same tactile–kinesthetic tokens of experience, the behavior is clear straightaway to the male howler monkey: he too knows—"inherently" or prereflectively—"that the function of the gesture is to invite copulation." Were this not so, the gesture would hardly "stimulate appropriate responses in the male."[66] Prereflective corporeal experience —Carpenter's, his readers', the female and the male howler monkeys' —is the basis of the gesture's sexual meaning. In Altmann's terms, it is the basis of its functioning as a comsign.

The same is true of the sexual meaning of early hominid bipedality in association with an erect penis. Bipedality in the service of sexual display behavior did not arise as a result of reflective deliberations on optimal sexual signaling behavior. The assumption of an erect posture was a prereflective act which, in mirroring the spatiokinetic dynamics of an early hominid male's own genitalic experience, symbolically reinforced the sexual signaling power of penile display itself. The augmented signal was unequivocally meaningful to the female(s) to whom it was addressed for the same reason that the female howler monkey's symbolic behavior is unequivocally meaningful to the male(s) to whom her display is addressed: the behavior is iconically anchored in species-specific tactile–kinesthetic invariants. In the evolutionary perspective of hominid communication, an early hominid male's symbolic behavior exemplified the pervasive biological disposition toward iconic corporeal representation. In this respect bipedal penile display was a significant step along a semantic pathway connecting ultimately to primordial language.

NOTES

1. E. Sue Savage-Rumbaugh and R. Bakeman, "Spontaneous Gestural Communication among Conspecifics in the Pygmy Chimpanzee (*Pan paniscus*)," in *Progress in Ape Research*, ed. G. H. Bourne (New York: Academic Press, 1977), pp. 97–116.

2. Ibid., p. 114.

3. C. R. Carpenter, "Societies of Monkeys and Apes," in *Primate Social Behavior*, ed. Charles H. Southwick (New York: Van Nostrand Reinhold, 1963), pp. 49–50.

4. Charles H. Southwick, "Introduction," *Primate Social Behavior*, p. 2.

5. Phyllis J. Dolhinow, "The North Indian Langur," *Primate Patterns*, ed. Phyllis J. Dolhinow (New York: Holt, Rinehart, and Winston, 1972), pp. 85–124.

6. See J. A. R. A. M. van Hoof, "The Facial Displays of the Catarrhine Monkeys and Apes," in *Primate Ethology*, ed. Desmond Morris (Garden City: Anchor, 1969), pp. 52 and 58.

7. Irenaus Eibl-Eibesfeldt, "The Myth of the Aggression-Free Hunter and Gatherer Society," in *Primate Aggression, Territoriality, and Xenophobia*, ed. Ralph L. Holloway (New York: Academic Press, 1974), pp. 435–57.

8. Wolfgang Wickler, *Mimicry* (New York: McGraw-Hill, 1968).

9. Wolfgang Wickler, "Socio-Sexual Signals and Their Intraspecific Imitation among Primates," in *Primate Ethology*, pp. 89–189.

10. Ibid.; and Desmond Morris, *The Naked Ape* (New York: Dell, 1967).

11. For a related discussion on the distinction between symbolic and

existential meaning, see Maxine Sheets-Johnstone, "Thinking in Movement," *Journal of Aesthetics and Art Criticism* 39 (1981): 399–407.

12. See Mary LeCron Foster, "The Symbolic Structure of Primordial Language," in *Human Evolution: Biosocial Perspectives*, ed. Sherwood L. Washburn and Elizabeth R. McCown (Menlo Park, Calif.: Benjamin/Cummings, 1978), pp. 77–121, and "Reconstruction of the Evolution of Language," in *Handbook of Symbolic Evolution*, ed. A. Lock and C. Peter, forthcoming from Oxford University Press; Morris Swadesh, *The Origin and Diversification of Language* (Chicago: Aldine-Atherton, 1971); Maxine Sheets-Johnstone, "On the Origin of Language," *North Dakota Quarterly* 51/2 (1983): 22–51 (see Chapter 6, this book); Edwin G. Pulleyblank, "The Beginnings of Duality of Patterning in Language," in *Glossogenetics*, ed. E. de Grolier (New York: Harwood, 1983), pp. 369–410; and see also Ivan Fonagy, "Preconceptual Thinking in Language," ibid., pp. 323–53.

13. Noam Chomsky, "The General Properties of Language," in *Brain Mechanisms Underlying Speech and Language*, ed. F. L. Darley and C. H. Millikan (New York: Grune and Stratton, 1967), pp. 73–88, and *Language and Mind* (New York: Harcourt, Brace and World, 1968).

14. Sigmund Freud, *The Basic Writings of Sigmund Freud* (New York: Modern Library, 1938), and *Complete Psychological Works of Sigmund Freud*, 24 vols., ed. and trans. James Strachey (London: Hogarth Press, 1953), vols. 4 and 5; Susanne Langer, *Philosophy in a New Key* (New York: New American Library, 1948), and *Feeling and Form* (New York: Charles Scribner's Sons, 1953); André Leroi-Gourhan, *Préhistoire de l'art occidental* (Paris: Mazenod, 1971); Foster, "Symbolic Structure."

15. Richard Dawkins and J. R. Krebs, "Animal Signals: Information or Manipulation?" in *Behavioural Ecology*, ed. J. R. Krebs and N. B. Davies (London: Basil Blackwell, 1978), pp. 282–309.

16. Charles F. Hockett, "The Origin of Speech," *Scientific American* 203 (September 1960): 89–96.

17. E. O. Wilson, "Animal Communication," *Scientific American* 227 (September 1972): 52–60.

18. See, for example, Ferdinand de Saussure, *Course in General Linguistics* (New York: Philosophical Library, 1959); Charles F. Hockett, "Origin of Speech," and "Logical Considerations in the Study of Animal Communication," in *Animal Sounds and Communication*, ed. W. E. Lanyon and W. N. Tavolga (Washington, D.C.: American Institute of Biological Science, 1960); Charles F. Hockett and R. Ascher, "The Human Revolution," *Current Anthropology* 5 (1964): 135–47; Charles F. Hockett and Stuart A. Altmann, "A Note on Design Features," in *Animal Communication* (Bloomington: Indiana University Press, 1969), pp. 61–72; Horst D. Steklis and Stevan R. Harnad, "From Hand to Mouth: Some Critical Stages in the Evolution of Language," in *Origins and Evolution of Language and Speech*, ed. Stevan R. Harnad, Horst D. Steklis, and Jane B. Lancaster, *Annals of the New York Academy of Sciences* 280 (1976): 445–55; H. S. Terrace and T. G. Bever, "What Might Be Learned from Study-

ing Language in the Chimpanzee? The Importance of Symbolizing Oneself," ibid., pp. 579–88; Ernst von Glaserfield, "The Development of Language as Purposive Behavior," ibid., pp. 212–26; Nancy Tanner and Adrienne L. Zhilman, "Discussion Paper: The Evolution of Human Communication: What Can Primates Tell Us?" ibid., pp. 467–80; Ralph L. Holloway, "Culture: A *Human Domain*," *Current Anthropology* 10 (1969): 395–412; and Sherwood L. Washburn and S. C. Strum, "Concluding Comments," in *Perspectives on Human Evolution* 2, ed. Sherwood L. Washburn and Phyllis J. Dolhinow (New York: Holt, Rinehart, and Winston, 1972), pp. 469–91.

19. See W. H. Thorpe, *Animal Nature and Human Nature* (New York: Anchor, 1974); von Glaserfield, "Development of Language"; and Pulleyblank, "Beginnings of Duality of Patterning."

20. Charles F. Hockett, *Man's Place in Nature* (New York: McGraw-Hill, 1973), pp. 106 and 414 respectively.

21. Hockett, "Origin of Speech," pp. 90, 93.

22. See J. T. Laitman, "The Evolution of the Hominid Upper Respiratory System and Implications for the Origin of Speech," in *Glossogenetics*, pp. 63–90.

23. Gordon W. Hewes, "The Current Status of the Gestural Theory of Language Origin," in *Origins and Evolution*, pp. 482–504.

24. Pulleyblank, "Beginnings of Duality of Patterning," p. 373.

25. See Stephen J. Gould and Richard C. Lewontin, "The Spandrels of San Marco and the Panglossian Paradigm: A Critique of the Adaptationist Programme," *Proceedings of the Royal Society of London*, Series B, Biological Sciences 205 (1979): 581–98.

26. For an analysis of these forms, see Foster, "Symbolic Structure" and "Evolution of Language"; Swadesh, *Origin and Diversification*; and Pulleyblank, "Beginnings of Duality of Patterning."

27. Hockett and Ascher, "Human Revolution," p. 144.

28. Emil W. Menzel, "Discussion," in *Origins and Evolution*, pp. 167–69.

29. Philip Lieberman, "On the Nature and Evolution of the Biological Bases of Language," in *Glossogenetics*, pp. 91–114.

30. See, for example, Vincent M. Sarich, "Pygmy Chimpanzee Systematics: A Molecular Perspective," in *The Pygmy Chimpanzee*, ed. R. L. Susman (New York: Plenum, 1984), pp. 43–48; and Morris Goodman, "The Chronicle of Primate Phylogeny Contained in Proteins," *Symposia of the Zoological Society of London* 33 (1973): 339–75.

31. For a justification of this methodological practice see Sherwood L. Washburn, "The Analysis of Primate Evolution with Particular Reference to the Origin of Man," *Cold Spring Harbor Symposia on Quantitative Biology* 15 (1950): 57–78; and Jane B. Lancaster, *Primate Behavior and the Emergence of Human Culture* (New York: Holt, Rinehart, and Winston, 1975).

32. See, for example, Tanner and Zhilman, "Discussion"; K. R. L. Hall and I. De Vore, "Baboon Social Behavior," in *Primate Patterns*, pp. 125–80; Emil W. Menzel and Marcia K. Johnson, "Communication and Cognitive

Organization in Humans and Other Animals," in *Origins and Evolution*, pp. 131–42; see also T. Sebeok, "Discussion of Communication Processes," in *Social Communication among Primates*, ed. Stuart A. Altmann (Chicago: University of Chicago Press, 1967), pp. 363–69.

33. Peter Marler, "Animal Communication Signals," *Science* 157 (1967): 769.

34. Von Glaserfield, "Development of Language." It should perhaps be noted that such an axiological anthropocentrism is to be distinguished from the corporeal anthropocentrism discussed in Chapter 10.

35. See, for example, Holloway, "Culture"; Jean Kitihara-Frisch, "Symbolizing Technology as a Key to Human Evolution," in *Symbol as Sense*, ed. Mary LeCron Foster and Stanley H. Brandes (New York: Academic Press, 1980), pp. 211–23; and Ashley Montagu, "Toolmaking, Hunting, and the Origin of Language," *Origins and Evolution*, pp. 266–74.

36. For an exception to the former omission, see Gordon W. Hewes's hypothesis of a gestural language existing prior to verbal language: "Pongid Capacity for Language Acquisition," in *Precultural Primate Behavior*, ed. Emil W. Menzel (Basel: Karger, 1973), pp. 124–43, and "The Current Status of the Gestural Theory of Language Origin," in *Origins and Evolution*, pp. 482–504.

37. Hockett, "Origin of Speech," p. 92.

38. Freud, *Basic Writings* and *Complete Psychological Works*, vols. 4 and 5.

39. Langer, *Philosophy in a New Key* and *Feeling and Form*.

40. Leroi-Gourhan, *Préhistoire de l'art occidental*.

41. Foster, "Symbolic Structure" and "Evolution of Language"; see also Pulleyblank, "Beginnings of Duality of Patterning"; Fonagy, "Preconceptual Thinking"; Swadesh, *Origin and Diversification*; and Sheets-Johnstone, Chapter 6, this book.

42. J. Z. Young, *Programs of the Brain* (Oxford: Oxford University Press, 1978), p. 135.

43. Adolph Portmann, *Animal Forms and Patterns* (New York: Schocken Books, 1967).

44. Ibid., p. 117.

45. See particularly Emil W. Menzel, "Leadership and Communication in Young Chimpanzees," in Menzel, *Precultural Primate Behavior*, pp. 192–225.

46. Ibid., p. 218.

47. Gordon W. Hewes, "The Anthropology of Posture," *Scientific American* 196 (February 1957): 123–32.

48. See, for example, Konrad Lorenz, "Comparative Studies on the Behaviour of *Anatinae*," in *Function and Evolution of Behavior*, ed. P. H. Klopfer and J. P. Hailman (Reading: Addison Wesley, 1972), pp. 231–59, and "The Comparative Method in Studying Innate Behaviour Patterns," ibid., pp. 3–36; and A. Daanje, "On Locomotory Movements in Birds and the Intention Movements Derived From Them," ibid., pp. 259–96.

49. For a general review see J. L. Gould, "The Dance-Language Controversy," *Quarterly Review of Biology* 51/2 (1976): 211–44; see also Donald R.

Griffin, *The Question of Animal Awareness* (New York: Rockefeller University Press, 1976), and "Prospects for a Cognitive Ethology," *Behavioral and Brain Sciences* 1 (1978): 527–38, and *Animal Thinking* (Cambridge: Harvard University Press, 1984).

50. Gould, "Dance-Language Controversy"; Karl von Frisch, *Bees* (Ithaca, N.Y.: Cornell University Press, 1950), and *The Dance Language and Orientation of Bees* (Cambridge: Harvard University Press, 1967).

51. Foster, "Symbolic Structure," p. 110.

52. Mary LeCron Foster, "The Growth of Symbolism in Culture," in *Symbol as Sense*, pp. 371–97.

53. In addition to Foster's "Symbolic Structure," see Philip Lieberman, "Primate Vocalizations and Human Linguistic Ability," in *Perspectives on Human Evolution* 2, pp. 444–68, and "Biological Bases"; and Laitman, "Hominid Upper Respiratory System."

54. Philip Lieberman, "On the Evolution of Language: A Unified View," in *Primate Functional Morphology and Evolution*, ed. Russell H. Tuttle (The Hague: Mouton, 1975), p. 535.

55. A. M. Liberman, F. S. Cooper, P. Shankweiler, and M. Studdert-Kennedy, "Perception of the Speech Code," *Psychological Review* 74 (1967): 431–61, and "The Motor Theory of Speech Perception Revised," *Cognition* 21 (1985): 1–36.

56. Lieberman, "Evolution of Language," p. 504.

57. Hockett, "Origin of Speech," p. 90.

58. Stuart A. Altmann, "The Structure of Primate Social Communication," in *Social Communication among Primates*, pp. 325–62.

59. Ibid., p. 336.

60. Dawkins and Krebs, "Animal Signals."

61. Sigmund Freud, *A General Introduction to Psychoanalysis* (New York: Liveright, 1963), p. 148.

62. Peter Marler, "On the Origin of Speech from Animal Sounds," in *The Role of Speech in Language*, ed. J. F. Kavanagh and J. E. Cutting (Cambridge: MIT Press, 1975), pp. 11–37, and "An Ethological Theory of the Origin of Vocal Learning," in *Origins and Evolution*, pp. 386–95; and Dawkins and Krebs, "Animal Signals."

63. Darwin, *The Descent of Man and Selection in Relation to Sex* (Princeton: Princeton University Press, 1981 [1871]), p. 258.

64. Jean Piaget, *La naissance de l'intelligence chez l'enfant*, 6th ed. (Neuchatel: Delachaux et Niestlé, 1968), obs. 180 (p. 294).

65. Carpenter, "Monkeys and Apes," p. 49.

66. Ibid.

6

On the Origin of Language

The greatest obstacle in any glottogonic theory is not that vocal sounds, or manual gestures, or whatever, could not be used as linguistic signs, but how any system based on seemingly arbitrary signs could have got started, and could have reached a condition in which sets or strings of such signs could be combined to form propositions.

GORDON W. HEWES

We will use the term *language*, ignoring its etymological speech-origins, to denote *a general system for encoding and communicating propositional information by arbitrary, syntactically-concatenated symbols.*

HORST D. STEKLIS AND STEVAN R. HARNAD

INTRODUCTION

To say that the beginnings of language[1] are not equivalent to its origin is not simply an acknowledgment of the *Oxford English Dictionary*. While it is true that origins have to do with derivations not commencements, the conceptual contrast goes deeper than a superficial temporal distinction. To reconstruct the origin of language is to reconstruct a living process that may be analyzed quite apart from circumstances such as hunting or increased brain size that have typically been thought of as marking the beginnings of language. The purpose of this case study is to examine the two major preconceptions that consistently permeate investigations into the origin of language and just as consistently obstruct a clear view of the terrain. As these preconceptions are examined the distinction between origins and beginnings will come into more penetrating focus. At the same time it will become apparent how a different methodological approach is needed to gain an understanding of language in an originary sense and that a sensory–kinetic model is the key to that understanding. In polemical terms, the purpose is to show why most present-day answers to the question of the origin of language cannot but fall short of a coherent account precisely insofar as they fail to recognize the essential reality of language—that no language can be spoken for which the body is unprepared—and its consequence: to understand the origin and evolution of a language is to understand a sensory–kinetic lifeworld.

A CRITICAL OVERVIEW OF THE TRADITIONAL TERRAIN

Explanatory chronologies do not illuminate origins but specify when, how, and why something happened. Whether a matter of language, placental births, or whatever, they place its beginnings at a certain time/place and offer an explanation of its presence on the basis of certain structural features and functional significances. Thus, the beginnings of human speech are dated and explained according to the presence of certain anatomical configurations and behavioral patterns that enhance survival. Regardless of the disciplinary track from which the question of beginnings is approached and regardless of the particular question of concern, the ultimate aim of such research is to bring together the two explanatory chronologies in such a way that they interlock consistently and thus corroborate and support one another. There is an assumption in this conceptual purview that if the structural and functional mappings are each successfully rendered and then satisfactorily merged, then what will finally be fully uncovered and understood is the origin and evolution of human speech. In other words, a structural–functional chronicle of beginnings and consequent development is taken as synonymous with an account of origin and evolution.

On the face of it there might seem to be nothing extravagant or absurd in such an assumption. Moreover, examined at closer analytical range, the assumption might appear eminently reasonable. On the one hand, it pinpoints certain structural features as requisite for the origin of human speech. On the other hand, certain functional significances having to do with enhanced adaptation are pinpointed as constituting adequate reasons for human speech to have originated and developed. To put together the anatomical and behavioral evolutionary chronologies is thus to spell out necessary and sufficient conditions for the origin of human speech.

What is the matter with this double-edged approach to the origin of language? It appears finely suited to a rigorous and consistent explanation of how human speech came to be. But appearances may be deceiving. Structural–functional analyses can recreate the *beginnings* of language but not its origin. They can give necessary and sufficient conditions for human speech to begin at a certain point in space-time but not for it to *originate*. Moreover even here the ground is not so firm as one might think.

While it is theoretically possible to add together the two sets of conditions and come up with a composite picture of the beginning of human speech, in point of fact that beginning is only a *possible* beginning, and this for two reasons. At the more obvious level, sufficient conditions are contingent ones. They carry no stamp of certainty; other conditions might be adduced in their place. Thus, while the functional significances of speech might be spelled out in terms of its value in hunting behavior and all that activity is typically thought to have involved—for example, tools, males, future orientation, and so on—its functional significance might theoretically be spelled out just as persuasively and reasonably in terms of its value in communicating dream images,[2] for example, or in assuaging feelings of loneliness or terror at night. More than this, however, and as unlikely as it might appear, what are given as *necessary* conditions may be called into question. Ethologist R. J. Andrew, for instance, has noted that "human speech is by no means the only way in which a vocal language might have evolved."[3] Other phonemes could easily have been utilized via higher pitches; tongue and teeth clicks could have been incorporated; and the like. In other words, even given a particular anatomical uniqueness in relation to speech, merely having a part (or parts) does not guarantee any particular usage. Neither, it might be added, does the possession of any non-unique anatomical feature guarantee any particular use of it—for example, of tongue and teeth with respect to particular sounds. Furthermore, if a different anatomical configuration, say head position, yields a different phonetic ability, as postulated with respect to Neanderthal hominids,[4] then there is no singular necessary relationship between hominid speech and anatomy, but only necessary relationships between phonetic ability and anatomy. One could thus only agree with Andrew and say further that if one takes hominid anatomical evolution seriously in terms of morphological change, then a variety of vocal languages appears likely.

In short, hominid speech was not a singular and absolute behavior from origin to present but a variable and relative one: what we know today as human speech *evolved* in a very real sense. In consequence, one cannot spell out necessary (in the sense of absolute) anatomical conditions for its achievement but only particular anatomical conditions necessary to particular phonetic capacities, and then only by inferential extension arrive at particular theoretical forms of human speech, that is, *possible* modes of speech. But furthermore, the shorter inferential jump from phonetic ability to human speech is actually no more certain than the much longer one from anatomical part to speech. In neither case does mere possession—whether feature or capacity—guarantee anything in the way of actual usage. Indeed, one could ask at what point sound becomes speech. Is a particular set or number of phonemes required, for example, prior to which acquisition a "deficiency" exists making "true speech" impossible?

Given the variability and contingency of necessary and sufficient conditions for human speech, a definitive answer to the question of its beginnings seems extremely difficult to come by, perhaps even impossible to spell out conclusively. Although its beginnings and origin clearly coincide at that point where preverbal hominids first spoke with one another, the question of the origin is, strangely enough, more accessible, and this because it requires a different methodology. Here we are dealing not with a decisive event—whether elaborated in the form of structural or functional happenings—but with a way of living in the world. To understand that way of living one must recapture the creature in question not by way of its bodily possessions per se—whether anatomical structures or behavioral repertoires—but by way of its living flesh: one must reconstruct the sensory–kinetic world of the once-living subject for whom speech became a mode of making one's way in the world.

Seen from this perspective, human speech could not have been initially *invented*; it must have been *discovered*. Like its predecessor—the distinction between origin and beginnings—this distinction is no mere acknowledgment of the *OED*. It is an acknowledgment of the two major preconceptions lodged at the heart of seemingly all writings on the origin of language. One of them has to do with a belief that arbitrary elements are the cornerstone of language. The other has to do with a distinction between expressive and propositional languages (or modes of communication). Because the preconceptions have remained unexamined, they have led quite naively to further assumptions that are misleading and that block a rigorously clear view of the question. If arbitrary elements and a propositional language are taken for granted as the *sine qua non* of language, then they will be assumed to have come into being at the time specified as "the origin of language." The only way they could do this of course is if preverbal hominids invented arbitrary sounds and propositionality at the moment of inventing language itself. Clearly such invention would, among other things, demand considerable conceptual sophistication: conceptual foreknowledge is necessary to invention. Not only did Lucretius, two thousand years ago, realize this necessity and on this count criticize the notion of language being invented, but some present-day philosophers do so as well.[5] Requisite foreknowledge would demand not only that preverbal hominids had a concept of language in advance of inventing it, but in terms of the issue here, a concept both of arbitrary and nonarbitrary systems and of truth and falsity in addition. Foreknowledge aside, a further major problem with this scenario is that while what is to count as human language is decreed in advance, by and large it remains unaccounted for in analyses of the origin of human language. In effect, what is assumed without question is precisely what needs to be explicated, as is apparent even in Hockett's now classic account of design features and Thorpe's elaboration of them.[6]

Let us examine the issue more closely.

ARBITRARY ELEMENTS

A SENSORY–KINETIC ANALYSIS OF THE ARBITRARY AND THE NONARBITRARY

To maintain that language was made up originally of arbitrary elements means first of all that preverbal hominids must have had a concept of the arbitrary as opposed to the nonarbitrary. That is, the hominids must have had a concept of *sound itself* such that they could distinguish a gratuitous vocalization from, for example, a practical one. To arrive at this *nonverbal* concept of sound, they would have had to have experienced arbitrary and nonarbitrary sounds, which is to say they would have had to have experienced their own or someone else's gratuitous vocalizations and in the process, or as a result of those experiences, they would have had to have realized that the sounds being made were not topical in any way but merely playful renditions. Sheer sound, in other words, would have had to have been experienced and a nonverbal concept of the arbitrary formed on the basis of those experiences.

Would one want to attribute such a seemingly sophisticated nonverbal concept to the hominids? Would one want to admit a nonverbal concept at all? The notion of arbitrary elements' being at the foundation of human speech requires unequivocal affirmation in both cases. It is relevant to note that in this affirmative context the claim that *all* concepts are language-dependent becomes absurd, for the concept of language itself is in this view a concept for which there is no language.

On the other hand, insofar as nonarbitrary sounds would also have had to stand out as such, one might ask, What is a nonarbitrary sound? Since no explicit answer is given in the literature, a distinction between arbitrary and nonarbitrary sound is apparently taken for granted. An explicit answer aside, it is clear that the intent is to distinguish quite emphatically between sounds used in human speech and sounds like mating calls and warning cries. In effect, to distinguish between arbitrary and nonarbitrary sounds is to distinguish between propositional and expressive modes of communication. But a distinction between the two kinds of sound can be made from a quite different perspective and one which has particular import if assumed in relation to a preverbal hominid world.

The sounds of human speech are commonly distinguished from nonhuman mating calls, warning cries, and the like on the basis of sound itself. That is, sound *as sound* can be perceived as either gratuitous or significatory, as *in itself* semantically non-sensical or sensical. In the preverbal hominid world significatory sounds such as warning cries were clearly sounds pregnant with a meaning beyond themselves, that is, beyond their sheer sonorous or physiognomic character. Sounds of worldly phenomena, for example of rain, wind, or thunder, would be included in this category. So also would sounds that hominids recognized as belonging to creatures other than their own kind. To say that all nonarbitrary sounds were already sense-bearing means that they were not neutral or free: if sounded or heard, they had certain effects, that is, certain behavioral repercussions in the form of actions being taken or not being taken. Sound and portent were thus firmly cemented. Context was also circumscribed: if certain sense-bearing sounds were uttered by a hominid, then a certain situation would obtain. Being socially significant and contextually bound, nonarbitrary sounds did not just hang in the air but moved things along in some way: they affirmed, entreated, warned, announced, and so on. They were not made capriciously or with what one might call a non-serious purpose in mind. From this vantage point, arbitrary sounds might be simply characterized as being all the remaining possible sounds that a creature might make or hear after the meaningful ones had been subtracted. While the classification might be mathematically sound, however, it is not particularly edifying. More important, it ignores a basic observation.

Gratuitous vocalizations may be arbitrary, but they are not wholly empty sensory forms. They have a certain character, a certain audible physiognomy: they are of a certain pitch, timbre, intensity, and duration; they are muffled or mumbled, whispered or wailed; they are stressed or unstressed, thick or thin; they are piercing, explosive, soft, brief; and so on. In short, arbitrary sounds have an identifiable qualitative character. The ability to identify qualitative characteristics of sound—*feature abstraction* as it is called in present-day research—in fact constitutes one of four primary steps in the recognition of speech, and by extension in the production of speech as well.[7] The requisite ability is of considerable interest. Arbitrary sounds are from this perspective complex objects. To repeat the same arbitrary sound, for example, requires a knowledgeable tongue as well as a knowledgeable ear. One need only think of initial experiences with a foreign language in which sound elements appear at first semantically vacuous. Until a fair amount of experience is had with the language one does not hear phonetic differences between one sound and another, and even hearing differences, one is not always able immediately to render them distinctively. What this analogy strongly suggests is that arbitrary sounds would not only have had to have been discovered, they would also have had to have been practiced in some way before a lingual dexterity and precision could be attained and in consequence a lingual habit achieved. In brief, the qualitative character of sound would have had to have been first recognized, and second, reiterable, before sound could come to function linguistically. Failing an acknowledgment of these sensory–kinetic powers of discrimination and articulation, one is forced to imagine arbitrary sounds arriving *deus ex machina* into the mouth of a waiting hominid, or perhaps more absurd still, a nonverbal hominid thinking apropos of nothing in particular, "Gee! I ought to use arbitrary sounds and start talking!"[8]

To cite the qualitative character of arbitrary sounds is not to imply that nonarbitrary sounds lack phonetic distinction. It means only that the significatory aspect of nonarbitrary sounds is ascendant, or conversely, that their physiognomic character—the particular way they resound—is in the background. In effect, sound is potentially meaningful in two ways: qualitatively as sheer sound and lexically as significatory sound. In light of these two possible modes of aural meaning, a hypothesis about the origin of language suggests itself.

As indicated earlier, significatory sounds in an ancestral hominid's world were in part clearly social: other creatures existed with whom or for whom soundings communicated in some way. Presumably that communication enhanced survival. In contrast, sheer sound, if present at all, would appear to have been simply personally meaningful, if meaningful at all, and devoid of survival value. Such sound was for the creature itself, though quite conceivably an individual could have played with sound with others in the same way that it played kinetically with them—by tumbling and rolling, wrestling and chasing, and the like. Yet if sheer sound is indeed the stuff of which human language was originally made, then one might reasonably wonder whether, in a strictly normative biological sense (that is, discounting deafness), the capacity for gratuitous vocalization is not a fundamental measure of the presence or absence of speech; more specifically, whether in evolutionary terms that capacity was not the basis for distinguishing nonarbitrary sounds from arbitrary ones. For example, would not precisely that capacity have made possible the realization that socially meaningful sounds were socially meaningful sounds? If so, then the capacity for gratuitous vocalization made possible a realization of sound itself and in turn, a realization of the aural contrast necessary to recognizing nonarbitrary sound *as such*. In the same way that a domain of the arbitrary came to exist in virtue of the capacity for gratuitous vocalizations, so also a domain of the nonarbitrary came to exist. The two domains in fact were mutually dependent: conceptually, the one did not exist without the other. From an evolutionary perspective and quite apart from the babbling hypothesis (see below), one might then ask whether individual vocal play—gratuitous vocalization—was not a pivotal factor in the origin of language in the form of human speech. In support of this possibility it might be noted that infant primates other than humans do not vocalize gratuitously; they do not babble or coo.[9] On the other hand, the fact that bird subsong appears to share certain features with infant babbling[10] does not nullify the possibility. On the contrary, it makes mandatory a differential explanation of both phenomena in terms of the particular sensory–kinetic worlds each species creates and inhabits.

EVOLUTIONARY IMPLICATIONS OF THE ANALYSIS

It is reasonable to infer that if sheer sounds were distinguished from significatory sounds, as they must have been if arbitrary elements were nonverbally conceived, then preverbal hominids played with sounds, which is to say that gratuitous vocalizations were not uncommon but part of their everyday living world. In a sense it seems peculiar that this behavior has not been postulated before. Perhaps it is because in admitting this possibility something is thrown askew in the received evolutionary picture, askew to the point of introducing a conceptual inconsistency into the typical representation of ancestral hominid life.

The survival of ancestral hominids is regularly pictured as a dog-eat-dog, cut-throat affair. By and large there is little suggestion of hominid play in paleoanthropological texts, and the possibility of play so seemingly frivolous in character as that of gratuitous vocalizations is rarely discussed,[11] or if mentioned, suggested only in passing.[12] Yet as we have seen, gratuitous vocalizations would have had to have been not only made but explored in order for both the *idea* and the *practice* of speech to arise: Knowledge of, and a lingual facility for, a range of arbitrary sound possibilities would have had to have existed. But it is not only the introduction of play into the received evolutionary picture that is jarring and problematic. It is also the acknowledgment of nonarbitrary sound as something more than expressive utterance. The latter subject will be presently taken up more fully but it must be considered here from the viewpoint of assigning meanings to arbitrary sounds.

While it seems obvious that arbitrary sounds would have had to have been experienced as such before any could have been assigned lexical meanings beyond their phonetic ones, it is perhaps not so obvious that the idea of assigning a meaning to an arbitrary sound would have had to have been rooted in an awareness of nonarbitrary sounds as *sound-meanings*. Only then might arbitrary elements pass from being sheer sounds to being significatory ones. Only then might one go from *playing* with sound to *using* sound. More specifically, if the language that is human speech originated in the articulation of arbitrary sound elements, then clearly there was an epistemological relationship between what was experienced as lingually–aurally arbitrary and lingually–aurally nonarbitrary, and it is reasonable to hypothesize that that relationship was one in which nonarbitrary sounds were taken as the prototype upon which arbitrary sounds were modeled;

that is, they served as paradigms of signification. Thus, if arbitrary elements were in fact the original building blocks of language, then clearly preverbal hominids could distinguish between sheer sound and significatory sound, which means (1) they must have experienced, perhaps primarily in the form of play, a range of arbitrary sounds, and, in the form of social interactions, certain nonarbitrary sounds; and (2) they must have used that compound experiential knowledge in attaining to the idea of assigning certain meanings to certain arbitrary sounds. In brief, they realized that a sheer sound could stand for something in the same way that an already significatory sound stood for something. To acknowledge this realization is to acknowledge the lifeworld of ancestral hominids as experientially and conceptually richer and broader than the received evolutionary picture typically represents it to be.

Arbitrary elements seen in conjunction with the typical survival scenario create a second conceptual inconsistency, one that arises from an unwitting contradiction. On the one hand it would have to be maintained that in light of a dog-eat-dog survival situation everything about their immediate world was significant to preverbal hominids. On the other hand, it is staunchly maintained by present-day researchers that arbitrary elements in the sense of *wholly meaningless* sounds were conceived and utilized by preverbal hominids. As for the former claim, the typical picture is one in which expedient and economical actions are always in the foreground.[13] Yet if everything is of moment, if everything is measured in terms of a rigorously and unrelentingly demanding survival situation, then sheer sound must also have been taken seriously, if not in play, then certainly in *naming* things or *symbolizing* certain actions or relationships by certain sounds. If everything in the world had portent of some kind, then it would not be called just anything; *any* sound at all would not do. In short, if everything in a preverbal hominid's world was alive with meaning— perhaps in a way similar to that in which a human world came to be alive with spirits and in which explanations of worldly events came to rest upon mythical forces and deities—then it appears contradictory to that world to introduce something that is *wholly meaningless* and especially to link it to something that is meaningful, and in fact, in terms of the typical picture, *critically* meaningful. What this logical inconsistency strongly suggests is that, on the contrary, so-called arbitrary sounds designated things according to the quality of their sound. They were experienced not as wholly meaningless elements but as qualitatively meaningful and as such could reflect the quality of the worldly referent they symbolized.[14] The word would sound like its referent, not necessarily in the way of a strict onomatopoetic rendering, in which case language would be limited to designating only audible phenomena, but in the way of a physiognomic onomatopoeia. The word would not imitate but qualitatively *intimate* the thing it stood for, and this in virtue of its sheer sound: its timbre, force, duration, and so on—its felt and heard qualitative character. A *physiognomic congruency* would thus be the ground upon which so-called "arbitrary" sound elements would have come to have linguistic meaning.

CONCLUSION

The traditional conception of arbitrary elements cannot be assumed with either epistemological or scientific impunity. Until the origin of language is accounted for by reconstructing a particular lifeworld, there is no way of understanding how arbitrary sounds could come to be made at all let alone serve as carriers of assigned meaning. What is essential is first that arbitrary sounds be distinguished from nonarbitrary sounds, and second that a paradigm of signification exist. Given the distinction and paradigm, physiognomic and significatory meanings become apparent and assigned meanings become a concrete possibility. The presence of nonarbitrary sound is thus essential to the utilization of arbitrary sounds as the building blocks of language. Moreover the very idea of a spoken language based upon arbitrary sounds demands that gratuitous vocalizations be incorporated within the evolutionary picture of the origin of language.

At the same time, given a world in which everything matters and that is physiognomic through and through, it is difficult to conceive how the original elements of language could have been wholly arbitrary to begin with. On the contrary, to be compatible with the received evolutionary picture and with a preverbal world, a physiognomic congruency of sound and meaning would appear to have been essential.

THE EXPRESSIVE/PROPOSITIONAL DISTINCTION

PRELIMINARY REASONS FOR DOUBTING THE VALIDITY
OF THE DISTINCTION: INCOMPATIBILITIES

The notion of a proposition as distinct from an expression dates back to Aristotle who defined the former as "a statement, with meaning, as to the presence of something in a subject or its absence,"[15] which definition, incidentally, shows why it is nonsensical to speak of "propositional statements." Aristotle's separation of thought and speech into two modes, one involving truth and falsity and the other not, was hardly linked to evolution. It might thus be thought peculiar that the separation is regularly and directly appropriated by evolutionists without a concrete examination of both its general validity and its specific meaning and implications for ancestral hominid life and the origin of language. To be sure, not all embrace the separation. For example, Peter Marler, an avian zoologist, is cautiously skeptical of the claim that linguistic utterances are absolutely distinct from emotional ones, and Bryan Robinson, a neuroanatomist, affirms outright that "normal speech appears to represent a harmonious mixture of both."[16] Still, the almost uniform acceptance of the separation by numerous scientists from a variety of disciplines cannot be denied. For example, in all the nine-hundred-odd pages of the 1976 interdisciplinary work, *Origins and Evolution of Language and Speech*, Aristotle's separation is virtually unanimously invoked but nowhere fleshed out.[17] No example is given of each kind of utterance, specifically as it might have been made by a pre- and a post-verbal hominid. Presumably the difference is adjudged as transparent as the difference between humans and non-humans, a presumption that of course begs the question at issue since to be human is already to be able to speak and to speak is already to be human.

If one were skeptical about there being an absolute and immediately discernible difference, one might begin with eighteenth-century philosopher Etienne de Condillac's reason for insisting upon the centrality of inflection to speech.[18] The sounds that are speech are not uttered in a monotone; on the contrary, spoken language is characterized by modulations of voice that shade and color what is uttered. Although Condillac's emphasis was upon the hearer—her/his interest requirements, so to speak—emphasis can clearly be placed as well upon the speaker—her/his convictions, attitudes, expectations, and so on, which are transparent in her/his statements. In effect, it would seem that whatever the first speaker's pronouncements on the world and however ponderous they might have been, they were not delivered in a monotone, not only because no one would have listened, but because of the speaker's commitment to the statement she/he was making: what was spoken to others was not detached from its living owner's interests, beliefs, and concerns about the world.

There is a second reason for skepticism following clearly upon the first. If one adheres to the typical evolutionary scenario, it is apparent that ancestral hominids' first uses of language could not have been neutral utterances—bald pronouncements on the world devoid of any felt significance. The fact that it was raining, for example, would not be noted with an armchair investigator's abstractness; neither would the fact of needing help or of there being a predator nearby. If the received evolutionary picture is credible at all, then a pure statement of purported fact has no place within it. Real-life feelings of fear, hostility, pain, pleasure, surprise, curiosity, and the like could not be peeled from immediate experience and thrown away like banana skins. From this perspective as well, the preconception that language can be cleanly divided into propositional and expressive forms is inconsistent with actually living subjects in a real-life world. Speech is essentially a *living* dialogue. To think that an ancestral hominid would have replied to a request from a fellow hunter, "Ah! The spirit is willing but the flesh is weak!" is absurd. The disjunction between utterance and speaker here matches the absurd disjunction of an objectively delivered, "There's a lion coming up on your right"—or even "It is raining." Clearly if one is critically and ceaselessly involved in the everyday reality of survival, then one cannot be commenting on that reality from the wings, as it were, uttering purely propositional asides on the situation at hand.

FURTHER REASONS FOR DOUBTING THE VALIDITY: CONSEQUENCES

The picture of a purely propositional language in collision with both Condillac's observation and with the received evolutionary picture disposes one to question the validity of the view that human language is essentially propositional and absolutely distinct from expressive utterances. This questioning of course is not to be taken as grounds for maintaining that, originally, spoken language was purely expressive. The challenge is not to find sound and reasonable grounds for aligning everyday language on the one side or the other of the distinction but for maintaining the distinction itself. If there are good reasons for doubting its everyday validity, then there are good reasons for repudiating and abandoning it.

Further reasons for doubt become apparent if one examines consequences as well as incompatibilities. If one claims, for example, that the expressive and propositional are two clear-cut and wholly distinct forms of language, then surely one would have to entertain the likelihood that prior to the development of the propositional language, hominids communicated in a manner similar to other primates: preverbal hominids would have made—per common belief—"purely expressive" utterances via particular patterns of sound. But if preverbal hominids did in fact make such utterances, then the earlier, that is, expressive, mode of communication presumably would not have disappeared altogether with the advent of the propositional language. Indeed, it seems inconceivable that all of a sudden (or even gradually), with the first spoken words, ancestral hominids would have stopped using any previous mode of communication, as if one day there was a "naming party" and from that day forth, all that issued from the mouths of the hominids was a propositional language. If the other language served them in the name of survival, then certainly it would count for something crucial and not be peremptorily abandoned. If, on the other hand, one denies any crucial meaning to the prior expressive language, then the auditory channel of the received evolutionary picture becomes unintelligible. A pandemonium of meaningless sound must be said to have existed, a pandemonium inexplicable by any conceivable stretch of the principle of natural selection. Put in this perspective of an *actual* evolutionary history, the connection between the two purported kinds of language can no longer be understood at the level of reified modalities of communication. Instead, the relationship must be examined from the concrete, empirically grounded viewpoint that there is no such thing as a language apart from a speaker —or potential speaker—of the language, which means that it must be looked at within the context of a particular sensory–kinetic world.

Within this living context, the likelihood of preverbal patterns of sound becomes the ground for the reasoned speculation described earlier, namely, that insofar as certain significations already existed in the form of certain sounds, the passage from an unspoken world to a spoken one was marked by new experiences centered on differentiating gratuitous sounds from significatory ones and on the idea of assigning meanings to the former. But over and above this suggested continuity it would appear that a relationship existed and continued to exist between the two systems of sound-meanings. There is no reason to think that the patterns of significatory sound that existed previous to the assignment of meanings to gratuitous sounds would be replaced by the formalized system of gratuitous sounds. On the contrary, it would seem much more natural to assume that those patterns were enfolded into the formalized system. Indeed, it would otherwise seem peculiar that we should today cry out in pain, gasp when startled, and the like. Why would we not instead always *say* in each case, "I am in pain" and "I am startled"? There is every reason to believe that expressive patterns of sound have a long line of descent. The question then is, If there were in fact two systems of sound-meanings, how were they specifically related?

If one acknowledges that hominids made "purely expressive" utterances, then it seems likely, especially in the early stages of a propositional language (and whether that language originally named things or specified certain actions or relationships), that whatever was spoken of was something of immediate moment—in the same way that what was expressively uttered was of immediate moment. There would not, in the early stages at least, seem to be any likelihood of abstract musings, weighty discourses, casual social chats, and so on. Thus, what appears likely is that particular and already significatory sounds became renderable in the new sound-meaning system. A particular cry of alarm could be equally rendered verbally as "Snake!" for example, or a particular shriek could be equally rendered as "Help!"[19] In other words, originally, the new language would have been used to symbolize precisely those experiences that mattered, experiences that were of immediate consequence (whether for the present or future), thus experiences colored by a *felt* significance. A significatory sound was not replaced by the formalized system of gratuitous sounds, but its meaning became renderable in that system. This is not to say that the newly developing language was *nothing but* a translation of already significatory sounds, but only that the new system of sound-meanings was at times *semantically congruent* with the older system. Indeed, since new meanings, that is, new ways of living in the world, did not erupt overnight with the advent of the new system, what else would be spoken of initially if not the critical, but familiar, meaning-charged everyday experiences sometimes captured in patterns of already significatory sound?

Now if the nature of the relationship between the two orders of sound-meanings may be explicated in terms of a translatability of meanings, then clearly the new language cannot be described as purely propositional. It was not only naturally inflected but substantively expressive. Moreover if the meaning of already significatory sounds was in fact renderable by gratuitous sounds or sequences of sound and vice versa, then the basic distinction to be made is not between an expressive and propositional language at all but between *one system of sound-meanings and another*. In effect, to understand the *origin* of language, a distinction would be made not at the abstract level of language as an already determined verbal system, but at the concrete level of sound as a sensory–kinetic phenomenon. By beginning with that phenomenon one situates oneself at the very spawning ground of a verbal language.

But the status and fate of the "prior language" has in fact been envisioned otherwise, in particular as existing alongside, totally separate from the newer form.[20] This view is confuted by the incompatibilities and consequences described above. If entertained nonetheless, its conceptual kinships alone would make it highly suspect if not totally unconvincing. The idea that two totally different and self-contained orders of language existed and have continued to exist side by side with no possible connection with one another is strikingly similar both to an outmoded and abandoned conception of the mind/body relationship (psycho-physical parallelism), and to a not unrelated nor unchallenged dichotomous categorization of behavior as either cognitive or emotive. Indeed, a noted paleoanthropologist criticizes the idea of an emotive/cognitive division in communicative behavior on neurophysiological and neuroanatomical grounds.[21]

In sum, to answer to the status and fate of the prior system of sound-meanings is to spell out ways in which what is decreed *the expressive* and what *the propositional* are or are not related. In the end it would appear that an absolute separation of the two systems may be conceptually upheld only insofar as one relegates an older expressive system to pure bodies, which is to say to mindless, nonrational, non-human animals, or to hominoid animals when they are in a mindless, emotional, or preverbal state. For the view to be taken seriously, what is wanted at the very least is a full-fledged scenario that would show concretely how a propositional language originated and evolved in absolute isolation from an expressive language.

It is in fact curious that since a concern with the origin of language necessarily entails paleoanthropological reconstructions, the full-fledged scenarios needed to lend credence to proposed theory are not commonly generated. In contrast, Condillac began his eighteenth-century account of the origin not with a certain *view* of language but with a living scenario by which he literally fleshed out his theory. His scenario thus provides direct access to the roots of language insofar as it recreates the lifeworld of living beings. One can readily see from his reconstruction that if the origin of language is to be accounted for—in his words—"according to the ordinary course of nature" and not by divine providence,[22] then it must rely on an understanding of the passage from one kind of sensory–kinetic world to another. Though not spelled out in detail, Condillac's reconstruction shows how the new sound language was patterned on already existing natural sounds; he describes how certain lingual sensitivities and capacities were vital to its development; he indicates the nature of correlative modes of communication; and so on. The spawning ground of the new language is, if not fully described, adumbrated sufficiently that a sensory–kinetic logic is apparent in the passage from one form of living to another. For example, Condillac points out that the development of articulate sounds was slow precisely because the adult tongue was not flexible and because "the child's organ for want of exercise quickly lost all its flexibility."[23] Thus in addition to the natural sounds, the older gestural form of communication continued with a few new words being added from time to time by chance. Condillac concludes, however, that "in proportion as the language of articulate sounds became more copious, there was more need of seizing early opportunities of improving the organ of speech, and for preserving its first flexibility."[24] Condillac thus implicitly affirms that no language can be spoken for which the body is unprepared and that an understanding of the origin and evolution of language is founded upon an understanding of a living sensory–kinetic process.

However deficient or naive Condillac's reconstruction might appear today, it nevertheless illustrates why, lacking a living scenario, one has no grounds for saying how language began much less how it can be characterized. One must first discover the *origin* of language; one must first reconstruct the story of how it originated. It is at this level of reality that the distinction between an expressive and a propositional form of language, if it exists at all, must be described. A reconstruction of the origin is no flight of fancy or nursery tale—or at least it need not be. It can be a scientific history, scientific precisely insofar as it is founded upon a sound and comprehensive grasp of the creature for whom speaking became a mode of living in the world.

A CRITIQUE OF THE DISTINCTION:
UNMASKING THE EVOLUTIONARY PREMISES

To examine the expressional/propositional distinction at face value in terms of incompatibilities, consequences, and methodology is to evaluate it at a pragmatic level: Is the distinction viable and if not, why not? Such an examination does not penetrate to a finer critical appraisal of the distinction itself. What the latter requires is an elucidation of "expressive" and "propositional" in evolutionary terms. Put in such terms the distinction may be seen to turn on two premises: (1) that certain creatures came to have the capacity to make true and false assertions, and (2) that expressive utterances cannot be true or false. Seen in this sharper and more penetrating evolutionary light, the distinction is ready-made but at the expense of assuming the veracity of the two premises. When either premise is critically examined, serious problems become apparent. A yelp, for example, while not usually taken as true or false, could quite conceivably be so taken: the creature could be dissembling. The same is true of a wail ("I'm hurt!") or a grunt ("Okay") or a shriek ("A snake is over there!"). All such purported expressive communications could be asserting something that is false which is to say they could be expressive and propositional at the same time. Moreover what might be decreed as purely propositional—statements such as "I need help," or "A predator is coming"—are statements that are likely to be expressively uttered at the same time that they are assertive of something true or false. Lying and pretense are not then inherently emotion-free acts nor is the "emotional part" an epiphenomenon of the lying. An utterance can be at the same time patently expressive and propositional by definition —which of course explains why in a successful act of lying one cannot separate the sham from the real—in effect, why one is duped—and why in a successful act of pretense, one cannot separate belief from affect—in effect, why the play goes on. In these real-life situations, the expressive and the propositional are minted simultaneously.

A DEEPER QUESTIONING OF THE PREMISES:
THE CASE FOR BEHAVIORAL PROPOSITIONALITY

It is precisely because in a living situation the boundary between "the expressive" and "the propositional" can be ambiguous that an absolute division between the two is difficult to defend. The soundness of the division may be further and more radically weakened by a finer consideration of acts of deception and pretense. When such acts are attributed to nonhuman primates—or nonhuman animals generally —the boundaries of propositionality itself are thrown into question. While it is obvious that a creature that lies is *ipso facto* a creature capable of formulating propositions, the questions raised by the attributed acts have no quick and easy answer at all. For example, Are behavioral propositions possible? Can nonhuman animals make propositional assertions? The answer in both cases would seem to be, "Only if movement and/or physiognomic versatility can be considered a language or a nascent language." A brief examination of this possibility will show at the least that the questions cannot be summarily dismissed as absurd and at the most that a persuasive case may be made for a pan-evolutionary behavioral propositionality.

To begin with, in playing dead, nonhuman animals may be said to be lying, feigning something to be so when it is not *really* so at all. The animal might be said to be impersonating (or perhaps better, imanimating) a dead animal. Forms of mimicry might thus be construed as prototypical of propositionality. The animal is claiming to be something it is not and in consequence lying to creatures in its immediate social environment. From this perspective the notion of mimicry would seem to merit deep and careful inquiry with respect to the possibility of a behavioral propositionality.

A richer and perhaps more compelling example of behavioral propositionality is apparent in the range of mimicry in the female firefly *Photuris versicolor*.[25] This female can impersonate five other species of female firefly. By adjusting its flashing behavior in form (number and duration of flashes), and in timing between flashes, it gives false signals as to its identity. It might thus be said to know the vocabulary and syntax of six different languages and to use five of these languages in a highly selective fashion to give misleading information to particular male fireflies. Given its selectively deceptive behavior and its considerable signaling sophistication, it is difficult not to consider its behavioral mimicry as proto-propositional if not outrightly propositional.

The animal that plays dead is also giving false information but in a peculiar and far less sophisticated idiom. Freezing on the spot after a fall or lying inert where one is, results actually in a negation of behavior for the onlooker. Like dead animals themselves, animals playing dead do not appear to behave at all. They are thus successful precisely insofar as they are seen not to *behave* but simply to *be*, and to be what they are not actually, namely, dead. In this sense their mimicry might be construed as similar to morphological mimicry: in both cases definitive information is conveyed physiognomically. The animal playing dead takes on a particular physiognomy in order to deceive. In cases of what might be called natural morphological mimicry, a certain physiognomy is immutably given. But morphological deception also includes those cases in which a transient physiognomy may be assumed. In such instances animals show themselves in a different form. An insect that congeals its naturally elongate body into a ball, for example, or an amphibian that puffs up its body to increase its actual size twofold, changes its form to appear as some *other* thing or some *other* creature in the world respectively. Given a minimum of physiognomic versatility—two possible forms of appearance—an animal has the possibility of using one of these forms of appearance to deceive others. There is, in consequence, a rudimentary physiognomic vocabulary available which, insofar as it makes deception possible, suggests a nascent language. Even if wanting in syntax and in a separation of signified and signifier, "[an] assertion of something about something"[26] is being made.

If mimicry is deceptively employed, then falsity is, by definition, engendered in the mimetic act. For this reason it is difficult to dismiss altogether the possibility that propositional assertions may be made by nonhuman animals. At the least it must be acknowledged that nonhuman animals can and do claim at times to be something or some kind of creature other than what they really are and in this sense can and do mislead others. The veracity of the first premise thus seems to be in serious question. The first creatures to make true and false assertions may not have been those creatures who discovered speech at all but those creatures capable of mimicry.

By a similar token the second premise is no less in question. In many types of ludic behavior, both human and nonhuman, pretense is again involved. Playing animals feign predatory chases, teeth to neck combat, and the like. Its didactic value notwithstanding, such play behavior would be most commonly characterized as wholly expressive: the animals are frolicking; they are not doing things in earnest but in sport. Yet there is a good deal more involved here than "purely expressive" behavior. A sophisticated form of mimicry is evident, one that verges on or perhaps even constitutes behavioral symbolism.

Animals playfully engaged in predatory chases or teeth to neck combat are engaged in a representational form of activity. The actual gestures and movements being made represent other gestures and movements that would be made in a *real* chase or a *real* fight. Furthermore, the animal represents itself as having feelings that it has not— fear, belligerence, curiosity, and so on—and to be a creature that it is not—a predator, an aggressor, a victim, an intimidator, or the like. Yet it would be difficult to maintain that the animals involved in the play situation are lying since, although there is pretense, there is no apparent intent to deceive and in fact no deception at all. For example, no playing animal actually sinks its teeth into the neck of the other animal thus actually wounding it. The purported claims then do not seem to add up to a propositional behavior. If the vantage point is slightly shifted, however, it is not only possible to view the behavior as propositional but it appears necessary to do so in order to explain the play situation itself.

With a minimally modified perspective it becomes apparent that while one can rule out lying, one cannot rule out the fact that something false is being behaviorally asserted: "I am going to bite you," or "I am going to catch up with you and rip you to bits." How is such information being conveyed? A persuasive case can be made for claiming that the movement repertoire of certain forms of behavior can be symbolically generated and read linguistically. Fighting behavior, for instance, can be seen as a language. Certain movements and gestures belong to it; it has a certain vocabulary the units of which may be variously combined but in circumscribed ways. Thus it has certain syntactical rules. For example, in the middle of a chase one animal does not stop and begin scratching itself. A particular sequence of gestures and movements obtains that is flexible but within determined limits. It is these movements and gestures that are represented in play-fighting. The represented behavior may thus also be seen as a language but a language once-removed from the *real* language— which is why in the play situation an animal *can* stop running and begin scratching. So long as the appropriate movements and gestures are made, however, the behavioral assertions peculiar to play-fighting convey the necessary information: "I am going to catch up with you and rip you to bits" or "I am going to bite you." The question is, Can such assertions be considered propositional?

Given that the assertions conveyed by the gestural–kinetic language are false, what is unusual is that at the same time the animals make those false assertions they nullify them by a seemingly tacit social consensus. While recognized as false, the claims are at the same time taken by all involved to be true. Every playing animal assumes the others to believe in the urgency of its plight, the strength of its attack, and so on; play would otherwise cease. Indeed, the play situation does not work at all if any animal reacts to the behavior of others as *merely* pretend. But neither does it work if any animal fails to make *false* claims itself or reacts to the behavior of others without acknowledging *its* falsity. In either case, actual combat might ensue. Stated positively, the play situation works precisely insofar as no animal subverts the delicate linking of conflicting beliefs (or whatever one might wish to designate as akin to beliefs): No animal takes the play behavior as anything but pretense behavior and no animal takes the pretense behavior as anything but real. Every creature involved agrees to take in, as it were, and to be taken in. The behavioral assertions of the play situation are thus transformed by a tacit communal belief in the non-falsity of the false. That belief structure transforms what would otherwise be pretense-deception into pretense-play.

Pretense-deception has in fact been documented in nonhuman primates,[27] and it of course forcefully supports the idea of a behavioral propositionality. What makes the question of propositionality in the play situation more complex, over and above its supposed antithesis to "expressive behavior," is that pretense here is *not* misleading; it is *not* transient; and it is *not* limited to experimental studies with nonhuman primates. From this perspective the doubling back of belief turns what would otherwise be either deceptive pretensions or disjointed movement patterns and molds them about a certain symbolic matrix. To paraphrase the anthropologist Gregory Bateson, the symbolic activity of play-fighting does not denote fighting but it does denote ideas for which fighting is an appropriate symbol.[28]

A difficult question nevertheless remains. To be propositional the behavior must be inherently rather than indirectly symbolic. Put in Piagetian terms, the question is whether play movement is only sensorimotor activity or whether it is truly symbolic. According to Piaget the distinction between signified and signifier (which is necessary to true symbolic behavior) begins to be empirically evident in children's play when "the action is unfinished, and moreover, only done for fun." The distinction is accomplished in situations where "the actions . . . are . . . not only taken out of their ordinary context and left uncompleted . . . but are now applied to new and inadequate objects and are carried out with strict attention to detail although they are entirely make-believe."[29] Finely focused field research studies would be needed to determine whether in animal play the separation between signified and signifier is embryonic or fully formed. Yet present-day evidence is not altogether lacking. If "an ape may pound on a tree when it cannot pound on another ape that annoyed or frightened it,"[30] then action is being taken out of its ordinary context and applied to a new and inadequate object. If gestural–kinetic patterns appear in fragments in the play of growing monkeys,[31] then incomplete actions are present and are ostensibly being "done for fun."

In sum, certain forms of ludic behavior appear to be either prototypical of, or to constitute behavioral symbolism. Propositionality is thus not categorically precluded by expressive behavior but may be engendered by it. Of course it could be objected that in view of *pretend* emotions, expressive behavior is not actually present at all, but this would presumably mean that the play activities described are really cognitive sport, an ironic view given the context.

PROPOSITIONALITY IN EVOLUTIONARY PERSPECTIVE

Over and above constituting a serious questioning of the second premise, the above observations and discussions again indicate that if it is true that certain creatures came to have the capacity to make true and false verbal statements, it is not necessarily true that until that time no such thing as truth and falsity existed. On the contrary, the notion of truth and falsity would seem to have had to have been grasped prior to purposefully deceitful verbal statements' being made. How could a creature come to make false verbal statements unless it first had direct experiences of falsity and on the basis of those experiences, came to entertain the idea of falsity and its usefulness? In fact, in view of the critical reasons given for doubting the veracity of the two premises, one might wonder whether it was not at the biologically astute knees of nonhominid animals that hominid ones first experienced false assertions, realized the value of lying, and learned to dissemble and mislead accordingly. It is not unreasonable to think that preverbal hominids stumbled upon dissembling creatures in the world about them and, in the process, found that telling the difference between a really dead creature and a feigning one, for example, could spell the difference between a ready and succulent meal or an imminent and fatal attack. Similarly, at the level of organic form, telling the difference between two species, one of which mimics the other, is of critical adaptational significance in the biological world generally, and there is no reason to think that mimicry did not exist or that its critical adaptational significance was any less at the time of preverbal hominids. Moreover if mimicry is widely observed in the natural world it would have to count, and to have counted in many instances for survival. If it is indeed survival that hangs in the balance, then the correlative notions of truth and falsity are of foundational biological import and an answer to the question of the genesis of propositionality cannot be ignored.

One final point should be made in connection with a more detailed look at the erstwhile division between propositional and expressive modalities of communication with respect to evolution. While it is true that verbal statements may be true or false, and while it is assumed that verbal hominids had the ability to make false statements, one wonders what false verbal statements would have been made by them and to what end. We can presume the hominids could only be speaking to one another and that given the ceaseless demands of eking out a living, there would be nothing but the cooperative social interactions typically claimed for ancestral hominid societies. It is thus difficult to conceive what misleading statements might have been made—about a purported food source or predator nearby? about a certain stone's being eminently suited to a certain task? about a new technique for skinning or for sharpening? about the whereabouts of a lost child? about the weather? about copulating? about directions "homeward"?—and why it would have been judicious to mislead another in the first place.

To answer that it is the possibility of misleading that is the defining feature of a verbal language is to say nothing at all. If false statements were in fact *not* made, if there was only the *possibility* of making them, then there is no use in narrowly circumscribing the newly developing verbal language of ancestral hominids as propositional. A host of other equally vacuous definitions could serve as well. In sum, to define the language as propositional on the basis of *possible* use is to say nothing about the language or the creatures who spoke it. And it makes no sense either, as noted, to claim that what was merely possible was in fact actualized. To cooperate is to work together, for example, not to lead each other astray by saying something is so when it is not.

CONCLUSION

So long as truth and falsity are taken as the basis for distinguishing between "true" language and any other form of communication, then grounds for maintaining the distinction are seriously compromised for a number of reasons, all of which indicate that truth and falsity with respect to verbal and nonverbal behavior is the basic issue to be rigorously examined and resolved, and with it such questions as, What are the evolutionary antecedents of truth and falsity prior to human speech? What is the full range of possible propositionality in verbal/nonverbal expressive acts? What are the social conditions and variables of propositionality? If the basic but unplumbed issue were seriously studied, deeper insights could undoubtedly be had into language that would significantly enhance an understanding of its origin and evolution. In the meantime, on the basis of the evidence presented here it is evident that propositionality—"the possibility of misleading, of claiming something false"[32]—is neither an exclusively human possibility nor is it necessarily an expressively vacant act.

A SENSORY–KINETIC MODEL OF THE ORIGIN OF LANGUAGE

The model assumes the validity of the preceding critique of both arbitrary elements and a propositional/expressive distinction. It furthermore engenders concepts generated in the course of the critique, particularly gratuitous vocalizations as a touchstone of language and an original physiognomic congruency of sound and meaning. The model is rooted in a literal understanding of the tongue as a lingual organ, that is, as the locus of sensory–kinetic lingual powers. Evidence of these powers and their intermodal development is had in observations and studies of infant behavior. The model may be extrapolated phylogenetically insofar as no creature can speak a language for which the body is unprepared. In other words, a certain sensory–kinetic world is essential to the advent of verbal language. An examination of human infant lingual behavior will progressively illuminate the characteristic features of that sensory–kinetic domain.

To begin with, the possibility of verbal language lies in the tactility of the tongue. Studies in oral anatomy give particular testimony to the tactile mission of the human tongue: "The muscles of the tongue are peculiar in that they do not operate in association with joint movement. Hence control of skillful movement cannot be guided by special neural information fed back from joint terminals. . . . The problem of lack of position information from joint endings seems admirably replaced by 'particularly sensitive exteroceptive systems,' namely, the numerous touch and pressure receptors all over the tongue."[33] Indeed, the tongue is the most tactilely sensitive area or part of the human body. While it might seem appropriate to say that in the very early days of infant life the tongue is being touched by things rather than that it is touching them, its own rhythmical movement in nursing nevertheless brings about certain tactile experiences. In the act of manipulating itself, the tongue causes a certain world to flow into and out of being. Moreover the sense of touch is here not colored by the sense of taste: in the oral experience of nursing, "the tongue is still entirely a tactile organ and is utterly devoid of the ability to taste."[34] Piaget's observational record of infants implicitly bears out this affirmation of the tongue as preeminently an organ of touch. At the age of one month, Piaget writes, Lucienne "plays with his tongue, sometimes by licking his lower lip, sometimes by sliding his tongue between his lips and gums." Piaget goes on to note that the behavior "is frequently repeated and always with the same expression of satisfaction."[35] Clearly the tongue is a felt presence, and it is on the basis of its being a felt presence that it becomes an animate organ, a mobile power in the world, a locus of exploratory gestures. The entire mouth area and the lips especially are of course part of the explorative experience. But the mobility of the tongue is distinctive. While the tongue can glide over the lips, for example, the lips cannot glide over the tongue. What is discovered in the tactile mobility of the tongue are certain physiognomies: a certain jaggedness or smoothness, hardness or softness, flatness or roundness, a certain beginning and ending, a certain warmth or coolness, a certain dryness or moistness. Whatever the thing touched, it is not a matter of contemplating it first and then discovering its tactile qualities as hidden features. The tactile character of the thing is immediately given. Indeed, for the infant, the tactile character is the very thing itself.

Emphasis upon the physiognomic immediacy of touch calls attention to the fact that the act of verbal identification could not take place at all, much less originate unless attention were first given to the qualitative presence of things. Short of perceiving their physiognomies, there is no way of distinguishing one thing from another and there are in consequence no forms to identify. In the experience of touch, humans—like all creatures—have their first introduction to a physiognomic world. Thus not only is the tongue an animate organ—the locus of exploratory gestures toward the world—it is the *first* animate organ, the *first* sensory–kinetic power or gestural center in relation to which a qualitative world arises.

An infant's beginning play with sounds in the first year of life is a further elaboration of its primordial communion with the world by touch. While babbling is obviously a total mouth phenomenon, the status of the tongue in the coordinated drama of movement and sound cannot be minimized. The tongue is the mobile midpoint between lips and larynx and as such is the mediating center of sound. If the tongue is held perfectly still, for example, lips can be moved and vocalizations from the throat may be made, but no variable vowel sounds can be produced and neither can any range of consonants. Philip Lieberman's studies document this phonetic centrality of the tongue: "The shape of the pharyngeal region constantly changes during the produc-

tion of human speech as the tongue moves backwards and forwards.
. . . These variations in pharyngeal cross-sectional area are characteristic for consonants as well as vowels and they are essential in the
production of human speech."[36]

In babbling, a human infant is discovering the tongue as a source
of sound as well as touch, and it is the tongue's capacity to create
sounds that ultimately becomes the infant's primary focal point of
attention; the tactile tongue becomes a tactile/aural tongue. In the process it does not cease to be a way of feeling and knowing the world
by touch, but there is a transfer of priority in which the ratio among
the senses is gradually transformed.

What is of moment in light of the tongue's movements and positions in babbling is not that it might happen upon sounds that are the
precursors of human speech, but that there is an inherent continuity in
the passage from one sensory prominence to another. A purely tactile
world awakens a world of sound, and in consequence, a new range of
powers is discovered. It might in fact be well to spell out briefly what
is known as the "babbling hypothesis" merely to distinguish it from
the thrust of the present discussion.

W. H. Thorpe has summarized the hypothesis as follows:

[It] assumes that the "random" babbling and jabbering of the human baby
comprise a great variety of sounds and so will include most if not all of the
sounds which are employed in the language of whatever culture it happens
to be reared in. Mothers often talk or croon to their children when attending
to them, and so the sound of the mother's voice will become associated with
comfort-giving measures. From this it is to be expected that when the child,
alone and uncomfortable, hears his own voice, this will likewise have a con-
soling, comforting effect. So it is supposed . . . that the infant will be rewarded
for his own first babbling and jabbering without any necessary reference to
the effects produced upon others. Before long, however, the infant will learn
that if he succeeds in making the kind of sound his mother makes, he will
get more interest, affection, and attention in return; so the stage is set for the
learning of language.[37]

Thorpe notes that there are difficulties in accepting the theory,
"perhaps the major one . . . [being] the difficulty, if not impossibility,
of characterizing the kind of reinforcing event which could adequately
account for the acquisition of language in such a learning situation."[38]
But apart from this deficiency, babbling is explained as a rehearsal
for a future of which the infant is entirely ignorant. In the blindered
concern for where it is going, the hypothesis says nothing of develop-

mental sensory–kinetic continuities and integrations that happen in the present and of which the child would have to be aware in order to capture and reiterate "the kind of sound his mother makes" and thus "get more interest, affection, and attention in return." Clearly in the process of growing an infant discovers and builds up a bodily compendium of *I can's*.[39] Babbling arises within the life of the infant as it is lived. It is a continuation of a sensory–kinetic process already underway. What the infant is doing in babbling is discovering its capacity for making sounds. Before there can be verbal language at all, there must be not only a capacity to make sounds, but also an awareness of oneself as a potential and actual sound-maker. The necessity of this latter requirement is obvious in the case of children born deaf. To be able to speak, touching/sounding and touching–sounding/hearing must come together. The double bisociation is crucial.

What is necessary to the human infant for verbal language must also have been necessary at the very origin of verbal language. Although the phylogenetic picture is vastly more complicated than the ontogenetic one insofar as no ready-made verbal language already existed, sensory–kinetic continuities and integrations remain foundational facts of organic life. A voice must be discovered and with it, both a world of possible lingual movements and positions and a world of possible corresponding pitches, textures, amplitudes, and so on. Clearly ancestral hominids would have had to have made such tactile/ aural discoveries before the possibility of verbal language could arise. While they may not have babbled, they must have approximated this ontogenetic stage in the sense of discovering their capacity to make sounds and to discriminate among them. The two capacities in fact feed off one another. What is discovered in perception flows back into burgeoning powers of articulation and vice versa. There is a complex of active awareness rooted in physiognomic perception. What moves and articulates and what is tactilely and aurally sensed are ultimately an indissoluble whole. Every new lingual *I can* is witness to this wholeness.

In the passage to verbal language, a further and final stage along a sensory–kinetic continuum and in sensory–kinetic integration is achieved. The tactile/aural tongue becomes witness to a preeminently visual world: the tactile/aural tongue becomes a tactile/aural/visual organ. Its enunciations are of things—or *relationships* seen. The most distant sensory world is thus brought within the realm of touch. This linkage of tactility and visuality might in fact explain why verbal language is sometimes thought of as having magical powers, why incantations, for example, are believed to be effective, or why the mere saying of a certain word is parentally proscribed and constitutes a punishable offense. Through the tongue, the body is in intimate contact with the things of which it speaks. By the same token, at the moment the tongue attains its visual powers, the visual world is no longer a multitude of foreign objects, a perhaps consistent but nevertheless strange out-thereness whose strangeness can be tempered only by touch. A verbally capable creature can tame the visual world —however out of reach it might be—and make it her/his own. The appropriation is not metaphorical. What is distant and not ready to hand must be corporeally appropriated in some way if it is to be part of a shared world, indeed, if it is to have a fixed place in a creature's world to begin with. Here the corporeal appropriation of the visual is a double sensory–kinetic awakening, a tactile/aural achievement.

In sum, the origin of language lies in the discovery of certain sensory–kinetic powers, the discovery of certain bodily *I can*'s in the form of lingual articulations and discriminations. The original elements of language were a consequence of that discovery. Whatever the sound made, it had a certain resonating character such that a physiognomic pairing of sound and meaning was made. This reconstruction is not unrelated to linguist Mary LeCron Foster's theory of the structure of primordial language.[40] If the meaning of the original sound elements of language was the analogue of their articulatory gestures, as Foster's theory holds, then what the theory actually postulates is a physiognomic congruency of sound as *tactile–kinetic* phenomenon and meaning. In other words, the articulatory spatial relationships that Foster analytically identifies are tactile–kinetic in nature. Thus not only are sound and meaning physiognomically congruent, as this study has suggested; the tactile–kinetic gesture—the bodily making of the sound—is also physiognomically congruent with the meaning. The one congruency does not preclude nor conflict with the other but in fact emphatically reinforces it. That this is so is apparent, for example, in the synaesthetic congruency of articulated sound and lingual touch, in the making of *soft* sounds, for example, or *explosive* sounds, and so on. It is of particular significance to point out once again that studies of the perception of human speech have shown that "the listener responds as though he is interpreting the acoustic signal in terms of the articulatory gestures that a speaker would employ to generate the word"—in other words, "The perception of human speech is generally structured in terms of the articulatory gestures that underlie the acoustic signal."[41] The primordial sounds of language were equally filled with just such *tactile* values. Hence, the act of sounding, the sound itself, and the meaning of the sound were all physiognomically related. At the origin of language, articulatory gesture, sound, and referent were physiognomic cognates of one another.

NOTES

1. Three clarifications should be made at the outset. (1) The terms "language" and "speech" are used interchangeably at times in the text not because it is being claimed (or assumed) that language is exclusively a matter of human speech but in the sense that to speak is to know and utilize a language. (2) The term "language" is also used, particularly in the latter half of the study, in a generic sense ("mode of communication") and should be so understood in such contexts; that is, the question of whether any other form of communication than speech may be properly called a language is not addressed here. (3) The place of a gestural language within an evolutionary scheme of language is not being ignored but is rather not at issue here. The concern of the study is with the origin of language in the form of human speech, i.e., the origin of a particular system of sound-meanings.

2. See Nancy Tanner and Adrienne L. Zhilman, "The Evolution of Human Communication: What Can Primates Tell Us?" in *Origins and Evolution of Language and Speech*, ed. Stevan R. Harnad, Horst D. Steklis, and Jane B. Lancaster, *Annals of the New York Academy of Sciences* 280 (1976): 467–80.

3. R. J. Andrew, "Use of Formants in the Grunts of Baboons and Other Nonhuman Primates," in *Origins and Evolution*, pp. 673–93.

4. Philip Lieberman, "Interactive Models for Evolution: Neural Mechanisms, Anatomy, and Behavior," in *Origins and Evolution*, pp. 660–72.

5. Lucretius, *De rerum natura*, trans. W. E. Leonard (New York: E. P. Dutton, 1957). See, for example, J. N. Findlay: "What I am saying is that the apprehension of Senses [in a broad sense, "meanings"] is a *precondition* of the attachment of such Senses to linguistic expressions and that there must be *some* pre-linguistic Senses if any are to be given to linguistic expressions." "An Ontology of Senses," *Journal of Philosophy* 79 (October 1982): 547.

6. Charles F. Hockett, "The Origin of Speech," *Scientific American* 203 (September 1960): 88–96; W. H. Thorpe, "The Comparison of Vocal Communication in Animals and Man," in *Non-Verbal Communication*, ed. R. A. Hinde (Cambridge: Cambridge University Press, 1972), pp. 27–47, and *Animal and Human Nature* (Garden City, N.Y.: Anchor Press, 1974).

7. R. L. Masland, "Some Neurological Processes Underlying Language," in *Perspectives on Human Evolution* 2, ed. Sherwood L. Washburn and Phyllis J. Dolhinow (New York: Holt, Rinehart, and Winston, 1972), pp. 421–37.

8. Actually, the thesis has been advanced that language was "abruptly acquired," presumably at the moment a nonverbal hominid realized some-

thing on the order of "Gee! I ought to use arbitrary sounds and start talking!" According to this thesis, the passage to a system of arbitrary sounds would have occurred "when the number of call [sic] and cries that could be made with the available vocal mechanism increased to the point where it was more efficient to code features. . . . If the computational abilities of the species were sufficiently advanced, it would have been efficient to recode . . . phonologic features leading to an arbitrary relationship between sound and meaning." Philip Lieberman, "Primate Vocalizations and Human Linguistic Ability," in *Perspectives in Human Evolution* 2, pp. 444–68. Computational abilities quite apart, since sensory–kinetic powers of articulation and discrimination go unrecognized, the basic problem remains.

9. See Suzanne Chevalier-Skolnikoff, "The Ontogeny of Primate Intelligence and Its Implications for Communicative Potential: A Preliminary Report," in *Origins and Evolution*, pp. 173–211.

10. Peter Marler, "Animal Communication," in *Nonverbal Communication* in *Advances in the Study of Communication and Affect* 1, ed. L. Krames, P. Pliner, and T. Alloway (New York: Plenum Press, 1973), pp. 25–50.

11. For a notable exception see Peter C. Reynolds, "Play, Language and Human Evolution," in *Play—Its Role in Development and Evolution*, ed. Jerome S. Bruner, Alison Jolly, and Kathy Silva (New York: Basic Books, 1976), pp. 621–35.

12. See, for example, Morris Swadesh, *The Origin and Diversification of Language* (Chicago: Aldine-Atherton, 1971); and Fernando Nottebohm, "Discussion Paper: Vocal Tract and Brain: A Search for Evolutionary Bottlenecks," in *Origins and Evolution*, pp. 643–50.

13. See, for example, Milford H. Wolpoff, *Paleoanthropology* (New York: Knopf, 1980); and David R. Pilbeam, *The Ascent of Man* (New York: Macmillan, 1972).

14. For a complementary, i.e., *articulatory* rather than *aural*, account of "arbitrary" elements, see Mary LeCron Foster, "The Symbolic Structure of Primordial Language," in *Human Evolution: Biosocial Perspectives*, ed. Sherwood L. Washburn and Elizabeth R. McCown (Menlo Park, Calif.: Benjamin/Cummings, 1978), pp. 76–121. The nature of the complementarity is brought out and discussed in the last section of this case study, "A Sensory–Kinetic Model of the Origin of Language."

15. Aristotle, *On Interpretation*, trans. E. M. Edghill, in *The Basic Works of Aristotle*, ed. R. McKeon (New York: Random House, 1968), pp. 17^a 22–23.

16. Marler, "Animal Communication;" Bryan W. Robinson, "Contrast Between Human and Other Primate Vocalizations," in *Perspectives on Human Evolution* 2, p. 442.

17. See note 2 above.

18. Etienne Bonnot de Condillac, *An Essay on the Origin of Human Knowledge*, trans. T. Nugent (Gainesville, Fla.: Scholars' Facsimiles and Reprints, 1971 [1756]).

19. By summarily categorizing nouns and verbs in isolation as nonpropositional, Aristotle failed to consider the possible propositionality of single words in living speech. The exclamation, "Snake!" for example, might mean, "There is a snake," or "Move quickly: a snake is coming toward you." As Wittgenstein notes, a word may function in a variety of ways depending upon the particular language-game: as an order, a report, a speculation, and so on (*Philosophical Investigations*, trans. G. E. M. Anscombe [Oxford: Basil Blackwell, 1963]). He notes in fact that the difference between a statement and a nonstatement, that is, between a proposition and a nonproposition, is a function of the language-game being played, which is to say of the different ways in which a word or words are uttered or used: "No doubt the tone of voice and the look with which they [the words] are uttered, and much else besides, will also be different [depending upon the game being played]. But we could also imagine the tone's being the same—for an order and a report can be spoken in a *variety* of tones of voice and with various expressions of face—the difference being only in application" (p. 10^e). For Wittgenstein, then, the difference between a proposition and a nonproposition is a function of its actual *living* context.

20. See, for example, Alison Jolly, *The Evolution of Primate Behavior* (New York: Macmillan, 1972); and George G. Simpson, "The Biological Nature of Man," in *Perspectives on Human Evolution* 1, ed. Sherwood L. Washburn and P. C. Jay (New York: Holt, Rinehart, and Winston, 1968), pp. 1–17.

21. See Ralph L. Holloway, "Early Hominid Endocasts: Volumes, Morphology, and Significance for Hominid Evolution," in *Primate Functional Morphology and Evolution*, ed. Russell H. Tuttle (The Hague: Mouton, 1975), pp. 393–415.

22. Condillac, *Essay*, p. 171.

23. Ibid., p. 175.

24. Ibid.

25. J. E. Lloyd, "Mimicry in the Sexual Signals of Fireflies," *Scientific American* 245 (July 1981): 139–45.

26. Aristotle, *On Interpretation*, 17^a 25.

27. Emil W. Menzel, "Leadership and Communication in Young Chimpanzees," in *Precultural Primate Behavior*, ed. Emil W. Menzel (Basel: Karger, 1973), pp. 192–225.

28. Gregory Bateson, "A Theory of Play and Fantasy," in *Play—Its Role in Development*, p. 124.

29. Jean Piaget, "Symbolic Play," in *Play—Its Role in Development*, pp. 562, 563.

30. Phyllis J. Dolhinow, "At Play in the Fields," in *Play—Its Role in Development*, p. 317.

31. Ibid.

32. Horst D. Steklis and Stevan R. Harnad, "From Hand to Mouth: Some Critical Stages in the Evolution of Language," in *Origins and Evolution*, p. 451.

33. E. L. Du Brul, "Biomechanics of Speech Sounds," in *Origins and Evolution*, p. 640.

34. Ashley Montagu, *Touching: The Human Significance of the Skin* (New York: Columbia University Press, 1971), p. 109.

35. Jean Piaget, *La naissance de l'intelligence chez l'enfant*, 6th ed. (Neuchatel: Delachaux et Niestlé, 1968), p. 51 (my translation).

36. Lieberman, "Primate Vocalizations and Human Linguistic Ability," p. 450.

37. W. H. Thorpe, *Animal and Human Nature* (Garden City: Anchor Press, 1974), p. 286.

38. Ibid.

39. See Chapter 2, note 8, p. 63.

40. Foster, "Symbolic Structure," pp. 76–121.

41. Philip Lieberman, "On the Evolution of Language: A Unified View," in *Primate Functional Morphology and Evolution*, p. 535.

7

Hominid Bipedality and Sexual Selection Theory

Male structures that are specialized to contact females in sexual contexts have an extraordinary propensity to evolve rapidly and divergently. . . .

The ability [of females] to discriminate among males using mechanical or stimulatory genitalic cues could . . . spread genetically through the females of a population. Once such female discrimination was established, selection would favor any male that was better able to meet the females' criteria (by squeezing her harder, touching her over a wider area, rubbing her more often, and so on) even though his genitalia were no better at delivering sperm than those of other males.

My hypothesis, sexual selection by female choice, proposes that male genitalia function as "internal courtship" devices.

WILLIAM G. EBERHARD

INTRODUCTION

Eberhard's evidence for sexual selection through female choice of male genitalia[1] accords closely with Darwin's original and preeminent concern with morphological aspects of sexual selection. Given the ambient Victorian culture of his time, it is not surprising that Darwin himself did not remark openly and directly upon male primate genitalia.[2] His cryptic and oblique references to "naked parts . . . oddly situated," to "a part confined to the male sex," or to "large surfaces at the posterior end of the body,"[3] all belie his usual descriptive precision and clarity. Eberhard's thesis that male genitalia function as " 'internal courtship' devices,"[4] that is, as tactile stimulators, that they evolve through female choice, and that this sexual selection by females occurs in runaway fashion, reinvigorates a Darwinian focus on evolutionary sexual morphology at the same time that it gives new meanings to comparative anatomy through its recognition of differential spatial/tactile–kinetic (and tactile–kinesthetic) genitalic potentialities. Eberhard's practical and theoretical separation of the act of copulation from the processes of insemination and fertilization constitutes a critical methodological step. The more usual lumping of the three phenomena leads less to a consideration of morphological characters and their possible display value than to a concern with economic, political, and social factors,[5] with the result that analyses and explanations of the sexual characters themselves—for example, the evolution of an atypically large penis like that of the human primate[6]—are bypassed.

The purpose of this study is to show first that bipedality and penile display are inextricably linked. Second, it is to show in elaboration of Eberhard's thesis (a) how a large penis—the most conspicuous feature of hominid reproductive anatomy[7]—and bipedalism—the most conspicuous hominid behavioral character by Darwin's original account[8]—might originally have been linked through sexual selection; and (b) how their evolutionary bond was cemented by pleasure: by the hominids' finding "sweet"[9] the activities in which they engaged. The thesis is *not* that hominid bipedality originated *exclusively* in sexual selection, but that given its incontestable link to penile display, sexual selection was a prime and critical factor in the move to consistent bipedality. Several major concepts attach to the undertaking and will be considered in turn: (1) the bipedal incentive; (2) the inverse relationship of nonhominid vulva to hominid penis; (3) the biological significance of tactile pleasure; and (4) the large human penis as evolutionary product.

THE BIPEDAL INCENTIVE

Set within a motivational perspective, the inverse visual/morphological relationship between quadrupedal and bipedal female genitalia and quadrupedal and bipedal male genitalia shows that a bipedal incentive would not attach to female primate sexual behavior as it would to male primate sexual behavior. Indeed, as a feature already engendered in many extant primate displays—sexual as well as non-sexual[10]—bipedality appears to be practiced more often by males than females. The comparatively substantial incentive for males to maintain a consistently erect posture follows from the fact that in its entailment of penile display, in particular the display of an erect penis, erect posture attracts female attention and potential response in the same way that a quadrupedal female's presenting posture attracts male attention and potential response. The entailment perfectly exemplifies the kind of matrix structural relationship described by Stephen J. Gould and R. C. Lewontin in their article, "The Spandrels of San Marco and the Panglossian Paradigm: A Critique of the Adaptationist Programme,"[11] and referred to in Chapter 4. As pointed out there, consistent bipedality imposes as specific and rigorous a *Bauplan* vis-à-vis visible male hominid genitalic features as does the fan-vaulted ceiling of St. Mark's Cathedral vis-à-vis structural design features. Granted that displays count for nothing apart from the animal to whom the display is directed,[12] a display is nonetheless a two-term relationship: the incentive is as important a component of the display as the response, particularly so where the question is how a behavior on the order of bipedality might have been reinforced and have come ultimately to be consistently established.

A male hominid's incentive toward bipedality is empirically evident in both the heightened force of his sexual display—both erect posture and erect penis substantially increase apparent size, for example, and the two erections are vectorially linked with respect to upward movement—and in his correlative new power of *ambulatory* sexual display. Bipedality for primate females holds the possibility of neither of these sexual optimizations; in terms of *display*, it minimizes rather than optimizes advertisement of their sexual powers.[13]

A male primate's incentive toward consistent bipedality is in effect qualitatively greater than that of a female. *Consistent* bipedality is not simply a question of *more* but of (among other values) sexual enhancement. The thesis that it arose in conjunction with male behavior, specifically sexual display, accords with the assessment of J. T. Stern and R. L. Susman that terrestrial bipedality was more common among male than among female earliest known hominids.[14] Their assessment is based upon an inferred sexual dimorphism, fossil evidence indicating that males were larger than females. If the postulated dimorphism proves correct as more fossil evidence is accumulated, then there is further reason for maintaining that the initial bipedal incentive was on the side of the male rather than of the female: the shorter stature of the female would make even more sexually disadvantageous the assumption of a bipedal posture for display. The directional facing of female genitalic swellings would no longer coincide with the male's line of vision. In contrast, initial bipedal posture in the male would not only optimize his greater size, but would position his genitalia in the (shorter) female's line of vision—in a way precisely similar to that in which a female chimpanzee's genitalia (by a relative lack of sexual dimorphism) are on a line with the male's line of vision. The thesis that bipedality arose in conjunction with male behavior is also supported by research which shows that male primates are more prone toward exploratory behavior than females, and that males are more mobile, physically active, and engage in contact play and threat behavior more often than females.[15]

The bipedal incentive warrants further discussion within the context of primate bipedality generally. Primates are bipedal in a variety of circumstances.[16] What then from a common primate heritage standpoint explains the bipedal incentive? To use primatologist David Pilbeam's estimations, what is the critical difference between a 55 percent terrestrial bipedality in australopithecines and a 10 percent terrestrial bipedality in their ancestor?[17]

Since tools, once associated with the beginnings of bipedality, are no longer associated with earliest hominids[18] (which is not to say that ready-made or nonfossilized tools could not have been used by earliest hominids for scavenging, nutcracking, and extractive foraging generally),[19] tool-making/tool-carrying cannot be postulated as the major incentive toward consistent bipedality. The idea that the earliest hominids were nonetheless motivated toward consistent bipedality in order to carry things, and to carry them regularly, that is, more often and habitually than their ancestors or co-speciating confreres, nevertheless prevails. For example, recent explanatory models of the origin of bipedality center on food-carrying behavior, specifically provisioning[20] and nuptial feeding,[21] males in each case supplying the females. An odd irony is evident in that the latter model, although rooted in sexual selection theory, makes scant reference to sexual morphology while postulating material resources and benefits as the pivotal factor; while the former model, although rooted in natural selection theory, postulates "the unique sexual and reproductive behavior of man" as the pivotal factors at the same time making scarcely any more reference to sexual morphology.[22] In neither account is the *exposed* hominid body considered except to remark (in the provisioning model) that strong selection pressure would be exerted on anatomical characters reinforcing pair-bonding, "the conspicuous penis of human males" being among these,[23] and (in the nuptial-feeding model) that "bipedal carrying and presentation of nuptial gifts" would have been favored by females because it would "allow them to accurately assess the size of the male and the size of the gift; . . . [and it would] also allow females to assess the size and tumescence of the male's genitals."[24] Both accounts illustrate the generally pervasive failure of "transport" explanatory models of bipedality to take into account the spatio-kinetic bodily transformations entailed by upright posture and the sexual significance of those transformations.

In contrast to transport models of bipedality, a basically corporeal model takes into account the fact that bipedality did more than free the hands for carrying. It freed the whole body in the sense of exposing it, and in so doing *changed male and female genitalic valencies*.[25] Acknowledgment of the radical shift in genitalic valencies leads directly to a consideration of the relationship of nonhominid primate vulva and hominid primate penis, a relationship ultimately critical to an understanding of analogies and disanalogies between hominid and nonhominid primates.

THE INVERSE RELATIONSHIP OF NONHOMINID VULVA TO HOMINID PENIS

A human primate's "distinctive and oversized penis," as Eberhard describes the male organ,[26] is the sexual inverse of a nonhuman primate's distinctive and oversized vulva. With hominid bipedality, the vulva loses its public status; in its stead the penis becomes a public sexual object. *Its* swellings—size and shape differentials, degree of tautness —directional orientation, and upward movement become natural foci of attention and potential response. Bipedal females indeed no longer have a sexual *organ*, an object on visual par with a penis, a fact that perhaps explains why exhibitionism is regarded a sexual deviation possible only to males.[27] While it might be deemed curious that both the stark visibility of male genitalia and the comparative invisibility of female genitalia in the shift from quadrupedal to bipedal posture have not been acknowledged, it is even more curious that recent research attention to sexual *concealment* (of ovulation in hominid females) has not raised the correlative question of what *is* sexually visible in hominids.[28] Clearly the public *object* about which sexual behavior centered necessarily shifted from pudenda to penis with upright posture. Loss of estrus—understood with respect to its visual manifestations—is in consequence explainable on morphological grounds. It no longer served any sexual function since a male could no longer immediately see and inspect female swellings and changes in coloration. Presenting behavior was in turn no longer advantageous and its physiological correlates became modified. As hominid menstrual cycles became established, male display replaced female presenting.

It is important to call attention to, and make explicit the underlying rationale for, the difference in sexual nomenclature. Relatively speaking, the habitually bipedal male does nothing in order to display his penis. He does not present it to a female; it is already there—a public object, plainly visible. The difference between male hominid display and female nonhominid presenting is in other words a difference between natural and modified socio-sexual bodily orientation. Its import is sizable. The frontality of the penis, its anterior positioning in bipedal posture/locomotion, makes it a cynosure on three counts: it is always facing whatever and whomever the male addresses; it is perpetually oriented in the direction of the male's forward movement; it is on the socially as well as kinetically and sensorily strongest surface of the body. Not only this but correlated primate anatomical changes maximize its conspicuousness. Hip-joint flexion typical of nonhominid ape anatomies contrasts markedly with the relative flushness of frontal abdominal/thigh surfaces of hominids. In effect, the hominid hip joint brings the frontality of the hominid penis to even greater visual prominence. In evolutionary terms, *anatomical changes correlated with bipedality*[29] *correlate with optimal penile display*.

The contrasting posterior orientation of presenting involves a repositioning of the body relative to normal direction of movement and social address such that the vaginal area is *"exposed."*[30] Moreover a presenting posture is a vulnerable one in that the animal faces away from and thus cannot concurrently assess the immediate reaction of the animal to whom it is presenting. As noted in Chapter 4, primatologists K. R. L. Hall and I. De Vore have observed that "presenting . . . is often accompanied by nervous, even fearful behavior on the part of the presenting animal."[31] The frontality of bipedal penile display is clearly of stronger positional advantage than posterior presenting.

The nonhominid primate vulva is nonetheless a public object on par with a hominid phallus. It is readily and immediately visible; its dynamic changes in appearance make it a ready object of attention and potential response; it is readily accessible to tactile and olfactory exploration. Of interest in this regard is J. Hanby's data on tactile–manual genitalic exchanges among adult male and female chimpanzees.[32] Females touch male genitalia far less than males touch female genitalia. (The exact percentages are: female/male 25 percent; male/female 67 percent; female/female 70 percent; male/male 52 percent.) The visual and tactile accessibility of female genitalia by males in contrast to male genitalia by females provides an empirical explanation of the low female/male contact. The high incidence of male/male contact can be explained on similar spatio-corporeal grounds, specifically with reference to a male's visual/tactile experience of his own body. (See for example Jane van Lawick-Goodall's description of a juvenile chimpanzee's thrusting movements as it stood quadrupedally: "[he looked] back between his arms and legs as his scrotum bounced against his penis; this always occurred when he was frustrated.")[33] While present-day humans might react quite differently to concealed genitalia of the opposite sex, it is reasonable to conclude that what is not tactilely or visually accessible in a nonhominid primate's corporeal world—what is not a readily available public sexual object so far as other animal bodies are concerned—is not a corporeal object commonly sought out for sexual touching. Further documentation of this fact is had in Jane van Lawick-Goodall's description of a chimpanzee mother's consistent fondling of her infant son's readily accessible genitals.[34] Where quadrupedal primate females *do* have immediate access to male genitalia, they are more likely to touch them.

THE BIOLOGICAL SIGNIFICANCE OF PLEASURE

Tactility is a source of pleasure. Eberhard's evidence showing that male genitalia function as tactile stimulators, and his related thesis that "selection for tactile stimulation [is] the most likely selective factor explaining the human males' distinctive and oversized genitalia," are both of seminal import. To begin with, they provide empirical support to otherwise speculative reflections—for example, to primatologist R. V. Short's surmise that "perhaps the large size of the erect penis is related to the act of intercourse," and his ensuing estimation that the human penis developed "to entice the opposite sex" and "to enhance enjoyment of the copulatory act."[35] They furthermore call into question analytical accounts in both classic and recent ethological studies. Wolfgang Wickler's original and influential descriptions of the use of the primate penis for display center on intrasexual competition, not on intersexual attraction. Apart from a passing reference to cross-cultural data on human sitting postures—in which males, if unclothed, would be clearly displaying their genitals, while women, if unclothed, would clearly be hiding theirs—there is not the slightest intimation that penes could or do function in intersexual display, much less as tactile stimulators.[36]

More recent research utilizing Wickler's ethological studies within the purview of sexual selection theory goes no further in relating "human males' distinctive and oversized genitalia" either to intersexual display or to tactile stimulation. In spite of inquiries into its "adaptational value," the size of the human penis remains an unexplained mystery. For example, ethologist J. H. Crook, while raising the question of the purpose of "the large (among primates) phallus," briefly discusses its possible significance only in a Wicklerian perspective: as an intraspecific symbol of power and dominance.[37] There is a peculiar silence about the uncommonly large phallus in his discussion of both visual and contact signals as human sexual releasers. While noted *visual* signals emanating from women and arousing men are relatively numerous (e.g., "high heels enhancing the provocative body movements of the walking female, breast deportment—the 'sweater girl' . . . voice quality and tone . . . areolar tumescence, body flush, eye glitter"), *visual* signals emanating from men and arousing women are minimal ("athletic deportment and movement, buttocks, eye glitter and pupillary distention"), and noticeably unrelated to male genitalia. This is puzzling since, as some of the enumerated female visual signals clearly indicate, Crook's model subjects are naked as well as clothed. In effect, penile tumescence would be as much a releaser—if not more of a releaser, since it is noticeable at a greater distance—as female areolar tumescence, which Crook mentions. (One might also recall sociobiologist Donald Symons regarding the potency of penile tumescence as a sexual signal for females: "photographs of men with erect penises will be far more effective than photographs of men with flaccid penises in sexually arousing women. The former suggest an actual sexual interaction, not just the possibility of a future interaction.")[38] Furthermore, while "genital sensation" is among those female *contact* signals Crook lists as arousing to men (others include "epidermal touch quality, breast tumescence, lip-feel, . . . and body scent"), no such specific genital reference is listed for women.[39] In fact no itemization of *contact* signals arousing to women is given at all. The result is that while tactile stimulation ("genital sensation") of the penis by the labia and vaginal walls is implicitly acknowledged, tactile stimulation of the clitoral–labial–vaginal complex[40] by the penis is not. The same peculiar omission is found in the original Hite reports on female and male sexuality, with males being questioned explicitly about "the pleasure of the vagina on the penis," but females not being explicitly questioned equivalently about the pleasure of the penis in the vagina.[41] While a reluctance to put the penis on the measuring line, not of reproductive competence but of arousal, pleasure-giving competence, has perhaps been fed by the notion that "female animals are mere egg repositories waiting for something to happen,"[42] fixation on orgasm—on whether females have orgasms, and on where anatomically they come from[43]—appears to blot out straightforward acknowledgment and investigation of the penis as a tactile stimulator. (Fixation on orgasm can also lead to preoccupations—and airy speculations—about the kind of mating system early hominids might or might not have enjoyed.)[44]

Though anchored predominantly in studies of insect male genitalia and mating behaviors, Eberhard's analyses and references are directly relevant to primate sexual anatomy and behavior precisely insofar as insects, unlike birds—Darwin's predominant sexual selection model—mate through *internal* fertilization. His detailed data on genitalic tactility and focus on genitalic tactile pleasure strongly support the growing body of observations on the primacy of primate tactility and tactile pleasure,[45] and, in addition, provide strong empirical grounds for otherwise speculative reflections regarding the central role of tactility in the evolution of sexuality in general and of human sexual behavior in particular.[46]

What Eberhard's theory explains is in a fundamental sense the obvious. Like the genitalia of other males in the animal kingdom who procreate by internal fertilization, the "distinctive and oversized human males' genitalia" has species-specific tactile powers. The obvious appears indisputable and is in fact corroborated both indirectly by fossil evidence suggesting increased cortical areas for tactility with the advent of hominids, and directly by laboratory evidence graphically depicting cortical representation of tactility body part by body part, including genitalia.[47] What is less obvious is what Darwin first attempted to show: that females choose certain males over others— that they exercise "female choice"—and that "it is to a large extent the *external attractions* of the male" over "vigor, courage, and other mental qualities" that determine her choice.[48] Put in evolutionary hominid perspective, and in a refocused conceptualization of *competence* (see below), what can be termed *contact resonance*—tactile–stimulatory competence—was assessed by early female hominids through penile display and determined their choice of copulatory mate. Pleasure— the promise of pleasure and the experience of pleasure—was thus a key variable in hominid female choice, and in consequence, in hominid reproductive effort and success.

A number of points attach to this relationship between somatic pleasure (or its anticipation) and sexual selection in the literal sense of choosing a copulatory partner. First, choice by definition is exercised in the context of possible alternative selections. It is the end result of perceptual experiences and judgments. Hence female choice must be considered part of a global phenomenon, viz., sexual signaling-and-response behavior: female choice is the culmination of those initiatory behaviors—for example, *penile displays*—by which motivated males propose copulation to females. But penile initiatory behaviors may themselves be the end result of perceptual experiences and judgments. When females are partially or fully bipedal (the question of the female incentive toward bipedality is treated below) such that genitalic swellings and changes in coloration are either no longer present or no longer immediately and publicly visible as indications of sexual readiness, then the male's field of possible mates enlarges. Virtually *any* female may be chosen as the object of the male's display attentions. In such circumstances, intrasexual competition is similarly a female as well as male phenomenon. Females compete among themselves for male attention, indeed, compete in Darwin's terms to attract the "best-armed" or "well-armed"[49] male in virtue of his pleasure-giving competence. The twin questions are, On what specific grounds would proto-early hominid females have competed, and on what specific grounds would proto-early hominid males have competed? and alternatively, What was the exact nature of the criteria of male choice and of female choice?

Male choice and intrasexual female competition will be considered first. Both were a matter of sexual signaling behavior by females in response to penile display. Bipedality, *specifically the female incentive toward bipedality*, provides the context for identifying that behavior.

Primatologists E. Sue Savage-Rumbaugh and B. J. Wilkerson state that ventro-ventral mating is preferred over dorso-ventral mating by female pygmy chimpanzees (*Pan paniscus*) when the females are in less than their maximally tumescent state. They suggest in consequence that "increased positional flexibility" is linked with an increased disposition toward copulation at times other than at the height of the estrous cycle.[50] It is reasonable on these and other (to be identified) grounds of "flexibility" to assume that the most likely proto-early hominid female behavior signaling an increased disposition toward copulation and the promise of greater pleasure through ventro-ventral copulation was a *bipedal*, face-on response and approach to an erect penis-displaying male. Not only was the female showing herself a ready and willing source of pleasure by her bipedal approach toward him, but the approach suggested to the male a relatively greater sexual pleasure through more variable, novel, and arousing bodily contact.[51] The point warrants detailed analysis in order to show clearly how consistent bipedality, ventro-ventral mating, tactile pleasure, and sexual novelty are related.

Ventro-ventral mating offers "increased positional flexibility" with respect to more than just dorso-ventral mating as noted by Savage-Rumbaugh and Wilkerson. The spatio-corporeal orientation in ventro-ventral copulation itself makes a variety of coupling positions possible and an equal variety of tactile contacts possible in the way of particular body-on-body, or body-to-body, touchings including facial touchings. (For examples about two thousand years old, see the Hindu classic, *The Kama Sutra of Vatsyayana*.) The orientation is furthermore *kinetically* as well as positionally enhancing of tactile pleasure. Significant in this respect is the fact that *thrusting* is an essentially *forward* movement, not a backward one. A bipedal female, one approaching and mating with a male ventro-ventrally, is capable of thrusting movements *during copulation* as a quadrupedally presenting female—for the sake of relevant comparison, a chimpanzee—is not. True thrusting movements on the part of a quadrupedally presenting female chimpanzee during typical dorso-ventral copulation would *disengage* her genitals from those of the male. Yet thrusting is a well-documented female as well as male primate movement pattern. Male and female chimpanzee infants thrust, and female chimpanzees engage in thrusting behavior when they mount a conspecific just as males do.[52]

Successful dorso-ventral chimpanzee copulation precludes female thrusting movements on the grounds of directional incompatibility; successful ventro-ventral chimpanzee copulation precludes them on the grounds of structural incompatibilities. The incompatibilities center on loss of contact *in the withdrawal phase* of the movement—the exact inverse of the phase at risk in dorso-ventral copulation. Female chimpanzee thrusting during successful ventro-ventral copulation is contravened (1) by natural anatomical hip-joint flexion (male and female), (2) by a posterior or less than fully anterior vagina, and (3) by the average length of the male chimpanzee's penis. Hominid female thrusting during successful ventro-ventral copulation is facilitated either directly or indirectly on all three counts by consistent bipedality; namely, by (1) anatomical restructuring of the hip joint toward extension such that abdominal/thigh bodily surfaces are virtually flush, (2) a more fully anterior positioning of the vagina, and (3) a longer average penis length (see below for a further discussion of this factor). Consistent bipedality thus enhanced proto-early hominid female movement possibilities during copulation by reinforcing the practice of ventro-ventral copulation. Such kinetic flexibility as thrusting during copulation is clearly in the service of tactile pleasure—for male and female alike. With the advent of female hominids, kinetic flexibility during copulation was no longer the unique prerogative of male primates generally, but only of quadrupedal male primates in particular. Were present-day evidence called for to suggest vestiges of this fact, belly dancers and female strippers would be obvious (if differentially sanctioned) showcases of female hominid enhancement of male tactile pleasure through kinetic flexibility.[53]

Along with other aspects of optimal contact resonance already identified, greater flexibility of the female made ventro-ventral mating qualitatively different from dorso-ventral mating. In addition to a bipedal approach toward the male, these qualitative aspects constituted tactile desiderata underlying male choice. Put in terms of sexual selection theory, proto-early hominid males copulated less or not at all with those females who responded to their display quadrupedally, by presenting; they chose less to copulate with females with posteriorly aligned vaginas than with those with more anteriorly aligned ones, and less with those with naturally flexed hip joints than those with extended ones. Choice females were those who approached males frontally, whose genitalia were more frontally accessible, and who, in copulating, were positionally and kinetically stimulating to the male. Those females were at reproductive advantage. Those females were also most likely to be *consistently* bipedal.

Corollary to these tactile desiderata, those males with "larger" (see next section and Afterword) penes promised greater tactile–stimulatory competence. As with male choice, female choice hinged also on the promise of more variable, novel, and arousing bodily contact, contact that would not be compromised by greater female kinetic flexibility through consistent bipedality. Males competed on the grounds of penile display—size and shape, tautness, directional orientation, and upward movement—and of penile prominence and full-body contact through natural hip-joint extension. As Eberhard points out, "Once . . . female discrimination was established, selection would favor any male that was better able to meet the females' criteria (by squeezing her harder, touching her over a wider area, rubbing her more often, and so on) even though his genitalia were no better at delivering sperm than those of other males." It is pertinent to spell out "the females' criteria" in greater detail.

Sex researcher Frank Beach points out that the possibility of female orgasm at any time through clitoral stimulation "tends to reinforce and increase the frequency with which she [the human female] desires and accepts intercourse."[54] He also suggests a concrete link between clitoral stimulation and ventro-ventral (as opposed to dorsoventral) mating. The point is not to establish whether proto-early hominid females had orgasms—a question in any case best left to prehistoric clairvoyants—but that female genitalic tactile pleasure is significantly enhanced by penile stimulation of the clitoral–labial–vaginal complex.[55] Genito-genital rubbing by female pygmy chimpanzees, and Hanby's data cited earlier, are important considerations in this regard.

Genito-genital rubbing (by which clitoral stimulation is effected) is a sexual behavior widely and regularly practiced by female pygmy chimpanzees.[56] It begins in infancy.[57] Savage-Rumbaugh and Wilkerson report in fact that clitoral intromission is occasionally achieved, and that in such cases, *thrusting* behavior preempts *rubbing* behavior. In addition, Kuroda reports that genito-genital rubbing appears to last longer than male/female copulation,[58] a fact that would confirm the role of tactile pleasure in choice of sexual positioning.

Hanby's data showing female/female (*Pan troglodytes*) tactile–manual genitalic contact higher than any other partnering contact also strongly supports the notion that female chimpanzee tactile pleasure is centered on clitoral–labial stimulation and in effect, that it is both facilitated and enhanced by ventro-ventral copulation. In light of both genito-genital and tactile–manual intrasexual practices—and of the fact that *both* chimpanzee species are represented—it is reasonable to assume that proto/early hominid females also found pleasure in clitoral stimulation. Again, the point is not whether these intrasexual female tactile contacts led to orgasm, but that given the anatomical focus of genitalic pleasure in nonhuman female primates, ventroventral copulation significantly enhanced sexual pleasure in female as well as male proto/early hominids. In such enhanced male/female copulatory circumstances, genito-genital rubbing and hand-to-genital contact, that is female/female sexual behavior, would become more and more a secondary mode of sexual pleasure for females.

A radical pleasure of the flesh thus served to perpetuate hominid ventro-ventral mating at the same time that it reinforced consistent bipedality. Together with the inherent positive value of size in display behavior—as discussed in Chapter 4—tactile pleasure ranked high. Those males who first of all displayed bipedally promised the most tactile satisfaction, that is, they promised ventro-ventral mating. In effect, proto-early hominid females chose less to copulate with sitting or diagonally recumbent males—invitational postures typical of both present-day chimpanzee species—than with *ambulatory*, bipedally-displaying males. They chose males with longer penes, and males with more fully extended hip joints, both for maximal stimulation and minimal risk that genital contact would be lost during copulation. (With respect to *longer* penes, primatologist R. V. Short has called attention to the fact that "Leonardo da Vinci showed in his magnificent drawing [of human intercourse titled, 'I display to men the origin of the second —or first or perhaps second—cause of their existence,' that] the size of the penis ['a mean length of 13 cm'] makes ventro-ventral copulation possible.")[59] Such choice males were at reproductive advantage.

Males, like females, competed actively and passively on the basis of sexual anatomical and behavioral characters. Penile length and degree of hip-joint extension were passive competitive characters; bipedal display and mobility were active competitive ones. The complete cycle of male–female/female–male sexual signaling-and-response behaviors was thus clearly self-reinforcing with respect to ventro-ventral copulation and to consistent bipedality.

The above analysis of the role of tactile pleasure in male and female choice and its relationship to bipedality focuses solely on "the corporeal facts of the matter." The facts describe a situation of fundamental sexual parity:

1. Tactile stimulation, an entailment of internal fertilization, was necessarily experienced by both male and female proto/early hominids in copulating.
2. Tactile stimulation is a source (or potential source) of pleasure.
3. Both males and females chose partners who offered them maximal tactile stimulation, and both competed intrasexually on the grounds of tactile stimulatory competence.

The corporeal facts document Darwin's brief suggestion of the possibility of "a double process of selection, . . . the males having selected the more attractive females and the latter the more attractive males." Darwin's follow-up remarks on the possibility are in fact of particular interest:

This process . . . though it might lead to the modification of both sexes, would not make the one sex different from the other, unless indeed their taste for the beautiful differed; but this is a supposition too improbable in the case of any animal, excepting man, to be worth considering.[60]

When *attractiveness* is transposed from the visual to the tactile, that is, when the criterion of sexual selection shifts from *a taste for beauty* to *a taste for optimal contact resonance*, male/female morphological sexual differences are explained at the most fundamental level. An alternative way of putting this same fact is by observing that Darwin's theory of sexual selection involves only female choice and male/male competition because it rests mainly on avian anatomy and behavior, that is, on the anatomy and behavior of animals who do not reproduce by internal fertilization. When anatomical structures and behavioral practices peculiar to internal fertilization are taken into account—as in Eberhard's research—it is clear that contact resonance is potential for both sexes. The conclusion to be drawn from both perspectives is that pleasure-giving competence was the criterion for male and female proto/early hominid choice and the ground upon which intrasexual female and male hominid competition took place.

THE LARGE HUMAN PENIS AS EVOLUTIONARY PRODUCT

When bipedality and its entailment of a permanently exposed penis are reckoned with literally in reconstructions of the hominid past, the fundamental and far-reaching sexual significance of penile display becomes obvious. Permanently enlarged breasts, hypothesized to have evolved as an advertisement of "lactational competence," and to be in consequence a prime factor in male choice,[61] can also be tied to an enhanced exposure of the body through bipedality. As lactational advertisements, however, permanently enlarged breasts are a *reproductive*, not properly sexual signal. They were furthermore not a visual datum immediately entailed by the move to consistent bipedality. As the theory itself proposes, permanently enlarged breasts *evolved* in their purported role as signals. That the penes of the Great Apes are not permanently exposed but are extruded when erected[62]—and that in this sense the permanently exposed hominid penis may also have evolved—does not contravene immediate bipedal entailment of penile display but on the contrary supports it. Hominid penile erection and flaccidity are equivalent to nonhominid penile visibility and invisibility. In both cases, the *erect* penis (together with its flaccidity or invisibility) is a visual datum—a sexual signal—immediately entailed by bipedality.

In Eberhard's interpretation, "male structures that are not modified in some way to consistently hold or contact females do not evolve rapidly and divergently, while those that *are* modified for this function show clear signs of rapid and divergent evolution."[63] (It should be noted that Eberhard explicitly uses *rapid* and *divergent* in a relative, not absolute sense.) In this evolutionary context, three interrelated analogies and disanalogies can be identified that flesh out further the evolutionary significance of an atypically large primate penis:

1. analogies and disanalogies in ventro-ventral coital positioning behaviors between female pygmy chimpanzees and hominids
2. analogies in morphological and behavioral paedomorphisms between pygmy chimpanzees and hominids
3. disanalogies in external female genitalia, particularly labia, between nonhominid and hominid primates

1. For penes to be maximally effective tactile stimulators, intergenital tactile fit is critical. In ventro-ventral copulation, coital positioning by female pygmy chimpanzees requires either leaning back, or lying down and wrapping the legs around the male's waist[64]— presumably to tilt the pelvis upward—or sliding under the male.[65] Quite apart from a more anterior positioning of the vagina, tactile fit in these instances is the result of behavior, specifically *female* behavior. A longer penis would mean the female's behavior need be less mechanically accommodating (recall Short's comment on Leonardo da Vinci's drawing of humans in copulatory position);[66] in positive terms, it could be the more pleasure-accommodating. Genitalic variation in the direction of greater penile length thus had short- and long-range consequences relative to speciation. It immediately facilitated sexual signaling. A longer penis was more visibly prominent in bipedal penile display than a shorter one. It furthermore immediately facilitated frontal coital positioning and maintenance of that position without risk of loss of contact as shown earlier. Long-range value is evident

with respect to the latter facilitation, viz., the female was no longer of necessity *statically* positioned; *mechanical accommodation was no longer a female behavioral constraint but a built-in of male genitalic anatomy.* In effect, a longer penis freed the female posturally and kinetically. *Mutually* stimulating pelvic movements (thrusting) and embracing postures were ultimately facilitated. Not only genital areas were in contact but entire frontal surfaces were. Arms and hands were furthermore free to develop a repertoire of touching gestures and movements. The overall result was that tactile stimulation potentially radiated throughout the whole body. Thus while increased penile length functioned immediately as a stronger, more arousing sexual signal and one promising uninterrupted *en face* copulation, it ultimately functioned to enhance tactile pleasure generally by opening up female postural and kinetic possibilities.

2. The fact that there is greater variability in male than in female secondary sex characters as Darwin showed,[67] lends credence to Eberhard's theory that rapid and divergent evolution of male genitalia can set the tempo and mode of speciation such that female characters catch up quickly with changes in male genitalic anatomy. The theory is based on the original work of geneticist Ronald A. Fisher, specifically, his well-known model of "runaway" selection of "extravagant" male features as the result of female choice.[68] Greater natural variability in male than in female secondary sexual characters supports the further hypothesis that the anterior positioning of female hominid genitals, while definitively linked to consistent bipedality and ventro-ventral coital positioning, was not rooted basically in female intrasexual genetic variability, but in a paedomorphic morphology similar to that in female pygmy chimpanzees. In other words, it was less the result of selection acting on a distributional extreme than of selection for the retention of a juvenile genitalic character: ventral orientation of the vaginal canal, a paedomorphic trait in fact typical of female pygmy chimpanzees. As Stephen J. Gould has pointed out, "When development is retarded, a mechanism is provided (via retention of fetal growth rates and proportions) for bringing these features [bodily shapes and structures] forward to later ontogenetic stages."[69] Reinforcing just such a paedomorphic female hominid genitalic morphology was a behavioral paedomorphism common to both male and female pygmy chimpanzees: ventro-ventral mating. While not classified outright as paedomorphic, ventro-ventral mating in pygmy chimpanzees is recorded as being more typical of juveniles than adults and is consistently interpreted as paedomorphic.[70]

Viewed comparatively in terms of analogies and disanalogies as above, the evolution of human sexuality begins with an explanation of the move toward stark visibility of the primate penis, and the sizable increase in penile length and girth—the chimpanzee penis, for example, is "pencil-thin" or "filiform"[71] and averages eight centimeters as opposed to thirteen centimeters in length. The explanation shows how, at the same time that the larger hominid penis liberated females kinetically and posturally, it both reinforced ventro-ventral copulation and optimized the reproductive success of females with morphologically paedomorphic genitalia. Such an analysis provides empirical, that is, corporeal, grounds for Short's general statement that "undoubtedly, increased penile length has made a wide variety of copulatory positions not only possible, but enjoyable, and may have increased female satisfaction from intercourse by increasing the probability of female orgasm."[72] Orgasm probabilities aside, tactile pleasure is a quite sufficient reason for early hominid females to have chosen males with longer penes as copulatory partners.

3. The sexual paedomorphisms discussed above are relevant to disanalogies in external genitalia, specifically in labia majora, between adult nonhuman and human primates. Labia majora are an infant-to-juvenile trait that disappears in adult female nonhuman primates.[73] Though a variable trait in human adult females, labia majora are in general retained, and their general retention is considered paedomorphic.[74] No explanation has been given for this infant-to-juvenile holdover. An eminently simple but powerful one can be given in terms of differentially visible male/female primate sexual morphologies, and in turn radically different primate sexual signaling behaviors.

Sexually immature nonhuman female primates have no need of a visible vaginal orifice since pudendal swellings and changes in coloration are not yet hormonally triggered. In other words, the *sexual* signaling value of her vulva is not yet central to the social relations of the female. From this perspective, the labia majora serve as a protective covering that deflects purely sexual interests. Support for this view is found in the fact that "in [nonhuman primate] females, there is a clear positive relationship between the onset of regular menstrual cycles and the appearance of mounting, reception of mounts by males, presenting to males, and certain vocalizations and gestures."[75] In effect, only with maturity does the vulva become an abiding focus of sexual attention; only then do the labia majora disappear.

Where genitalic visibility is not of signal priority, there is no functional reason for the disappearance of the labia majora. That they are retained in adult female hominids is a function of the nonvisibility of female hominid genitalia. What is not in view is not seen; what is not seen does not serve as a visual signal. While an analogy can be drawn between nonhuman (*Pan paniscus*) and human adult females with respect to a paedomorphic orientation of the vaginal canal, a disanalogy with both chimpanzee species exists with respect to the overall visual appearance of the vulva: "At no age does the chimpanzee (*Pan*) present a vulva resembling the human pudenda, i.e., a *slit-like* rima *guarded* by swollen labia majora, with the labia minora and other parts *all hidden within*" [76] (italics added). The evolution of hominid female genitalia is, from this perspective, an evolutionary move toward greater invisibility, beginning with bipedality and morphologically ending with the closing over of the vaginal orifice by the labia majora.

With the above examination of primate sexual analogies and disanalogies, the reappraisal of upright posture vis-à-vis human sexuality begun in Chapter 4 is completed. It has shown that consideration of the primate *Bauplan* imposed by consistent bipedality clearly and forcefully mandates a reappraisal of hominid sexuality. *Homo exhibere* was an undeniable ancestor of present-day humans. An understanding of how this hominid affected the course of hominid sexuality *and* hominid evolution necessarily rests on an examination of corporeal matters of fact: animate form and a concomitant species-specific tactile–kinesthetic/kinetic body.

AFTERWORD

The descriptive adjective *large* (and the phrase "larger than all other primates") customarily used to describe the human penis is actually inapt. It is a generalization not only lacking precision, but a generalization that masks a crucially significant observation, one in fact made above in passing, *viz.*, there are two major ways in which a nonhuman primate penis differs visibly from a human one: in thickness and in length. The two distinctive differences are suggestive with respect to the two major speciation events that define hominids, the first event being the original evolutionary divergence of hominids and pongids from a common ancestor, the second being the evolutionary divergence of *Homo* from an existing australopithecine lineage.

Empirical grounds support the thesis that in the first major hominid speciating event—divergence of hominids from a common hominid/pongid ancestor—rapid and divergent evolution of the hominid penis occurred in the direction of increased length; and that in the second major speciating event—the evolution of *Homo* from an australopithecine stock—rapid and divergent evolution of the hominid penis occurred in the direction of increased girth. As shown in the main text of this chapter, increased penile length was tied to a sexual morphology and behavioral practices coincident with the advent of consistent bipedality, for example, a more fully anterior vagina and ventro-ventral copulation. Increased penile girth can similarly be tied to changes in sexual morphology and behavior, and ultimately to modifications in female reproductive anatomy leading to the possibility of expanded fetal crania. The two distinctive genitalic changes accord precisely with fossil evidence that substantiates bipedality as the earliest diagnostic of hominid speciation, and a large neocortex as a much later diagnostic of hominid speciation.[77]

The purpose of this Afterword is to present evidence for the latter half of the thesis—divergence of *Homo* from an existing australopithecine lineage—but less with a view to making a definitive case than to insisting on the necessity of addressing the question of hominid sexuality and speciation in the new and concrete corporeal terms of primate sexual morphology introduced and elaborated in this chapter and in Chapters 4 and 5. It is axiomatic in evolutionary theory, after all, that speciation is contingent upon reproductive isolation. One critical aspect of this isolation concerns genitalia. In fact, as Eberhard points out, genitalia are frequently used taxonomically by biologists to distinguish one species from another. He furthermore points out—with compelling evidence—that "any structure that is a consistently useful taxonomic character at the species level must have evolved rapidly and divergently . . . that is, it acquires a new form in each new species."[78]

In what follows, Eberhard's thesis will again be taken as a theoretical framework. It should be emphasized that, as with the relationship set forth earlier between penile display and bipedality, the relationship set forth below between speciation and the "large" human penis does *not* purport to explain the latter phenomenon *conclusively* by the former. What it aims to show and show incontrovertibly is that animate form *in toto* must be taken into explanatory accounts of hominid speciation. Species-specific male hominid genitalia were at the very least a necessary and decisive condition for evolutionary divergencies and on that account must figure prominently. Furthermore, as will be evident, recent evidence on the value of novelty and its relation to the development of premating signals, thus to speciation, make consideration of penile display as an entailment of consistent bipedality mandatory.

CONCEPTUALIZING THE PROBLEM OF THE DIVERGENCE OF *HOMO*

With respect to penile substitutes—and to the contact resonance of male hominids evolving from an australopithecine stock—virtually any rod-like instrument can open labia and expand the normally collapsed, elastic vaginal walls. In neither case therefore is optimal tactile pleasure a question primarily of mechanics. It is primarily a question of tactile–stimulatory competence. Mary Jane Sherfey, a medical doctor whose work is based on the findings of Masters and Johnson, emphasizes that the girth of the penis is instrumental to human female sexual excitement and orgasmic intensity: "Not only does a widened penis create more tension on the distended [vestibular] bulbs, but it presses the corpus spongiosum . . . against the pelvic bone . . . so that the blood flow to and from the bulbs and the clitoral shaft is blocked, thereby increasing the pressure in both organs." She notes furthermore that penile substitutes, though not very effective or popular objects, are "a close facsimile of the erect penis, primarily in diameter, not length."[79] Put in terms of female anatomy, the greater the width of the vaginal orifice, elasticity of the vaginal walls, and distensible breadth of the surrounding genitalia, the greater the girth of the penis necessary to stimulate the external genitalia and vaginal walls (specifically the lower third).[80] While any rod-like instrument could produce the back and forth movements of thrusting, it would not thereby necessarily create the essentially lateral kind of displacements and frictions (or surface genital contacts) that flesh against flesh creates and that results in an impressive degree of vasocongestion. Vasocongestion produced by thrusting movements is the *physiological* source of significantly high levels of female and male sexual excitement and pleasure—what is *felt* as "pelvic sexual tension."[81] In effect, a thin, filiform penis would mean significantly less distension and significantly less pleasure.

The sexual significance of penile girth to optimum tactile pleasure in present-day female hominids suggests that while the initial increase in hominid penile length (apart from its fundamental signal value) was essentially a *mechanical* modification for measurably enhancing tactile pleasure by securing tactile contact while opening up postural and kinetic possibilities for the female as described earlier, the subsequent increase in girth was a *stimulatory* modification for enhancing tactile pleasure directly. The suggestion is based on Eberhard's slim but viable distinction between mechanical and stimulatory discrimination by females. The problem is not that Sherfey's facts regarding penile girth, vasocongestion, and sexual pleasure do not jibe with the simple distinction. It is that the notion of increased girth as *stimulatory* enhancement oversimplifies recognized factors in the second major hominid speciating event by reversing the more credible sequence of anatomical modifications.

THE VARIABLES

At first glance it might be simply assumed that increased penile girth was a sexual adjustment to female reproductive modifications for larger-brained infants, infants that would ultimately be classified under the genus, *Homo*. On the one hand female pelvic expansion commonly associated with larger fetal crania was not characteristic of earliest known australopithecines.[82] On the other hand significant cortical expansion began to occur two to three million years ago.[83] The beginning of marked cortical expansion coincides precisely with the estimated divergence of *Homo* from an australopithecine stock.[84] It furthermore coincides with accredited tool-making capacities of early *Homo* individuals, that is, habilenes.[85] As suggested above, the problem with the simple assumption is in the relational causalities it postulates among the following: male sexual anatomy, female sexual anatomy, female reproductive anatomy, large-brained infants, the advent of *Homo*. These relational causalities cannot be anatomically substantiated, not only because adaptationist morphology is pushed to the brink of open-sesame enchantment—"the coronal diameter of the birth canal (pelvic outlet) increase[d] *in response to* greater term fetal cranial capacity"[86] (italics added)—but because *sexual* morphology and *sexual* morphological change are ignored, and with them, speciation implications. When taken together into account, a more credible sequence of anatomical modifications becomes apparent. Male genitalia were not modified to accommodate changes in female reproductive anatomy. On the contrary, those females whose *sexual* anatomy accommodated an increased penile girth were reproductively at advantage. *That* advantage in turn both accommodated the birth of larger-brained infants and the possibility of speciation.

Eberhard's central thesis validates just this resolution of anatomical/evolutionary factors and of facts presented by Sherfey. Rapid and divergent changes in male genitalia—the result of female choice on the basis of greater tactile stimulation—constitute the initial sexual requirements for speciation. In other words, *viewed from the vantage point of sexual selection theory rather than of an excessively adaptationist natural selection theory by which reproductive outlets respond seemingly miraculously to "the demands of bigger brains,"* larger female birth canals and larger-brained infants on the one hand, and hominid speciation on the other, were respectively a possibility following upon, and the terminal result of, a major modification in hominid male genitalia. A review of the corporeal facts of the matter—morphological and behavioral—within the context of sexual selection theory, and a review of fossil evidence of hominid speciation within the same context, will provide an explanation of increased penile girth. It will answer the basic question: Why would males with "large" penes be at reproductive advantage? It will show that a more credible relationship among the variables hinges fundamentally on a recognition of intrasexual male/male competition through penile display, and associated changes in male genitalia.

INCREASED GIRTH AND INTRASEXUAL DISPLAY

When increased girth is added to increased length, the positive biological value of size gains a second, or more precisely, third dimension. Both increments enter into the characterization of the human penis as *large*. A significantly thicker erect penis is not simply a more prominent, clearly visible datum, it constitutes a more powerful biological *display* than a thin, long erect penis. That the largest of primate penes might well have originated in intrasexual as well as intersexual display is supported by this basic corporeal fact. It is supported by other corporeal facts as well.

An upright creature whose genital organ is perpetually exposed has the possibility of using it for social purposes, just as nonhuman primates use *presenting* in a variety of social circumstances—to appease, to greet, and so on—and not just sexually; and just as they use *mounting* for social as well as sexual purposes—to demonstrate dominance, for example. The appropriation of the penis as a vehicle for agonistic displays thus follows *a biological primate tradition:* that of conjoining sexual and agonistic signals in a single behavior. The tradition is not actually limited to primates, as sociobiologist Gerald

Borgia's discussion of the close relationship between intrasexual and intersexual communication in insects shows, and as geneticist R. A. Fisher's "war propaganda" model of male display shows more generally.[87] It furthermore follows *biologically patterned use of male genitals* for intrasexual agonistic display, as documented by a number of primatologists.[88] It is also confirmed by representations of penile display in human artifacts, as will be shown below. Moreover the appropriation of the penis for intrasexual display is formally linked to *the biological tradition of corporeal representation*. An erect penis of whatever size is hard and unyielding. It has the character of something that holds its ground and does not give way—just like a strong combatant. It is an iconic signal of threat in this sense. A *thick* erect penis augments the signal of implacable power. Hardness combined with greater girth constitutes a substantially greater show of power than a comparable hardness of thinner dimensions.

When the above corporeal facts are put in evolutionary perspective, it becomes clear why two creatures who are already upright, whose canines are reduced (or reducing) in size, and who have no other natural corporeal weaponry such as claws or antlers, might threaten each other by penile display. The larger the display, the more likely it would intimidate. The more it intimidated, the more competitively successful it would likely be. The more competitively successful, the more likely it would contribute to the reproductive advantage of the displayer, as Darwin originally showed in the evidence he brought forth in support of sexual selection. Darwin's original evidence, substantially augmented by others since,[89] showed that females are sexually attracted to males who impress them with their "charms" or with a show of force in intrasexual combative encounters.

A variety of cross-cultural artifacts, literature, and ritual/religious symbolizations from present and past human societies gives evidence of the use and power of penile display. In the context of his already cited study, "Socio-sexual Signals and Their Intraspecific Imitation among Primates," Wickler, for example, gives an account of cross-cultural usages of the human penis as a symbol of power. Together with graphic reproductions of statuary and ornamentations (including charms), his account gives ready testimony to the potentially formidable impact of penile display.[90] Ethologist Irenaus Eibl-Eibesfeldt presents similar cross-cultural evidence.[91] In the instances cited or graphically reproduced, an erect penis appears unequivocally tied to an assertive show of power. The possibility of intrasexual intimidation through penile display is strongly suggested even in the genital-less drawings depicting cross-cultural, thigh-spreading human male sitting postures.[92] Apart from other ethologically gathered evidence,[93] further documentation is had in Santha Rama Rau's prefatory remarks to *The Kama Sutra*: "In the very heart of a Siva temple you will find the *lingam*—a classic phallic symbol of the god that is both the creator and destroyer."[94] Moreover within our own Western Greek heritage, there is the phallic god, Priapus. Virgil is credited with writing three of the eighty poems written in his honor. Some of the poems center directly on Priapus's role as keeper of the garden, statuary depicting him being placed in gardens to deter thieves from stealing fruit. The statuary is described as follows: "[Priapus] was represented holding a sickle. . . . His distinguishing attribute was an unnaturally large erect penis, usually painted red."[95] As one scholar has remarked, "The general stance of this figure is that of a threatening male."[96] In brief, cross-cultural evidence together with the corporeal facts discussed above suggest that penile display could have functioned as readily as intrasexual agonistic threat as intersexual invitation in ancestral hominid society.

Put precisely in this hypothetical evolutionary perspective, intrasexual penile display marked the potential for the beginning of a new species of hominid. When, as Darwin showed, spontaneous variations are sexually selected, they can give rise to speciating events. Eberhard's data on animal genitalia support the same thesis in the exacting terms of internal fertilization. But the thesis can be put in broader social terms as Darwin himself indicated. Biologist Mary Jane West-Eberhard has in fact carried out Darwin's theoretical program by showing that new and distinctive *signals* (and/or weapons) are as potent sources of speciation as spontaneous variations. Put in highly abbreviated form, her findings are that (1) "socially selected characters [for attraction and combat] may sometimes put a premium on novelty per se, and this may considerably increase the rate of evolution of weapons and display"; and that (2) "the evolution of divergent signals potentially serving as pre-mating isolating mechanisms can be an early rather than late event in the speciation process . . . and divergence of social traits may be the basis of breeding incompatibility . . . between populations that have diverged very little ecologically."[97] Corporeal facts regarding intrasexual penile display can be examined in greater detail in the light of West-Eberhard's socially expanded sexual selection theory. The examination will provide both a

credible temporal sequencing of change in female sexual and reproductive anatomy, and a credible context for early hominid intrasexual
male/male competition.

That a female early hominid would readily discriminate between
thick and thin penes and that such discrimination could have sizable
evolutionary consequences are hypotheses well supported by analogy
to evidence of female discrimination in other species.[98] Female hominids would choose males with thicker penes on the basis of *both* novel
stimuli—"the very distinctiveness and conspicuousness of a novel signal might be advantageous in display"[99]—and intrasexual male/male
competition. At the same time, females with genitalia accommodating
thicker erect penes would be more likely to be chosen as sexual partners—displayed-to—since they would in all likelihood allow easier
intromission and in turn be more pleasurable partners. In fact, male
choice of females with genitalic variations toward the larger distributional extreme is a necessary corollary of increased penile girth. The
latter would have been equivalent to a sexual, and hence *reproductive*,
dead-end if no female genitalia could accommodate it. But once mechanical fit was secured and sexual selection eliminating smaller or
narrower vaginal variants and thinner penes was established, a further evolutionary shift in hominid sexual behavior would have been
encouraged. The shift is best put in the perspective of a striking disanalogy with chimpanzee sexual behavior.

Given the physiological basis for "felt sexual tension," the relatively short copulation time of both species of chimpanzee (8 seconds
in *Pan troglodytes*, 12.2 seconds in *Pan paniscus*)[100] can be explained as a
function of lesser distensibility—of the pencil-thin chimpanzee penis
—and even of no distensibility—of the already *naturally* distended vulval area of female chimpanzees in estrus. Increased penile girth and
vulval distensibility *coincident with intromission* became in developing
hominids a potential source of increased sexual pleasure, culminating
ultimately in prolonged copulatory activity. (Such an explanation does
not exclude the very likely possibility that prolonged copulation time
in humans is tied to radically greater leisure, that is, to the relative
absence of continuous attention to subsistence/survival.)

As Eberhard's theory indicates (and Fisher's runaway model pre-
dicts), rapid and divergent evolution of male genitalia in the direction
of further increases in penile girth would follow both initial intrasexual competitive successes and initial mating successes. Selection of
females having genitalic proportions coincident with increased penile
girth—a wider vaginal orifice, broader and/or lengthier external geni-

talia, more elastic vaginal walls, possibly even transverse as opposed to longitudinal (or oblique) folds of the vaginal mucosa insofar as the latter might lead to greater tactile stimulation[101]—not only would have followed rapidly as suggested above, but would have laid the anatomical groundwork for changes in female reproductive anatomy. This temporal order of female anatomical change is expected on empirical grounds. Anatomy text designations notwithstanding, "the external organs of generation in the female . . . : the mons Veneris, the labia majora and minora, the clitoris, . . . and the orifice of the vagina"[102] are first and foremost *sexual*, not reproductive (generative), organs. The priority of sexual function is well stated in a book on childbirth: "Thanks to its great elasticity, it [the vagina] adjusts to the penis during sexual intercourse as well as to the baby's head and shoulders during delivery."[103] Female genitalic *sexual* selection in conjunction with increased penile girth in other words became an *exaptation*— to use Stephen Gould and Elisabeth Vrba's term[104]—with respect to reproduction; the new female sexual anatomy was "co-opted" for the birth of larger- (and larger-) brained infants. Had female reproductive anatomy been directly *adapted* for larger-brained infants—birth canals miraculously increasing in size "in response to greater term fetal cranial capacity"—it is questionable whether the "shockingly crowded conditions" that prevail[105] would have been the result, and this in spite of the fact that anatomical adjustments for parturition could not negatively affect consistent bipedality.[106] Furthermore, like the reverse situation of increased penile girth in the absence of female variations toward the larger distributional extreme, direct adaptation in the absence of changes in male genitalia might well have resulted in a sexual and in turn reproductive dead-end. Males with long, thin penes would not likely have been able to provide sufficient tactile stimulation to copulate successfully. In consequence, ejaculation might not have resulted. Even in the event that it did, sperm transport would not likely have been helped along by female genitalic response, a response that has been shown to affect actual fertilization.[107] In effect, a new hominid lineage might well not have appeared.

The divergence of *Homo* from australopithecine stock is not clearcut. It is just this ambiguity that provides a credible context for intrasexual male/male competition, and that demands serious consideration of sexual selection as the driving force for the divergence. Fossil evidence indicates precisely that *Homo habilis* and *Australopithecus africanus* were strongly resemblant both cranially and post-cranially,[108] and that they were contemporaries of one another as well.[109] Strong

resemblance was at the hub of the controversy that surrounded classification of *"Homo" habilis* as *Homo* to begin with.[110] Strong likeness suggests that socio-behavioral rather than ecological changes provided
the primary impetus for the divergence of *Homo* from an australopithecine lineage, that is, for speciation. (This is not to say that ecological factors are to be totally discounted.)[111] The implication, perhaps
particularly with the ultimate extinction of australopithecines, is that
early hominids and australopithecines were competitive for the same
resources. In such a situation new behaviors could foster a decisive
selective advantage. It is just this process of social selection leading
to speciation that West-Eberhard has spelled out and that provides
the concrete context for early hominid intrasexual male/male competition.

When the primary impetus for the divergence of *Homo* from *Australopithecus* is put in the context of social competition—when it is
seen from the perspective of male/male rivalry, that is, of competition
for food or other material resources, for social status, or for mates—
then novelty, the unending nature of change, and the potential for
runaway change, *all* are factors in fostering rapid and still more ex-
aggerated evolution of the structural/behavioral character by which
the rivalry is concretely embodied and carried out. The result of the
rivalry, in this case a sharper and sharper division between males with
thick and males with thin penes, would lead to increasingly distinctive *premating* signals readily discriminated by females. In serving to
exaggerate penile differences, the rivalry would ultimately lead to differential reproductive success between the two groups, and ultimately
to speciation.

The fact that hominid sexual signaling behavior already centered
on penile display would facilitate its use in the new social context.
Moreover as pointed out above, a conjoining of sexual and agonistic
meanings in a single behavior is an economy of nature common to
primates; it is a biological tradition. In addition, as noted earlier, the
use of a thick erect penis as a threat-weapon in male/male competition
follows biologically patterned use of male genitals by certain primates
for agonistic display, and is an extension of that original practice of
corporeal representation by which the spatio-kinetic iconicity of erect
posture and erect penis was used to reinforce and make ambulatory
the signal of sexual readiness and potency. In short, all of the corporeal facts cited above support the new usage—and by extension the
attendant thesis.

When both the advent of bigger brains and hominid speciation are interpreted in terms of corporeal facts and of sexual selection theory, they are provided a concrete morphological and behavioral evolutionary context. In turn, a credible sequence of "hominidizing" events is possible. Even tool-using/tool-making, the associated functional product of bigger brains and a *Homo* lineage, is cast in a new light. The use of a club or similarly formed artifact as an instrument of threat or attack may have been an early evolutionary manifestation of the same kind of iconic phallic symbolism—the same kind of iconic corporeal representation—as that recognized in later archaeological artifacts— decorated rods and spears, for example—that have been classified as male symbols.[112] From this evolutionary vantage point, *Homo exhibere* and *Homo faber* clearly meet in those long-ago products fashioned by hominid hands.

NOTES

1. William G. Eberhard, *Sexual Selection and Animal Genitalia* (Cambridge: Harvard University Press, 1985).

2. But see Julian Huxley's remark that "for some curious reason Darwin hardly refers to these [copulatory organs] at all." "The Present Standing of the Theory of Sexual Selection," in *Evolution*, ed. G. R. de Beer (Oxford: Clarendon Press, 1938), p. 21.

3. Charles Darwin, *The Descent of Man and Selection in Relation to Sex* (Princeton: Princeton University Press, 1981 [1871]), pp. 313, 291, and 376, respectively.

4. Eberhard, *Sexual Selection*, p. 14.

5. See, for example, Gerald Borgia, "Sexual Selection and the Evolution of Mating Systems," in *Sexual Selection and Reproductive Competition in Insects*, ed. M. S. Blum and N. A. Blum (New York: Academic Press, 1979), pp. 19–73; and R. L. Trivers, "Parental Investment and Sexual Selection," in *Sexual Selection and The Descent of Man, 1871–1971*, ed. B. Campbell (Chicago: Aldine, 1972), pp. 136–79.

6. See, for example, Wolfgang Wickler, "Socio-Sexual Signals and Their Intraspecific Imitation among Primates," in *Primate Ethology*, ed. Desmond Morris (Garden City, N.Y.: Doubleday, 1969), pp. 89–189; Desmond Morris, *The Naked Ape* (New York: Dell, 1967); R. V. Short, "Sexual Selection and Its Component Parts, Somatic and Genital Selection, As Illustrated by Man and the Great Apes," in *Advances in the Study of Behavior* 9, ed. J. S. Rosenblatt, R. A. Hinde, C. Beer, and M-C. Busnel (New York: Academic Press, 1979), pp. 131–58, and "The Origins of Human Sexuality," in *Reproduction in Mammals* 8, ed. C. R. Austin and R. V. Short (Cambridge: Cambridge University Press, 1980), pp. 1–33; and J. H. Crook, "Sexual Selection, Dimorphism, and Social Organization in Primates," *Sexual Selection and the Descent of Man*, pp. 231–81.

7. Short, "Human Sexuality."

8. Darwin, *Descent*.

9. David P. Barash, *Sociobiology and Behavior* (New York: Elsevier, 1982), p. 147.

10. See, for example, Jane van Lawick-Goodall, "The Behaviour of Free-Living Chimpanzees in the Gombe Stream Reserve," *Animal Behavioural Monographs*, vol. 1, pt. 3 (1968), pp. 165–311, and "A Preliminary Report on Expressive Movements and Communication in the Gombe Stream Chimpanzees," in *Primate Patterns*, ed. Phyllis J. Dolhinow (New York: Holt, Rinehart, and Winston, 1972), pp. 25–84; Yukimaru Sugiyama, "Social Behavior of Chimpanzees in the Budongo Forest, Uganda," *Primates* 10 (1969): 197–225; George B. Schaller, *The Mountain Gorilla* (Chicago: University of Chicago Press, 1963), and "The Behavior of the Mountain Gorilla," in *Primate Patterns*, pp. 85–124; David A. Hamburg, "Aggressive Behaviour of Chimpanzees and Baboons in Natural Habitats," *Psychiatric Research* 8 (1971): 385–98.

11. *Proceedings of the Royal Society of London*, Series B, Biological Sciences, 205: 581–98.

12. Thelma Rowell, *The Social Behaviour of Monkeys* (Middlesex: Penguin, 1972); see also Wolfgang Wickler on the same point with respect to mimicry in *Mimicry* (New York: McGraw-Hill, 1968).

13. Crook's positive estimation of the sexual display power of women in high heels—the latter "enhanc[e] the provocative body movements of the walking female" ("Sexual Selection," pp. 250–51)—fails to take into account a major point in Gould and Lewontin's above-cited article: the necessity of distinguishing (possible) current utility from reasons for origin.

14. J. T. Stern, Jr., and R. L. Susman, "The Locomotor Anatomy of *Australopithecus afarensis*," *American Journal of Physical Anthropology*, n.s. 60 (1983): 279–317.

15. See, for example, Trivers, "Parental Investment"; Harry F. Harlow, "Development of the Second and Third Affectional Systems in Macaque Monkeys," in *Research Approaches to Psychiatric Problems*, ed. Thomas T. Tourlentes, Seymour L. Pollack, and Harold E. Himwick (New York: Grune and Stratton, 1962), pp. 209–29; F. D. Burton, "The Integration of Biology and Behavior in the Socialization of *Macaca sylvana* of Gibraltar," in *Primate Socialization*, ed. Frank E. Poirier (New York: Random House, 1972), pp. 29–62; and V. Reynolds, "Open Groups in Hominid Evolution," in *Primates on Primates*, ed. D. D. Quiatt (Minneapolis, Minn.: Burgess, 1972), pp. 31–43.

16. See, for example, David R. Pilbeam, *The Ascent of Man* (New York: Macmillan, 1972); van Lawick-Goodall, "Free-Living Chimpanzees," and "Chimpanzee Locomotor Play," in *Play–Its Role in Development and Evolution*, ed. Jerome S. Bruner, Alison Jolly, and Kathy Sylva (New York: Basic Books, 1976), pp. 156–60; and A. H. Schultz, "The Physical Distinctions of Man," *Proceedings of the American Philosophical Society* 94 (1950): 428–49.

17. David R. Pilbeam, "Distinguished Lecture: Hominoid Evolution and Hominoid Origins," *American Anthropologist*, n.s. 88 (1986): 295–312.

18. For an example of the earlier belief, see, for example, Sherwood L. Washburn, "Tools and Human Evolution," *Scientific American* 203 (September 1960): 63–75; for a recent estimation of the relationship see Donald C. Johanson and Maitland A. Edey, *Lucy* (New York: Warner, 1981).

19. Re: scavenging, see Lewis R. Binford, *Bones: Ancient Man and Modern Myths* (New York: Academic Press, 1981), and *In Pursuit of the Past* (New York: Thames and Hudson, 1983); Pat Shipman, "Scavenging or Hunting in Early Hominids: Theoretical Framework and Tests," *American Anthropologist*, n.s. 88 (1986): 27–43. Re: extractive foraging, see Sue T. Parker and Kay R. Gibson, "A Developmental Model for the Evolution of Language and Intelligence in Early Hominids," *Behavioral and Brain Sciences* 2 (1979): 367–408.

20. C. Owen Lovejoy, "The Origin of Man," *Science* 211 (1981).

21. Sue T. Parker, "A Sexual Selection Model for Hominid Evolution," *Human Evolution* 2 (1987): 235–53.

22. Lovejoy, "Origin of Man," p. 341.

23. Ibid., p. 346.

24. Parker, "Sexual Selection Model," pp. 243–44.

25. Consistent upright posture in fact freed the legs as well as the hands, and the body as a whole with respect to movement. See Maxine Sheets-Johnstone, "Evolutionary Residues and Uniquenesses in Human Movement," *Evolutionary Theory* 6 (1983): 205–9. See also John Devine on the tendency to one-dimensionalize human bipedal locomotion: "The Versatility of Human Locomotion," *American Anthropologist*, n.s. 87 (1985): 550–70.

26. Eberhard, *Sexual Selection*, p. 79.

27. R. J. Stoller, "Sexual Deviations," in *Human Sexuality in Four Perspectives*, ed. Frank A. Beach (Baltimore: Johns Hopkins University Press, 1976), pp. 190–214; R. Green, "Variant Forms of Behaviour," in *Reproduction in Mammals* 8, pp. 68–97; and Short, "Sexual Selection."

28. See Sarah B. Hrdy, *The Woman That Never Evolved* (Cambridge: Harvard University Press, 1981), for a general summary and discussion of concealment of ovulation.

29. See John T. Robinson, *Early Hominid Posture and Locomotion* (Chicago: University of Chicago, 1972).

30. See Frank A. Beach, "Cross-Species Comparisons and Human Heritage," in *Human Sexuality in Four Perspectives*, p. 302.

31. K. R. L. Hall and I. De Vore, "Baboon Social Behavior," in *Primate Patterns*, p. 174.

32. J. Hanby, "Sociosexual Development in Primates," in *Perspectives in Ethology* 2, ed. P. P. G. Bateson and P. H. Klopfer (New York: Plenum, 1976), pp. 1–67.

33. Van Lawick-Goodall, "Free-Living Chimpanzees," p. 273.

34. Ibid., p. 221: "The frequency with which Flint handled his penis may have been related to the fact that his mother continually played with his penis when he was younger."

35. Short, "Human Sexuality," pp. 14 and 16, respectively.

36. Wickler, "Socio-Sexual Signals."

37. Crook, "Sexual Selection," p. 251.

38. Donald Symons, *The Evolution of Human Sexuality* (Oxford: Oxford University Press, 1979), p. 183.

39. Crook, "Sexual Selection," p. 251.

40. See Mary Jane Sherfey, *The Nature and Evolution of Female Sexuality* (New York: Random House, 1966); W. H. Masters and Virginia Johnson, "Orgasm, Anatomy of the Female," in *Encyclopedia of Sexual Behavior*, 2 vols., ed. A. Ellis and A. Abarbanel (New York: Hawthorn Books, 1961), 2: 702, and "The Sexual Response Cycle of the Human Female, III, The Clitoris: Anatomic and Clinical Considerations," *Western Journal of Surgery, Obstetrics and Gynecology*, 70 (1962): 248–57.

41. Shere Hite, *The Hite Report* (New York: Macmillan, 1976), and *The Hite Report on Male Sexuality* (New York: Knopf, 1981).

42. Bettyann Kevles, *Females of the Species* (Cambridge: Harvard University Press, 1986).

43. See, for example, Sherfey, *Female Sexuality*; Symons, *Evolution of Human Sexuality*; Hrdy, *Woman*; Frank A. Beach, "Human Sexuality and Evolution," in *Reproductive Behavior*, ed. W. Montagna and W. A. Sadler (New York: Plenum Press, 1973), pp. 333–65; and Hite, *Hite Report*.

44. R. G. Whitten, "Hominid Promiscuity and the Sexual Life of Proto-Savages: Did *Australopithecus* Swing?" *Current Anthropology* 23 (1982): 99–101.

45. See, for example, Jane B. Lancaster on the importance of tactile satisfaction to mothering in, "Play-Mothering: The Relations Between Juvenile Females and Young Infants among Free-Ranging Vervet Monkeys," in *Primate Socialization*, pp. 83–104; and David A. Hamburg on the centrality of pleasure to survival in, "Emotions in the Perspective of Human Evolution," in *Human Evolution*, ed. N. Korn and F. Thompson (New York: Holt, Rinehart, and Winston, 1967), pp. 415–27. See also the following researchers on the positive sensual experience of grooming: van Lawick-Goodall, "Free-Living Chimpanzees" and "Expressive Movements and Communication"; C. A. Bramblett, *Patterns of Primate Behavior* (Palo Alto, Calif.: Mayfield, 1976); Harry F. Harlow, "Love," *American Psychologist* 13 (1958): 673–85; and Harry F. Harlow and R. R. Zimmerman, "The Development of Affectional Responses in Infant Monkeys," *Proceedings of the American Philosophical Society* 102 (1958): 501–9. See also Ashley Montagu on the general evolutionary significance of tactility and the specific importance of tactility in the mother/child relationship in, *Touching: The Human Significance of the Skin* (New York: Columbia University Press, 1971); Harry F. Harlow on the singular importance of "contact comfort" to healthy socio-sexual development in primates in, "The Effect of Rearing Conditions on Behavior," in *Sex Research: New Developments*, ed. J. Money (New York: Holt, Rinehart, and Winston, 1965); Konrad Lorenz on sensual pleasure as an important aspect of appetitive, stimulus-releasing behavior in, "The Comparative Method in Studying Innate Behaviour Patterns," in *Function and*

Evolution of Behavior, ed. P. H. Klopfer and J. P. Hailman (Reading: Addison Wesley, 1972); Frank A. Beach on the unlearned "positive effect" or "mutual physical gratification" of human intercourse in, "Cross-Species Comparisons" and "Human Sexuality and Evolution"; and Alison Jolly on the role of pleasure in the evolution of female sexual response [orgasm] in, *The Evolution of Primate Behavior* (New York: Macmillan, 1985).

46. See, for example, Morris, *Naked Ape*; and Crook, "Sexual Selection."

47. Wilder Penfield and T. Rasmussen, *The Cerebral Cortex of Man* (New York: Macmillan, 1950), p. 214.

48. Darwin, *Descent*, p. 100 (italics added).

49. Darwin, *Descent*, p. 262.

50. E. Sue Savage-Rumbaugh and B. J. Wilkerson, "Socio-Sexual Behavior in *Pan paniscus* and *Pan troglodytes*: A Comparative Study," *Human Evolution* 7 (1978): 327–44.

51. On the value of sexual novelty, see M. J. West-Eberhard, "Sexual Selection, Social Competition, and Speciation," *Quarterly Review of Biology* 58 (1983): 155–83; and Eberhard, *Sexual Selection*.

52. Hanby, "Sociosexual Development"; and J. Hanby, L. Robertson, and C. Phoenix, "Sexual Behavior in a Confined Troop of Japanese Macaques," *Folia primatologica* 16 (1971): 123–43.

53. See also the eminent American art critic Bernard Berenson on the essentially tactile–kinetic values of visual aesthetic form, in "The Central Italian Painters of the Renaissance," in *The Bernard Berenson Treasury*, ed. H. Kiel (New York: Simon Schuster, 1962).

54. Beach, "Human Sexuality and Evolution," p. 360.

55. Sherfey, *Female Sexuality*; and Masters and Johnson, "Orgasm, Anatomy of the Female" and "Sexual Response Cycle of the Female."

56. S. Kuroda, "Social Behavior of the Pygmy Chimpanzees," *Primates* 21 (1980): 181–97.

57. N. Thompson-Handler, R. K. Malenky, and N. Badrian, "Sexual Behavior of *Pan paniscus* under Natural Conditions in the Lomako Forest, Equateur, Aire," in *The Pygmy Chimpanzee*, ed. R. L. Susman (New York: Plenum Press, 1984), pp. 347–68.

58. Savage-Rumbaugh and Wilkerson, "Socio-Sexual Behavior"; Kuroda, "Social Behavior."

59. Short, "Human Sexuality," p. 14.

60. Darwin, *Descent*, p. 276.

61. Jane B. Lancaster, "Evolutionary Perspectives on Sex Differences in Higher Primates," in *Gender and the Life Course*, ed. A. S. Rossi (New York: Aldine, 1985), pp. 3–27.

62. See Short, "Sexual Selection," on the relative visibility of Great Ape penes.

63. Eberhard, *Sexual Selection*, p. 175.

64. Thompson-Handler, Malenky, and Badrian, "Sexual Behavior."

65. T. Patterson, "The Behavior of a Group of Captive Pygmy Chimpanzees (*Pan paniscus*)," *Primates* 20 (1979): 341–54.

66. Short, "Sexual Selection."

67. Darwin, *Descent*.

68. Ronald A. Fisher, *The Genetical Theory of Natural Selection* (New York: Dover, 1958 [1930]).

69. Stephen J. Gould, *Ontogeny and Phylogeny* (Cambridge: Belknap Press, 1977), p. 375.

70. Kuroda, "Social Behavior"; and Thompson-Handler, Malenky, and Badrian, "Sexual Behavior."

71. Tim Halliday, *Sexual Strategy* (Chicago: University of Chicago Press, 1980); Franz de Waal, *Chimpanzee Politics* (New York: Harper Colophon, 1982); and Short, "Sexual Selection" and "Human Sexuality."

72. Short, "Sexual Selection," p. 149.

73. W. C. Osman Hill, *Evolutionary Biology of the Primates* (New York: Academic Press, 1972).

74. Gould, *Ontogeny and Phylogeny*.

75. Hanby, "Sociosexual Development in Primates."

76. W. C. Osman Hill, "External Genitalia," *Primatologia* 3 (1958), p. 698.

77. See Lovejoy, "Origin of Man," for a review of this chronology.

78. Eberhard, *Sexual Selection*, p. 1.

79. Sherfey, *Female Sexuality*, pp. 162 and 125 respectively.

80. Ibid. See Sherfey's summary chart of Masters and Johnson's extensive clinical findings.

81. Ibid., p. 73.

82. C. Owen Lovejoy, "Biomechanical Perspectives on the Lower Limb of Early Hominids," in *Primate Functional Morphology and Evolution*, ed. Russell H. Tuttle (The Hague: Mouton, 1975), pp. 291–326.

83. Donald C. Johanson and Tim D. White, "A Systematic Assessment of Early African Hominids," *Science* 203 (1979): 321–30; and Lovejoy, "Origin of Man."

84. Johanson and Edey, *Lucy*.

85. Mary D. Leakey, "A Summary and Discussion of the Archaeological Evidence from Bed I and Bed II, Olduvai Gorge, Tanzania," in *Human Origins: Louis Leakey and the East African Evidence*, ed. Glynn L. Isaac and Elizabeth R. McCown (Menlo Park, Calif.: W. A. Benjamin, 1976), pp. 431–59.

86. Lovejoy, "Biomechanical Perspectives," p. 318.

87. Borgia, "Sexual Selection and the Evolution of Mating Systems"; and Fisher, *Genetical Theory*.

88. See, for example, K. R. L. Hall, "Social Vigilance Behaviour of the Chacma Baboon *Papio ursinus*," *Behavior* 16 (1960): 261–94; Wickler, "Socio-Sexual Signals"; Detler W. Ploog, J. Blitz, and F. Ploog, "Studies on Social and Sexual Behavior of the Squirrel Monkey (*Saimiri sciureus*)," *Folia primatologica* 1 (1963): 29–66; van Lawick-Goodall, "Free-Living Chimpanzees"; and Frank E. Poirier, "Colobine Aggression: A Review," in *Primate Aggression, Ter-*

ritoriality, and Xenophobia, ed. Ralph L. Holloway (New York: Academic Press, 1974), pp. 123–57.

89. See, for example, P. O'Donald's analysis in *Genetic Models of Sexual Selection* (Cambridge: Cambridge University Press, 1980).

90. Wickler, "Socio-Sexual Signals."

91. Irenaus Eibl-Eibesfeldt, *Ethology*, 2nd ed. (New York: Holt, Rinehart, and Winston, 1975).

92. Gordon W. Hewes, "Anthropology of Posture," *Scientific American* 196 (February 1957): 123–32.

93. See, for example, Crook, "Sexual Selection."

94. Santha Rama Rau, "Foreword," *The Kama Sutra of Vatsyayana* (New York: E. P. Dutton, 1964).

95. Hugh Lloyd-Jones, review of *Priapea: Poems for a Phallic God*, trans. W. H. Parker (New York: Routledge/Croom Helm, 1988), in *New York Review of Books*, 10 November 1988, p. 21.

96. Ibid., p. 23, quoting Ann Richlin, *The Garden of Priapus: Sexuality and Aggression in Roman Humor*.

97. Mary Jane West-Eberhard, "Sexual Selection, Social Competition, and Speciation," *Quarterly Review of Biology* 58/2 (1983), pp. 159, 177.

98. Darwin, *Descent*; Eberhard, *Sexual Selection*; West-Eberhard, "Sexual Selection"; and Borgia, "Sexual Selection"; see also J. A. Cohen on the psychophysics of female discrimination and mate choice, and on sensory processes as determinants of evolution as well as products of natural selection, in "Sexual Selection and the Psychophysics of Female Choice," *Zeitschrift fur Tierpsychologie* 64 (1984): 1–8.

99. West-Eberhard, "Sexual Selection," p. 159.

100. Short, "Sexual Selection" and "Human Sexuality"; and Thompson-Handler, Malenky, and Badrian, "Sexual Behavior," respectively.

101. See P. Eckstein, "Reproductive Organs," *Primatologica* 3 (1958): 542–629.

102. Henry Gray, *Anatomy, Descriptive and Surgical*, ed. T. P. Pick and R. Howden (Philadelphia: Running Press, 1974), p. 1025.

103. M. A. Furuhjelm, C. Ingelman-Sundberg, and C. Wirsen, *A Child Is Born* (New York: Delacorte Press, 1979), p. 21.

104. Stephen J. Gould and Elisabeth S. Vrba, "Exaptation—A Missing Term in the Science of Form," *Paleobiology* 8 (1982): 4–15.

105. A. H. Schultz, "The Recent Hominoid Primates," in *Perspectives on Human Evolution* 1, ed. Sherwood L. Washburn and P. C. Jay (New York: Holt, Rinehart, and Winston, 1968), p. 177.

106. Robinson, *Early Hominid Posture*.

107. Jolly, *Evolution of Primate Behavior*; and Eberhard, *Sexual Selection*.

108. Pilbeam, *Ascent*, but see also P. V. Tobias, "The Distinctiveness of *Homo habilis*," *Nature* 209 (1966): 953–57, on evidence of narrower cheek teeth in habilenes than australopithecines.

109. Johanson and Edey, *Lucy*.

110. See E. L. Simons, David R. Pilbeam, and P. C. Ettel, "Controversial Taxonomy of Fossil Hominids," *Science* 166 (1969); and Robinson, *Early Hominid Posture*.

111. See G. H. Denton, "Did the Antarctic Ice Sheet Influence Late Cainozoic Climate and Evolution in the Southern Hemisphere?" *South African Journal of Science* 81/5 (1985): 224–36; and Elisabeth S. Vrba, "African Bovidae: Evolutionary Events Since the Miocene," ibid., pp. 263–66, and "Testing Models of Macroevolution: Examples from Miocene-Recent African Mammals," *South African Journal of Science* 81/6 (1985): 300.

112. See André Leroi-Gourhan, *Préhistoire de l'art Occidental* (Paris: Mazenod, 1971).

8

On the Conceptual Origin
of Death

The human race is the only one that knows it must die, and it knows this only
through its experience. A child brought up alone and transported to a desert
island would have no more idea of death than a cat or a plant.

VOLTAIRE

INTRODUCTION

Maurice Merleau-Ponty described the objective body as the "impover-
ished image" of the phenomenal body.[1] In an earlier work, Jean-Paul
Sartre drew a similar distinction when he described the body being-
for-itself and the body-for-others as existing "on different and incom-
municable levels" with one another.[2] Many existential philosophers
have gone on to extol these critical determinations and to incorporate
the distinction in their work as a fundamental verity of human existence. Thus, Calvin Schrag, for example, has insisted on the necessity
of consistently contrasting "the body as *concretely lived*" with "the body
as *objectively known*."[3] On the other hand, Herbert Plügge, and more
recently, Richard Zaner, have spoken of the entwinement of the physical and lived bodies: "The bodily as physical," says Plügge, "also exists
phenomenally within the frame of the bodily as live."[4] Zaner uses the

203

concept of the uncanny to describe the intrinsic entwinement peculiar to embodiment.[5] More recently still, Maxine Sheets-Johnstone has examined the physical and lived bodies from an existential–evolutionary perspective and described their quintessential coherence in terms of "existential fit."[6] Together, these latter works suggest a reassessment is underway, modest in impact perhaps still at this point, but with substantial implications for a more just hermeneutics of the body, a more exact *Leibkörper phänomenologische*.[7]

An examination of death within the context of this apparently nascent reassessment might at first glance seem counter-productive. Death, after all, commonly means not an entwinement but a separation: a cessation of the lived body and a slow decay of the physical one. But the initial impression misses the point: what *was* unitary— what was entwined or quintessentially coherent in the everyday flow of corporeal life—is in death sundered. An understanding of the conceptual origin of death thus rests upon an understanding of how a certain Other came into the world, an Other in the form of a physical body perceived and ultimately conceived *as such*.

Along with the above remarks that situate this chapter within the context of phenomenology and existential philosophy, a few words should be said regarding methodology and methodological implications. To begin with, being an examination of the origin of the concept of death, the concern is not ontological but epistemological. How is it that we humans came to be aware of death? More precisely, since the concept of death did not originate with modern *Homo sapiens*—burial practices of Neanderthals, for example, point toward an older genesis —how is it that our long-ago ancestors came to an awareness of death? To answer this question is to elucidate an existential–evolutionary history: it is to show in an existential–evolutionary sense the origin of the chiasmatic notions of animate and terminal existence. To this end both a hermeneutical and a phenomenological analysis are needed: the former to root the investigation in evolutionary perspective, the latter to flesh out the complex structures of awareness discovered in the paleoanthropological hermeneutic.

The detective work at times necessary to the hermeneutic enterprise is in principle no different from that necessary to other similar existential studies: clues are gathered and interpreted. What might be deemed unique here is that in part a wholly different realm of clues is used. Existential significations will be extracted neither from pathological or medical findings nor from customary everyday ontic sources. In order to chart the origin of certain strikingly human awarenesses, what is needed are evolutionary clues, some of which are discoverable through a bracketed examination of given evolutionary behaviors; some of which are discoverable through an examination of the everyday worlds of nonhuman animals; and some of which are discoverable through an interpretation of certain behavioral practices in preliterate societies.

The gathering and using of such clues assume the essential correctness of evolutionary theory. More than this, they indicate that evolutionary theory is being taken *seriously:* it is not just organs and systems that evolved, but sensitivities and powers, awarenesses and behaviors. In other words, evolutionary changes are not partial or disembodied alterations—survival is not a matter of the mere *having* of a certain anatomical part—but organic variations of *whole, living* creatures; an evolutionary history is permeated through and through with existential significations. But furthermore, if evolutionary theory is to be taken seriously, it is clear that existential philosophy can no longer disregard the fact that humans did not suddenly descend from the treetops, neither as freedom (Sartre) nor as *Dasein* (Heidegger) nor as any other wholly isolated evolutionary being. Or, to put the point more emphatically, humans did not spring *undescended* into the evolutionary world. Whatever humans are—in an existential sense, whatever ontological structures might be described as theirs and theirs alone—they are evolutionary creatures: ontological structures are necessarily ones that evolved and ones that, for all we know, are still evolving and will continue to evolve. While humans might admittedly be too shortsighted to appreciate that long-range bio-ontological relativity, they cannot be too shortsighted to acknowledge their evolutionary heritage short of espousing a creationist doctrine of human existence. Thus, if self-disclosedness is what makes *Dasein Dasein,*[8] then the evolutionary origin of self-disclosedness is an issue. In default of evolutionary grounding, the concept of *Dasein* either collapses in the face of evolutionary theory or it sustains itself through a creationist doctrine. Neither of these alternatives is attractive. But neither need be taken. By extending the range of genetic phenomenology, that is, by employing a phenomenological hermeneutics with respect to paleoanthropological reconstructions, it is possible to ground *Dasein* in evolutionary time and in so doing, illuminate the onto-epistemological structures that constitute the opening of its Being-toward-Death.

Something similar can be said with respect to the being-for-itself that is human freedom. As with *Dasein,* the entrance of such a being onto the worldly scene necessitates a *deus ex machina* in the wings.

Such backstage manoeuvering clearly undermines the credibility of the very being for whom it is being undertaken. What is crucial to the ontology is evolutionary grounding. As with the grounding of self-disclosedness, the grounding of being-for-itself is to be sought in a phenomenological hermeneutics that, in its application to paleoanthropology, is akin to genetic phenomenology: in both undertakings, it is a question of uncovering and elucidating *origins*.

NONHUMAN ANIMAL DEATH: THE QUESTION OF LANGUAGE AND BEHAVIORISM

It might be thought that the reason nonhuman animals do not know death as such—that is, as a conceptually distinctive phenomenon—is that they have no verbal language; and correlatively, that we humans know death because we speak. Only through the having of such a language could the recognition of death be conceptually fixed. Thus, it might be said that the reason Olly and her daughter, Gilka, chimpanzees of the Gombe Stream area,[9] traipsed about with Olly's dead four-week-old new baby was that they had no verbal language by which they could conventionally identify the state of the baby as dead. Had they such a language, their behavior would conceivably have been different: Olly would not likely have carried the corpse along with her in the days following the infant's death, slinging it over her shoulder, letting it drop to the ground with a thud when she sat down, or dangling it from an arm or leg when she stood up; presumably neither would Gilka have tickled the corpse, played with it, or groomed it. Interpreted at face value, these behaviors suggest that although the infant was no longer behaving "properly," it was being treated as if it were still living: however carelessly, it was still being carried about by its mother; however unresponsive, it was still being groomed; and so on. The body as a lifeless specimen of flesh, a fly-ridden carcass, a physically present but non-moving being was not apparently recognized as such. Would the word *death* have sufficed to change all this?

On the other hand, if Olly's and Gilka's behaviors cannot be said to be indicative straight off of an awareness of death, they might perhaps be seen as an expression of loss. Consider, for example, the behavior of Humphrey toward Mr. McGregor after the latter had become paralyzed and eventually died. Humphrey stayed with his old friend almost constantly. When Mr. McGregor was literally no longer present—after euthanasia, his body was secretly removed—"it looked as if Humphrey did not realize he would never meet his old friend again. For nearly six months he kept returning to the place where Gregor had spent the last days of his life, and would sit up one tree or another staring around, waiting, listening. During this time he seldom joined the other chimps when they left together for a distant valley; he sometimes went a short way with such a group, but within a few hours he usually came back again and sat staring over the valley, waiting, surely to see old Gregor again."[10]

Was Humphrey wondering what had happened to his friend? Was he grieving his loss? Was he at a loss to explain his loss? Was he thinking his friend would return if only he waited long enough? Is Humphrey's wondering, or mourning, or confusion, or expectation dependent upon language? Certainly it would seem not. Certainly too it would seem that one cannot deny some such cognitive–affective experience as wondering, expecting, grieving, and the like, to Humphrey. Why otherwise would a social animal such as a chimpanzee spend six months away from its confreres, returning instead to the site where he last saw his friend and sit solitarily, staring over the valley? There is in fact something subtly familiar about Humphrey's behavior, else it would not be conjectured that "Humphrey did not realize he would never meet his old friend again," or that "Surely, he was waiting to see old Gregor again, listening for the deep, almost braying voice . . . that was silenced forever." [11]

The stunning noncomprehension of death that humans sometimes feel at the sudden loss of a loved one is apparent in the sudden cessation of the everyday world with its typical behaviors. The loss is a shock that loosens—even severs—ties to customary concerns and practices. Humphrey's behavior seems to recall such experiences; it seems woven of the same existential cloth. What, then, is lacking to Humphrey's experience of loss such that he might have a concept of death? The "no-moreness" of loss, after all, appears similar to the "no-moreness" of death: in both cases, an Other is no longer vitally present. From this perspective, Olly's and Gilka's behaviors might be seen as on a continuum with Humphrey's: Olly and Gilka, although not conceptually awakened as such, are confronted by the no-moreness of death, Humphrey, in a more humanly evocative way, by the no-moreness of loss. The problem, however, is that no matter how conceptually similar the experiences might appear, no mere conceptual leap can bridge the gap. The concept of death—whether verbal or nonverbal—is not fully derivable from an experience of loss. Such a concept would have too narrow a compass: the deeper and wider no-moreness peculiar to death would be missing. What is lacking to Humphrey for a concept of death—or to Olly and Gilka—is not a word that would anchor all their experiences of lifeless Others—a singular identifying verbal epithet that could be cast like a net over any experienced lifeless forms—or conceivably, even a singular *non*linguistic concept of lifeless being. While it could be said that the word *death* is used (or even that a certain nonlinguistic concept comes into play) whenever an individual becomes permanently inert and unresponsive —that is, whenever this sort of individual is met with, one knows one is in the presence of death—such a usage does not reflect the richer notion customarily associated with death. Death does not just *name* a certain state of affairs relative to another body—that is, inert, unresponsive, even putrid, grotesquely colored, and so on—nor does it merely mean that such a state of affairs obtains. Conceptually, it connotes an awareness of terminality, of a punctuated existence which is inevitable and which is mine and the lot of all living creatures. Where does this awareness of punctuated existence come from? What are its conceptual origins? Clearly, the aspect of death that such an awareness grasps, and that such an awareness must once have grasped in an originary sense, cannot simply be pointed to, any more than it can be conceptually derived from and verbally fixated upon the experience of loss. Clearly, the origin of this awareness lies neither in a readily available nor ready-made language, but in a particular kind of awareness of bodily life, one in which, as illustrated by the previous examples, a body can be either present or absent in the death sense of no-moreness.

If the above examination of nonhuman animal death calls into question the claim that short of language there are no concepts, it also forces the hand of any behaviorist who claims knowledge of death resolves itself into an awareness of inert, unresponsive bodies. If the question, How is it that our long-ago ancestors came to be aware of death? is answerable at all, behavioristic perspectives need to be surpassed if not relinquished. In other words, one has to go beyond accounts of the Other's death, or perhaps more aptly still, one has to find in the Other's lifeless form the path leading to an awareness that one's own existence is on the line. Thus, before coming to designate the concept of punctuated existence in language, our hominid ancestors would have had to have had a complex of nonlinguistic notions of bodily life, and these notions, of course, on the basis of particular kinds of awarenesses of bodily life. Short of acknowledging such foundational awarenesses and notions, we are left with a problem akin to that characterized by Thomas Nagel in respect to the point of view of a bat: we, like our death-recognizing hominid ancestors, have a certain concept beyond the reach of substantiating facts. Thus, as Nagel points out, "We can be compelled to recognize the existence of . . . facts without being able to state or comprehend them." [12] Certainly we know death when we see it and certainly, by definition, our death-recognizing ancestors knew death when they saw it. What we do not know in the least, and what they did not know either, is what death is like—in the Nagelian sense of the experiencing creature itself—even if it is *nothing*. How, then, could we or they possibly come to have a concept of it? If we believe nothing is there—indeed, if we know death to be the end of our possibilities—surely we must have some bodily sense for believing so, and surely that sense of the body must have precipitated our long-ago ancestors' originary notion of death. Otherwise, however inert, unresponsive, putrid, and grotesquely colored the bodies (and however rich our verbal vocabularies), neither we nor our ancestors should have any reason to conceive of *death*, but only of inert, unresponsive, putrid, grotesquely colored bodies.

NONHUMAN ANIMALS AND PHYSICAL BODIES

What does it mean to say that for themselves, nonhuman animals do not have physical bodies as such? It means that by and large they do not appear to themselves nor do their fellow creatures appear to them as analyzable and manipulable bodies. In the visual spectacle of themselves and creatures about them, what appears is not a mere physical object—an object of such and such parts, for instance, or of this or that degree of rotational possibility. What appears is a certain portentous physiognomy of some kind: threatening, caring, playful, fearful, curious, and so on. What appears, in short, is not a material body abstractively separated or separable from a living body. Consider, for example, the phenomenon of recognition in a penguin rookery. There is no reason to think penguins recognize their own mates and offspring among thousands of others in any way other than the way we humans, searching for a familiar face in the crowd, come finally to recognize an overall facial form or style of walking—to recognize a certain "pattern of wholeness." [13] This pattern is not a matter of analysis but of physiognomic form: it is not an assemblage of discretely and serially distinguished physical features but a singular and immediate qualitative *Gestalt*.

Now the having of a physical body as such, that is, an analyzable and analyzed, manipulable and manipulated body, is what makes twentieth-century biology and medical science possible. Short of a separation of *this* body from the living body, there would be no temperatures to be taken, no organs to be transplanted, no cells to be counted. There would be no body to *inspect*, to examine and to study to the end that one could deduce certain relationships, certain cause and effect sequences—such as that which might be seen to obtain, for instance, between a limp and a swollen ankle. Certainly this separation of physical and lived bodies has been described in many ways before. What has not surfaced, however, is precisely the fact that in nonhuman animal societies there is no such kind of inspection. Whatever bodily inspections are carried out in the infancy or adulthood of nonhuman animals, they do not appear to go beyond a qualitative noticing: what emerges from the inspections is not an abiding material thing in the world but a certain physiognomic form. How then does one get from not distinguishing a physical body *as such* to the distinguishing of one? To answer "through having a different kind of brain" is, of course, to opt for a reductionism that evades the question entirely: it is not a question of laboratory distinctions but of first-person sensory–kinetic worlds.

However bizarre it might appear at first glance to say that nonhuman animals do not have physical bodies as such, the truth of the statement is borne out in many ways—including the observation that even the more intelligent of nonhuman animals—as twentieth-century Westerners estimate chimpanzees, orangutans, and gorillas —do not have witch doctors, shamans, or other kinds of medical practitioners among them. Medicine—in whatever form—can only be practiced on, or with reference to, physical bodies. If physical bodies do not exist, no one can minister to them clinically, no matter how hurt or in pain a creature might appear to be. The licking of wounds is not the result of an examination and diagnosis but the dispositional tactile response of a living body in face of suffering—its own or another creature's. The human response of embracing and stroking is an elaboration of that tactile consolation; it is a manual expression of a once-lingual gesture.[14]

Further corroboration is had in considering what happens when a very young nonhuman primate is wounded. Its mother appears to notice changes in its behavior straightaway and may compensate for the youngster's inability to get about in the way it has in the past, but she does not investigate the source of its difficulty; she does not look to see what is the matter; she does not set about analyzing why it is the youngster is unable to keep up with the group and thereby discover that its leg is broken or otherwise injured in such a way as to make walking impossible. She does not know what an injured leg looks like because she has never inspected in an analytical sense a normal leg and come to know what *it* looks like. In a word, the youngster's physical body *as such* does not exist for her any more than a physical world *as such* exists for her. If nonhuman animals do not have a medical practice—or a full-scale geology or astronomy—it is not that they lack a language in the form of human speech or a culture by human standards. It is because in an evolutionary–existential sense they have no physical bodies as such. The having of a physical body and a physical world are a matter of apprehending physicality in a preeminently material rather than physiognomic sense.

This is not at all to say that there are no instances or intimations of physical thinghood in a nonhuman world. To begin with, consider the following account quoted by Adolph Portmann in his book *Animals as Social Beings*:

The position of a male with high social standing is abruptly shattered as soon as he loses his antlers. In the spring of 1951, in the Basel Zoo, I was able to watch the moment when a fallowbuck sank to a lower level (alpha, beta, gamma, here describe the levels in social rank). On April 18th, at 3:45 P.M. the herd of five males and eight females were begging for food from the zoo visitors. Suddenly they were slightly startled by a playing child, so that some of them trotted off, including the alpha male. He happened to graze with the right side of his antlers the branch of a fir-tree lying in the enclosure. Immediately this half of the antlers fell clattering to the ground. Obviously upset, with tail raised, he sniffed at the piece he had just lost. Almost at the same moment the beta buck realized what had happened, and attacked and pursued him vigorously. The other three yearling antler-less gamma bucks took scarcely any notice of the occurrence nor did the does. After about half an hour both the alpha and beta bucks had more or less calmed down and were again begging for food. But the former buck was not tolerated at the fence by his rival, and therefore kept right at the back of the enclosure. . . . Up to the evening the one-palmed animal carried out peculiar head movements, as were observed by Heck (1935) after the loss of antlers. On 23rd April the beta buck also had shed his first antlers. From this time on there was the same social ranking as had prevailed before the alpha animal shed his.[15]

One would be hard-pressed to deny an inchoate sense of materiality to the fallowbucks, be it ever so colored over physiognomically. The literal piece of the deer that has fallen off is out there in the world, on its own, so to speak; but it is a thing the deer recognizes as some-*thing mine*. Marjorie Grene's comment on the report corroborates the notion of a rudimentary apprehension of a physical body as such in some nonhuman animals: "That the stag 'knows' about his antlers," she writes, "is confirmed by many other studies, notably, for example, those of Hediger on the psychology of animals both in captivity and in the wild."[16]

As a further instance of materiality, it can be said generally that tool-making and tool-using among nonhuman animals clearly demonstrate a use of things *as things*, that is, as material and not *merely* or *only* as sensuous objects, for example, the use of leaves to wipe oneself after defecating.[17] But in addition to this tool-using behavior, as it is reported in the literature, there is also a more direct manipulation of things as things. Japanese macaques who wash their sweet potatoes in water to rid them of sand deposits before eating them are clearly manipulating things *as things* in their world. English tits who discovered they could puncture milk bottle tops and skim off the cream are also manipulating things as things. Curiosity fosters investigations and manipulations. Yet these discoveries of thinghood do not seem to generalize into a physical world as such, into a cosmology, so to speak. All are intimations of a material world, they do not found it. And indeed, they cannot found it. The point from which such a world could come into view is missing. One's own body itself must first come into view as a consistent and permanent physical reality. In the case of the deer, the visual body of the other might be said to have come into a partial such view, but the visual body that is one's own has not. What there is of that latter body lies not only detached on the ground but must seemingly be sniffed in order to be verified as one's own: it is not straightaway recognized. Of course the point could be made that so far as mammals are concerned, a quadruped cannot see its body as readily as an upright creature can. What is actually visible of its visual body comes into view naturally in a less immediate way. It is certainly true too that if *we* had antlers, upright posture would allow us no better visual vantage point upon them than the deer's. But the point could also be made that smell—a dominant sense in non-primate and nonmarine mammals—is not a sense that can objectify things in the world as consistent and permanent realities "out there." The smell of "mine" is not only an ingested awareness, a quasi-tactile entity, it is a one-dimensional object: it has no parts. In contrast, the vision of "mine" is "out there" and it remains "out there," a complex, multi-dimensional object, and one that in turn can be analyzed and manipulated.

DEATH AND THE VISUAL BODY

If it appears that the having of a physical body is linked to the having of a *visual* materiality, it is because the physical body as such and as we know it is above all a visual specimen. Certainly a physical body can be awakened and subsequently examined by touch, smell, movement, sound, and even taste—we can feel the downy texture of its skin, smell its sweat, kinesthetically reckon its joint mobility, listen to its heart, taste its tears—but its *inspection* is preeminently the work of two eyes, and this not on etymological grounds, but quite the reverse: because two hands, nostrils, ears, or a tongue cannot approximate to the corporeal wholeness and profusion of detail grasped by two eyes. In effect, what more natural way to have come to an awareness of the physical body than visually and what better way to have begun inspecting its physicality than by *looking* at it?

When one inquires into certain decisively hominid practices that single out a physical body, it becomes apparent that in the origin and evolution of these practices, visual meanings were indeed being asserted, meanings having to do with decidedly visual analyses and visual manipulations. Counting by the body and counting on the body —the latter practice observed in preliterate cultures and predating the exclusive use of the fingers to count[18]—and caring for the injured are paradigmatic instances of these two modes of visual meaning. What is remarkable is that counting by the body and caring for the injured seem to reach far back into hominid history. Let us consider briefly each practice in turn.

Milford Wolpoff, a paleoanthropologist, remarks of a break line in the femur of an East African australopithecine that "the fact that the break *healed* indicates that the individual was taken care of by others."[19] Now of course by the notion "care by others," Wolpoff does not mean splinting or casting, but rather that in this Pliocene period of hominid evolution, members of a hominid group apparently protected and ministered to the needs of the injured. That this evolutionary picture of caring contrasts markedly with descriptions of the treatment of injured members in extant nonhuman primate societies is significant: whereas the usual method of paleoanthropologists is to draw analogies to the latter societies in rendering reconstructions of early hominid ones, only a disanalogy can be drawn here. The disanalogy is rooted in a difference in sensory–kinetic worlds; namely, the ascendancy of the visual body as a separate reality. In order to minister to an injured individual, it is first necessary to see concretely that something is wrong. It means not merely sensing that something is peculiar or amiss in the way that an individual is acting, but apprehending what that something is and ministering to the individual accordingly, for example, bringing food, protecting against predators. The situation of the injured hominid is thus quite different from that of a paralyzed Mr. McGregor shunned by his confreres save for his friend Humphrey, who protected him from the aggressions of others, but who left him to fend for himself so far as food was concerned and who ceased to groom him. These latter omissions are not neglected social niceties; they are the measure of a certain sensory–kinetic domain of sensitivities and powers. The situation is equally dissimilar from that in which chimpanzees who, initially frightened by the queerness of a polio-stricken confrere, "rushed for reassurance to embrace and pat each other while staring at the unfortunate cripple." Eventually their fear subsided, "but, though they continued to stare at him from time to time, none of them went near him, and eventually he shuffled off, once more on his own."[20]

The dawning emergence of the visual body as physical object necessarily meant a dawning awareness of the everyday appearances of the body—the concrete everyday functioning of its "members"; and correlatively, a dawning awareness that those everyday functional appearances could change—that the living powers of the individual could be altered. These dawning visual awarenesses were certainly not a matter of language but of the gradual materialization of physiognomic perceptions. What before might have been perceived as queer, for example, moving in an abnormal manner, came to be perceived as a visibly physical injury.

As to numerical awareness, there are, as suggested earlier, two modes that warrant comment. To begin with, the practice of counting by the body is evidenced in ancestral hominid tool-making—both in the bifacial Oldowan artifacts and the later Acheulian axes. A rudimentary visual notion of "how many" is apparent in each, a notion not necessarily verbalized at all but, on the contrary, one most likely to have been felt as enacted by the body. Recall Ashley Montagu's observations of certain Acheulian handaxes (cited in Chapter 3), for example:

It is clear that each flake has been removed in order to produce the cutting edges and point of the tool with the minimum number of strokes. . . . If one examines this tool carefully, one may readily perceive that no more flakes have been removed than were minimally necessary to produce the desired result.[21]

Montagu's observations strongly suggest that a numerical awareness was connected both with the tool itself as a visual object—it had a certain regular appearance in terms of its surfaces and consequent shape—and with bodily movements as tactile–kinesthetic realities— they too had a certain regular numerical as well as dynamic character. Given descriptively detailed accounts of the preeminently physiog- nomic nature of preliterate societies[22]—and the standard paleoanthro- pological practice of drawing analogies to these societies—it is likely that the felt tactile–kinesthetic numerical character was perceived by early hominids as *transferred* to the visual object in its own right. A distinctive visual object—a tool—was, after all, being created before someone's very eyes. Thus there must have been an awareness of a distinctively physical object coming into existence: a certain visual form *qua* physical object must have been recognized as being achieved.

When accounts of enumeration in extant non-Western cultures are interpreted in terms of sensory–kinetic worlds, the situation ap- pears remarkably similar. That is, with respect to counting on the body, visual meanings, while anchored in and solidified by tactile– kinesthetic gestures, are nonetheless visual meanings. While numbers are brought to life by touching particular parts of the body and in sequence, yet at the same time, the numerical awareness is clearly a visual phenomenon. It is the visual body perceived as a system of parts, a numerically divisible entity, that anchors the enumeration. Whatever the body parts tactilely enumerated—finger, nose, ear, fore- arm—and in whatever sequence, a visual corporeal standard grounds the practice. In fact the visual body is counted on as a physical object in both a literal and a metaphorical sense—it is amenable to such an analysis and in turn is analyzed and manipulated as such. The practice of counting on the body is rooted in the dawning emergence of just such an object. Indeed, what else but a physical object in the form of the visual body could furnish the analytical and manipulational per- manency and consistency necessary to the formation of a numerical standard?

If it is the visual body that came to be abstracted and distinguished from the living body and to stand out from it as a distinctly physical entity, then the question is how this visual body came to be so dissociated. In concrete terms, How would our early ancestors have stumbled upon the visual body as a material thing in the world? The answer would seem to lie in an understanding of the aura of strangeness pervading a perceived difference in something heretofore familiar, a perceptual shift not unlike that of the chimpanzees' perceptions of change in the visual appearance of their polio-stricken confrere: thus, initially, an understanding of how fingers, seen in the familiar act of picking seeds or fruit, or a hand seen in the familiar act of gathering stones or of touching another's hand, or feet seen in the familiar process of watching one's footing, or even particular parts of the body seen in the process of learning a new skill—how such everyday visual apparencies turned suddenly strange, and in a way unmatched by any other sensory modality, particularly the tactile–kinesthetic. A given movement coordination, for example, might have felt strange, but only because it was a new technique being learned—forging a tool for the first time perhaps, or trying to adhere to a set standard in forging it. Similarly, a feeling of dizziness or of pain might have appeared strange, but again, only in the sense of not having been experienced before, not in the sense of something familiar's having been suddenly experienced as *alien*. When perceived as strange in this latter sense, aspects of the visual body were no longer enfolded in the overall lived action; they were momentarily cut from their familiar moorings; the naturally forged coordination of the tactile–kinesthetic and the visual bodies was perceptually sundered. A radical separation was born.

Whatever the innumerable sudden glimpses and however drawn out the gradual insights, the visual body in time came to be seen as an outsider, a thing out there, a materiality, ultimately a full-fledged physical object in a world of full-fledged physical objects.[23] In fact it seems likely that whatever the particular cultural practices at any particular time and place in hominid history, the growing sense of the physicality of the body was consistently reflected in a proportionally growing sense of the physicality of the world: the material complexity of the one was no less and no more strange and wondrous than that of the other.

Perhaps it should be emphasized more strongly that the physicality of the body was not forged overnight nor was the visual body from some very early time onward seen only and wholly as a purely physical specimen. Accounts of physiognomic perception in preliterate societies clearly confute both notions as do our own everyday twentieth-century Western lives in which our visual bodies are normally melded into the task at hand, the visual body being an element within the totality of the lived body—as in driving, playing tennis, hammering, washing dishes, writing, or playing the violin. The physicality of the visual body was a dawning awareness stretching over perhaps millions of years and in fact only since the rise of Western medicine and science has the visual body as physical specimen become, and in relatively hurried fashion (in the last second to midnight on the now proverbial cosmic time clock) a truly separable and separated reality—literally, *a thing*, an object analyzed and manipulated in its own right. Moreover, it is not that "once" perceived as such, the visual body was (or is) never seen as anything more than a material thing. The point is simply that "once" perceived as such, its perceptual and ultimately conceptual separation from the felt body marked a radical turning point in hominid history: it was the spawning ground of revolutionary new practices—caring for others and counting by and on the body; and it was the spawning ground of revolutionary new beliefs—the conceptual measure of death was made on a visually mattering body.

The question then is, How did death enter into a visually mattering world? If a human were isolated completely from birth onwards, with no living beings about, he or she would have no reason to conceive of death. Nothing in experience would lead to such a concept. By itself, a living body does not know death; nothing in its experiences of the world or of itself prepares it for such an eventuality. Whether caught up in the world at hand, or reflecting on its singular universe, there is seemingly nothing that would precipitate it toward such an awareness. An emerging awareness of the visual body as physical specimen would not in these circumstances adumbrate a notion of death either. While this body might be awakened in moments of casual inspection or through injury, these momentary insights would not suffice to conjure a sense of death: the mere perception of a physical body as such does not lead a creature to conceive of death. The conceptual origin of death lies in something more, that is, in a social world, or at least an interanimate one, and this because to meet with death is not only to be a physical body; it is also to be other than what one is now, other in a way similar to the way in which others are other for me: they are visual bodies unconnected to what I know directly as my own felt body. Clearly this originary sense of otherness needs amplification.

FROM A PALEOANTHROPOLOGICAL HERMENEUTICS
TO A HUSSERLIAN PHENOMENOLOGY

The distinct move to a Husserlian phenomenology in this particular context demands a shift to a first-person account, for unlike the concept of a tool or of a verbal language, the concept of death does not refer to something palpably out there in the world in some way. Accordingly, a corporeal journey is required—from the preceding hermeneutics of the concept of death to that hermeneutics' foundational source in corporeal experience. The *I* that makes its appearance here is to be understood as a "phenomenologically reduced" *I*, that is, as the *I* of any reader who takes the journey him- or herself.

How were fellow creatures likely to appear to our long-ago hominid ancestors? An approximation to their viewpoint is had in part by bracketing: putting out of play twentieth-century cultural expectations, attitudes, assumptions, and beliefs. Interpreted in evolutionary contexts, insights from this bracketed world can be of seminal significance. Bracketed perceptions, in other words, are amenable to "primitive" interpretations insofar as everyday twentieth-century Western theses are temporarily suspended.[24] Thus, when bracketed, others appear not as persons, or human beings, or males, or females, for example. They appear simply as visual forms, forms in-animation and of-ever-changing-physiognomies. There is no *inside* to these moving visual forms; there is only threat, entreaty, comfort, playfulness, and the like, that is, physiognomic aspects palpably present in their gestures and expressions, posturings and amblings. That I see *these* physiognomies is an aspect of their appearance that would require its own analysis, but that elucidation is not critical or at issue here. What is critical here is that, seen as sheer visual appearances, these forms have no interiors. Nothing that I see of these moving visual forms and changing physiognomies suggests an interior—an inner material depth. There is, in effect, not actually an *outside* that I see: there is only the moving visual form of ever-changing physiognomies.

Now were any one of these moving visual forms opened up and made visible to me by accident or injury of some kind, what I would see are entwined, moist, layered, reddish objects of various shapes: hard and soft things bearing no resemblance at all to the moving form I just saw with its ever-changing physiognomies. There is no reason for me to connect these appearances or to ponder their relationship: the moving visual form is one thing, these hard and soft things quite another. Hence I do not conceive of inside and outside *as such* at all, much less think that *I* have an inside like the one before me. On the contrary, I have twinges, pressures, pains, nodules of tension, and so on, not in so many words, of course, and not by a reflective nonlinguistic comparison either, but as *sheer somatic experiences*. In effect, I hardly begin to wonder what these tubules, bones, sinews, and fibers have to do with me.

In evolutionary contexts, these observations take on all the more weight since in their daily lives, our hominid ancestors must have seen moving visual forms and hard and soft things on many occasions without connecting them: as hunters they would have seen them regularly; yet not *as such*, that is, not as outsides and insides. What was eaten, for example, was more than likely to have been a matter of edibility, not spatial relationship. Yet on some occasions, relative to their own flesh and blood kind, these hominids must also have seen moving visual forms and hard and soft things. At some time, then, the perception of hard and soft things must suddenly have been fraught with strangeness. This primordial experience of strangeness can be captured by a return to a bracketed world.

From a bracketed perspective, the moment I apprehend the two appearances of a visual Other to be appearances of the *same* spatio-temporal object, I am aware of an inside and outside as such. I am aware of the same visual form in two seemingly conflicting guises: one animated and affectively charged, the other inanimate and a pastiche of pulpy masses and rocklike solidities. The lack of connection appears strange, as strange as, or perhaps even stranger than the initial awareness of my own visual hand *qua* physical object. In the latter experience I can at least discover my felt hand and my visual hand to be connected in the singular experience of moving it and seeing it move. In the course of picking fruit, for example, or of watching my step, I have some sense of a felt–visual correspondence. In the experience of the other, however, there is no sense of a relationship at all, there is no perceived correspondence between the two realities; yet the two appearances are appearances of the same spatio-temporal object. Hence the stronger sense of strangeness. Here inside and outside are *queer*. There is something unaccountably peculiar in this juxtapositioning of inside and outside: they are strange bedfellows, so to speak, as strange as would be the juxtapositioning of my twinges and pressures with those tubules and bones, sinews and fibers. These awarenesses are not of course language-dependent—any more than are the awarenesses of a preverbal child who sees and understands that a round knob does not fit into the square opening in a chain of detachable beads with round and square knobs and holes. Unlike the chain of beads, however, no ultimate collateral matches are to be found between inside and outside, or between twinges and tubules: the other's inside and outside simply do not match in any coherent way, and my inside and the other's inside do not match in any coherent way either. The only things that match in a general way are our intact moving visual bodies with their ever-changing physiognomies: only outsides match.

Now when we remember that these thoughts are thoughts without words, that the experience is a sense of queerness, not its verbalization, then it is clear that I am caught up in the peculiarity of certain relationships—or far more precisely, certain nonrelationships. It is not a matter of explaining these nonrelationships, but only of sensing their queerness. When confronted with the natural death of the other—a phenomenon I of course do not yet know as such—the strangeness is heightened in the extreme and the complexity of the situation augmented. Here what I witness is a radical transfiguration of the moving visual form; its ever-changing physiognomies are gone; it is no longer gesturing, opening its mouth, squinting, running, or carrying things about. It is utterly still. The other that I knew is yet *another* other. Strangeness is compounded by change. However queer the earlier experiences, they were not radical and stark in the way this queerness is: this queerness is an utter change of being that is extraordinary. Commerce with *this* other is no longer possible. I cannot play with this other; I cannot be entreated, comforted, or threatened by it any longer. Its visual form is no longer the same.

Yet it *is* the same. Though unanimated and of an unchanging physiognomy—even as unmoving and unexpressive—the form I now perceive is distinctively but not wholly different from the moving visual form I not long ago perceived, wholly different, that is, in the way that the inside of another is different from the outside, or in the way that the inside of another is different from my inside. The two terms of this relationship—moving visual form and nonmoving visual form—are identical and not identical; the visual form is at the same time two forms and only one form. Described in this way, the experience is in fact conceptually similar to the experience of duality–unity that obtains in preliterate societies: a corpse is perceived to be both a single and dual object. It is a unitary phenomenon, but it is also dual insofar as it is adjoined at the same time and without felt contradiction whatsoever to its ghost. Here, of course, the phenomenon of death has been elaborated. A belief system for understanding and dealing with death is well beyond the originary experiences of strangeness and change. Yet the belief system clearly indicates, and in a most forceful way, the radical queerness attaching to the originary experience in its very attempt to explain it. In the originary experience, one is confronted by something that is all there, yet that is not all there: something is missing; and alternatively, something is missing, yet everything is all there. What the corpse/corpse–ghost concept does is to nullify the missing factor on the one hand and to attest to its missingness on the other. Extraordinary change is thus accommodated by having it both ways, so to speak.

Both the queerness of the Other and the transfiguration of the Other into yet Another describe stages in an awareness of fellow creatures apprehended simply as moving visual forms. Together with an awareness of one's own visual body *qua* physical object, these awarenesses can be seen to converge in the concept of death. Yet even with a burgeoning notion of the materiality of the visual body, even with the sensed queerness of insides and outsides of the Other, even with the Other's extraordinary transfiguration into Another, the concept of death is not yet attained. Only with the notion of *my* punctuated existence do the threads of the concept weave together; that is, the concept of death is ultimately rooted in a certain realization of *my* being. Death is "out there," but it is also in me. In a strongly Sartrean sense of Otherness, death is plaited in my very being; in a strongly Heideggerian sense, it is my own. What must be shown is how the materiality of the visual body, the queerness of insides and outsides, and the sense of extraordinary change come together, and in such a way that there is a realization that, like the Other, I too will change radically and become a merely visual body.

To approximate most closely to this realization, we must differentiate between the experience of natural and of accidental death and follow through its methodological implications. In the lives of the early hominids, accidental deaths would likely have been commonplace. Whatever the fatal maimings and disembowelments, however, and whatever the sense of no-moreness, a concept of death as inevitable, as mine, and as the lot of all living creatures would not have been thereby grasped. On the contrary, there might well have been a vague sense that "barring such a fate, I will go on 'forever.'" In other words, only with experiences of natural deaths might the concept of death have taken root. Only through such experiences might it have been realized that a certain nullifying fate was inevitable and mine. If this realization is put in the perspective of the Husserlian analytic of the constitution of Other Egos, a considerable clue is found as to how it might have come about, and this because prior to a realization of death, there must first have existed just such Others, that is, Others-than-I constituted and understood on the basis of "my own animate organism."[25] Without these Others—without an interanimate world, as noted earlier—there would have been no ground upon which the concept of death could have arisen. Indeed, short of granting an innate idea of death, a possibility that is absurd in logical as well as evolutionary/genetical terms, there would be no concept of death at all. Put in Husserlian terms, in the experience of another's natural death, there would have been a dissolution of the primal instituting of the other as animate organism similar to my own, and a consequent breakdown of the passively generated pairing of I and Other. The Other would no longer have the same sense for me as animate organism that it previously had; similarity would no longer be apparent as before; the associative pairing of I/Other and the mutual transfer of meanings carried by the pairing would be annulled by overwhelming difference. Clearly, the Other could no longer continue "to prove itself as actually an animate organism, solely in its changing but incessantly *harmonious* '*behavior*.'" Clearly, the Other would no longer be apperceived as an analogue of myself, an "intentional modification" of my own animate organism. Clearly, the mutual transfer of sense vouchsafed by pairing would be nullified "with the consciousness of 'different.'"[26] At the same time, however, and still holding to a Husserlian perspective, it is clear that with the experience of the Other-in-death, all intersubjective significance is hardly lost. Although it no longer has the same sense for me as animate organism, a residual sameness lingers in the appearance of the Other-in-death; our bonds are tenuous but they are not completely dissolved. I experience the Other as a muted and distant Thereness, a Thereness that is now unfulfilled and unfulfillable, not simply because of the mutedness and distance, but because there is no longer the familiar crossing over to "such as I should be if I were There."[27] What is to be understood, then, is precisely how a lingering sameness, or residual pairing, founds an experience of an apperception *manqué*, that is, an aborted or failed making co-present of something that is not actually given in perception.

THE EXPERIENCE OF THE OTHER-IN-DEATH

In the appearance of the Other-in-death, a no-moreness of similarity is set against a persistence of similarity. It is of course an initial sense of likeness that awakens both—the still resonating and the dilute similarity of self to Other. As Husserl points out, "It is clear from the very beginning that only a similarity connecting, within my primordial sphere, that body over there with my body can serve as the motivational basis for the 'analogizing' apprehension of that body as another animate organism."[28] In the Husserlian analytic, analogical apperception results in a grounding of the life processes of the Other in my own life processes, not as a reasoned-out correspondence, a one-by-one recounting to myself of our similarities, as it were, but through a passively generated synthesis reaching beyond what is actually perceived, an intentionality that itself is grounded in the beforehand givenness of my own ongoing subjective life. Husserl speaks of this beforehand givenness as the primally institutive original: it is this I myself who is "always livingly present"[29] and it is this I myself who thereby sees apperceptively in the Other a similar flow of living presences. The flow is made co-present with what is given perceptually of the Other and in a single act. The question, then, is, What happens to this pairing in the experience of the Other-in-death where similarity fades but is not wholly extinguished?

In Husserlian terms, death is a nonoriginary experience. It is appresentationally perceived in the form of Others who have changed radically and who are no more than merely visual bodies, that is, they are no longer moving visual forms of ever-changing physiognomies. A methodological point derives from this insight and it turns on the fact that death is always so perceived: the perception could not be otherwise and still be a perception of death. Thus a descriptive account of the experience in twentieth-century terms is not tied to a particular way of seeing the world. Whatever the evolution in conceptualization, that is, in whatever direction our hominid ancestors might have eventually been led to explain and to understand death, their concept of and beliefs about death would have had to have been grounded in nonoriginary experience. Let us, then, pursue the description in keeping with the Husserlian analytic.

What is apparent in death is a stillness, a radical behavioral change, a sleeplike demeanor from which the Other is unrouseable. What is present, in other words, is an Other I can no longer know, an Other whose being escapes me. In effect, this merely visual form, this impenetrable façade marks a cessation of community, a no-moreness of intersubjective life. As described earlier, I can no longer play with this Other, be entreated or threatened by this Other. But the no-moreness is double-edged: the Other's stillness is coincident with my stillness toward him; the Other's no-moreness of entreaty is as much mine as his. As Husserl points out, the transfer of meanings grounded in the passive generation of pairing is a *mutual* transfer. Not only this but "every successful understanding of what occurs in others has the effect of opening up new associations and new possibilities of understanding; and conversely, since every pairing association is reciprocal, every such understanding uncovers my own psychic life in its similarity and difference, and by bringing new features into prominence, makes it fruitful for new associations."[30]

Now the central problem is precisely one of understanding how a "successful understanding" of death was originally achieved. A "successful understanding of what occurs in others" in death was certainly not had by our early ancestors in straightaway fashion, much less simply in virtue of their being hominids. If substantial clues are to be found, they must be sought in an analysis of the close-up and not infrequent views of natural death our ancestors must have had. To describe such an experience through a bracketing of our own face-to-face view of death is to describe an awareness of utter separation. In this experience, the Other is closed off in his or her impenetrable solitary silence; but so also am I. In the suspension of a communal life, the other is alone; but so also am I. A reciprocality of meanings is singularly apparent in this utter separation. Let us begin by describing the former set of meanings first. What does the other's utter separation from me signify?

The cessation of community with the Other stirs an inchoate sense of ending amidst life, of an island of stillness in the midst of movement. On the other hand, in the aloneness of the Other from me there is a sudden end of sharing, an unexpected parting of ways. With the Other's solitary stillness there is no longer the possibility of a mutually created togetherness of projects in the world. In fact, a radical transformation marks the solitary and impenetrable appearance of the Other: in place of the Other I once knew is *Another*, a stranger with whom no community is possible. In my face to face meeting of the Other-in-death, I come up abruptly and continually against this *Another* whose presence I cannot fathom but whose presence separates me completely from the Other I once knew.

At the same time, there is a sense of former encounters with this now still and solitary Other; there are images of commonly lived moments. No matter the radical transfiguration, the Other remains Other. A particular past creeps in and with it a sense of ongoing consistency enduring through change. Throughout the variety of recollections and images, a persistent sameness anchors a once-communal life. An aura of continuity impresses itself upon the kaleidoscope of remembrances and images, however fleeting or vague. The temporal sweep of our communal life begins to solidify; the island of stillness in the midst of movement is tied to a commonly lived past.

A further dimension is present beyond these dual significations of a once-communal life, one that sustains and at the same time transcends the "common time form"[31] of our past. It is through this further dimension that Other and Another, past and present, recollections and ending, come together. In fact, only when the Other's present ceases to be strange—when the Other ceases to be Another or when endings are understood as continuous with the past—that awarenesses central to the concept of death arise. To grasp these awarenesses in an originary sense, we need to reenter the descriptive analytic.

In my face-to-face meeting of the Other-in-death, the awakened vestiges of the past give rise not only to an awareness of a communal life; they also gather together, as it were, and converge upon a single point: upon the unmoving visual body before me. Were it not for the impenetrability of that body these remembrances would enter into its stillness. Yet so much are these vestiges of the past vestiges of *that* body, they slip into its flesh; they fill out its form. I apperceive the Other as a density of being-in-the-past. The façadelike repose of the Other remains impenetrable but gives way to a growing temporal thickness. At this moment there is no longer an Other and an Another, recollections and ending, a past and a present. There is a continuity separable from, but enfolding our communal life. The very persistent sameness that called forth a past-and-now-ended communal life calls forth a temporal continuity that is not ours but that belongs wholly to the Other. The visual form that is the Other is apperceived as a change that exists in continuity with its own past. What appears in the aloneness of the Other is thus a heightened sense of individuality. No matter how still the figure, it has temporal girth; those vestiges of the past that have converged upon the Other and entered into its flesh have given it a historical density of its own. Thus, in the Other's utter separation from me I find ultimately not only a temporal continuity and ending of our communal life, but I also find an individual temporality that is ended.

THE EXPERIENCE OF THE OTHER-IN-DEATH AND
SELF-UNDERSTANDING

In the ongoing encounter with and understanding of the Other-in-death, new associations and new possibilities of understanding indeed open up: Other and Another, recollections and ending, past and present become joined; temporal solidifications point the way toward the realization of a common time form; a burgeoning awareness of an individual temporal continuity points the way toward a new composite understanding of change and sameness. How does this successful understanding of the Other reverberate within my own "psychic life"? If the notion of my own "temporality-toward-death" can arise only on the basis of an experience of the Other-in-death, not myself-in-death, then the concept of death is clearly born in a *reverse* analogical apperception: though I do not know in the least what it is like to be There in place of the Other, I know that it is ultimately and inevitably my fate to be There where the Other now is. How could this knowledge have come about? How could the Other's aloneness present me with such knowledge of myself, in particular when the Other is no longer "governing somatically" in a manner coincident with "my own organismal governing," [32] that is, when I no longer can effectively associate my actions and responses, my conduct and general style of being in the world with the Other who is now before me? How, in Husserl's terms, is my understanding of the Other-in-death a "reciprocal . . . understanding of my own psychic life in its similarity and difference"?

Precisely because the experience of death is never mine originally, and in turn, because the concept of death is rooted in a reverse analogical apperception, the apperception is an analogical apperception *manqué*. It is a matter, in other words, of my never quite achieving an apperception of myself in death, of my never successfully and completely making co-present something that is not actually there in any given perception of myself, something that in fact, invariably eludes my grasp. To uncover the structures of this analogical apperception *manqué*, let us begin with my failed analogical apperception of the Other.

Whatever the Other's processes might be—even if they are nothing, and indeed, precisely if they are nothing—I cannot fill them in. Whatever the degree of residual pairing, it is insufficient to ground a fulfilled intentionality. No change in point of view—no different stance taken and no new profile gained—suffices to modify the suddenly truncated meanings in any way. I do not and cannot know what the Other's stillness means beyond its literal meanings of being still: an end of what was both a communal and an individual temporal form.

An attempted imaginal projection of myself There, in place of the Other, bears out this unfulfilled and unfulfillable intentionality. In any strivings toward meaning through an imaginal projection of myself toward the Other's Thereness, my lived body follows me; that is, in the course of imagining my being there, I find my felt body creeping into the image. On the one hand, in a spectated image, what I first take to be "myself over there"—eyes closed, still, a visual body, a façade, an outside—turns out to be not necessarily me at all. "My" body over there could in fact be *Any Body:* the visual body over there is an amorphous form lacking the precision of detail that would definitively identify it as mine. So long as it is unanimated, a merely visual body, an aura of arbitrariness hangs over it. Any attempts to make it my body result in subtle intrusions of my somatic body. In delineating the closed eyes as mine, for example, I find my actual eyes crossing over the threshold from the real to the imaginary, thus animating the "merely" visual form. The problem of course is that I cannot imagine myself as a merely visual form, a form without movement, a form devoid of even the slightest motions of breath. I cannot imagine myself, *that body over there,* as not breathing, for example, without actually holding my breath, or at the least, causing actual confusion in my normally regular and usually unheeded breathing pattern. In short, I cannot imagine myself-in-death in spectator fashion. By itself, the imaginal body's identity is obscure; with enforced ownership, it is no longer a *merely* visual form.

On the other hand, neither can I imagine myself There in utter stillness from the inside. It is impossible to silence my living body completely, both in terms of movement and of feelings. Although I do not know that the Other is not feeling anything, there are no indications that anything is being felt at all, indications that would be harmonious with a past in which analogical apperceptions of feeling *were* present. The Thereness that is present now and that I aim at emulating imaginally is a queerness that eludes me completely: I am to be There, utterly still as the Other is, *but also* utterly emptied of movement and of feeling—a shell felt from the inside and at the same time not felt at all since the shell covers nothing in the way of a felt body. Such a Thereness is in fact, exactly as Husserl would describe it, a kind of mock creature: "Precisely if there is something discordant about its behavior," Husserl writes, "the organism becomes experienced as a pseudo-organism."[33] No matter how strong the concentrated aim, I cannot grasp myself imaginally as such a creature; I cannot fulfill such an image. Here my living body is not an intruder but an impediment. It blocks my every aim to be the Other's stillness imaginally by an assertion of its livingness, its assertion of movement and of felt presence.

The failed imaginal projections bring into striking focus the fact that the merely visual body of the Other and my own visual body no longer mirror each other in a fulfilled manner. Even though they remain structurally coincident, our visual bodies are no longer mutually paired or pairable as before. The basis of our former analogical pairing was precisely a *moving* visual form; visual form *tout court*—structural coincidence alone—is a necessary but by itself insufficient condition for our continuingly fulfilled associative pairing. This insight is borne out by Husserl's analysis of the verificatory procedures vital to ongoing paired association. "The first determinate content" that supports verification of the Other as *my* Other has to do with movement, with bodily modes of engaging the world: "Consistent confirmation," Husserl says, comes in "the understanding of the members [i.e., structural organs of the body] as hands groping or functioning in pushing, as feet functioning in walking, as eyes functioning in seeing, and so forth."[34] By themselves the Other's "members" are *not* the first determinate content. In effect, the fundamental stratum vital to a fulfilled pairing and to a mutual transfer of meaning is nowhere evident in my encounter with the Other-in-death. Where I fall short of the Other in my failed imaginal projections, so the Other falls short of me in its failed appearance as a moving visual form. Both failures are confirmations of our utter separation. Both failures are in fact mirror images of each other and as such are descriptive of the nature of the analogical apperception *manqué*, an apperception bereft of its formerly coincident analogical structure.

There is a still deeper significance to be uncovered in the unyielding differences I find now between myself and the Other. While the Other is dumb, as it were, to my concernful gaze and gesturings, there is no longer either, and reciprocally, a sense of care or concern from the Other *toward me*. The Other's muteness is an emphatic cessation of what I have experienced until now: continuous and consistent pairing *with me*. No longer do I find myself mirrored in the Other; no longer does the Other's regard look back toward me. In place of a mirror, there is a void. With the cessation of community, there is an end of the Other as analogue of myself. While there is no longer the familiar "such as I would be if I were There," there is now an awakening sense of the isolatedness of my Hereness, a Hereness that is stranded, and that no imaginal projections can repair or reconcile. This awakening sense of solitude that comes back to me from the Other deepens proportionally in the burgeoning sense of my own Hereness, my own individuality and temporality. My own flow of experiences stands out in relief against the stillness of the Other. *I too* have a continuity separable from but enfolding our communal past; *I too* am a persistent sameness across a manifold of change; *I too* am a present in continuity with a past. At the same time, however, I am wholly distinct from this Other. Unlike the present of the Other, my present is a felt and moving present. In this most discordant and irreconcilable of differences, this utter incompatibility of presences, I find the sense of my livingness heightened. In this experience I find myself not just a certain *livingness,* but embarked upon a *life:* I am not just this contrasting presence here and now but a continuing continuity of being; I am not only a moving present in continuity with a past, but this ongoing flow of feelings and movement. I not only have temporal girth but a certain temporal open-endedness. I am at the center of a distinct temporal flow that is wholly mine. This inchoate sense of a life, *my life,* is decisive. I am at the conceptual threshold of death.

That threshold is crossed in a moment of insight. The concept of death is born when the sense of *I too* and the sense of distinctive contrast are heightened in equal measure. With the sense of *I too* I ultimately grasp *my* punctuated existence; with the sense of distinctive contrast, I grasp the inevitability of my death. The concept of death is thus as grounded in my experience of utter likeness to the Other I once knew as it is in my experience of utter contrast to the Other here before me. The felt similarities and felt differences reverberate with the existential dissonance of life and death, of *my* life and *my* death. A radical new understanding is born. This temporal stretch of being that I am is not just animate: it is a life, my life. And this life which is mine and which I am—*this more than just animate being*—is not a never-ending expanse of being but a punctuated one. In this moment I realize that it is precisely my possibility to be There where the Other is now, but *in time.* It is in this moment that I grasp both my living temporality and my ultimate end.

In my encounter with the Other-in-death, pairing is faded; yet however mute and distant, it suffices to carry forward for me the double meanings of an analogical apperception *manqué:* my own livingness and my own death, my own moving and felt presence and my own ultimate end. It is thus not simply that the Other is unmoving, but that its stillness has created a vacuum in me; it is not simply that the Other is remote from me but that its separation has created a hollow in me. What comes back to me finally from the Other becomes a cleft in the very marrow of my being, an unlived and unlivable moment of my own history, a transfiguration of myself into a merely visual form I will never know.

AFTERWORD

The ascendancy of the visual body *qua* physical object—a body wholly distinct from the lived body—marks critical turning points in the history of hominid life. No matter how culturally engrained and appropriated the concept today, there was a time when flesh and blood hominid creatures came to conceive of death—as they came to conceive of caring for the injured, of counting, of tool-making—even of language. These originary conceptions are sedimented in our own awarenesses and thinking; indeed they are the bedrock of current beliefs and practices. Hence, if an exact and rigorous philosophical understanding is to be had of what it is to be human, then the importance of "historical disclosure"[35] in the Husserlian sense of making these originary concepts explicit and bringing them to self-evidence cannot be denied. In fact, the foregoing analysis strongly suggests that a Heideggerian metaphysics needs grounding, at least in this instance, in a Husserlian epistemology. As Dan Magurshak pointed out several years ago in relation to Heidegger's metaphysics of death, "Epistemological issues need resolution."[36] It would seem that if the metaphysics is to gain concrete resonance, recourse must be had to a genetic phenomenology in the inclusive sense of a paleoanthropological hermeneutics. The analysis strongly suggests too that were Sartre's account of death and the Other a literally fleshed out thematic, one in which an epistemological hermeneutics of the body figured as prominently as an existential ontology, striking points of coincidence would be found. "If the Other did not exist," Sartre says, but without concrete elaboration, "[death] could not be revealed to us, nor could it be constituted as the metamorphosis of our being into a destiny"; death, Sartre writes, "transforms us into the outside."[37] In sum, it would appear that short of a paleoanthropological hermeneutics, an understanding of such seemingly simple yet unique human concepts as that of death will always remain shrouded; and correlatively, that given a paleoanthropological hermeneutics, understood as an extension of, or complement to, a Husserlian genetic phenomenology, the deepest of deep structures, those having to do with evolutionary–existential origins, will come gradually to light.

NOTES

1. Maurice Merleau-Ponty, *Phenomenology of Perception*, trans. Colin Smith (London: Routledge & Kegan Paul, 1962), p. 431.

2. Jean-Paul Sartre, *Being and Nothingness*, trans. Hazel E. Barnes (New York: Philosophical Library, 1956), p. 305.

3. Calvin O. Schrag, "The Lived Body as a Phenomenological Datum," in *Sport and the Body: A Philosophical Symposium*, ed. Ellen W. Gerber and William J. Morgan (Philadelphia: Lea & Febiger, 1979), p. 156.

4. Herbert Plügge, "Man and His Body," in *The Philosophy of the Body*, ed. Stuart F. Spicker (Chicago: Quadrangle Books, 1970), p. 296.

5. Richard M. Zaner, *The Context of Self* (Athens: Ohio University Press, 1981). See particularly pp. 47–66.

6. Maxine Sheets-Johnstone, "Existential Fit and Evolutionary Continuities," *Synthèse* 66 (1986): 219–48. An abridged version of this paper was presented at the Merleau-Ponty Circle, Binghamton, New York, October 1982.

7. Zaner's *Context* suggests just such a domain of study, p. 55.

8. For a discussion of *Dasein* see Chapter 10, this book.

9. Jane van Lawick-Goodall, *In the Shadow of Man* (New York: Delta, 1971), pp. 214–17.

10. Ibid., pp. 218–24.

11. Ibid., p. 224.

12. Thomas Nagel, "What Is It Like to Be a Bat?" *Philosophical Review* 83 (1974): 441.

13. Max Scheler, *The Nature of Sympathy*, trans. P. Heath (New Haven: Yale University Press, 1954), p. 264, quoted in Zaner, *Context*, p. 210.

14. Ashley Montagu, *Touching: The Human Significance of the Skin* (New York: Columbia University Press, 1971), p. 37.

15. Adolph Portmann, *Animals as Social Beings*, trans. O. Coburn (London: Hutchinson, 1961), pp. 182–83.

16. Marjorie Grene, *The Understanding of Nature* (Dordrecht: D. Reidel, 1974), p. 272.

17. Claudia Jordan, "Object Manipulation and Tool-Use in Captive Pygmy Chimpanzees *(Pan paniscus)*," *Journal of Human Evolution* 11 (1982): 36; Jürgen Lethmate, "Tool-Using Skills of Organutans," ibid., p. 53.

18. Lucien Lévy-Bruhl, *How Natives Think*, trans. Lilian A. Clare (New York: Washington Square Press, 1966). It might also be pointed out that ac-

cording to accepted linguistic theory, a one–two counting system predated the decimal system, i.e., predated the use of the fingers to count. See Morris Swadesh, *The Origin and Diversification of Language* (Chicago: Aldine-Atherton, 1971). It is possible that the original binary system was tied to the evolution of hominid upright posture. The possibility was first examined by Maxine Sheets-Johnstone in a paper, "On the Origin of Counting: A Re-Thinking of Upright Posture," presented at the 65th annual meeting of the American Association for the Advancement of Science in San Francisco, June 1984. See this book, Chapter 3.

19. Milford H. Wolpoff, *Paleoanthropology* (New York: Knopf, 1980), p. 150. See also Frank E. Poirier, *Fossil Evidence*, 2nd ed. (St. Louis, Mo.: C. V. Mosby, 1977) on much later fossil remains (in the Shanidar cave in Iraq), which also show evidence that caring treatment by others was given.

20. Van Lawick-Goodall, *In the Shadow*, p. 221.

21. Ashley Montagu, "Toolmaking, Hunting, and the Origin of Language," *Origins and Evolution of Language and Speech, Annals of the New York Academy of Sciences* 280 (1976), p. 271.

22. Lévy-Bruhl, *How Natives Think*; see also his *The Notebooks on Primitive Mentality*, trans. P. Rivière (New York: Harper & Row, 1975).

23. The common experience of full-fledged physical objects in Western cultures today contrasts strikingly with the participatory mode of experience that dominates in preliterate societies and that has been described in detail by Lévy-Bruhl. See above, note 22.

24. Maxine Sheets-Johnstone, "What Was It Like to Be Lucy?" (Paper presented at the 58th annual meeting of the American Philosophical Association in Long Beach, California, March 1984).

25. Edmund Husserl, *Cartesian Meditations*, trans. Dorion Cairns (The Hague: Martinus Nijhoff, 1973). The phrase is found throughout the Fifth Meditation.

26. Ibid., pp. 114, 115, and 113 respectively.

27. Ibid., p. 119.

28. Ibid., p. 111.

29. Ibid., p. 112.

30. Ibid., pp. 113, 120.

31. Ibid., p. 128.

32. Ibid., pp. 119–20.

33. Ibid., p. 114.

34. Ibid., p. 119.

35. Edmund Husserl, "The Origin of Geometry," in *Husserl: Shorter Works*, ed. Peter McCormick and Frederick A. Elliston (Notre Dame, Ind.: University of Notre Dame, 1981), p. 265.

36. Dan Magurshak, "Heidegger and Edwards on *Sein-Zum-Tode*," *The Monist* 62/1 (1979): 116.

37. Sartre, *Being and Nothingness*, p. 545.

9

On the Origin and Significance of Paleolithic Cave Art

Urged on by my eagerness to see the many varied and strange forms shaped by artful nature, I wandered for some time among the shady rocks and finally came to the entrance of a great cavern. At first I stood before it dumbfounded, knowing nothing of such a thing; then I bent over with my left hand braced against my knee and my right shading my squinting, deep-searching eyes; again and again I bent over, peering here and there to discern something inside; but the all-embracing darkness revealed nothing.

Standing there, I was suddenly struck by two things, fear and longing: fear of the dark, ominous cavern; longing to see if inside there was something wonderful.

LEONARDO DA VINCI

The painter "takes his body with him," says Valery. Indeed we cannot imagine how a *mind* could paint.

MAURICE MERLEAU-PONTY

INTRODUCTION

Like the practice of stone tool-making that long preceded it, paleolithic cave drawing originated in a particular kind of tactile–kinesthetic activity, and one similarly giving rise to the creation of spatial forms. With cave drawing, however, the spatial forms entailed concepts tied to pictorial rather than sculptural space. In traditional discussions of cave art where functional or semantic interpretations dominate, little if any attention is given to these concepts. Instead, theories are advanced—and disputed—concerning the representation of animals and the practice of hunting-magic; figural representations in general are analyzed in the context of fertility rites, sexual symbolism, and "art for art's sake"; patterns designated "geometric signs" are deciphered and classified mainly as symbols of sexual gender, and to a lesser extent interpreted as traps and weapons used in hunting, as symbols of primitive shelters, or as notations of lunar phases and seasonal change.[1] Even analyses of the origin of "image making" say nothing of the bodily act of *making* but instead focus on *seeing*—on an "inaugural seeing as"—to explain the origin and development of paleolithic cave art.[2] The various theories and interpretations are frequently permeated with assumptions, some of them straightforwardly affirmed, but in the main most commonly buried in the theoretical superstructure of the particular analysis offered. Two absolutely critical and intimately related assumptions—one of them nowhere acknowledged—specifically need to be brought to light and examined: the earthly physical reality that fundamentally defines a cave, and the conceptual infrastructure requisite to the original practice of engraving and painting on cave walls. To take for granted either the experiential reality of caves or the experiential dimensions of the original acts of drawing on cave walls is to risk undermining the ultimate interpreted significance accorded paleolithic cave art. The experiential values together constitute the properly empirical as well as logical starting point of an examination of the origin and significance of paleolithic cave art. They necessarily ground all other values attributed to the art, whether statistical, semiotic, pragmatic, or aesthetic. Moreover only these experiential values have the explanatory scope and power to account for fundamental pictorial facts, facts identified by virtually all cave art researchers regardless of their orientation. This is because the facts are tied to tactile–kinesthetic values. They have to do with the act of drawing and with the empirical nature of the cave drawings themselves. In sum, a viable theory of the origin and significance of paleolithic cave art must begin at the beginning: first with caves as earthly physical entities, and then with the pictorial act of drawing on their walls.

CAVES: GETTING TO THE BOTTOM
OF "SOMETHING WONDERFUL"

What is taken for granted in the first instance lies under such considerable cultural overlay that it is not surprising that the knowledge assumed is nowhere acknowledged. Art historians, anthropologists, paleoanthropologists, and archaeologists consistently approach the *cave* aspect of paleolithic cave drawing as a *geological* given: they take for granted that to be in a cave is to be *inside*. Thus they take for granted a radically different earthly landscape with its radically different sensory and spatial qualities—the underfoot terrain, the silence, the natural formations, and so on. Moreover, they take for granted their ready-made—or readily accessible—knowledge as to how the particular speleological features they see and feel are formed, indeed, how caves themselves are formed and what kind of life—floral and faunal—to expect within them. In consequence, when they go into a cave to explore it and examine its artworks, in fact when anyone conversant with twentieth-century geology goes into any cave to explore or examine it, they are not surprised at the physical features—visual, audible, tactile—of a cave. In proceeding deeper and deeper inside they anticipate finding passages that are tight, that twist and turn, and that seem interminable; finding caverns that are expansive and areas that seem like "rooms"; finding stalagmites and stalactites; finding moisture, water drippage, water flows; and so on. In short, because they have a twentieth-century concept of *caves* prior to entering into any one cave, they find the experience of *being inside* neither remarkable in itself nor remarkable with respect to perceived features. Even associations such as feeling oneself to be inside the bowels of the earth, for example, are not remarkable but bear testimony to a certain logic of resemblance, what Langer would term a "logical congruity of form":[3] animal bowels also twist and turn, are seemingly endless, are moist, and so on.

Now undoubtedly paleolithic cave artists also took many things for granted on the basis of *their* accumulated knowledge, both direct through personal experience and indirect through cultural transmission. For instance, they likely assumed that they could go out the same way they went in; that the cave floor would support them as they descended deeper and deeper into the cave; that some paths through the cave would require bending; that the interior would be unremittingly dark; and so on. Such fulfilled expectations notwithstanding, *being inside* was here both remarkable in itself and with respect to experienced features and associations. Where no geology and in particular no earthwide or even partial geography inform accumulated knowledge, a cave is not necessarily one among many in nature's landscape nor is it entertained as a possible structure one might find in a given area. Where life proceeds literally on the surface of the earth, the inhabited terrain is a determinate expanse regularly illuminated by day and covered over by darkness at night. The terrain can be dug into —for grubs, termites, or tubers, for example—but it has no *insides* as such. In consequence, *being inside* is a thoroughly unique, even primal experience. To enter a cave—not simply for habitation purposes near the mouth, but to follow passages into darkness—is to penetrate into an extraordinarily different world. It is to feel one's way within an eerie interior; it is to be surrounded by queer forms, and enveloped by a space opaque to natural vision and everyday sound. This culturally uncluttered sense of *being inside* has conceptual affinities with descriptions given by Piaget and other child psychologists of young children's primary understandings of, and fascinations with, *insideness*.[4] The conceptual affinities are substantiated by studies of language acquisition in children as well as by studies of infant and childhood behavior. The former demonstrate the prepositional primacy of *in* as both locative state and locative act, the preposition *in* being the first spatial concept understood both perceptually as signifying certain spatial relationships and behaviorally as signifying certain spatial acts.[5] To show the conceptual affinities is to show how *in, inside,* and *insideness* generally, are first of all corporeal concepts and in fact invariant hominid ones, as far back as artifactual evidence and comparative primate studies document their existence. It is also actually to show how the body has been as much overlooked in studies pertaining to the development of concepts in infants and children as it has been overlooked in studies of ancestral hominid artifacts and ancestral hominid life in general.

Putting one thing inside another has an attraction for small children. Even in the absence of toys expressly geared to putting one thing inside another, like nests of boxes, children will regularly put keys inside dishes, for instance, and watchchains inside boxes.[6] Although psychologically explained in terms of learning the rule that "two objects can be in the same place provided one is inside the other,"[7] a child's natural penchant for putting one thing inside another is not thereby explained nor is its fascination with *in, inside,* or *being inside*. Indeed, the essence of the concept of "insideness" is neither acknowledged nor comprehended by the rule. Neither in studies of infant and child behavior nor in studies of children's linguistic acquisition of locatives is the primacy of "insideness" analyzed in an experiential sense. Interpretations of data in both kinds of studies stop well short of the body. It is because corporeal understandings are ignored that in comparing the two current and contrasting views of how a child acquires language—the "name priority" view and the "concept priority" view—psychologists can write that by the latter view, "the child's conceptual scheme . . . is due either to the operation of an innate 'concept program' which determines the series of emerging concepts, or to a more flexible processor which is responsive to the particular characteristics of our world."[8] In virtue of the computerlike image they evoke, the terms "concept program" and "flexible processor"—by present-day cybernetic and robotic standards at least—tacitly evoke a brain mechanism of one sort or another, a cerebral concept-maker so to speak, but clearly they have no actual biological empirical reality whatsoever.[9] Present-day studies of infant and child behavior might find more empirically justifiable paths of explanation (and certainly be less constrained and biased by a vainglorious cerebral pomp) if brains were invoked less and experiential bodies taken more seriously. In particular, the fact that at ages as early as one and a half years, children have a conceptual mastery of *in* as locative act is less plausibly explained by "programmers" and "processors" than by the fact that their experience of *in, inside, putting inside,* and *being inside* is (and has been) reiterated many times over every day of their lives in such acts as sucking, eating, defecating, urinating, being held in the arms of others, being put into a crib or other spatially enclosed structure, having a stomachache, grasping something in the hand, putting a foot into a shoe, an arm into a sleeve, a thumb into a mouth, and so on. Precisely because they are in many instances biological and not just cultural, such fundamental experienced varieties of *insideness* warrant extended comment and examination. They strongly suggest a pan-cultural, pan-*Homo* tactile–kinesthetic invariant concept of *insideness*.

To begin with, in birth an infant is propelled from an enclosed, dark space into a nonbounded, light space. That such a radical transition is not remembered in adulthood does not mean that it was not once experienced. Following its journey from an inside to an outside, an infant is commonly enclosed in a wrapping of some sort; and it is furthermore recurrently enclosed in the arms of those who nurse or feed it, soothe it, or otherwise minister to its needs. It is thus more often than not enveloped in something such that it is still *inside*. But there is a second equally significant sense of insideness. Not only is the infant still *inside*, but its own insides are awakened in radically new ways. In its first act of nursing, an infant takes a nipple into its mouth; its spontaneous actions cause something warm to flow forth—inside. Internal discomforts such as those caused by air or cramps are directly felt internal disturbances, ones that indeed generate crying or fussing. Insides are in effect felt as uncomfortable or comfortable, painful or warm and pleasurable. It is not that the disturbed or contented infant —newborn or older—has a full-blown concept of *insideness* as opposed to *outsideness*, but that its body is the source of growing spatial aware-nesses: concepts of *in*, *inside*, and *being inside* develop over time with reference to bodily happenings, bodily sensations, and bodily acts. In short, what is by one and a half years actively distinguished as *in* has been actively and passively nourished by a myriad of experiences of *in*.

When Piaget writes of a sixteen-month-old infant opening its mouth in conjunction with its attempt to open a matchbox,[10] he gives evidence of just such corporeally rooted spatial understandings and principles of action—of a developing tactile–kinesthetic spatial bodily logos. He does not interpret the evidence in this way because he does not recognize an experientially resonant thinking body in his theory of the development of human intelligence. The lingual act is interpreted as a *faute de mieux:* "Lacking the power to think in words or clear visual images, the infant uses, as 'signifier' or symbol, a simple motor indi-cation."[11] The problem is that the tactile–kinesthetic analogy between lingual gesture and manual gesture is far too powerful to be reduced to "a simple motor indication." The "indication," after all, could have been a *pursing* of lips, or a *protrusion* of tongue instead. In fact so long as the astuteness and precision of the analogy is ignored, the "simple motor indication" could as well have been a gesture with the leg or head. Moreover disclaiming the possibility of thinking in words and clear visual images on the one hand, but at the same time averring the use of a "'signifier' or symbol" on the other, suggests straight-away that a bias toward the lingual and the visual precludes outright affirmation of the obvious: nonlinguistic corporeal concepts.

But even earlier than sixteen months, evidence of a developing bodily logos is consistently apparent. In weeks and months follow-ing birth, an infant's mouth is a center of growing sensitivities and powers. Its tongue becomes an inside agent of the first order, its lips mediators between inside and outside (sometimes to the dismay of parents). More specifically, it is during this time that the infant discovers its tongue as maker of tactile apparencies. It brings features of worldly objects to life as it explores them lingually; it brings aspects of its own mouth to life and in the process discovers its tongue as a maker of sounds. What is of moment in these latter experiences is not "prespeech emanations" or "linguistic foreshadowings," but corporeal awarenesses and capabilities: through *inside* actions the world is ultimately articulated in speech just as through tactile–kinesthetic understandings of *insideness* the outside world is first explored and understood.

Other bodily acts come to bear out, extend, or reinforce a growing infant's lingual awarenesses of insideness. That bodies go inside clothes (however minimal) and food goes inside mouths are concepts fundamental to childhood experience. People even earlier than paleolithic cave artists are credited with wearing clothes—they "undoubtedly made clothing with pieces put together with lacing." [12] It should be noted that clothes are *on* only from the perspective of an observer who sees the body covered over; for the experiencing person, the body is felt *inside* whatever is worn. Thus while one might say "I have my hat on" or "Put your coat on," the actual experience is of being inside. When a child is told to put its arm *in* the sleeve, its foot *in* the shoe, or the spoon *in* its mouth, linguistic repetition simply bears out and reinforces the already experienced tactile–kinesthetic spatial similarity among such acts. Being *under* the covers is analogous to having clothes *on*. Here again, the primary experience is of *being inside*—enveloped or enclosed rather than a visual object in an ordered vertical stratification. That bodily experience and observer experience are not always coincident explains the extraordinary privileging of *in* over *on* and *under* in a child's acquisition of language. [13]

Certain spontaneous bodily happenings and acts coalesce conceptually to emphasize insides. Sounds come from insides; sneezes come from insides; so also do coughing and spitting; the breath comes from insides; excretory products come from insides; and so on. All such corporeal happenings and acts involve passage in the same direction: from inside to outside. Western psychoanalytic theory that explains a child's reluctance to use a toilet, especially for defecating, and to flush the toilet after use, focuses on possessiveness, but the possessiveness is clearly not a simple case of object ownership—feces being "an *additional* part of the body" (italics added) or a personal "donation" as Freud describes them. [14] What is "possessed" or "donated" are objects internally created—and created recurrently—by the body itself: they come from within. The corporeal concept of *insideness* is similarly over-looked in investigations and discussions of prehension, a bodily act integral to hominid evolution and ontogenetical development. Hands that learn to grasp succeed in holding something *inside* them. But what is additionally remarkable is that whether with or without an object, the act of opening and closing the hand—of prehending and letting go —regularly makes an inside come to life. A third-person focus on the acts as simple physical movements, *merely* opening and *merely* closing the hand, overlooks the creation and fascination of the insideness of the act. Indeed, judging from a young infant's rapt attention to the proceedings, there is good reason to think that the "object" that first visually disappears in an infant's play with "worldly objects" is the inside of its own hand, and in fact the hands of others as well.[15]

Given all the above-described corporeal experiences of insideness, it is no wonder that insides are fascinating and that *in* is the first locative state and act to be linguistically understood. There is already a literal body of knowledge subtending the linguistic understanding. In fact, the linguistic priority of *in* over *on* and *under* is not adequately explained by the invocation of "cognitive rules" at all. In the literature on linguistic development in children, the primary acquisition of *in* is explained in terms of learning the rule that "if *x* is a container, put *y* inside it."[16] The rule is identified as a "nonlinguistic strategy." Where the strategy comes from is a question never asked and thus nowhere investigated. Yet surely the "strategy" or "rule" is motivated: by knowledge gained from bodily experience, not just in the sense of *doing*, but in the sense of *being a body*. The cognitive rule from this perspective is in fact a rational extension from corporeal experience. Putting one thing inside another is how an infant has lived its active life from the beginning. There is thus a direct and powerful analogy between the behavioral rule and bodily life. It is of interest in this context to note that when given some of the cultural paraphernalia of Western humans, some chimpanzees apparently operate by the same powerful analogy. They have a propensity to put themselves or objects inside chalk circles,[17] and their ready use of cultural tools involving a concept of *in, inside,* and *being inside* is exemplary.[18]

It is imperative for a number of reasons—all of them equally critical—to take the concept and above analysis of insides seriously, and the fascination with insides as well in an attempt to understand the origin and significance of paleolithic cave art. First, as the analysis has shown, there is clearly a concrete *bodily*—and not merely a hypothesized "developmental intelligence"—connection between present-day human infants and children and paleolithic hominids. Second, caves are by definition a unique kind of insides. Third, an inherent human attraction to caves has in fact already been singled out as "justification" for paleolithic cave art. In a recent peer-reviewed article on the significance of paleolithic art the anthropologist-author declared, "I would not venture a reason that people are attracted by caves, but there is no doubt that they are, and that is perhaps sufficient, for clearly the attraction was the same in prehistoric times."[19] Rather than taking the fascination for granted (and its "sameness" in ancestral and modern hominids likewise), it is requisite as well as proper to question the physical reality of caves, and, without treating them as readily comprehended geological or geographical givens, analyze their essential character. If there *is* an attraction, especially one present in paleolithic times and enduring to the present, then clearly there are experiential grounds for it, and those grounds need to be investigated and clarified. But this is not the whole story. As peer criticism of the article suggests, a fascination with caves might be a necessary but not a sufficient condition for engraving and painting on their inner surfaces. "The suggestion that people simply like to explore does not explain why, having explored, they carried painting equipment into the caves or, alternatively, why they were carrying their equipment in the first place."[20] There is thus additional reason for pressing forward to a fuller understanding of the essential character of caves. Not only are *insides* attractive and explored, but it is *insides* that are engraved and painted upon. In other words, there is something in the original experienced character of caves that explains both their fascination *and* the impulsion to engrave and paint on their surfaces. A further experiential analysis of *insideness* will bring this deeper character to light.

Corporeal insides have extraordinary powers. They have the power to transform one thing into another. In fact they are the source of a diversity of powers: the voice transforms silence into sound; dreams transform the nothingness of sleep into images and chimerical events; teeth transform substances by breaking them into pieces and then pulverizing them; saliva transforms what is otherwise relatively dry into something juicier; bodily insides transform imbibed fluid into urine; phosphenes transform darkness or the lack of visual stimuli into patterns of light; bodily insides transform cold air into warm air; and so on. Some of these corporeal powers are directly controllable, others involuntary, others both. Yet even with immediately controllable powers a sense of the extraordinary can pervade as it most certainly does in the case of involuntary powers. This is in part because the source of the power is not readily explicable. It comes from *insides*, but is as mystifying as, say, feces—or the voice which, like dreams and phosphenes, arises from within and is "an airy nothing." That breath, articulatory gestures, and "throat activity" can combine to make a verbal language possible is a complex awareness much less readily apparent than that teeth, for example, combine to make chewing possible. The material reality of teeth is part of the everyday material world as voices, dreams, and phosphenes are not. Moreover the latter are not enduring ready-mades but veritable spontaneous creations of bodily insides. Where a sense of the extraordinary attaches to the transforming powers of insides—as in the production of dreams, phosphenes, excretory products, the voice, and a warm breath—insides are, or can appear to be, magical, not in the sense of sorcery or conjuring acts, but in the sense of being something beyond one's immediate ken and powers of understanding. It is just this character of insides that Leonardo da Vinci evoked when he anticipated the possibility of "something *wonderful*" inside "the great cavern" before him. It is just this character that both casts further light on paleolithic fascinations with caves and suggests why paleolithic hominids would have been motivated to paint on their walls. What would otherwise be part of the typical everyday world with its familiar flora and fauna is transformed simply by being *inside*. The form and power of things inside is precisely *extra*ordinary—whatever is there appears magical, awesome, dumbfounding. To engrave or paint on the inside surfaces of a cave is precisely to enter actively into the potential magic of insides. To draw on the inside walls of a cave is to be part of the potential transforming powers of insides.

Corporeal insides have a further experiential character. They can be experienced as transformable as well as transforming. Their transformability is qualitatively manifest—most obviously in everyday experienced changes in the felt character of the body. Eating transforms a feeling of emptiness or discomfort into a feeling of fullness and satisfaction, for instance; sexual consummation transforms the flush and urgency of sexual desire into the repose of sexual fulfillment. The change in feelings in each case has locative significance; it is felt *inside*. But the transformability of insides is not limited to changes in the felt character of the body. Bodily insides are also spatially mutable. As pointed out earlier, they can literally pass outside—in bleeding as well as excretory acts, for instance. The location of insides is thereby relative, that is, spatially transformable. The same is true of outsides: what is normally outside can be put inside—a thumb, for instance, or a penis, or an entire body inside a shelter. Whether passage is from inside to outside or outside to inside, bodily feelings are commonly implicated. What was before cold is now warm, for example, or what was before vulnerable is now safe. In effect, a given felt character can be metamorphosed into its experiential opposite through a personal act.[21]

The concept of the *transformability* of insides is implicit in paleolithic cave drawing. To draw on the walls of a cave was, after all, to change their perceived character. It was also to bring forms formerly found in the outside world inside and thereby transform *their* character. But transformability is at the heart of paleolithic cave art in a twofold sense. It not only describes the character of the cave walls and of the forms drawn thereon, but it also describes the powers of the artists themselves. Indeed, the act of drawing was an extraordinary discovery, a new-found power by which "a surface nothing" was transformed into something wonderful.

The conceptual stage is thus set for an understanding of that original act by which paleolithic cave art came to be. The transforming powers of insides together with their transformability explain the fascination of insides. Insides are fascinating because they are *wonderful*. They provoke awe and astonishment in equal measure; they are complex, unexpected, not readily or easily explainable or understandable phenomena. They can in all these senses appear quasi-magical. When the physical reality that defines a cave is put in the perspective of the multiple everyday bodily experiences of insides, there is indeed a constellation of reasons, all firmly anchored in the concrete evidence of corporeal life, to explain paleolithic hominids' entering into caves, and with tools and paint in hand. What is yet to be illuminated, however, is precisely that extraordinary act by which the walls of caves were originally transformed. In particular, the discovery of the power to transform a surface, and the wonder of pictorial line as concrete agent of aesthetic transformation, both need elucidation. A critical overview of current and past approaches to, and interpretations of, paleolithic cave art will provide the context for examining these fundamental discoveries and concepts. It will at the same time provide the context for a much-needed clarification of an *aesthetic* descriptive account of paleolithic cave art.

AN AESTHETIC OF PICTORIAL LINE
IN PALEOLITHIC CAVE ART

What figures centrally in virtually all descriptions, analyses, and discussions of paleolithic cave engravings and paintings (hereafter, "cave art"), and what is at the same time conceptually taken for granted, is pictorial line and pictorial depiction, the latter more commonly and presumptively termed "representation." What rivets the attention of cave art researchers is the semiotics, not the aesthetics, of line and "representation"; pinning down the meaning of the drawings to the point of being able to say what the drawings signified to the "signifiers" is ultimately the all-consuming concern. Even where there is a discussion and analysis of *form*, reputedly an aesthetic category, the concern is far from aesthetic. When André Leroi-Gourhan, for example, the eminent doyen of paleolithic cave art, considers the formal elements, he does so under the progressive headings of "the pure geometric" ("groups of lines constituting geometric figures unidentifiable because of an absence of oral or written context"); "the geometric figurative" ("geometric lines or areas whose grouping allows at least the relative identification of the subject," [e.g., "reindeer or ibex heads seen from the front and reduced to four 'brackets' of which two represent the horns and two the ears"]); "the synthetic figurative" ("the lines express the essentials of the form of the subject without representing the fine detail of the contours seen by the eye"); and finally, "the analytical figurative" ("characterised by research into visual reality, . . . the analytical figurative tends toward a total representation of the anatomically natural morphology").[22] As is evident, the concern is actually with *content*, that is, with a recognizable subject or figure in an object-specifiable sense. This concern, together with the concern for each drawing's degree of representational accuracy vis-à-vis "visual reality," effectively passes over an understanding and analysis of line itself. In effect, the purported formal categories are blind to an essential pictorial and biological truth: line is the key to pictorial art, but not a key paleolithic hominids had (or present-day hominids have) in hand at birth.

Semantic comparison puts this point in further perspective. In a too logocentric or too geometric—and too little aesthetic—approach to cave art, a linguistic/mathematical rather than pictorial semantics dominates. As suggested above, the former semantics is anchored in the notion of *standing for*. Let x stand for y, and p for q, for example, or *rabbit* for furry, small, pointed-ear creatures, and by paleolithic extension, this drawing of a horse for "maleness," this drawing of a bison for "femaleness," this drawing of an ox for hunting magic, a meaning being postulated in each case, and in each case always exceeding, that is, always analytically looking past or ignoring, the actual drawing —in the same way that the conventionalized meaning of a word exceeds its actual sound. Thus the view that "whether we call it hunting magic or something else, the fact is that the paintings and drawings on cave walls had a transcendental purpose";[23] or again, that "if one has photographs of animals, one can accurately assess what they are doing; but here we are dealing with drawings by artists with a message to convey."[24] In short, everything on the walls of the caves is treated as a representative counter that needs deciphering.

Representative counters are basic to a linguistic/mathematical semantics—as they are not basic to a pictorial semantics. It is for this reason that the term *depiction* is conceptually preferable to *representation* in assessments of paleolithic cave art. It is a straightaway graphic concept; it does not entail the notion of one-on-one counters or of one thing going proxy for another; and it has a narrower intentional compass: the emphasis is on the intentional act of making lines rather than on "the meaning" intended in drawing them. In a too logocentric or too geometric approach, line and representation are in fact both taken for granted as the underlying vehicle and *modus operandi* respectively of cave art, whereas the very idea of *drawing*, an idea combining an awareness of the power to make lines, and an awareness of the possibility of depicting something by lines or not depicting something by lines (including the possibility of merely scribbling), had first to arise as a possible project. In short, drawing had first to be *conceived*. Only with the discovery of this concept, the concept of line as tactile–kinesthetic act, can the origin of cave art be understood. Cave art originated in the discovery of the *wonder* of line, in the very real sense of discovering what lines could do.

G.-H. Luquet, a French professor of philosophy writing in the first half of this century and well known for his research both on children's art and paleolithic art,[25] is regularly acknowledged and with great esteem, in discussions and debates about the meaning of cave art. The acknowledgment centers mainly on present-day concerns with researcher classifications. Luquet is classified as an adherent both of an "art for art's sake" interpretation and of a magico-religious interpretation of paleolithic art insofar as a historical sequencing of the artifactual evidence led him to postulate a derivation of the latter from the former. Today the two interpretations are generally considered antithetical (as indeed, the hunting-magic interpretation is regularly considered antithetical to the art-for-art's-sake interpretation), there being commonly a single and absolute meaning postulated for all paleolithic cave art from the very beginning. Unfortunately, the essential core of Luquet's work is overlooked in a merely classificatory estimation of his thesis. His central concern—one that in fact anchored and solidified the whole of his theoretical analysis—was, Where did the idea of cave art come from? In his words, how did "a consciousness of the power to create images" arise?[26] Only by concretely specifying the historical source of paleolithic art could one accede to its meaning with any sense of rigor and precision. As he explicitly pointed out, "Determination of its origin would allow the rather vague and arbitrary speculations of aesthetic metaphysics to be founded on a more objective basis."[27] In brief, Luquet was aware that in order to grasp the significance of cave art it was necessary to catch it at its source. What he cogently and logically argued is that "the intentional execution of a figured work . . . supposes two conditions. . . . It is necessary on the one hand to have the desire to create, . . . on the other hand [to have] the idea of the performance itself, *the understanding of this act as simply possible*" (italics added).[28] In emphasizing the importance of both conditions, Luquet clearly emphasized the centrality of the sense of *I can* to the concrete acts of engraving and painting. In other words, it was in the discovery of corporeal possibilities that paleolithic hominids originally discovered their power to create pictorial forms.

Luquet did not elaborate on the conceptual significance of "the understanding of this act as simply possible," yet he clearly raised the seminal question and at the same time indirectly drove home a seminal point: to arrive at the possibility of cave art, it is not enough to "see" forms in nature, to project "representations" where there is only a certain "schema," to use art historian E. H. Gombrich's terms.[29] In order to arrive at what Luquet describes as the "consciousness of an ability to modify preexistent material by work,"[30] it is necessary to be *bodily* involved in the production of form. The indirectly made point is of critical moment because the opposite view is often given central status in present-day literature on the origin of cave art. There is no question but that in some instances certain natural, visually perceived conformations suggested aspects of animal form to paleolithic hominids,[31] but the idea that it was the sight of such conformations that gave rise to cave art is very much to be questioned. To this end, the deficiencies of *projection* as an explanation of the origin of paleolithic art, that is, the deficiencies of the "schema to representation" viewpoint, need to be exposed. At the same time Luquet's insistence on the discovery of "the power to create images" needs to be taken seriously; namely, as the context for a detailed analysis both of what in the most basic sense is there on the walls of the caves, and of what the fundamental significance is of what is there.

Clearly in the most empirical sense possible, what paleolithic cave artists were doing from the very beginning was *making lines*. Even earlier, in paleolithic mobiliary art (decorated objects), what was being made were lines. Any explanation of the origin or of the significance of cave art that fails to take this fundamental fact into account cannot succeed in explaining the origin or the significance of cave art. To say in the interest of ascertaining origins, for example, that the paleolithic discovery of an animal shape "somewhere in a rock," is analogous to the "South American Indians' " discovery of lobsters "in the stars"[32] is to make a false analogy on several counts. To begin with, a geometric one-dimensional continuous line imaginatively limned by the eyes against a remote "surface area" is confused with a concrete three-dimensional sculptural conformation appearing in relief on a three-dimensional solid, and in which outline is given by shape rather than pictorial line. The distinction between a geometric and aesthetic line aside for the moment, an experience in which figure is prominent is not the same as one in which volume is prominent. To see an animal shape on a rock face is primarily to see a contoured volume, not a line that defines a volume; to see lobsters in the sky, on the other hand, is primarily to see linear contours, not contoured volumes. Moreover it is to see contours in a quite sophisticated sense insofar as the lines that are drawn, are drawn not by the hand but by the eyes, a considerable pictorial abstraction. Finally, while projection may clearly lie at the origin of such astrological objects as lobsters, where it is a question of solids or of sheer surfaces rather than stars (or dots), the concept of line does not make either an easy or clear-cut visual appearance. Inkblot projections (which Gombrich actually uses as documentation for "the propensity of the mind to project")[33] quickly confirm this fact: what is filled in by interpretation is ordinarily controlled by a presenting physiognomy that depends primarily not on line but on general mass for its character. To give a more precise example, if it is true that "to the primitive, the tree trunk or rock which looks like an animal may become a kind of animal,"[34] it is not because of *line* but again, because of a certain presenting volume-centered physiognomy, that is, a particular shaped and textured bulk or mass. In sum, projection does nothing to supply the line that is precisely necessary to a conception of *drawing*. Merely seeing animal shapes "somewhere in a rock" gives nothing of the sense of the power to create pictorial images—a sense of pictorial *I can*'s relative to those shapes.

There is yet a further basic sense in which the analogy is false. The lines drawn by paleolithic cave artists were not geometric lines but pictorial ones. In effect, they were not one-dimensional idealized entities but two-dimensional actualized ones. A geometric line is in essence a visual artifact; a pictorial line is a manual one. The terminology in cave art literature is misleading in this respect. What are now commonly called *signs*[35] are nondepictive linear forms, that is, drawings that are not unambiguous pictures of readily recognized objects in the world but in essence simply shapes, sometimes with linear embellishments or "non-figurative lines" as Luquet terms them. The point is that they are not *geometric* forms as they are now regularly described and classified. To describe and classify them as such is to prejudge what is actually there on the walls of the caves; it is to inform the lines with a twentieth-century mathematical reading and to bypass an analysis of the lines as pictorial phenomena. To describe them as such can also bring questionable values to the artifactual record as when "pure geometric" lines of the Mousterian (pre-paleolithic) period are described as "straight lines or confused curves."[36] For someone seeing the lines from the point of view of a "pure geometry" of line, interwoven curves may indeed be judged confused. For someone trying out or playing with the linear possibilities of pictorial space, the lines may not be confused at all.

Rather than representations, and whether the latter are cast in the perspective of schema or not, what most aptly describes what is actually there on the walls of the caves is *linear forms*. A pictorial analysis of these forms properly focuses first on the fact that some of them are straight lines forming open figures—as when mere strokes are evident; others are straight lines forming closed figures—sometimes complex ones like compartmentalized quadrangles. The same is true of arced lines. Some are open, as where the dorsal curve of animals is depicted; others are closed, as in the drawings of complete animals. That some linear forms are relatively straight-edged and others curved, that some are open and some are closed, are fundamental pictorial facts about paleolithic cave art. Openness and enclosure are indeed particularly thematic of paleolithic engravings and paintings. The theme is of considerable significance in the context of Piaget's experimental research on the development of spatial concepts in children.[37] As noted in Chapter 2, the acts of drawing and of knot-tying figure prominently in this research. As Piaget remarks, and in fact emphasizes but without drawing any significance, the earliest pictorial distinction a child makes is between lines that enclose and lines that do not enclose: at the very first stage when models begin to be copied (ages 2.11 to 3.6), open shapes are regularly distinguished from closed ones. Of very young children—up to four years—Piaget writes that "it is obvious that the task of controlling the actual drawing of the shapes must, at this stage, devolve upon perceptual–motor and intuitive regulating mechanisms. . . . What types of figure are the main outcome of such mechanisms? . . . Open shapes like the cross are distinguished from closed shapes [like the circle] much more clearly than straight-sided angular shapes [like triangles] are distinguished from curved ones [like circles]."[38] Because Piaget's prime interest is in the latter distinction—as discussed in Chapter 2, he wants to chart the development of Euclidean spatial concepts and finds the concepts of a topological geometry merely primitive stepping stones to that end—"perceptual–motor and intuitive regulating mechanisms" are not pursued in any way or even minimally defined. If analyzed in the perspective of the previous experiential analysis of *insides,* they would not remain untethered or unidentified. Open and closed figures are the result not of vague and abstract "mechanisms" but of a concrete body of experience that conceptually determines the distinction, and impels the child to draw accordingly. The *geometric* notion of enclosure given by Piaget in both his experimental work with children's drawings and with their knot-tying is in fact patently wanting in corporeal recognition. The geometric notion is as far removed from the concept of enclosure generated by the spatiality of the body—the three-dimensional spatiality of animate form and the tactile–kinesthetic body—as the notion of seeing animal shapes in the textural conformations of a rock is from the concept of drawing. As Piaget himself states, ironically enough in terms of his investigation of *enclosure* via the tying of knots, "In three dimensions enclosure takes the form of the relation of 'insideness', as in the case of an object in a closed box."[39]

A separation of the pictorial from the geometric underscores again the fact that a bona fide aesthetics of cave art properly begins with an analysis of the lines themselves, a bona fide evolutionary aesthetics with the discovery of the wonder of line, that is, with the discovery of the concept of *drawing.* In this connection, one does not have to espouse the whole of R. G. Collingwood's aesthetic theory to recognize the correctness of his observations regarding "the forgotten truth" of painting, a truth rediscovered at the close of the nineteenth

century in the works of Cézanne and later in the critical writings of
the art critic–historian Bernard Berenson. As Collingwood put it, "Of
course Cézanne was right. Painting can never be a visual art. A man
paints with his hands, not with his eyes." [40] The forgotten truth is of
critical moment to an understanding of the origin and significance
of paleolithic art. If there are artifacts to be *seen* in a cave, it is because they have been *made*. Cave art is in this respect an extension
of ancestral stone tool-making: both were generated by manual concepts; both were the result of "handiwork" with an instrument; both
resulted in the creation of spatial forms. Whatever the *whatness* of a
particular linear form—whether an animal, an oval, or meandering
lines—it was tied to certain tactile–kinesthetic powers. What is to be
emphasized in this generation of new-found powers is that paleolithic
hominids found what they could do by doing, or having done. Indeed, it is in the context of doing and having done that projection
gains credibility as a factor in the evolution of paleolithic cave art.
Luquet indirectly stressed this point when he examined possible ways
in which paleolithic hominids might have originally discovered their
power to create images of animals. The power had to have been concretely manifest in some prior activity. Thus he reasons that "figured
art" did not derive from decorative art but from the interlaced scrabble
of lines drawn by paleolithic fingers on the clay walls of the various
caves. In this cacography of line, or "macaroni" as it is called, certain
animal parts were suggested: a muzzle, a tail, hindquarters, and so
on. From what in one instance Luquet aptly terms "a game of lines," [41]
paleolithic hominids discovered their power to create animal images,
to depict. The contemporary art historian Whitney Davis makes the
same point when he states *contra* Gombrich's thesis that "in my view,
it is useful to reverse the standard idealist claim [i.e., 'image-making
is just something the mind of *H. sapiens sapiens* is capable of doing'],
immediately simplifying it and rendering it psychologically and historically credible. Objects are not seen as marks; rather, *marks are seen
as objects*." [42] In short, the wonder of line *to envelop shape* was discovered
and conceptualized in the making of lines themselves.

   Its significance notwithstanding, the point raises a difficult question. As Luquet went on correctly to observe, "We are not at the end
of our pains, and the difficulty of solution still remains before us. If
digital lines may have brought about intentional figured drawings,
they themselves, nevertheless, remain to be explained." [43] In other
words, *the mere animation of a surface* as an intentional production must
also be accounted for. Yet here again, that is, even with the very ori-

gin of the discovery of pictorial line, Luquet insists many times over that paleolithic artists discovered what they could do in the course of already having done something. Whatever the lines he examines, notably handprints and finger streaks, Luquet in each case adduces their intentional production to the intentional repetition of an originally *un*intentional act: stumbling and making an accidental swipe at the wall with the hand; putting the hand on the wall and leaving an imprint. What is of moment in this account is not *what* the precise unintentional action was, but *that* it was. What is critical is a rational conceptual chronology.

Luquet clearly had the critical understandings necessary to solving the puzzle of the origin of paleolithic cave art, but he left them conceptually unelaborated. He put his analytical findings in the direct service of his previously proposed and argued theory that magical uses of art were preceded by "a disinterested activity": earlier engravings and paintings "had no object other than beauty"; they were "art for art's sake."[44] The present task, then, is to eschew theory for a continuing aesthetics of pictorial line. Before continuing with that analysis, a few clarifying remarks need insertion with respect to an *aesthetic* descriptive account of paleolithic art.

It should be obvious by now that the belief that aesthetic inquiry into paleolithic art is fruitless, that, as one paleolithic archaeologist stated, "simple aesthetics explains nothing and has no bearing on meaning,"[45] is patently false. "Simple aesthetics" thus far suggests quite the contrary, and on both counts. This is because simple aesthetics was what paleolithic cave art was all about to begin with: the wonder of line, and with it, the discovery of drawing. Moreover it should be obvious too that it is a misuse of aesthetics to equate what is identified as paleolithic "artistic representations [that] exist in their own right" with "a free play of signifiers,"[46] as if paleolithic pictorial art were a developing language, a half-baked one on the way back to the bakery. It is equally a misunderstanding of aesthetics to equate "art for art's sake" with meaninglessness.[47] Such conceptions, arrived at by a paleolithic art anthropologist, indicate again that confusion of a linguistic semantics with a pictorial one—or an outright substitution of the former for the latter—is a major obstacle in the way of the most perspicuous and least speculative account of the origin and significance of paleolithic art. Clearly what is consistently referred to in one way or another as the "meaning" of the drawings[48] is not reducible to a set of counters each of which is matched or matchable against some objective—or subjective—"signified" in the manner of a referential language capable of designating pots and pans or sad and happy facial expressions. At the same time neither does aesthetic creation —the creation of something with no informative or practical value— result in semiotic nonentities, especially ones envisioned as inspiring contemplation in their makers and spectators, and furthermore credited with awakening "conscious, reflective thought" further down the evolutionary road.[49] It is difficult if not impossible to conceive of *meaningless* entities having such powerful effects.

A further aesthetic point and one with methodological implications warrants clarification. That paleolithic hominids did not consider what they did to be *art* is of no moment in the present context. To insist on the necessity of *aesthetic* understandings is no more than to insist on the pictorial nature of what is actually there on the walls of the caves—linear forms—and on their pictorial analysis. In other words, it is not classifications of hominid activity that are of concern, it is origins. In particular, through the concrete evidence of the cave drawings themselves, there is the possibility of uncovering conceptual foundations, a possibility not similarly available to other arts—to music and dance, for example—since no such concrete evolutionary evidence is available for them. Given the pictorial nature of what is there on the walls of the caves, it is logical as well as aesthetically mandatory to take the creation of lines as primary. In this regard, statistical analyses of lines cannot replace aesthetic ones, nor can aesthetic understandings be derived from statistical ones. Various meanings of cave art can certainly be postulated on the basis of gathered statistics, but those meanings are necessarily parasitic on the aesthetic forms themselves. This necessary priority of an aesthetics of line is well exemplified in Leroi-Gourhan's acknowledgment of two sets of "signs" in paleolithic cave art: *"enclosed"* (his quotation marks) and *dots and strokes*. According to Leroi-Gourhan, "enclosed" and dot and stroke signs— a classification actually based on a purely spatial characterization of linear form—were found only "after an exploratory series of statistical tests."[50] But in fact these two most basic kinds of linear form are there to begin with for any eyes seeing the forms themselves—forms that, after all, are all that are empirically there and have been empirically there all along. They are not statistical constructs but aesthetic realities.

Finally, something on the order of a defense of aesthetic analysis is called for precisely in the context in which such an analysis was explicitly rejected by Leroi-Gourhan in his classic and impressively detailed book, *The Treasures of Prehistoric Art*. His reason for rejecting aesthetic analysis is best understood in the full context of his lead statement that "the systematic presentation of paleolithic works of art can be a tricky business,"[51] and of his ensuing methodological rationale, which proceeds as follows. First, a chronologically based presentation is not reliable because precise and consistent dating is extremely difficult, in the case of cave art virtually impossible: "direct dating . . . rests on extremely insecure foundations." Second, an analysis animal by animal, that is, by the representation of the horse, the bison, etc., does not do justice to possible interrelationships: "one runs the risk of forgetting to ask if the artist or artists have not chosen to group them together on the same wall." Third, a classificatory analysis by technique fails: "engraving, sculpture, and painting . . . though apparently justified in a book on art" would not be valid since "men of the Old Stone Age might not have made the same distinctions among techniques that we do." In light of the ostensible shortcomings of these three possible approaches, Leroi-Gourhan opts for a structural–semiotic approach: "In order not to force the finds into a preconceived pattern and at the same time to avoid repetition as far as possible, I made an effort to discover how the works were classified—unconsciously of course— by the men of the Old Stone Age themselves. Study of the meaning of the works and the purposes they served provided a guiding thread."[52]

The metaphysical not to say epistemological problem of reaching back into the unconscious thoughts of paleolithic hominids aside (and the puzzling question aside as well as to how it is possible to arrive at unconscious classifications with respect to meaning and purpose, but not with respect to distinctions in aesthetic technique), the problem of paleolithic meaning itself appears to go unrecognized. At one level it is clear that the meaning(s) of an artwork must be known before its meaning(s) can be studied, yet it is precisely the meanings of paleolithic artworks that are in perennial question and dispute. At quite another level it is clear that the perennial search for *meaning*—Were the art works tied to hunting magic, fertility rites, or totemism?— veers off the aesthetic mark; it exceeds the aesthetic facts of the matter. Precisely in dissociating an aesthetic semantics from a linguistic one, Susanne Langer was led to use the term *import* over *meaning*, *import* signifying significance "without conventional reference."[53] Just as with Collingwood, one does not have to espouse the whole of Langer's aesthetic theory to recognize the astuteness of her distinction. To say aesthetic forms have import is to say that they have a certain perceptual character or quality in virtue of their formal structure or dynamic character. Accordingly, if the import of a particular cave art drawing can be known, and known at all in a paleolithic sense, it is through attention to what in the most basic possible sense is actually there, that is, to what actually transpired aesthetically in terms of worked surface and what was actually created in the act of drawing. Precisely from an aesthetic perspective, whether Old Stone Age men (or women, or children) made "the same distinctions among techniques that we do" is immaterial. The techniques themselves and what they give—lines, dots, imprints, gouges, and so on—are known. Of such empirical matters there can be no doubt. A systematic presentation of the *meaning* of paleolithic art—parietal or mobiliary—that takes no account of such basic, intentionally created aspects of aesthetic form—while ironically enough categorizing the works themselves as *art*—is not starting from paleolithic scratch but from twentieth-century culturally inundated interpretations of scratch. What is critical then—and with respect to both parietal and mobiliary art—is an analysis that focuses on the aesthetic facts of the matter, in particular on the two main kinds of created form, sculptural and linear—art objects having either a predominantly three-dimensional or two-dimensional character in virtue of the manner of their creation, of the material being artistically transformed, and of the size and potential mobility of the surface worked on. In such an aesthetic analysis the key to understanding paleolithic art is not through the head, so to speak, especially the remote heads of paleolithic hominids, but through the hand. Pictorial line, a line that is *drawn*, is the quiddity of the majority of paleolithic artifacts.

With the above clarifications of an aesthetic descriptive analysis of paleolithic cave art, it is possible to turn to an aesthetics of pictorial line.

Susanne Langer has said that "the first effect of formal design is to animate a surface."[54] But the same is true of any line—formally decorative or not—on a blank surface. As with the first paleolithic cave drawings, where before there was nothing, there was now a linear form. Moreover with respect to these early drawings, not only was there something rather than nothing, but that something had unique spatial significance. In fact that lines first and foremost animated a surface was no more significant than that they created shapes. In other words, while lines drawn by paleolithic hominids—scribbles, successive strokes, ovals, quadrangles, lines depicting parts of animals or complete animals—radically transformed an inner surface of a cave simply by being drawn on it, the character of the lines drawn transformed the surface further by the delineation of shape, particularly through curved lines and enclosed figures. In effect, *lines were discov-*

ered to have formidable transforming powers. They brought an otherwise blank and unremarkable surface to life, and they had the potential of suggesting or defining a variety of enclosures, contained spaces depictive of animals and possibly of traps, shelters, or vulvas (as per various researchers' assessments), or not depictive at all, but in either case the potential of capturing *insides* as it were. The momentousness of this discovery cannot be overestimated. Several comparisons will show why it cannot.

What differentiates present-day children's drawings from paleolithic ones to begin with—leaving aside for the moment that children do not paint in caves—is that children are given pencils, crayons or paint, and paper. They have ready-made and readily available materials with which and on which to draw. Many Western or West-influenced children have furthermore lived amidst a plethora of visually impelling cultural objects such as picture books, comic strips, paintings, and the like. By comparison, paleolithic hominids not only lived a radically deprived cultural life, but with respect to actual drawing itself, they had literally to start from scratch. They had first to discover that lines could be made on a blank two-dimensional surface, and that tools as well as fingers could be used to make these lines. No ready-made models in the form of picture—or art—books existed. Presumably no model of pictorial linear form such as an alphabet yet existed either. For individuals unaccustomed to two-dimensional graphic design, and to the technological apparatus supporting such graphics, the discovery of pictorial line and of what it can do, is a startling one—even for a child. That by drawing a continuous line one can capture the likeness of an animal such as a dog or a horse, for example, can be a revelation. In particular, *that shape is created by pictorial line* and that pictorial lines *have the power to enclose*—that drawn lines can outline figures or objects found in the everyday world—is an extraordinary discovery, one conceptually akin to a very young child's discovery of, and fascination with, *insideness*. A continuous line that returns to its starting point not only can capture likenesses; *it necessarily captures insides*.

Another way of putting the momentousness of the discovery in perspective is to differentiate between imprinting and drawing. It is one thing to see a footprint, for example—a possibility both Luquet and the noted art historian Henri Breuil mention in discussing the possible source of the first intentional digital lines[55]—and quite another to realize that shape can be created by line. This distinction was not made by either Breuil or Luquet nor has it been made by other researchers on paleolithic cave art. It is a peculiar oversight in that handprints on cave walls are regularly distinguished as being either negative or positive. In the one instance, they are made by placing spread fingers and hand against the wall and drawing around them as in stenciling, in the other by spreading fingers and hand with pigment and then pressing them against the wall. That there is a creative difference between delineating fingers and hand by stenciling, and imprinting fingers and hand, is obvious. That there is a conceptual difference should also be obvious. A sense of enclosure is given directly in the former act, and only indirectly in the latter one. This is because although shape is given in both instances, it is given through line in *drawing*, through surface impression in *imprinting*. Thus while there is every reason to believe that paleolithic hominids were aware of, and used, footprints in the course of hunting—that they regularly tracked animals—animal imprints cannot explain the origin of paleolithic cave art; not only because they were not made by the hominids themselves and thus had no tactile–kinesthetic connection to the felt powers of the body, that is, they were unconnected to any *manual* concepts, but because they called forth a recognition of shape through surface impression rather than an awareness of shape through contour delineation.

Comparison of parietal with mobilary paleolithic art highlights the momentousness of the discovery of the transforming powers of pictorial line even further. The presenting surface of a cave wall is vast in comparison to the surface area of works of mobiliary art—stones and organic materials (horns and bones) that were artistically transformed by engraving, painting, or sculpting. The presenting surface of cave walls is furthermore relatively flat in contrast to the rounded character of horns and bones, and it remains characteristically flat after being artistically transformed. The flatness contrasts also with the indentational character of line in bas-reliefs. What is most like the flatness of cave walls is the presenting surface of engraved stones and bone discs, in other words, relatively flat objects that, like the cave walls, remain relatively flat even after being worked. Finally, cave walls are stationary. If their artistically worked surfaces were objects of use in any sense—if they had a sexual or magical mission, for example—they were of use only *in situ*.

The above comparisons seem obvious to the point of being trivial. Their significance lies in the way size, flatness, and location of worked surface influence and delimit the possibilities and effects of pictorial line. Where the effects of the differential in surface size and surface conformation is most striking is in the drawing of animals. Where the latter are depicted on hand-held objects, enclosed shape is not set off against a broad flat expanse. The bearing of depicted animals in mobiliary art is in consequence less impressive. Added to this lessened impact is the fact that while lines can enclose shape in any pictorial drawing, shape in mobiliary art is necessarily miniature. This is not to say that animals depicted in caves are all lifesize; they are not. It is simply to call attention to the fact that where surfaces are vast and surface conformation is flat, the bearing of depicted animals is enhanced. Whether small or large, enclosed figures—insides—stand out against flat, continuous surfaces. The impact or "aura of presence" of an animal drawn inside a cave thus comes not only from its being drawn *inside* but also from the fact that as an enclosed figure, it has an extraordinary physical setting from which it stands out to begin with, and that with few if any constraints placed on bodily proportions, it may also appear more lifelike.

The significance of the difference in location of worked surface has to do literally with where the surface is found prior to being drawn on. Horns, bone discs, stone slabs—all materials from which mobiliary art was fashioned—were found in the everyday external world; they were part of the landscape. Caves too are part of the landscape but only at the point where a minimal geography and geology of the earth begin to inform experience of them. They are more properly landscapes themselves, inside rather than outside ones. They are thus not part of common everyday external reality. As pointed out earlier, they are queer in this sense. For lines to be drawn in such a place methods of illumination were necessary, for example. In some instances, scaffolding was necessary in order to reach a surface. In contrast to the ease with which individuals could pick up items in an outdoor landscape and draw on them, individuals wishing to draw on cave walls had to make advance preparations—at least where more than fingers were used on soft surfaces. Even with finger-created "macaroni," however, pictorial lines in caves were out-of-the-ordinary, special creations. For instance, unlike the process of engraving lines on a stone or bone, engraving lines on the pristine surface of a cave wall was not a readily public event. Unless executed at the entrance of the cave or unless daylight extended some distance inside the cave, the drawing was hidden away and no one without access to an artificial light source could see it. Most importantly, the lines were made on a foreign landscape and became part of it, a landscape bearing little or no resemblance to the familiar, everyday external one. It is at this juncture particularly that aesthetic analysis sheds light on a critical difference between parietal and mobiliary art and at the same time conclusively highlights the momentousness of the discovery of pictorial line in cave drawings and what it could do.

Pictorial line transformed blank surfaces into animate ones in both parietal and mobiliary art, but in the former, its power was substantially augmented. Transformation carried with it the possibility of making the strange familiar, both by the replication of forms found in the everyday external world, and by the very act of drawing itself. Finger streaks or a handprint on a wall, for example, leave behind something at once both familiar and radically new. In addition to the visible hand (or fingers) and the felt hand, there is a third hand, detachable and detached from the body and left there on the wall. Something similar is true with the drawing of other linear forms. Animals drawn on cave walls resemble animals seen and touched in the everyday external world. Linear forms on the walls of caves could in general replicate forms or objects seen and touched in the familiar outside world—traps, shelters, arrows, flora, and even formal designs already made on mobiliary objects. By such acts of drawing and leaving behind, paleolithic hominids could appropriate the foreign landscape of a cave, not in the sense of possessing it (though such a conception might have been possible), but in the sense of extending the bounds of the everyday world. What was extraordinary, queer, and unfamiliar was animated by what was known. What was strange was thereby brought into the folds of the familiar. The act of drawing lines on a pristine surface in an alien, un-everyday-like landscape was in this sense a quasi-magical transformative act. To put the aesthetic insight in broader perspective, the drawing of lines on the walls of caves need not have been connected with hunting or fertility rites, nor have referred in any other ritualistic or symbolic way to specific behaviors in the everyday lifeworld in order to be experienced as magical. To be magical, the lines simply had to be made and *to be there*. *Being there* was in itself momentous. The wonder of line in cave art was thoroughly unique in this respect.

What might be designated existential import—as distinguished from referential meaning or symbolic import[56]—is neither foreign to, nor atypical of, twentieth-century Western life. It is akin to the significance Sir Edmund Hilary affirmed when he climbed Mount Everest, an act moreover that similarly extended the bounds of the everyday world and brought the extraordinary into the folds of the familiar. It is furthermore akin to the significance of many twentieth-century artworks—Merce Cunningham's *Sounddance*, Balanchine's ballet *Jewels*,

Jackson Pollock's drip paintings, and Artaud's dramas. It is equally akin to some non-Western interpretations of the body—those in Chinese medicine, for example, where the significance of functional readings is not tethered to the state of a particular material organ. To think that in cave art, pictorial line needs to mean *some-thing*, that over and above depiction (or nondepiction), it must *represent* or *refer* to a concrete entity or practice in the everyday world in order to have semiotic value, and that short of this referential connection it is without significance—it is "meaningless"—is to overlook precisely the fundamental and formidable aesthetic powers of pictorial line: to transform a surface, to delineate shape, and potentially to extend the bounds of the everyday world. It was in these fundamental aesthetic realities that the momentousness of the discovery of pictorial line was originally centered, and where the potential for magical import resided.

THE THINGS THEMSELVES

It is fitting now to turn to the particulars of cave art itself and demonstrate the justness of the preceding analyses of caves and of pictorial line. To begin with, it is consistently pointed out that little or no sense of movement is present in early cave drawings: the animals depicted are static figures.[57] Concentrated focus on the shape-giving power of line, rather than on, or with, the kinetic power of line explains why animals are not pictured in the act of doing something like walking or grazing but simply pictured. What fascinated paleolithic hominids was clearly the power to render spatial form—the shape of things. Innumerable other facts about cave art—all of them consistently acknowledged—are explained by this same fascination. Shape-through-pictorial-line has the scope and power to explain why much of what was originally drawn on the cave walls has the recognized characteristics it has; and further, why much of what is actually there on the walls of the cave is there at all, not in terms of *causes* but in terms of *reasons*, for what must finally be understood are not *facts*, but *motivations*. In what follows, evidence will be progressively adduced to show how and why the shape-giving power of line is the most fundamental common explanatory denominator for the origin and significance of paleolithic cave art.[58]

Exclusive focus on the shape-giving power of line explains the virtual lack of drawings of scenes from everyday life. Narrative depiction is radically limited, and each animal tends to be depicted separately rather than in a group. Moreover where juxtapositioning does occur, there is no attempt to scale size to a common standard nor to relate the animals as living entities to each other, whether as members of the same or different species. As one researcher pointed out, "A horse may have a tiny bison placed among its hooves, or as at the main hall at Lascaux, huge bulls, three meters in length, may dominate oxen and deer of moderate size with tiny ponies below."[59] The linear drawing of each animal is essentially an enclosure of a particular form. It captures a particular inside. The blank surface of the wall is in effect transformed by the sheer presence of shapes rather than by behavioral dramas of everyday life.

In further contrast to readily apparent aspects of the everyday world there is no suggestion of an environmental setting at all. A base line suggesting the ground, for example, is nowhere to be seen. Indeed an interesting aspect of the fascination with the shape-giving power of line concerns the fact that animals are not always presented in an upright position with respect to the cave floor but are drawn upside down or in a vertical alignment. The fact clearly calls into question the propriety of assessing paleolithic art in terms of visual accuracy, as if the latter were either a central aim or the proper arbiter of pictorial paleolithic art. The evaluation actually stems both from Luquet's original research on the development of verisimilitude in children's drawings and his use of classifications derived from that research to posit a historical sequence of development in paleolithic art, and from the earlier distinctions made by Max Verworn vis-à-vis verisimilitude in paleolithic art.[60] Whether paleolithic cave art arose with "visual realism" and developed into "intellectual realism," however, or whether the historical situation was the reverse, is not cogent to the aesthetic facts of the matter. Indeed, that the one view can be as readily espoused as the other would seem to indicate the irrelevance of verisimilitude to an understanding of the origin and significance of paleolithic cave art. The aesthetic facts of the matter give evidence simply of a concern with pictorial line and what it can do: transform a surface, envelop shape, and make the strange familiar.

The shape-giving power of line in particular also explains the fascination with the curvilinear dorsal line of animal bodies. All depicted large herbivores—horse, bison, oxen, and mammoth—have similarly shaped dorsal curves, the withers or hump of which is often given emphasis by additional, wider, and/or darker paint lines, or accentuated by deeper engraving. In fact, in Leroi-Gourhan's chronology, the drawing of all Style II animals (see note 57) is based upon the same cervico-dorsal line, a characteristic defining a particular species being added to the basic curvilinear form.[61] The dorsal line is furthermore frequently drawn by itself. Moreover its similarity to the dorsal line of hominid figures drawn in half-bent postures was pointed out by Luquet. Leroi-Gourhan, after acknowledging the probable correctness of Luquet's assessment, goes on to emphasize not only that "the same dorsal line plus a few details of horns, trunk, or mane, is sufficient to define a bison or mammoth or horse," but that "Paleolithic artists were so well aware of this that they engaged in plays on form, a sort of graphic punning."[62] To acknowledge the commonality of the linear form is clearly to affirm the shape-giving character of pictorial lines and the concept of same in the artists who drew them.

The fact that the sex of animals is unspecified despite their being otherwise completely drawn, and the fact that though rare, there are more drawings of female hominid genitals than male ones, are also tied to the fascination with the power of line, in particular, with the power to create insides on the one hand, and to create a symbol of insides or of entrances to insides on the other. With respect to the former, it is the bodily bulk of the animal that is captured: head and legs are in some instances strikingly out of proportion to a voluminous body; sometimes, in fact, an animal's head is missing. More compelling still is the fact that there are comparatively few if any bodily markings. Insides are pure insides. As Peter Ucko and Andrée Rosenfeld point out, "The bodies of animals were commonly left blank."[63] Clearly what is of moment is *the contour line defining an inside*. Nothing detracts from that inner form created by line. The result is that, irrespective of gender, a particular kind of animal takes shape. It is difficult to imagine that sex—Leroi-Gourhan's fundamental male/female opposition[64]—is at the origin of paleolithic art when in fact its phallic underpinnings are not in evidence—and in fact when animals in the act of copulating are not in evidence either. On the other hand, certain oval and triangular shapes with median or vertically bisecting lines running down the center (or from base to apex) could well be vulvas as Leroi-Gourhan and others urge. It is not necessary, however, to postulate a "female sign" typology oppositional to a "male sign" typology to explain the depiction of vulvas. It is possible to take the female genitalic outlines for what they are: vulvas give entrance to miraculous insides. From them issue both blood and tiny living beings. A vulval shape depicts a bodily opening from which emanates *extraordinary* substances and forms. Males are not the source of such extraordinary happenings; males have no such *insides*. The spatial theme of *insideness* has an affinity only with the female body. (That vulvas are also a source of pleasure is irrelevant since intercourse is not thematic in paleolithic art.)

The relative abundance of female over male genitalic depictions is readily explained by the fascination of insides as transforming and transformable—and with the wonder of *being inside* a cave to begin with. As for forms otherwise interpreted as derivative from female signs—notably, variously compartmentalized rectangles—they too are most simply and directly understood as the enclosures they are. That they may on this account depict animal traps is certainly possible: a trap catches something inside it. That "tectiforms" may also on this account depict shelters is likewise possible for the same reason: shelters contain people and things. What is to be reckoned with in an understanding of paleolithic cave art is in each case the character of the linear form itself.

Superimposing one drawing upon another such that little care or notice appears to be taken of what has already been drawn is regularly acknowledged as the least explicable aspect of the art: "The care taken in producing a lively, recognizable and elegant drawing does not extend . . . to preserving it intact in its finished state, for engravings and paintings are often superimposed. To twentieth-century eyes this is one of the most puzzling aspects of Palaeolithic art, that a drawing should be created with such care and then obscured or obliterated by another, particularly when the walls to right and left may be quite free of decoration, but it is a persistent characteristic of all aspects of this art." [65] Exclusive fascination both with the power of line to transform a surface, and with the shape-giving power of line, holds the most fitting key to the puzzle. Acknowledgment of the wonder of pictorial line makes unnecessary questions of whether superimposition was "stratigraphically" significant, that is, whether it may be used as the basis of a chronology of cave art [66] or whether it was compositionally intentional. There is no need to posit a system of "associated themes," for example, such as Leroi-Gourhan does in the name of "mythographic assemblages"—"a specific form of representation . . . which points to a mental step of the artist, a very important step which is that of the framing of figures in relation to available surfaces." [67] As the earlier quotation points out, wall-space surrounding superimposed drawings "may be quite free of decoration." Analogy to children's drawings is apt in this respect. In drawing, a child is often so caught up in the sheer act of creating lines that, whether in the rush or in the raptness of the moment's activity, it will often draw over what has already been drawn. That more paper is readily available or that free space exists on the present piece are equally immaterial. What has already been drawn is simply not treated as sacrosanct.

A further aspect of the analogy makes a further relevant point. To assume that adults created paleolithic art is as adultist as it is sexist to assume that men created it. When the possibility is considered that paleolithic art was executed by more than one individual, it is regularly assumed that the hypothetical individuals were adult males. Yet there is no empirical reason whatsoever to think that the group of individuals involved did not include children (or females), particularly since handprints in caves are consistently regarded as belonging to children—"In most cases the hands are too small to have belonged to men"[68]—since children regularly accompany adults, particularly their mothers, and since mothers as well as fathers could have gone as a family group into a cave to draw inside it. "Macaroni" lines that swirl around and through animal forms strengthen this possibility. Judging both from present-day Western children's delight in finger-painting and from the tendency of primate children to engage in the same activity as their caretaking elders—that is, their tendency to imitate, and in higher primates, to learn by imitating, especially from their parents—paleolithic children would have been fascinated by the activity of swirling fingers or a paint-laden brush on a soft surface such as to leave a scramble of lines on it irrespective of overlappings, as readily as they would conceivably have been fascinated by the discovery of the power of line to animate a surface and to envelop shape. In fact, insofar as the macaroni lines and animal forms are not infrequently superimposed one on the other, it is quite conceivable that they were the joint and simultaneous work of a family, the children busily engaged in the same occupation as their elders.

The lack of animal size-scaling mentioned earlier is correlatively suggestive. Smaller forms such as "a tiny bison placed among a horse's hooves," might well have been the creation of children. Supportive analogical evidence shows that children up to their teenage years who have had no graphic experience and little or no visual experience of pictures, but who live among animals—who indeed are dependent upon animals for survival—are not only capable of drawing them straight off, but draw them in apparent preference to drawing anything else.[69] Handprints, insofar as they are thought to be children's, are also correlatively suggestive of the role of children—and families— in superimpositioned drawings. Handprints are not found in all caves (there are approximately twenty caves in Spain, France, and Italy in which they are found) and are in some caves quite isolated drawings. In many instances, however, "hands are . . . often shown close to representations such as dots, animals, etc.,"[70] a fact that again strongly shows that paleolithic cave art could conceivably have been the work of family groupings, children working in close proximity to adults.

In sum, superimposing is the result of an exclusive fascination with line. What has the power to animate a surface, and where the surface is not only vast but in itself an extraordinary other-worldly phenomenon, the *making* of pictorial line is (or can be) more impressive and compelling that what is made in the sense of an enduring memorial of creation. In a word, process outstrips product; it is aesthetically cherished more highly. Viewed from this perspective, the wonder of pictorial line for paleolithic hominids was in what it left behind at the time of creation: an enchantment of the moment, akin possibly to the aesthetic appeal of *happenings*—and of chance aesthetic events generally—that were typical of art in the 1950s and 1960s, and that, interestingly enough, can be traced back once again to Cézanne. "Since Cézanne, it has become evident that, for the painter, what counts is no longer the painting but the process of creation."[71]

Ucko and Rosenfeld approximate to the idea that what was of moment was the sheer being-there of pictorial line when, in considering explanations for superimposing vis-à-vis the question of paleolithic hominids' respect for the "visual effects of their (and their forebears') artistic works," they suggest that "if superpositioning means that previous, but more or less contemporary, representations were disregarded then it seems plausible that in some cases the act of painting and engraving was more important than the final visual result."[72] Pictorial line, however, never surfaces in their account because of the way in which "the act of painting and engraving" is conceived. Rather than opposing "visual effect" with "the act of painting and engraving," as if it were necessary to *choose* between them, the two need to be conceptually conjoined just as they are experientially conjoined for the artist in the act of drawing. The tactile–kinesthetic act of drawing clearly has visual impact; a line drawn is *ipso facto* a line seen. Hence, to say that the process of drawing was more important than an enduring product does not necessitate estranging act and effect, or in broader perspective, making and thinking, the latter in the Cartesian sense of perceiving, judging, contemplating, and the like. It is to say that existential import is engendered in the very stuff of which the artwork is made. Ovals, for example, are *ovals*. They have pictorial significance as *enclosures, curved* enclosures. Import emanates from the sheer tactile–kinetic play of pictorial line and the figures and patterns it draws. To understand the artistry of paleolithic art *in paleolithic terms* is thus again not a matter of recognizing figures and patterns as representative contents, identifying and tallying them as representing a "such and such." Neither is it a matter of assaying them on the scale of visual accuracy, whether for the purpose of historical ordering or for purportedly "aesthetic" evaluation. It is a matter of seeing more primitively and deeply into the wonder of pictorial line itself. It is at this level of experience that the beginnings of art are to be found.

In the same section that they consider explanations of superpositioning and make the pointed dichotomy between "visual effect" and "the act of painting and engraving," Ucko and Rosenfeld also consider the question of the location of artworks. They note that "the technically most difficult works, the bas-relief sculptures, are almost exclusively found in daylight shelters with habitation debris but . . . they occasionally extend beyond the entrance shelter into the dark regions of the cave just as the various engraving and painting techniques do." In light of this latter placement, Ucko and Rosenfeld point out that "it cannot validly be argued, therefore, that the most difficult techniques could only be worked in daylight so that inside caves, where lighting had to be provided by oil/fat lamps or resinous torches, the artists had to restrict themselves to painting and engraving." [73]

Ucko and Rosenfeld's answer to the question of why drawings and not bas-reliefs proliferate deep inside caves (an art location they categorize as 3) begins as follows: "Before it can be accepted that category 3 representations are *only* Art for Art's Sake" (italics added), and it goes on to suggest that

much of category 3 art might have been placed inside caves in passages and niches just because these locations were difficult to reach. This would not, in itself, imply that the reasons for so doing were magical or mystical for the aim in some cases could have been to impress anyone who saw the artistic work by its very inaccessibility. . . . It is possible to imagine that once the "visitor" had been taken to a particular decorated wall in a cave the panel of superpositioning would impress; possibly as the visible expression of the energies of the particular group who "owned" or "used" the cave.[74]

The point is that when shape as defined by linear form is taken into account, in particular when the idea that pictorial line can capture insides is acknowledged as the key concept and reckoned with accordingly, a straightforwardly pictorial rather than circuitously functional explanation of the location of artworks becomes possible. That bas-reliefs are not frequently found in the interior of caves but that engravings and paintings are, has to do with the fact that line in the former instance is sculptural, not pictorial. Bas-reliefs do not give *insides*. Surface here is not flat: the works appear not *on* or *in* the surface but *out of* the surface with the result that *insides* are not captured by line. Bas-reliefs are three-dimensional works in which shape dominates line, that is, in which the created shape appears to define line rather than the reverse. Bas-reliefs are not then just more difficult technically. They are a different kind of artwork, which means that they entail working—and aesthetic—concepts different from drawing. For example, bas-reliefs readily emulate the everyday external world in their three-dimensionality. By comparison, to make a two-dimensional drawing on a relatively flat, that is, *two-dimensional* surface is extraordinary. Moreover to make it on a surface that, unlike flat stone slabs that could also be drawn on, was vast and part of an already extraordinary *inside*, verges on the magical. The wonder of line was, as shown earlier, not only to animate a surface and to envelop shape, but to capture three-dimensional forms from the external world on a two-dimensional surface—to make the strange familiar, or in reverse terms, to extend the bounds of the everyday world. In essence this is what written language does. It is likely in fact that the evolutionary origin of written language is rooted in the concepts of pictorial art.[75]

Given the above evidence of the explanatory scope and power of pictorial line, it is possible to clarify the aesthetics of line in the context of an art-for-art's-sake interpretation of paleolithic art. As conceived by most paleolithic researchers, "art for art's sake" precludes a grasp of hominid artistic beginnings because it opposes rather than conjoins act and effect (or making and thinking), and in consequence precludes a grasp of *pictorial line*—the very quiddity of the art in question. Being simply defined as "having no functional purpose," art for art's sake flits between two poles. On the one hand it is aligned with contemplation of the beautiful, that is, with "visual effect": "Paleolithic men were artists . . . because they appreciated beautiful things."[76] On the other hand, it is aligned with artistic expression, that is, with the act of drawing: it is identified with "the pleasure that the artist [takes] in creating images."[77] Unless the two strands are joined, the concrete aesthetic reality of pictorial line is not realized. While on the surface it might appear correct to say that the artist is not the viewer, and the spectator is not the maker of the work created, the surface turns out on closer inspection to be without foundation. "Paleolithic men [and women and children] were artists" because they drew on the walls of caves and in the process made aesthetic judgments about placement, shape, size, bodily features, designs, where to begin, where and when to end, and so on, all of which judgments were guided by the perception of lines in the process of drawing them, and all of which judgments were coincident with certain artistic acts.

In sum, the act of engraving and painting was not an empty-headed act, and neither, by the same token, was the act of aesthetic perception an empty-handed one—whether with respect to process or product. If paleolithic artists and their confreres cherished or came to cherish the finished works in an aesthetic sense, and if contemporary hominids do likewise, it is because *paleolithic artists and contemporary hominids necessarily saw and see back into the act of drawing itself.* It is there that first-order significances of paleolithic cave art are found. In effect, only by reaching back into what is actually there in an aesthetic sense is it possible to reach back to paleolithic understandings of paleolithic art. Talk of knowledge about the *beginnings of art* otherwise has no sense at all.

Twentieth-century eyes have a privileged overview of the beginnings of pictorial art. Unlike the paleolithic artists themselves who may or may not have known of cave drawings other than their own, and thus who may or may not have seen resemblances among drawings in different caves, twentieth-century eyes can survey the whole in one sweeping glance as it were and immediately grasp striking fundamental commonalities: animals are depicted, but in the beginning with little if any sense of movement, and with little sense of weight for that matter; narrative depiction is virtually nonexistent; the dorsal line of animals is a frequently drawn and emphasized line; few drawings specify the primary sexual characters of animals; vulvas are rare, phalluses even rarer; bodies are commonly left blank; superimposition is everywhere in evidence; bas-reliefs are rarely found deep within caves. In brief, all primary characteristics described in detail above are in general present in cave drawings throughout the Franco-Cantabrian area. The question is, What accounts for the similarity? What explains the fact that in a concentrated but still dispersed geographical area the same kind of drawings were made? The purported "obviousness" that many proposed explanations of paleolithic art invoke is not convincing because the *explanans* lacks a fully supportive and perdurable pictorial base. For example, at Lascaux, there is a drawing of a horse that has a partially compartmentalized open figure above it and some open and closed serrated forms below and to the side, forms that straight off resemble plant leaves but that have been interpreted as "barb signs." Thus the scholar writes, "The hunting-magic purpose of the picture is obvious: apart from the 'trap' emblem, the artists added flying arrows."[78] Another scholar leads into his purportedly obvious "mother" characterization of sculpted female figures by stating that

> the representation of the male figure plays a leading role only in cave paint- ing, where, as a hunter, he appears in his own sphere of action. The female figure, on the other hand, predominates in small sculpture, in her opposing role as the primary element in assuring the continuity of the species and of the group. The female image became a magical invocation of fertility, the race's *sine qua non* of survival. . . . The ample forms of the *Venus of Vestonice* and other female figurines which have survived intact unequivocally reveal that these were intended to be images of motherhood.[79]

What seems obvious in fact in such interpretations is a desire for hardtack meaning over what might likely be considered the tea-like flimsies and dainties of aesthetic import.

In conjunction with the above criticism, a final word should be said of Leroi-Gourhan's detailed analysis of paleolithic art since it has directly influenced—in part or whole—the thinking of so many researchers. Statements to the contrary, Leroi-Gourhan's analysis is actually rooted in pictorial values, that is, in his basic, putatively "sta- tistical" recognition of "dots and strokes" as different from "enclosed" signs. Because he does not pursue this basic *aesthetic* insight, his analy- sis veers away from a pictorial appreciation of the facts of the matter. Thus in his analysis of "signs," for example, he states that "it leaped to the eye that the ovals, triangles, and quadrangular signs were all more or less abstract variations on the vulvas which appear among the earliest works of prehistoric art."[80] As Ucko and Rosenfeld com- ment, "Unfortunately the situation is not really so simple; it cannot be assumed that just because triangles . . . appear to some modern eyes to resemble vulvas that they did also to Paleolithic man."[81] It is indeed a virtuoso jump from the ovals, triangles, and quadrangles to Leroi-Gourhan's key interpretation of paleolithic art: "Clearly, the core of the system rests upon the alternation, complementarity, or an- tagonism between male and female values, and one might think of a 'fertility cult.'"[82]

Leroi-Gourhan's quest for hardtack meaning appears to run away with itself rather than find a home in a solid and thoroughly support- ive body of evidence, one that properly begins with the momentous original act of drawing itself, hence with the discovery of pictorial line and its power to transform a surface. Only such an empirically demonstrable body of aesthetic evidence is capable of supporting the whole edifice of paleolithic art—including an explanation of *cave* art itself. Moreover only through such a body of evidence does the elucidation of each recognized characteristic of cave art remain tightly tethered to what is actually there on the walls of the caves. The interpretational significance of aesthetic analysis is in fact succinctly illustrated with respect to *signs*. To say that *signs* regularly appear with animals is already to say too much. *Signs* connote a complex semiotic system already in full operation whereas what is actually there on the walls are merely (1) depictions of certain animals and (2) certain linear patterns that are not representations of animals but that, like depictions of *complete* animals, are closed figures, and that, like depictions of *partial* animals (e.g., a stroke or a dorsal line), are open figures. Seen in this perspective, marks such as dots cannot properly be interpreted as "male signs" or reified as signs of anything else such as the proper path to follow through the cave, especially when, like a line that is drawn, dots in fact sometimes mark the contour of a horse or other animal, or simply festoon the area around an animal drawing or even the area around a certain declivity in the wall. At Chufin cave in the Spanish Cantabria, for example, "a hole in the rock, suggesting a vulva, is outlined with red paint and lines of dots."[83] As the painting strongly suggests, rather than being a *sign*, male or otherwise, dots can clearly function pictorially: to simulate line or to highlight. In conformity with one of the laws of dots in Japanese painting, "dots judiciously added [can] enliven and heighten the general effect."[84] More simply still, solely by being there, they can enliven a blank surface.

Whether a question of dots, open figures, or closed ones, the extraordinary similarity among drawings in different caves derives from concepts discovered in the act of drawing itself. Even in paleolithic times, painters "took their bodies with them." To reduce cave art to a system of abstract thought or to representations of hunting or other behavioral practices is to conceive the act of drawing as merely the act of *applying* system or practice to the walls of the caves. In such reductive explanatory schemes there is no concrete bridge from system or practice to the pictorial facts of the matter, thus no experiential understandings of motivation rooted in pictorial thought. Such reductive explanatory schemes furthermore leave a wider evolutionary context unconsulted. The omission is peculiar given not only the ready availability of evolutionary finds but their conceptual relevance to paleolithic *cave* art. The practice of burying dead individuals in caves is well documented in the Mousterian as well as the Upper Paleolithic, that is, in the period prior to, as well as contemporaneous with, cave drawing. This means that individuals living during these periods had a concept of death. The concept necessarily involves some basic rational understandings of insides and outsides, for with death, clearly something *inside* is gone. An outer form is there but it is unanimated. There is indeed a possible further connection. At La Ferrassie where it is generally agreed the earliest prehistoric artworks art are found— vulvas engraved on stone slabs—so also are found burial remains inside the cave. The spatial contiguity suggests a conceptual contiguity, a joining of the concepts of birth and death—of insides, and entrances to insides, with respect to both vulvas and caves.

Clearly, the *art* of the Paleolithic lies in the art of pictorial thinking; it owes its existence to concepts spawned by *le corps engagé*. Conceptually enlightened by this working body, it is not necessary to boost the intellectual character of paleolithic art by tying it to ostensibly "mental" operations. Physical "operations" do quite nicely when not erroneously categorized as unintelligent activity—"mere play" or "art for art's sake," as if these activities existed in a conceptual vacuum. At minimum, by penetrating insides and transforming their surfaces, our ancestors began exploring the mystery of enclosure, of contained space, of insideness, and brought the wonder of pictorial line, a wonder tied fundamentally not to a geometric eye but to a corporeal I, to an original prominence within the mainstream of hominid thinking and hominid evolution.

NOTES

1. See the following major sources: Count Begouen, "The Magic Origin of Prehistoric Art," *Antiquity* 3/9 (1929): 5–19; G.-H. Luquet, *The Art and Religion of Fossil Man* (New Haven: Yale University Press, 1930); Magin Berenguer, *Prehistoric Man and His Art* (Park Ridge; N.J.: Noyes Press, 1973); John Halverson, "Art for Art's Sake in the Paleolithic," *Current Anthropology* 28/1 (1987): 63–89; Alexander Marshack, *The Roots of Civilization* (New York: McGraw-Hill, 1972); Ann Sieveking, *The Cave Artists* (London: Thames and Hudson, 1979); Walter Torbrügge, *Prehistoric European Art* (New York: Harry N. Abrams, 1968); Henri Breuil and L. Berger-Kirchner, "Franco-Cantabrian Rock Art," in *The Art of the Stone Age* (New York: Crown, 1961), pp. 11–65; Andreas Lommel, *Prehistoric and Primitive Man* (New York: McGraw-Hill, 1966); Grahame Clark, *The Stone Age Hunters* (New York: McGraw-Hill, 1967); André Leroi-Gourhan, *The Dawn of European Art*, trans. Sara Champion (Cambridge: Cambridge Uni-

versity Press, 1982), and *Treasures of Prehistoric Art*, trans. Norbert Guterman (New York: Harry N. Abrams, 1967); *Larousse Encyclopedia of Prehistoric and Ancient Art*, ed. René Huyghe (New York: Prometheus Press, 1957); and for an overview of the literature and theories to circa 1967, Peter J. Ucko and Andrée Rosenfeld, *Paleolithic Cave Art* (New York: McGraw-Hill, 1967).

2. Whitney Davis, "The Origins of Image Making," *Current Anthropology* 27/3 (1986): 193–215. See also his "Replication and Depiction in Paleolithic Art," *Representations* 19 (Summer 1987): 111–47.

3. Susanne K. Langer, *Feeling and Form* (New York: Charles Scribner's Sons, 1953).

4. See, for example, T. G. R. Bower, *Development in Infancy* (San Francisco: W. H. Freeman, 1974); Jean Piaget and Barbel Inhelder, *The Child's Conception of Space*, trans. F. J. Langdon and J. L. Lunzer (New York: W. W. Norton, 1967); and Jean Piaget, *La construction du réel chez l'enfant* (Neuchatel: Delachaux et Niestlé, 1967), and *La naissance de l'intelligence chez l'enfant* 6th ed. (Neuchatel: Delachaux et Niestlé, 1968).

5. Eve V. Clark, "Building a Vocabulary: Words for Objects, Actions and Relations," in *Language Acquisition*, ed. Paul Fletcher and Michael Garman (Cambridge: Cambridge University Press, 1979), pp. 149–60; Nancy Cook, "In, On and Under Revisited Again," in *Papers and Reports on Child Language Development* 15 (Stanford, Calif.: Stanford University, 1978), pp. 38–45; Eve V. Clark, "Non-Linguistic Strategies and the Acquisition of Word Meanings," *Cognition* 2 (1973): 161–82; see also Robert Grieve, Robert Hoogenraad, and Diarmid Murray, "On the Young Child's Use of Lexis and Syntax in Understanding Locative Instructions," *Cognition* 5 (1977): 235–50.

6. Piaget, *La naissance*.

7. Bower, *Development in Infancy*.

8. J. Huttenlocher, P. Smiley, and H. Ratner, "What Do Word Meanings Reveal about Conceptual Development?" in *Concept Development and the Development of Word Meanings*, ed. Thomas B. Seiler and W. Wannenmacher (Berlin: Springer-Verlag, 1983), p. 211.

9. With respect to the psychologists' appeal to a concept-making brain, it is interesting that it took paleoanthropologists a good many years to call into question and finally invalidate their predilection for making the brain the fount of each progressive and radical change shaping human evolution, and instead to see *its* progressive and radical development as consequential to a revolutionary new body and revolutionary new behaviors such as consistent bipedality and stone tool-making, though of course the revolutionary new body and behaviors have not since been tied in any meaningful and consistent way to an experiencing body.

10. Piaget, *La naissance*, p. 294 (obs. 180).

11. Ibid. (my translation).

12. Milford H. Wolpoff, *Paleoanthropology* (New York: Knopf, 1980), p. 292.

13. Clark, "Building a Vocabulary" and "Non-Linguistic Strategies"; and Cook, "In, On and Under."

14. Sigmund Freud, *The Basic Writings of Sigmund Freud*, ed. A. A. Brill (New York: Modern Library, 1938), p. 589.

15. See Bower, *Development in Infancy*, p. 238: "Piaget's son was surely typical in finding the relation 'inside' fascinating. . . . One of my own daughters spent the best part of one night placing small objects in my hand, closing my hand on them, moving my hand to a new location, and then opening it up to see if the object were still there. This kept her happy and busy till nearly 4 a.m." That an inside can hold and carry something elsewhere is of course a discovery contingent upon the inside itself, i.e., the hand and its power to enclose (and hide).

16. Clark, "Non-Linguistic Strategies."

17. David Premack, "Symbols Inside and Outside of Language," in *The Role of Speech in Language*, ed. James F. Kavanaugh and James E. Cutting (Cambridge: MIT Press, 1975), pp. 45–61.

18. See, for example, E. Sue Savage-Rumbaugh, Duane M. Rumbaugh, and Sally Boysen, "Linguistically Mediated Tool Use and Exchange by Chimpanzees (*Pan troglodytes*)," *Behavioral and Brain Sciences* 4 (1978): 539–54.

19. Halverson, "Art for Art's Sake," p. 70.

20. David Lewis-Williams, "Comments," *Current Anthropology* 28 (1987): 79.

21. Insofar as such bodily transformations are experienced as oppositional—either *this*, or if I do *x*, then *this*—they presage a conceptual pairing. Experienced oppositionality can thus be seen to underscore the bodily provenience of the structuralist concept of binary opposition.

22. Leroi-Gourhan, *Dawn of European Art*, pp. 15–17.

23. Berenguer, *Prehistoric Man*, p. 75.

24. Paul G. Bahn, "Review of *La Contribution de la Zoologie et de L'Ethologie à L'Interpretation de L'Art des Peuples Chasseurs Préhistorique*," ed. H.-G. Bandi, W. Hunter, M.-R. Sauter, and B. Sitter, 3ᵉ *Colloque de la Societé Suisse des Sciences Humaines, 1979* (Fribourg: Editions Universitaires, 1984), p. 58.

25. Luquet, *Art and Religion*.

26. Ibid., p. 118.

27. Ibid., p. 114.

28. Ibid., p. 117.

29. E. H. Gombrich, *Art and Illusion*, 2nd ed., Bollingen Series (New York: Pantheon Books, 1961).

30. Luquet, *Art and Religion*, p. 119.

31. Ibid., p. 139, for example; see also, for example, Sieveking, *Cave Artists*, p. 49; Ucko and Rosenfeld, *Paleolithic Cave Art*, pp. 48–50; Torbrügge, *Prehistoric European Art*, p. 47; and Begouen, "Magic Origin," p. 8.

32. Gombrich, *Art and Illusion*, p. 108.

33. Ibid., p. 105.

34. Ibid.

35. See Leroi-Gourhan, *Treasures of Prehistoric Art*, pp. 136–44.

36. Leroi-Gourhan, *Dawn of European Art*, p. 15.

37. Piaget and Inhelder, *Child's Conception*.

38. Ibid., p. 65.

39. Ibid., p. 8.

40. R. G. Collingwood, *The Principles of Art* (New York: Oxford University Press, 1958), p. 144.

41. Luquet, *Art and Religion*, p. 127.

42. Davis, "The Origins of Image-Making," p. 199.

43. Luquet, *Art and Religion*, p. 127.

44. Ibid., pp. 148, 200, and 115, respectively.

45. Paul G. Bahn, "Comments" (on John Halverson's "Art for Art's Sake in the Paleolithic"), *Current Anthropology* 28 (1987): 72.

46. Halverson, "Art for Art's Sake," p. 69.

47. Ibid.

48. For a summary of the various interpretations of the meaning of paleolithic cave art, see Ucko and Rosenfeld, *Paleolithic Cave Art*, and Halverson, "Art for Art's Sake."

49. Halverson, "Art for Art's Sake," p. 71.

50. Leroi-Gourhan, *Treasures of Prehistoric Art*, p. 137.

51. Ibid., p. 54.

52. Ibid., pp. 191 and 54 respectively.

53. Langer, *Feeling and Form*.

54. Langer, *Mind*, p. 124.

55. Breuil and Berger-Kirchner, "Franco-Cantabrian Rock Art," p. 22; Luquet, *Art and Religion*, p. 128.

56. See Maxine Sheets-Johnstone, "Thinking in Movement," *Journal of Aesthetics and Art Criticism* 39 (1981): 399–407.

57. In Leroi-Gourhan's chronology, it is "between Style II and Style III . . . [that] movement begins to be expressed." Moreover when it is, "it is almost never by a general reshaping of the postures, but by a separate shifting of characteristic details, as in the stereotyped gaits of the Lascaux horses." In other words, movement in the beginning is for the most part limited to locomotor movement; the interior mass of the body captured by pictorial outline remains constant. *Treasures of Prehistoric Art*, p. 208. (Style II dates from the middle Gravettian to the middle Solutrean, 25,000 to 19,000 years B.C.; Style III dates from the late Solutrean and early Magdalanien—19,000 to 16,000 years B.C.)

58. Since there is agreement about virtually every characteristic to be discussed, a single rather than repetitive citation of sources is called for. See note 1. The following sources are in particular comprehensive: Leroi-Gourhan, Luquet, Halverson, Ucko and Rosenfeld, and Sieveking.

59. Sieveking, *Cave Artists*, p. 44.

60. G.-H. Luquet, *Les dessins d'un enfant* (Paris: Alcan, 1943), and *Le dessin enfantin* (Paris: Alcan, 1927); Max Verworn, *Zur psychologie der primitiven Kunst* (Jena: Fischer, 1908), and *Die Anfange der Kunst* (Jena: Fischer, 1909).

61. Leroi-Gourhan, *Treasures of Prehistoric Art*, p. 517.

62. Ibid., p. 122.

63. Ucko and Rosenfeld, *Paleolithic Cave Art*, p. 58.

64. Leroi-Gourhan, *Treasures of Prehistoric Art*.

65. Sieveking, *Cave Artists*, pp. 44–46.

66. See Henri Breuil, *Four Hundred Centuries of Cave Art* (Paris: Montignac, 1952).

67. Leroi-Gourhan, *Dawn of European Art*, pp. 23–24.

68. Leroi-Gourhan, *Treasures of Prehistoric Art*, p. 148.

69. Anna Schubert, "Drawings of Orotchen Children and Young People," *Journal of Genetic Psychology* 37 (1930): 232–44.

70. Ucko and Rosenfeld, *Paleolithic Cave Art*, p. 99.

71. Woks (a Russian artist), *Art News*, March 1959, p. 62.

72. Ucko and Rosenfeld, *Paleolithic Cave Art*, p. 172.

73. Ibid., p. 170.

74. Ibid., pp. 172, 173.

75. See Mary LeCron Foster, "The Birth and Life of Signs," in *The Life of Symbols*, ed. Mary LeCron Foster and Jayne Botscharow, forthcoming in 1990 from Westview Press.

76. Ucko and Rosenfeld, *Paleolithic Cave Art*, p. 165.

77. Luquet, *Art and Religion*, p. 113.

78. Lommel, *Prehistoric and Primitive Man*, p. 29.

79. Torbrügge, *Prehistoric European Art*, p. 15.

80. Leroi-Gourhan, *Treasures of Prehistoric Art*, p. 137.

81. Ucko and Rosenfeld, *Paleolithic Cave Art*, p. 215.

82. Leroi-Gourhan, *Treasures of Prehistoric Art*, p. 173.

83. Sieveking, *Cave Artists*, p. 153.

84. Henry P. Bowie, *On the Laws of Japanese Painting* (New York: Dover, 1951), p. 58.

Part III

Theoretical and
Methodological Issues

10

The Thesis and Its Opposition: Cultural Relativism

What, if anything, can the anthropologist be said to have come to understand about man? I take the question to call for some positive assertions about people. . . . What can be said now, not about differences but about prevailing resemblances?

ROBERT REDFIELD

WHY A FRESH APPROACH IS NEEDED

Ludwig Wittgenstein's question and sardonic remark on thinking quoted at the beginning of the first chapter underscores the fact that by current Western standards, thinking remains a more inaccessible mystery than either consciousness or intelligence, and this in spite of its immediate accessibility and ostensive prevalence throughout all human societies at the very least.[1] It is not surprising, then, that the origin and genealogy of thinking is not a prominent concern in philosophy or the human sciences, or that the relationship between the evolution of hominid thinking and hominid evolution has never been seriously examined. Yet in some respects the omission of these concerns from the academic register is peculiar. Descartes's sizable influence on Western conceptions of mind and body grew out of epistemological meditations that in part were originally formulated not in

277

terms of a mind, but in terms of thinking. But by thinking—*je pense, donc je suis*—Descartes meant a range of human capacities, perception and feeling among them. Thinking was in fact defined as conjoining consciousness and knowledge (*conscience et connaissance*). While the conceptual division between mind and body has endured as has philosophical interest in consciousness and knowledge, philosophical attention to thinking has not.

Claude Lévi-Strauss's primary preoccupation with classificatory systems serves as an equally striking example of the peculiar academic inattention to thinking. In focusing on basic conceptual categories in widely dispersed cultures, Lévi-Strauss was necessarily examining the structure of human thought, but his classificatory analyses are cast most often in abstract terms of a mind and its ways of representing the world, and not in concrete terms that spell out the nature of thinking itself. Matrix concepts such as numbers, direction, the cardinal points, odd/even, and in particular the concept of binary opposition that fundamentally governs structuralist classifications, are pregiven by the unconscious mind: "The mind contrives to introduce a principle of order and regularity"; "the unconscious . . . imposes structural laws upon inarticulated elements which originate elsewhere —[in] impulses, emotions, representations, and memories."[2] The origin of fundamental human concepts is in effect nowhere questioned. In the ultimate structuralist analysis the concepts presumably come ready-made with a human brain. Such a reductionism is implicit in Lévi-Strauss's writings, in his claim, for example, that "it is in the last resort immaterial whether in this book [*The Raw and The Cooked*] the thought processes of the South American Indians take shape through the medium of my thought, or whether mine take place through the medium of theirs."[3] In short, inquiry into the roots of human thinking is kept at bay by a theoretically invoked homogeneous human unconscious that churns out equally homogeneous fundamental human concepts. It is of course also kept at bay by Lévi-Strauss's insistence upon synchronic cultural studies to the exclusion of a concomitant evolutionary anthropology. The exclusion effectively counters investigation of the roots of hominid universals such as the use of tools or counting systems and thus effectively counters investigation of the origin of fundamental hominid concepts. The possible identification of pan-*Homo* invariants that would elucidate the provenience and nature of human thinking is in effect overridden as much by the resolute turn away from an evolutionary anthropology as by the invocation of an omnipresent conceptualizing unconscious.

What explains the mysterious aura of thinking? Clues lie not only in the influential Cartesian split between a thinking substance and a bodily substance—in more general terms, the separation of thinking and doing—but in the largely unspoken scientific split between corporeal experience and corporeal behavior—in finer terms, the scientific distinction between the unobserved/unobservable and the observed/observable, a distinction most frequently referred to by contrasting subjective with objective or what is private with what is public. With the division between corporeal experience and corporeal behavior, as between thinking and doing, it becomes understandable why thinking remains unclarified. By definition it is made inaccessible in a way that consciousness and intelligence are not. Consciousness can be evaluated in terms of a measurable corporeal on/off switch; intelligence can be graded along a scale (however controversial the scale). In brief, consciousness and intelligence can be defined in public terms and in turn investigated scientifically. Not so thinking. No material or behavioral residues and no theoretical constructs or models have been found that by consensus define thinking and put it on an equally measurable scientific map of the human. Indeed, contrary to Wittgenstein's suggestion, thinking *does* seem an event of astronomical proportions, precisely *immeasurable* astronomical proportions. Moreover while neither consciousness nor intelligence would seem possible *prima facie* in the absence of thinking, the majority of scientific assessments of consciousness and intelligence bring the astronomical no closer to inspection. They present no evidence of the thinking that might have spawned the concepts corresponding to a designated stone tool, for example, cave painting, or linguistic ability, or that might be associated with a designated cranial capacity, let alone with evidence as to the nature of thinking itself. A Piagetian might respond to the contrary, that human thinking has been shown via linkage with the development of intelligence to be rooted in action. But Piagetian theory does not support the linkage in the sense of giving the body its due. The conceptual correlates of tactile–kinesthetic activity—the *experiential* dimensions of observed behavior—are ignored. In Piagetian theory and experimental practice, mere tactile–kinesthetic experience lacks cognitive punch. Only through vision does perceptual space become conceptual space, for example.[4]

In sum, the split between corporeal experience and corporeal behavior is clearly as pernicious to an understanding of thinking as the split between thinking and doing. To unveil the mystery of thinking, a fresh approach is needed. The fresh approach taken in this book is one that attempts to crack the noetic code by tracing its evolutionary roots. By its very nature the approach is suspect—a foolhardy venture at minimum, a futile one at the extreme. This is because it affirms the possibility of uncovering a *history*. It affirms the possibility of "getting back."

THE OPPOSITION

THE QUINEAN SCENARIO

The notion of getting back to the conceptual origins of human thought goes against academically popular dogma. The now popular dogma was put in a particularly striking way by Otto Neurath, a philosopher of the logical positivist Vienna Circle in the 1930s, whose quest was to restructure everyday language to make it consonant with scientific knowledge, but who found in the end that it was impossible to do away with the object language of everyday life and get back to a pristine, neutral, sense-data language. He wrote: "No *tabula rasa* exists. We are like sailors who must rebuild their ship on the open sea, never able to dismantle it in dry-dock and to reconstruct it there out of the best materials."[5] The metaphor has been taken by cultural relativists as both a shibboleth and a caveat: we cannot assay the structure of our own culture in such a way either to uncover its basic foundations, or with an eye to reconstructing its basic tenets and premises. Being caught in the space/time warp in which our culture first ensnares us and progressively weaves ever more tightly about us, we lack the proper vantage point or foothold for either project.

Whether put metaphorically in terms of a raft or not, the relativist's dogma is prone to error in a doubly critical respect: it ignores evolution or trivializes it, in some instances extolling itself as a science at the same time; and it not infrequently stations itself exclusively on the pedestal of human language. Williard van Orman Quine, for example, an eminently regarded philosopher who regularly aligns himself with science, writes in support of Neurath's conclusion that "as scientists we accept provisionally our heritage from the dim past, with intermediate revisions by our more recent forebears; and then we continue to warp and revise. . . . We are in the position of a mariner who must rebuild his ship plank by plank while continuing to stay afloat on the open sea."[6] When he inquires about the *origin* of certain practices or beliefs in the provisionally accepted heritage—specifically the origin of language—he virtually dismisses the seriousness of the question with both an adaptationist wave of the hand and a giant Rubicon step:

What of the origins of all this ["language and lore"] in the race? It would be irrational to suppose that those origins were rational. The prehistory of science was probably a composite of primitive unconscious symbolism of the Freudian kind, confusions of sign and object, word magic, wishful thinking, and a lazy acquiescence in forms whose motivation had been long forgotten. Biases in our conceptual schemes may have great utility in the systematizing of science, and therewith high survival value, despite humble origins in the random workings of unreason—just as chance mutations in the chromosome may launch a sturdy and efficient new race. Natural selection through the ages tends to favor the happy accidents at the expense of the unpropitious ones, in the evolution of ideas as in the evolution of living species.[7]

This is indeed a queer scenario, and queer in a number of senses. It contradicts its own espousal of popular dogma by offering probabilities of "what it was like before language"; it proposes a faculty *de novo*, which by wide scientific consensus is *not* the way evolution works; it flies in the face of recent findings about primordial language; and it casts a Panglossian glow over the whole. Since the work of uncovering conceptual origins is ambushed from the start by such a scenario, it is worthwhile elaborating on the above four major points of rebuttal.

To begin with, it is obvious that if getting back to a preverbal or inchoately verbal world is impossible, then speculations about what that world was like are out of place, all the more so if those speculations are preceded by axiologically potent warnings about what could and could not have been. Furthermore, if it is claimed impossible to explain how language came to be, then it is not possible in good faith to offer an explanation of how it came to be. Thus language cannot be said to have originated in a process that, by extrapolation of natural selection theory to the domain of ideas, mirrors the workings of organic evolution. As a mechanistic principle, moreover, intellectual selection (as it might be designated) is an untenable principle. If "in the evolution of ideas as in the evolution of the living species," only propitious ideas tend to survive, surely people would not worry or indeed feel any cause for alarm about nuclear proliferation, nuclear accidents, or nuclear war, for instance, or feel at all apprehensive about the intellectual endowments of its leaders. Finally, conjectured probabilities on the order of confusion, primitive unconscious symbolism, wishful thinking, and lazy acquiescences, do not agree with facts that point rather dramatically to rational rather than irrational beginnings of "language and lore." For example, if the origin of language were really mired in irrational thought, then certain chronologies formulated on the basis of fossil evidence would be virtually inconceivable. A conservative estimate of the antiquity of tool-making places the inception of that obviously intelligent activity at two and a half million years ago, and of course tool-using is generally concurred to have taken place for perhaps millions of years before that.[8] A conservative estimate of the origin of language (based on certain anatomical relationships and measurements) places it one and one-half to two million years ago, its full development in terms of vocal abilities and verbal repertoires not being established until between three and four hundred thousand years ago.[9] In sum, quite apart from the connection often drawn by anthropologists between stone tool-making and language with respect to intellectual ability,[10] it is clear that the practice of tool-using and tool-making demanded precision rather than confusion, industrious hands-on thinking rather than wishful thinking, and creative exploration rather than a lazy acquiescence in habitual forms.

Second, there is wide scientific agreement that evolutionary characters do not arise *de novo:* there are no Caesars taking Rubicon-size steps in evolutionary history. To quote one well-known neuroanatomist: "What evolution brings about is increased refinement in the relationships between functions—'new' functions can be added only by changing the relationships between existing functions."[11] What this means, of course, is that words cannot suddenly be put in the mouths of waiting hominids to accommodate the preferred scenarios of twentieth-century philosophers any more than rationality can be catapulted onto the scene by a kind of twentieth-century Lamarckian *willing,* or *sentiment intérieur.*

Third, recent research into primordial language shows that it was structured on the basis of physiognomic likeness between articulatory gesture and referent, and in fact that utterances did not linguistically point to objects but to motional–relational complexes. Primordial language was "a representational system of classification by means of which states and movements in space [were] translated into spatiosonant, articulatory counterparts."[12] Such findings decisively refute the notion of an irrational origin.

Finally, the origin of language (and presumably all other fundamental and preeminently human practices and beliefs since in a Quinean world "conceptualization on any considerable scale is inseparable from language")[13] is presented simply as a happy ending. Where a Panglossian paradigm—first described by biologists Stephen Gould and Richard Lewontin[14]—reigns supreme, evolutionary origins are uniformly compressed into neat little pragmatic boxes labeled "adaptationally for the best," then laid to untroubled eternal rest. With the Panglossian burial of the origin of language, not only is evolution mocked, but language, like a ready-made Phoenix, is made to rise inexplicably from the seemingly trashiest and most unlikely of ashes.

There are other equally important formulations of the academically popular dogma that warrant detailed examination precisely to show that the theoretical obstacles they place in the way of getting back are in a robust biological sense biodegradable. Three principal formulations will be examined. Each will be put in the form of a counter to the claim that it is impossible to get back, and two of them will be discussed in terms of the work of a well-known adherent.

MERLEAU-PONTY'S SCENARIO OF AMBIGUITY

In the first instance, what prevents getting back is starting with the wrong body, that is, either a pathological body through which one attempts to identify what makes the normal body normal, or a generalized body with an emphatic bent toward the visual. These are essentially Maurice Merleau-Ponty's errors. In spite of a lavish attention to the body—lavish in contrast to the paucity of attention given it by other philosophers, and to its seemingly ignoble stature in the eyes of many—Merleau-Ponty is as blind to the richness and complexity of animate form as to the richness and complexity of everyday tactile–kinesthetic experience. When Hubert Dreyfus and Paul Rabinow, philosopher and anthropologist respectively, note in their joint commentary on his work that Merleau-Ponty failed to find the bodily invariants he sought, they suggest an examination of various other bodily phenomena that might have proved more promising and that "reading Merleau-Ponty one would never know [existed:] that the body has a front and a back and can only cope with what is in front of it, that bodies can move forward more easily than backwards, that there is normally a right/left symmetry, and so on."[15] This seminal insight notwithstanding, Dreyfus and Rabinow do not actually pinpoint the essential problem, viz., the path back to corporeal invariants (and thus to the origin of fundamental hominid concepts) lies not by way of a pathological or visually oriented body but precisely by way of that spatially articulate animate form they single out as more promising. A pathological body is an exception to the evolutionary rule; it is not typical of the species and in this sense exists outside evolutionary history. A visually oriented body on the other hand lacks immediate corporeal resonance. Unlike tactility and movement, vision is not a double sense, turning back always as much on the body as toward the world. In fact, being always at a corporeal remove from *both* the immediacy of the world and of the globally felt body, it cannot support a rich and complex gnostic system (*gnostic* from original *gnosis* meaning *knowledge*) that would serve as a fundamental standard for thinking. Indeed, Merleau-Ponty conceives his predominantly visual body to be ultimately a *functional* rather than gnostic system of meanings. A critical look at his existential reinterpretation of George Stratton's experiments with inverted vision[16] will document and clarify these various points in detail.

What Merleau-Ponty attempts to show through his reinterpretation is that ordinary spatial concepts such as top and bottom are actually ambiguous rather than normative dimensions. They shift according to the spatial situation—in his more favored phrase, according to the spatial *level*—in which we humans happen to find ourselves. In particular, top and bottom are not "made variable with the apparent direction of head and feet," that is, they are not "marked out in the sensory field by the actual distribution of sensations."[17] Thus they do not anchor our spatial experience but are merely part of the field of our experience. In consequence, the explanation of inverted visual experiences by reference to a top and a bottom fails because head and feet have no direction: they are "contents," as Merleau-Ponty calls them, without orientation.[18]

What Merleau-Ponty overlooks in this critique is that there is an intact, resonant body between head and feet, a globally felt presence in which per the experimental *visual* situation, a rush of pressure should be felt in the head—and it is not; and in which feet should feel no pressure spreading out uniformly against a solid surface— and they do. In other words, references to the experienced *weight* of the body—what Herbert Plügge in more strikingly experiential terms calls the *heft* of the body[19]—are nowhere to be found, an omission of considerable importance given that normal body positioning is experienced most readily by the experimental subjects when they are active. In short, normal experiences of top and bottom are rooted in felt experiences of the whole body, not just portions of it as head and feet. In broader terms, spatial concepts have localized corporeal meanings only by reference to the felt dimensions of animate form and the tactile–kinesthetic body as a whole.

There is a second criticism to be made against Merleau-Ponty's disavowal of a primary directionality. While it is true that subjects in Stratton's experiments may be said to situate themselves in a new spatial level as Merleau-Ponty says they do, he is incorrect in asserting that their adjustment to a new level means an absence of *fundamental* uprightness, an absence of a normal vertical with a sensed priority of top and bottom. When, in defense of his thesis that there is no primordial human orientation, he declares "faces are not often presented in a strictly vertical position, the 'upright' face enjoys no statistical preponderance,"[20] he stretches beyond limit his thesis of spatial levels without any primary foundation. A body may rise to the inverted occasion, but, like a momentarily tilted face, it loses nothing of its primordial form and upright orientation in the process. Moreover, unless Merleau-Ponty claims that a blind person has no concept of top and bottom at all, he cannot deny that experimental subjects, after all, have only to close their eyes to test out and affirm their fundamental verticality. Amplification of this latter point in the finer terms of Merleau-Ponty's thesis will make clear why what Merleau-Ponty calls "hidden acquisitions" fail in their mission to explain how there can be a bottomless space, and why their methodological consequence is ultimately to reduce his thesis to a series of purportedly logical, but in reality groundless, pirouettes.

The central quest in Merleau-Ponty's words is "to catch space at its source." He declares that "we cannot catch it in the ordinary run of living, because it is then hidden under its own acquisitions. We must examine some exceptional case in which it disintegrates and re-forms before our eyes."[21] Thus it is that he embarks on his reinterpretation of Stratton's experiment (see note 16 for a brief description of Stratton's own interpretation of his experiment). But thus too he indicates that space is essentially *visual;* and further, that understandings if not truths about spatial concepts can only be had indirectly, that is, by taking away, or creating deficiencies in normal visual perception. The generalized body with a visual bent is thus transformed into an essentially pathological body. The methodology is patterned after the technique used to map brain function. Where deficits occur, there lies the explanation for both peculiar and normal behavior. The unjustified privileging of the visual aside for the moment, readings of the normal from the pathological assume a great deal. Radical distortions do not always subtract something from the normal and, through ensuing behavior, thereby give clues to what normal intact functioning might be. Radical distortions can *add* something, something totally aberrant, and thus confound causal reasoning from the pathological to the normal. Walle Nauta and Michael Feirtag, for instance, writing on "The Organization of the Brain," point out that destruction of the subthalamic nucleus "leads to the motor dysfunction known as hemiballism, in which the patient uncontrollably makes motions that resemble the throwing of a ball." They ask, "Is the normal function of the intact subthalamic nucleus therefore the suppression of motions resembling the throwing of a ball?" and they answer, "Of course not; the condition represents only the action of a central nervous system unbalanced by the absence of a subthalamic nucleus." [22]

So with the body in its situation of inverted vision. Its experiences and consequent actions are the experiences and consequent actions of a body unbalanced by the absence of those normal experiences that are the visual correlates of its fundamental animate uprightness, a vertical directionality subtended by tactile–kinesthetic feelings of weight, heft, and solidity, and generating a certain orientation toward the world. In other words, what "disintegrates and re-forms before our eyes" is not "space at its source" but quite literally the passing visual scene. In the process of adapting to that scene, the hominid body loses nothing of its primary verticality—any more than its self-ministrations before a twentieth-century mirror efface its primordial left/right sidedness. It is in fact telling of its fundamental verticality that an experimental tactile–kinesthetic inversion analogous to retinal inversion, or even to mirror reversal, cannot be carried out. Unlike the visual body, in the most basic spatial sense, animate form cannot be made pathological and the tactile–kinesthetic body cannot be fooled. That the latter body is felt temporarily in an abnormal position during the second day in Stratton's week-long experiment does not mean —as Merleau-Ponty insists—that "as a mass of tactile, labyrinthine and kinaesthetic data, the body has no more definite orientation than the other contents of experience," for thereafter, in Merleau-Ponty's own words, "the body progressively rights itself, and finally seems to occupy a normal position." [23] In short, the body affirms what is fundamental to it.

Space at its source is not then a preeminently *visual* space nor even a space marked out by combined visual/tactile–kinesthetic co-ordinations, as Merleau-Ponty would have us believe. *Space at its source is a corporeal space defined by the intrinsic spatiality of animate form and the inherent spatial possibilities of the tactile–kinesthetic body.* (It might be added that space at its source is just so defined for all animate creatures: it is always corporeal and on that account always species-specific.) Moreover just as evolutionary history inherently demonstrates by the very process of speciation and as the capacity for successful adaptation directly shows—in the hominid shift to consistent bipedality, for example—the spatial priority of animate form and of the tactile–kinesthetic body is a *fundamental,* not absolute, priority. Merleau-Ponty is right in denying an absolute, altogether inflexible, spatial priority; but he errs in trying to show that its absence sentences us to conceptual ambiguities and hidden acquisitions "which cannot in principle ever be reached and thematized in our express perception."[24]

His error is compounded when, in a theoretical contradiction akin to that of Quine, he proceeds in fact to describe the primordial level of hidden acquisitions. The description has an unmistakable evolutionary ring to it, a ring Merleau-Ponty does not acknowledge because to affirm a scrutable historical foundation would clearly efface the line he regularly draws between humans and nonhumans. It would necessitate recognizing a *nonhuman* but still hominid ancestry. In effect, Merleau-Ponty first states that the principle that denies access to the first spatial level is a consequence of the nature of the primordial level itself. Being the origin of all levels, it can neither be specified as "a *certain* world, a *certain* spectacle,"[25] nor can it be disengaged from a previous level and analyzed. Merleau-Ponty is thus faced with the problem of initial spatial encounters with the world. His solution is to assert a sequence of logical "musts":

[Since the first level] cannot be orientated "in itself," my first perception and my first hold upon the world *must* appear to me as action in accordance with an earlier agreement reached between x and the world in general, my history *must* be the continuation of a prehistory and *must* utilize the latter's acquired results. My personal existence *must* be the resumption of a prepersonal tradition. There is, *therefore,* another subject beneath me, for whom a world exists before I am here, and who marks out my place in it. This captive or natural spirit is my body, not that momentary body which is the instrument of my personal choices and which fastens upon this or that world, but the system of anonymous "functions" which draw every particular focus into a general project. Nor does this blind adherence to the world . . . occur only at the beginning of my life. It endows every subsequent perception . . . with its meaning, and it is resumed at every instant. Space and perception generally represent . . . a communication with the world more ancient than thought. That is why they . . . are impenetrable to reflection (italics added).[26]

What Merleau-Ponty conjures into being in his sequence of logical musts is a corporeal history outside evolutionary time. Conceptual acquisitions will indeed remain hidden in such circumstances. A history that leaves no tangible traces behind cannot possibly be analyzed. What the free-floating logical musts and spatial levels reduce to are "anonymous functions" as far removed from the living tactile–kinesthetic body as cognitive maps. Thinking cannot possibly take root on such hypothetical entities or functions. They engender no gnostic system of meanings on which thinking could pattern itself. But logical musts fall by the wayside when a hominid evolutionary history —of tool-using/tool-making, cave painting, burial rituals, counting, and language—is acknowledged. Indeed, it is clear from that history that our hominid ancestors bequeathed to us *a corporeal legacy that is not more ancient than thought but coincident with it.* The methodological route back to those foundational structures of thinking lies not in an analysis of what is seen, pathologically or otherwise, but in what is felt—felt affectively, no doubt too, but in the most fundamental epistemological sense, what is felt by the tactile–kinesthetic body. Logical musts, like scenarios of the irrational, both of them contradictions in principle of the thesis they espouse, fall by the wayside when those animate structures are allowed into the light.

HEIDEGGER'S METAPHYSICAL SCENARIO

What prevents getting back is also starting with no body at all: leaving it behind or unattended. This is essentially Heidegger's error. Though the body is always implicated in Being (that is, in *Dasein:* quite roughly, "the Being who understands"), it never keeps pace with the uncovering of *Dasein's* existential structures and is never given concrete ontological attention in its own right. With respect to *Dasein,* the body is left stranded on a metaphysical reef, the corollary of the epistemological one Sartre describes in considering possible ways of accounting for the Other, a body that, in living terms, is never transparent in the way one's own body is for oneself. Although differently expressed, Heidegger's ontology in fact subserves the traditional dual Cartesian metaphysics of a mind and a body, and this in spite of references to everyday bodily acts such as hammering in which the theoretical and practical are interpreted as intertwined, and in spite of a vocabulary impressively oriented toward tactile–kinesthetic experience—for instance, "throwness," "de-severance," "falling." Even in a discussion of spatiality, of right and left, for example, Heidegger distinguishes between what originally belongs to *Dasein* and what to "bodily nature." Oddly enough, it is from the directionality of *Dasein*, not bodily nature, that "the fixed directions of right and left [arise]." Moreover although Heidegger mentions that "*Dasein's* spatialization in its 'bodily nature' is likewise marked out in accordance with these directions," he immediately advises the reader parenthetically that "this 'bodily nature' hides a whole problematic of its own, though we shall not treat it here."[27] The problematic is in fact not treated elsewhere either. In brief, the inferred intricate threads that bind bodily nature and Dasein are peculiarly—and surprisingly—left unexamined.

The consequence of leaving the body behind is unexplained concepts, that is, concepts that are simply taken for granted with no thought as to how they might have originated. For example, while Heidegger in so many words declares that we turn this way and that, toward and away from things in our environment, before we have a concept of right and left, he ignores the fact that turning toward and away are *bodily* acts, and most often tactilely as well as kinetically oriented, that is, toward contact or avoidance of contact with something. Turning toward and away are not acts of a pure spirit or Being. Short of a body, there is no turning—of anything—to begin with. In effect, the *concept* of directionality, like the *concepts* of right and left, are corporeally spawned concepts. To affirm, on the contrary, that these spatial concepts are spawned by "the Being who understands" not only perpetuates the errors of a partial and in consequence biased metaphysics, it also creates conceptual problems in the very real sense of assuming concepts to arise *sui generis*, Dasein miraculously and out of the blue presumably "secreting thoughts as the liver secretes bile."[28] In spite of its absurdity, this is in essence what Heidegger implicitly proposes. Neither everyday objects in the world nor Dasein have an epistemological, not to mention evolutionary, history. As to everyday objects, Heidegger tells us that "whenever something is interpreted as something [e.g., a car, a house, a hammer, a chair], the interpretation will be founded essentially upon fore-having, fore-sight, and fore-conception," these fore-structures of perception being absolutely opaque to analysis. As to Dasein, he tells us that "*The 'essence' of Dasein lies in its existence."* [29] There is no narrative of events describing the genesis of this existence. An analytic of *Dasein* is a question of purely ahistorical Being.

The possibility of getting back is thus not only intrinsically doomed by a dual metaphysics of which one-half remains unexamined; it is more particularly ruled out by ontological concerns. The roots of human thinking cannot be discovered through strictly ontological analyses. Conceptual origins can be exposed only by way of epistemological investigations. By their very nature, the latter enterprises are open to a conceptual history; through them it is possible to delve backward in time. Ontological investigations can only deal with what is (or is not). How certain concepts and attendant practices and beliefs originated is a question that does not properly arise. In consequence, the origin of concepts is as much taken for granted in doctrinaire ontological analyses as it is in partial and hence biased metaphysical ones. The result is a historical lacuna in a double sense: a historical blank with respect to each particular concept that anchors the ontology, and a historical blank in the ontology itself. The lacuna is most strikingly exemplified in Heidegger's fundamental ontological concept *Being-toward-death*, and in his pedestaling of a ready-made language. For example he writes of the latter: "In thinking Being comes to language. Language is the house of Being. In its home man dwells." [30] Nowhere does Heidegger question how this house came to be built. Nowhere does he consider how the *idea* of language arose and evolved. Dan Magurshak has justly pointed out the need to resolve epistemological issues in his otherwise sympathetic appraisal of Heidegger's concept of death. [31] Such issues may seem pedestrian alongside a concern with Being. They are nevertheless integral to an understanding of Being. A concern with conceptual origins is an essential dimension of a sound and complete ontology.

BROADER PERSPECTIVES

It should not be assumed that the error of starting with the wrong body or of leaving the body behind and unattended are peculiarly philosophers' errors. The errors have been cast in philosophical light only because their relationship to the question of getting back is most succinctly and clearly exemplified in the philosophies of Merleau-Ponty and Heidegger. Anthropologists and researchers in the human sciences generally are just as prone to starting with the wrong body or leaving it behind and unattended, above all when it is a question of assaying "mental" activities on the order of thinking and intelligence. On the one hand, described in behavioral terms, the body is categorically not regarded as a body of knowledge. On the other, tactility and kinesthesia are rarely given their due as modes of knowing the world, that is, as gnostic systems, and not merely perceptual–motor pathways.

For many anthropologists, the errors are in part due also to a desire to maintain a strict disciplinary division between anthropology and psychology, the anthropologist's objective determinations being considered amenable to much more rigorous and precise scientific validation than those of their academic colleagues. A case in point is Edmund Leach's criticism of Charles Berg's analysis of the difference between an Australian hair ritual and modern hair ritual.[32] Leach, an anthropologist, questions the validity of the psychoanalyst's—Berg's—statement that "in the former [Australian hair ritual] the symbols used (penis and incision of penis) are, as one would expect in a primitive degree of culture, certainly not far removed from their anatomical source, indeed their phallic origin is patent, whereas in our modern practice displacement and disguise are so extreme that to the average person the disguise is effective. He will not discern . . . that in dealing with hair so remote as that of his face and head he is unconsciously dealing with a phallic substitute."[33] Leach aims his criticism at Berg's distinction between primitive and modern societies, a distinction "most anthropologists find difficult to accept or even to understand." He asks, "Is it really the case that the weight of modern civilization always pushes the significance of sexual symbols deep into the 'unconscious'?"[34]

If this quasi-rhetorical question is viewed not as a criticism of what Leach takes to be an undocumented contrast between "civilized and uncivilized societies," that is, if it is viewed not from the viewpoint of comparative social anthropology but rather as a neutral question about the structure and possible modes of human thinking, then the question takes on deep and provocative significance, and Berg's contrast becomes an interesting point of departure for examining conceptual origins and the evolution of human symbols. In other words, passing quite unnoticed in Leach's criticism is Berg's claim that some symbols at least have their origin in bodily realities. The claim is not even peculiar to psychoanalysts. Mary Douglas, a social anthropologist, opens her book on comparative human socio-religious cosmologies with the statement that "most symbolic behaviour must work through the human body."[35] Leach himself emphasizes not only the fact that cross-culturally "certain kinds of symbols crop up much more frequently than others," but attributes the phenomenon to the body's being a "cultural universal."[36]

The claim that most human symbols can be traced back to an anatomical source suggests that the body plays a formidable role in the structuring of human thought. Indeed, it suggests that to understand human thinking is to trace back to their bodily source those fundamental concepts that have shaped human practices and beliefs. In anthropology, as in philosophy, when one starts with the wrong body or leaves it behind or unattended, the contours of that path never come to light.

THE PRIMACY OF CULTURE AND THE LINGUISTIC TURN

Corporeal inequities and Quinean misformulations of the hominid past aside, there is a final impediment to getting back, namely forsaking biology in favor of culture, in particular esteeming evolutionary hominid history so remote from present-day cultures (Western and non-Western) that it is dismissed on grounds of irrelevancy. Where such estimations can be shown erroneous and short-sighted is in their neglect of attention to the implications of fossil evidence in paleoanthropology and to universal patterns in cultural anthropology. A consideration of both topics points in essentially the same direction.

Present-day paleoanthropological finds and interpretations support the thesis that the physical appearance of hominids and their behavioral repertoire evolved hand in hand. Contrary to older hypotheses insisting that big brains came first—that is, that big brains were the generative force behind those physical and behavioral changes that made hominids hominids, most notably upright posture and tool-using/tool-making—fossil evidence shows that hominid upright posture is at least three million years old, tool-making (as noted earlier) two and a half million years old, and language (as noted earlier) one and a half to two million years old. Indeed, fossil evidence shows that larger cranial capacities began their modest initial development well after consistent bipedality had been established, and their greater subsequent development after tool-using/tool-making had become established behaviors. Clearly, then, our hominid ancestors did not think their way into looking and acting human by dint of an exceptional cranial capacity and inferred associated brain power. The reasonable implication—even sound conclusion—is that whatever their thinking at any stage, it was conceptually rooted not in a brain, but in the concrete realities of everyday bodily life: in a revolutionary primate animate form, and in the concomitantly revolutionary dynamics and corporeal possibilities of the tactile–kinesthetic body. The implication has substantial import. With respect to *essential* physical appearance and basic behaviors, the revolutionary form and body are near rather than remote from present-day humans. (This claim is substantiated in detail in Chapter 15, "The Case for Tactile–Kinesthetic Invariants.") Hence a fresh analysis of the shift to upright posture, for example, and of the practice of tool-using and tool-making in terms of their respective corporeal meanings can shed light on the roots and evolution of present-day human thinking.

A consideration of "the common denominator of cultures"—what was originally called "the psychic unity of mankind"[37]—places the issue in complementary evidential perspective. If it is true that "what cultures are found to have in common is a uniform system of categories, not a fund of identical elements,"[38] then it is also true that while differentially expressed (in different rituals, practices, namings, and so on), in the most fundamental sense human thinking is everywhere standardized on the same model. In other words, basic concepts, those undergirding or coincident with certain universal cultural categories—for example, marriage, funeral rites, cleanliness training, numerals—are forged on the basis of a common referent. George Peter Murdoch, a cultural anthropologist, comes close to just such an insight when, after observing that competent authorities agree "irrespective of theoretical divergences on other issues" that cultural universals exist, he goes on to say that the basis of the common denominator of cultures

cannot be sought in history, or geography, or race, or any other factor limited in time or space, since the universal pattern links all known cultures, simple and complex, ancient and modern. It can only be sought, therefore, in the fundamental biological and psychological nature of man and in the universal conditions of human existence.[39]

Once a standardized model is acknowledged on the basis of the cultural facts of the matter, and once Murdoch's close and accurate reasoning is similarly acknowledged concerning *where* the foundation is upon which the common denominator of cultures must rest, it is a small step to hypothesize the hominid body as model. What, after all, could be a more universal condition of human existence than animate form? What is more biologically fundamental than the body? What, in the most fundamental sense, is more psychologically resonant than the sensory–kinetic dimensions of tactile–kinesthetic experience?

The above considerations strongly suggest that a study of cultures—their artifacts and classificational systems—exclusive of evolutionary anthropology effectively cuts off the possibility of mapping hominid universals, specifically pan-cultural biological hominid invariants. When put in the perspective of the history of anthropology itself, the relatively recent and resolute turn toward culture might be readily explained as a reaction against earlier anthropologists (or in the eyes of many present-day anthropologists, against earlier *pseudo-anthropologists*) who without field training or studies of their own attempted to identify features common to all cultures by studying the reports of explorers, missionaries, and the like, or who attempted in general terms to explain differences between modern and primitive ways of thinking and behaving. Nonetheless, however earnest the motivation for the turn, allegiance to a strict cultural relativism is biologically and historically restricting. Not only is there no way of getting back under such circumstances, but there is nothing to get back to. There is no acknowledged hominid history to begin with.

Of further import is the fact that the decisive turn toward cultural studies is linked to the larger turn toward language, a turn made by anthropologists and philosophers earlier this century, and a turn that carried considerable if implicit force with respect to the general conception of thinking. It is well known that Lévi-Strauss patterned his structuralist approach to anthropology on methodology in linguistics, and that Wittgenstein catapulted language to philosophical prominence in his insistent attempts to show that philosophy was really a matter of understanding how we use—and misunderstand—language. As Wittgenstein's question and commentary on thinking ironically demonstrate, however, intense emphasis on linguistic and ultimately on conceptual cultural differences does—and has done—nothing to clarify the nature of thinking itself. This is in part because thinking is not language-dependent—there are modes of thinking not only other than verbal language but preceding verbal language as indicated earlier by the use and fabrication of tools—and in part because thinking *is* concept-dependent. While the headstrong turn toward language effectively cuts off an examination of thinking precisely because it subsumes all concepts within language, it also effectively hides the reverse relationship obtaining between concepts and thinking. Concepts are not invented by a linguistic wave of the tongue; they are themselves dependent upon thinking, in the most basic case, perhaps, the thinking present in the act of recognition.

Because "the mental" is often equated to language, some anthropologists and philosophers might be inclined to argue that thinking *is* a separate evolutionary development, that is, a faculty linked to cultural evolution, and even cultural speciation, so to speak. What is ignored in this argument, ignored in addition to evidence of non-linguistic thinking as well as evidence justifying the thesis that non-human animals think, is the *origin* of language. Only a creationist doctrine can explain it in the separatist's scheme of the world. Even if pushed to a genetic level, the separatist's view is untenable. Genes cannot put words into a creature's mouth. They are not up to *inventing* a verbal language, much less several thousand different ones. Linguistic anthropologists who have been concerned with primordial language have emphasized the role of the body in its origin and development. This role should actually be expected since speech is a tactile–kinesthetic/aural phenomenon. Whatever might be going on in the brain at the time an individual is speaking, it is the speaker, not the brain, who, rather than which, is uttering and choosing words, suggesting a place or a way to find food, expressing opinions, conveying sentiments, and the like. In fact, no stimulation of language areas in the brain has ever produced a word, let alone a suggestion of a place or a way to find food. It is not, then, a wild conceptual leap but a precise and meticulous step from research findings on primordial language to the thesis that thinking was originally modeled on the body, that both in a world without verbal language and in the beginnings of a literally lingual one, thinking was patterned on bodily motifs. It follows that if language is to be consulted in resolving the complexities of thinking, then the linguistic turn should properly be made first toward primordial language.

The pedestaling of language by both anthropologist and philosopher hides its mundane origin from view not only so far as research findings in primordial language are concerned, but with respect to vestiges and suggestions of its original corporeal character in present-day languages. The seventeenth–eighteenth century Italian philosopher Vico, for example, pointed out the role of the body in common metaphors for inanimate objects: "the brow and shoulders of a hill; the eyes of needles and of potatoes . . . mouth for any opening . . . the tongue of a shoe . . . the belly of a sail . . . the flesh of fruits . . . the bowels of the earth."[40] More recent examination by cultural historian Walter Ong has shown how much a sense of tactility and movement pervades many common English words having to do with knowledge: analysis, comprehension, order, outline, for example.[41] More recently still, Mark Johnson and George Lakoff, philosopher and linguist respectively, have detailed the physical experiential grounding of many everyday metaphorical concepts.[42] Clearly the world is frequently perceived and understood in bodily terms; it is *thought* in terms of corporeal being. The examples suggest not only that a less exalted view of language might be salutary to an understanding of its history, but they suggest further that a tempered, genuinely inquisitive scholarly reaction to anthropomorphism, specifically *corporeal* anthropomorphism, would be equally so. It is, after all, corporeal anthropomorphism that the anthropologist Douglas writes about in her earlier-cited study of how the body shapes socio-religious symbols in various cultures. It is corporeal anthropomorphism that the sociologist John O'Neill describes when he speaks of the reciprocal conceptual relationship between bodies and societies.[43] Finally, it is just such anthropomorphism that the well-known Japanese primatologist Junichiro Itani so eloquently if tacitly defended in his Huxley Memorial Lecture when he noted first that "Japanese culture does not emphasize the difference between people and animals, so it is relatively free from the spell of anti-anthropomorphism"; and second, that "the conviction that anthropomorphism is not to be discarded in elucidating the complex *specia* of primates . . . has led to many important discoveries."[44] In sum, if thinking in general and thinking-in-words in particular are at root anthropocentric—if the body in each case forges meanings in its own image, even to the extent of a systematized corporeal semantics—then the above examples are clearly not culturally idiosyncratic but are exemplaries of a biological tradition. To bring that tradition into view requires a readjustment of the focusing lens. As acknowledged and suggested in Chapter 1, the linguistic turn in anthropology and philosophy alike produced extraordinary insights. A corporeal turn would assuredly do no less.

NOTES

1. For an overview of evidence of thinking in nonhuman animals, see Donald R. Griffin, *Animal Thinking* (Cambridge: Harvard University Press, 1984), and his earlier book, *The Question of Animal Awareness* (New York: The Rockefeller University Press, 1976).

2. Claude Lévi-Strauss, *The Savage Mind*, trans. George Weidenfeld and Nicolson Ltd. (London: Weidenfeld and Nicolson, 1966), p. 156, and *Structural Anthropology*, trans. Claire Jacobson and Brooke Grundfest Schoepf (New York: Basic Books, 1963), p. 203.

3. Claude Lévi-Strauss, *The Raw and the Cooked*, trans. John and Doreen Weightman (New York: Harper Torchbooks, 1969), p. 13.

4. Jean Piaget and Bärbel Inhelder, *The Child's Conception of Space*, trans. F. J. Langdon and J. L. Lunzer (New York: W. W. Norton, 1967). See also Jean Piaget, *La naissance de l'intelligence chez l'enfant*, 6th ed. (Neuchatel: Delachaux et Niestlé, 1968).

5. Otto Neurath, "Protocol Sentences," trans. George Schick, in *Logical Positivism*, trans. A. J. Ayer (Glencoe, Ill.: Free Press, 1959), p. 201.

6. Williard van Orman Quine, "On Mental Entities," in *The Ways of Paradox and Other Essays*, rev. ed. (Cambridge: Harvard University Press, 1979), p. 223.

7. Ibid., p. 222.

8. Nicholas Toth, "The First Technology," *Scientific American* 256 (April 1987): 112–21.

9. Bruce Bower, "Talk of Ages," *Science News* 136/2 (8 July 1989): 24–26.

10. See, for example, Gordon W. Hewes, "An Explicit Formulation of the Relationship between Tool-Using, Tool-Making, and the Emergence of Language," *Visible Language* 7 (1973): 101–27; Ralph L. Holloway, "Culture: A *Human* Domain," *Current Anthropology* 10 (1969): 395–407; Jean Kitahara-Frisch, "Symbolizing Technology as a Key to Human Evolution," in *Symbol as Sense*, ed. Mary LeCron Foster and Stanley H. Brandes (New York: Academic Press, 1980), pp. 211–23.

11. Irving T. Diamond, "The Evolution of the Tectal–Pulvinar System in Mammals: Structural and Behavioral Studies of the Visual System," *Symposia of the Zoological Society of London* 33 (1973): 223.

12. Mary LeCron Foster, "The Symbolic Structure of Primordial Language," in *Human Evolution: Biosocial Perspectives* 4, ed. Sherwood L. Washburn and Elizabeth R. McCown (Menlo Park, Calif.: Benjamin/Cummings, 1978), p. 117.

13. Willard van Orman Quine, *Word and Object* (Cambridge: MIT Press, 1960), p. 3.

14. Stephen J. Gould and Richard C. Lewontin, "The Spandrels of San Marco and the Panglossian Paradigm: A Critique of the Adaptationist Programme," *Proceedings of the Royal Society of London B* 205 (1979): 581–98.

15. Hubert L. Dreyfus and Paul Rabinow, *Michael Foucault*, 2nd ed. (Chicago: University of Chicago Press, 1983), p. 112.

16. Stratton performed experiments on vision just before the turn of the last century. His subjects were fitted with devices that prevented normal inversion of the retinal image. He consistently emphasizes the pull of "pre-experimental vision" and of "pre-experimental representations [of the

body]" in explaining subjects' experiences. For example: "The difficulty of seeing things upright by means of upright retinal images seems to consist solely in the resistance offered by the long-established previous experience." He concludes that "only after a set of relations and perceptions had become organized into a norm could something enter which was in unusual relation to this organized whole and be (for instance) upside down." George M. Stratton, "Some Preliminary Experiments on Vision without Inversion of the Retinal Image," *Psychological Review* 3/6 (1896): 611–17; see also his "Vision without Inversion of the Retinal Image," *Psychological Review* 4/4 (1897): 341–60.

17. Maurice Merleau-Ponty, *Phenomenology of Perception*, trans. Colin Smith (London: Routledge & Kegan Paul, 1962), p. 246.

18. Ibid.

19. Herbert Plügge, "Man and His Body," trans. Erling Eng, in *The Philosophy of the Body*, ed. Stuart F. Spicker (Chicago: Quadrangle Books, 1970): 293–311.

20. Merleau-Ponty, *Perception*, p. 252.

21. Ibid., p. 244.

22. Walle J. H. Nauta and Michael Feirtag, "The Organization of the Brain," *Scientific American* 241 (September 1979): 88.

23. Merleau-Ponty, pp. 249 and 244 respectively.

24. Ibid., p. 253.

25. Ibid., p. 254.

26. Ibid.

27. Martin Heidegger, *Being and Time*, trans. John Macquarrie and Edward Robinson (New York: Harper and Row, 1962), p. 143.

28. For the original formulation of this simile, see Pierre-Jean de Cabanis, *Oeuvres Complètes*, 5 vols. (Paris: Bossange Frères, 1824), 3: 160–61.

29. Heidegger, *Being and Time*, pp. 191 and 67 respectively.

30. Martin Heidegger, "Letter on Humanism," in *Martin Heidegger, Basic Writings*, ed. David Farrell Krell (New York: Harper and Row, 1977), p. 193.

31. Dan Magurshak, "Heidegger and Edwards on *Sein-zum-Tode*," *The Monist* 62/1 (1979), p. 116.

32. Edmund R. Leach, "Magical Hair," in *Myth and Cosmos*, ed. John Middleton (Austin: University of Texas Press, 1967), pp. 77–108; Charles Berg, *The Unconscious Significance of Hair* (London: Allen and Unwin, 1951).

33. Quoted in Leach, "Magical Hair," p. 91.

34. Ibid.

35. Mary Douglas, *Natural Symbols* (New York: Pantheon Press, 1970), p. vii.

36. Edmund R. Leach, "The Influence of Cultural Context on Non-Verbal Communication in Man," in *Non-Verbal Communication*, ed. R. A. Hinde (Cambridge: Cambridge University Press, 1972), p. 326.

37. George Peter Murdock, "The Common Denominator of Cultures," in *Readings in Introductory Anthropology*, 2 vols., ed. Richard G. Emerick (Berke-

ley, Calif.: McCutcheon Publishing, 1969), 1: 323–26. See also Robert Redfield, "Anthropological Understanding of Man," ibid., 1: 36–48.

38. Murdock, "Common Denominator," p. 324.

39. Ibid.

40. Giambattista Vico, *The New Science of Giambattista Vico*, 3rd ed., trans. Thomas Goddard Berger and Max Harold Fisch (Ithaca, N.Y.: Cornell University Press, 1970), para. 405.

41. Walter Ong, " 'I See What You Say': Sense Analogues for the Intellect," in *Interfaces of the Word* (Ithaca, N.Y.: Cornell University Press, 1977), pp. 121–44.

42. George Lakoff and Mark Johnson, "Conceptual Metaphors in Everyday Language," *Journal of Philosophy* 77/8 (1980): 453–86.

43. John O'Neill, *Five Bodies* (Ithaca, N.Y.: Cornell University Press, 1985).

44. Junichiro Itani, "The Evolution of Primate Social Structures," *Man*, n.s. 20 (1985): 597.

11

The Thesis and Its Opposition: Institutionalized Metaphysical Dualism

From the point of view of how the whole thing actually worked, we knew how part of it worked. . . . We didn't even inquire, didn't even see how the rest was going on. All these other things were happening and we didn't see it.

BARBARA MCCLINTOCK

Anderson [a theoretical physicist] ends his discussion with the remark that when he was asked to write something about his personal scientific philosophy he discovered for the first time that he had one! Moreover he found that one of the central tenets was entirely different from what he would have expected, namely that the whole can be greater than, and very different from, the sum of its parts.

W. H. THORPE

UNNATURAL SPECIES

The choice of "the mental" by the philosopher—or its relegation to philosophers—and the choice of "the physical" by the scientist, establishes a division of the animate that is mirrored neither by a Darwinian scheme of the world, a Darwinian methodology, nor by everyday living reality. However restrictively or generously their genetic pro-

300

gramming is conceived, all creatures, humans and nonhumans, undeniably move about in purposeful ways. They make life-enhancing choices, at minimum not only about what and what not to eat (including the choice of a new food item) and when to eat (e.g., when it is safe to do so as well as when they feel hungry), they make choices as well in the very act of procuring food. Movements in hunting, for instance, are coincident with choices to pursue a certain animal as prey, to continue or discontinue a chase, to change tactics, and so on.[1] In no such behavior is there empirical evidence of a mental as opposed to a physical or a physical as opposed to a mental. There is only a creature using its native wits to outsmart its prey or outmanoeuvre its predator. Hunting creatures clearly live their lives as animate wholes.

If there were a law of nature to which to appeal in such a matter, surely it would decree first that academically propagated creatures are unnatural species; and second, that in order to render creaturehood properly, it is necessary to regard living forms as organic wholes, even if one is studying only partial aspects of a form. Such a law of nature is in fact exactly what the eminent biologist J. S. Haldane was at pains to formulate in his fundamental axiom of biology: what life scientists properly study is "the life of organisms," "manifestations of persistent wholes"[2]—what in concrete, empirical terms can be identified as *Darwinian bodies*. A full justification and elaboration of the term *Darwinian bodies* will be found below. It suffices to note at this point that in his exposition of evolutionary theory, Darwin started with physical attributes and behavior, but remained an organic wholist. He did *not* fail to recognize and acknowledge the whole animal, the living creature. It is precisely because he was an organic wholist that he did not conceive bodies to evolve in the absence of minds (mental powers), nor conceive mental powers to be vouchsafed to humans alone. When his organic wholism is preempted on the one hand by a biology of the body—or an anthropology of behavior—and on the other by a philosophy of mind, then the life of living organisms fades from view and Darwinian bodies fall through the crack.

Failure to think in persistent wholes or to tie one's thinking to intact living organisms results in queer statements revealing queer conceptions of the nature of creaturely life vis-à-vis the role of scientific analysis. A psychologist recently wrote: "It may seem strange that a conference on [brain] lateralization should have to concern itself with the essential unity of the individual but that is our fate, and this is a question which we cannot avoid facing."[3] A physical anthropologist recently pointed out in a college textbook that "many of the functions of primates can be classified as *behavior;* that is, besides biochemical and physiological functions of cells or organs there are many actions of the whole animal."[4] Such statements both begrudge and distort what is first and foremost in a living individual: its persistent wholeness. They ignore the fact that what evolves are not piecemeal parts but intact organisms—animate forms.

By and large, present-day philosophers do not so much begrudge the essential unity of the individual as omit fundamental aspects of it because of the skewedness of their subdisciplinary focus. Disquisitions on minds seldom touch on bodies, and if they do, it is commonly the body as a visual object or the source of visual perceptions. In contrast, when Aristotle wrote about the soul he underscored the necessity of finding the most adequate definition for each of its forms and in the process of doing so, had much to say about the body, in particular about the biological primacy of touch among all the senses.[5]

Now it might be thought naive to call attention to what are now traditional academic divisions. Most academics realize there is more to being human than what their particular discipline defines or particular approach reveals, even if that realization is not often buttressed by personal interdisciplinary breadth or efforts. If this generalization is true, then the problem is not academic divisions per se. They are a problem only when disciplinary choice is not simply an expression of personal interest, but is conceived in more lofty terms: as the hub of all human understandings, or even coincident with some universal axiology. The problem is with the partial beings that academic divisions tend to generate. With the proliferation of these partial beings, the Darwinian body continually loses ground and is ultimately lost sight of altogether.

But there is a secondary problem as well, namely the point from which typical academic investigations begin. There are at least two reasons for this problem. To avoid repetition, both will be discussed in terms of studies of "the mental" only. Corollary omissions, preconceptions, and conceptual/linguistic ensnarements beset studies of "the physical."

Present-day philosophers almost uniformly start with "the mental" and omit a concomitant, not to say complementary, philosophy of the body. When they do, "the physical" seems predictably foredoomed. It is reduced either to the status of a handmaiden or to a brain—the latter most often recently conceived as in a vat on some distant astronomical object or involved in complicated cerebral exchange programs.[6] The latter situations actually owe their reflective existence to science; that is, philosophers are merely taking science seriously. If the brain is the physical seat of "the mental" as present-day science teaches, then the possibility of detaching the mental on the one hand, and the possibility of changing corporeal drivers on the other, become logical possibilities engaging the attention of philosophers. More specifically, the possibilities make the reality of the perceived world on the one hand, and the criteria for personal identity on the other, problematic. But they also make the living body problematic. The living body seldom makes an appearance in these scenarios: squeezed out by pressing concerns with brains, the living body has become so much superfluous pulp.

The lack of a complementary philosophy of the body aside, no sooner is "the mental" disengaged for study than a worrisome problem arises. How is "the mental" connected to "the physical"? How, *in terms of everyday life*, do the two interact or form a union? In view of the metaphysical ease with which people normally lead their day to day lives, it is ironic that a separation into parts rather than an essential unity is so readily conceived and accepted as metaphysically sound. The latter is the difficult problem, not the former, just as it was for Descartes who is credited with the original conceptual separation.[7] There is a further irony in the fact that many second-generation existential and even phenomenological philosophers who deal with the still unresolved problem (a legacy left them, many times in compounded form, by seminal first-generation existential philosophers such as Heidegger) commonly solve it by way of *embodiment*. The solution is ironic since instead of discounting the ready-made division and starting with a fresh analysis of the experiential dimensions of existence, as is consistent not only with an existential approach but with the phenomenological tradition from which existential philosophy derives, the point of departure is actually Cartesian: the self is conceived as packaged in the flesh. The solution is in fact nothing more than a grammatical union. The body "embodies"—presumably as the mind "inspirits." Richard Zaner, for example, first declares that there are two kinds of matter, "bodily life and psychical life . . . which stubbornly refuse being taken as *merely* material." He then defines the first of these as "the living body *embodying*" and the second as "the subject (self/mind)" (italics added).[8] Where the original conceptual separation between the mental and the physical is mended by a grammatical union, an empirical frame of reference is lost from view. Nothing in experience is shown to tether the grammatical constructs of an *embodying* body and an *embodied* subject. In consequence, the conceptual gap between "the mental" and "the physical" remains unclosed.

Embodiment in such instances appears to be a matter of having one's metaphysical cake and eating it too, but with a forked tongue —not to malicious but to inadvertent effect. In other words, while broaching the long overdue investigation, even celebration, of the centrality of "the lived body" (in German, the *leib* as opposed to the *körper*), many existential philosophers simultaneously cling to the traditional Cartesian metaphysics that refuses to acknowledge the centrality.[9] The duplicity is covered over by the grammatical-raised-to-the-power-of-the-metaphysical concept of embodiment that, at the same time it hoists the body to new-found prominence, keeps it in its usual place with regard to a self, mind, or subject. Moreover without language it is doubtful the concept of embodiment would even arise; it is an abstract lexical offshoot of a flesh and bone body. "*Processes* of embodiment" (italics added),[10] for example, or "the Self's *incarnate* potential" (italics in original)[11] are empirically empty attempts at reification, both of an "embodying body" and of a self the latter purportedly embodies. The empirical deficiency is forcefully if negatively highlighted by eighteenth-century empiricist philosopher David Hume's conclusions about "the self"; all Hume could find when he looked for a self was "a flux of impressions."[12] Could this flux be what the living body embodies? It scarcely seems hardy enough stuff to interest an embodying body. What, then, is the *self* or *mind* that is embodied? What is this *act* or *fact* of embodiment? Statements about "our lived experience of being embodied"[13] need to be cashed in (as Husserl would say)[14] for evidence that *shows* embodiment to be an experienced fact. Unless and until such experience(s) can be described, the metaphysical (and logical) disjunction between on the one hand an incarnate subjectivity —or lived body—and on the other a Cartesian metaphysics, will remain, and with it the problem of how "the mental" and "the physical" are in fact united.

ON DARWINIAN BODIES

Because "the mental" can be conceived as estranged from, and even thoroughly independent of "the physical" (not as a brain in a vat but as a pure spirit or "thinking substance"), and in consequence, because the Darwinian body can easily fall through the crack, it is most reasonable to begin an investigation of the roots of human thinking from the perspective of a Darwinian body, that is, with intact living creatures in the throes, pleasures, industries, and curiosities of their everyday lives. The reasonableness of the approach is augmented on at least two counts. To start with a Darwinian body is to follow the path of evolution itself in the sense that the efflorescence of thinking in terrestrial creatures is chronologically keyed to the evolution of primates of which, so far as we know, hominids are the most recently evolved lineage. (To start with a Darwinian body also follows the hypothesized path of the evolution of evolution. Where the latter is itself understood as a process that evolves, the present-day world is conceived as at a particular stage [metacultural] in the bio-historical process. Within this perspective, the Darwinian body—originally a product at the stage of natural selection—is viewed not as displaced in subsequent evolutionary stages but as having undergone transformation at the hands of further selective mechanisms, namely, cultural and metacultural selection.) [15]

Second, to start with a Darwinian body is of course to proceed as Darwin did, that is, with neither academic allegiances nor strictures. Darwin's observations and descriptions were clearly not restricted by certain disciplinary perspectives, methodologies, and concepts, but were grounded in perspicacious and painstaking perceptions of creatures in the process of their everyday lives. Darwin described the bodily form, the actions, the emotions, and the mental qualities of living creatures. True, he observed only bodies, but he gave them their living due. A body that is given its living due is given as much as its bodily comportments and behaviors allow. A detailed example from Darwin will illustrate just how generous a just allowance was and should be.

In his second major work on evolution, *The Descent of Man, and Selection in Relation to Sex*, Darwin showed how the principles of selection apply equally to humans—that humans are not special creations, but have affinities in every respect to "the lower animals." [16] In his first chapter, he presents evidence showing that structural aspects of the human body are homologous to structural aspects of nonhuman bodies, that embryonic development is similar in both cases, and that humans, like "the lower animals," have rudimentary organs. In effect, in this first chapter, Darwin is recapitulating in human terms much of the corporeal evidence substantiating evolutionary theory that he presented in *The Origin of Species*, his first work on evolution. But Darwin obviously does not think he has made his full case. "The descent of man" involves much more than an evolution of physical features correlative to those of nonhuman animals. In the second and third chapters, Darwin presents evidence showing that *human mental powers are on a continuum with nonhuman mental powers*. In the first of these chapters, he points out affinities with respect to power of attention, memory, imagination, and reason. He is clearly untroubled by brain size with respect to the attribution of these "mental powers." He is concerned only with overt animate behavior. In this respect he gives a pragmatic, even Wittgensteinian, assessment of mental powers. Just as the meaning of a word is given in its use according to Wittgenstein, so the mental powers of an animal are given in *their* use. The criteria for affirming power of attention, deliberation, and so on, are in effect palpably present; they are there in the flesh.

Darwin goes on to affirm that the verbal language of humans is similar to the language of nonhuman animals in several important respects, and to question whether with "self-consciousness, mental individuality, abstraction, and general ideas," [17] the difference is not, as elsewhere, *in degree rather than in kind*. In each case he presents evidence for believing that just such a difference obtains. Thus just as there are differences in degree and not differences in kind between humans and nonhumans with respect to the evolution of physical features, so with respect to the evolution of mental powers.

It should be pointed out that Darwin intended his study of emotional expression in humans and nonhumans to be part of *The Descent of Man, and Selection in Relation to Sex*, but owing to the latter's already extended length, the material on emotions was published separately. Accordingly, *The Expression of the Emotions in Man and Animals* constitutes the third of Darwin's three major works on evolution. In this book, Darwin again presents evidence for the same thesis: humans and "the lower animals" are all creatures of evolution *in every respect*, in this instance, sharing the same emotional etiology, similar patterns of emotional behavior, and similar means of emotional expression. [18]

What is remarkable in Darwin's presentation throughout both *The Descent of Man* and *The Expression of the Emotions* is his tacit insistence upon the *observability* of "mental characters." "The lower animals, like man, *manifestly* feel pleasure and pain, happiness and misery" (italics added). [19] Moreover not only are these *observed* features not subjective gloss, they are not reasoned conjectures: "*The fact* that the lower animals are excited by the same emotions as ourselves is so well established, that it will not be necessary to weary the reader by many details. Terror acts in the same manner on them as on us, causing the muscles to tremble, the heart to palpitate, the sphincters to be relaxed, and the hair to stand on end" (italics added).[20]

From such statements it is clear that *though analytically divisible ex post facto,* Darwin conceives the mental and the physical to be experientially and behaviorally intertwined, and as much in the act of reasoning as in the feeling of terror. In reviewing the capacity of nonhuman animals to reason, for example, Darwin follows the statement, "Few persons any longer dispute that animals possess some power of reasoning," with the observation that "animals may constantly be seen to pause, deliberate, and resolve."[21] The putative jump (typically fancied by twentieth-century Western observers) from a so-called *physical* pause to a so-called *mental* deliberation and resolve is nowhere to be found. In effect, for a Darwinian observer, to live means not merely to survive in the struggle for existence, to have the more viable morphological, physiological and/or behavioral variation—the longer canines, the higher threshold for pain, or the swifter run, for example —but to live out in the fullest corporeal sense the struggle itself: to be not merely *un corps,* but *un corps engagé.* Behavior in Darwinian terms is thus not reducible to a series of inputs and outcomes. It is not equivalent to twentieth-century laboratory proceedings and results even though it may be shown to follow certain behavioral patterns described in those proceedings and results. It is, in the most basic and incontrovertible sense, a corporeal slate upon which much is written and written legibly. In sum, while Darwin clearly subscribes to a classificatory separation of mental and physical qualities—undoubtedly an unquestioned Cartesian legacy—he does *not* subscribe to their essential division. His meticulous and detailed analyses within those classifications notwithstanding, what he observes—and what he is bent on rendering—are "persistent wholes," "the lives of organisms," "the essential unity of individuals."

It is furthermore clear from a theoretical viewpoint that what Darwin is saying by his insistence on the observability of the mental is that the same rule of *analogical apperception*[22] applies to nonhuman bodies as to human ones. That analogical apperception is the rule among humans hardly needs documentation. When humans perceive one another's behavior they at the same time read in certain attitudes, dispositions, rationales, and the like, and certain feelings, such that the perception of other bodies is always filled in (*ap*-perceived)—by motivational ascriptions, for example. What is specifically read in—what is *analogically* apperceived—is empirically rooted in the cognitive and felt dimensions of one's own prior bodily experiences of attention, deliberation, reasoning, feeling, and so on. In effect, other human bodies are perceived not as empty shells of doings; observed living bodies are given their living due.

Analogical apperception is not only a built-in factual presupposition of a Darwinian metaphysics and biology, it is a built-in of corporeal life. It has its origin in the *biological disposition to use one's own body as a semantic template*—in the specific context under discussion, to understand the behavior of other creatures on the basis of one's own corporeal experiences. Moreover it is in the long run a necessary biological fact of life. Whatever the degree of genetic programming toward that end, correct readings of the cognitive and felt dimensions of the behavior of others are as critical to the evolutionary success of a creature as are typically morphological characters, all the more so for predominantly social creatures. Their biological necessity to a harmonious social order is often written between the lines in studies of primate social behavior, in Harry Harlow's deprivation and nondeprivation experiments with monkeys, for example, and Jane van Lawick-Goodall's observations of chimpanzees in the wild.[23] The principle is furthermore directly documented in primatologist Stuart Altmann's coinage and use of the term *comsign* to designate signals understood by all individuals of a particular species or social group on the basis of behaviors common to all members of the species or group.[24] Comsigns are in essence the result of analogical thinking based on a commonality of animate form and of tactile–kinesthetic experience. They are at the same time, and in a broad evolutionary sense, the result of the biological disposition to use one's own body as a semantic template. Accounts of social behavior (including the Tanzsprache of honeybees) found in the paleoanthropological case studies show that living bodies are consistently given their living due by creatures in nonhuman and human societies alike. Thoughts and feelings are indeed *manifestly* present in bodily comportments and behaviors. "The mental" is not hidden but is palpably observable in the flesh.

In sum, Darwin's metaphysical passage from homologous bodily structures to homologous mental ones is smooth and untroubled because it is undergirded by the biological principle of analogical apperception. The question should nonetheless be raised as to whether Darwin is giving too much credit. Is the practice of analogical apperception by humans misplaced in the case of their observations of *non*human animals? Is Darwin violating C. L. Morgan's famous canon: "we should not . . . explain any instance of animal behaviour as the outcome of higher mental processes, if it can fairly be interpreted as the outcome of mental processes which stand lower in the order of mental development"?[25]

ANALOGICAL APPERCEPTION AND
BIOLOGICAL REDUCTIONISM

The twentieth-century philosopher Thomas Nagel has long been concerned with conciliating the objective and subjective, to the point of securing a place for the subjective in the annals of behavior. He insists that an objective account is insufficient since "the subjectivity of consciousness is an irreducible feature of reality—without which we couldn't do physics or anything else—and it must occupy as fundamental a place in any credible world view as matter, energy, space, time, and numbers."[26] There are similar rumblings of disquietude from scientists as well, particularly those sympathetic to a Whiteheadian metaphysics—for example physicist David Bohm[27] and biologist James A. Marcum[28]—or to the tenets of hermeneutical analysis as, for example, biologist Gunther Stent.[29] Such philosophers and scientists are fundamentally in accord with Darwin: description at a merely physical level is not a complete description. Their joint answer to Morgan's canon might be formulated in the most basic way as follows: In no case may we interpret an action as the outcome of a lower psychical faculty if such an interpretation violates the integrity of the body in question. For Darwinian observers there is no metaphysical or methodological problem in identifying the integrity of a particular body since the mental is neither an epiphenomenon of behavioral evolution nor a thing evolving apart on its own. It is there in the living flesh of the creature before them. The viewpoint is mirrored in a tantalizing statement made by Merleau-Ponty: "It is no mere coincidence that the rational being is also the one who holds himself upright or has a thumb which can be brought opposite to the fingers; the same manner of existing is evident in both aspects."[30] Merleau-Ponty never actually brought this evidence to light. He never showed just how rationality and uprightness, or rationality and an opposable thumb, constitute "the same manner of existing," in part because as indicated earlier, he started with the wrong body, and in part because the conjunction of rationality, uprightness, and an opposable thumb points in an incisively Darwinian direction. The conjunction invites a bona fide existential *and* evolutionary perspective, one in which traditionally omitted evolutionary dimensions are acknowledged as part and parcel of an *existential* history, and in which traditionally omitted existential dimensions—Nagel's "subjectivity"—are acknowledged as part and parcel of an *evolutionary* history.

The latter acknowledgment is not only tenable; it is crucial. Too low a bow to the "purely objective" tends to end in a collapse. The reduction of *tactility* to *cutaneous stimulation* is a pertinent case in point. Biologist Samuel Barnett's attempt to behaviorize Darwin's descriptive label of a photograph of a cat rubbing itself against someone's leg[31] actually ends in self-defeat. In lieu of Darwin's "affectionate frame of mind"; Barnett would substitute "cutaneous stimulation." Clearly the latter label does not shed any new and penetrating light on the feline situation. Indeed, the word *rubbing*, and the phrase "affectionate state of mind" are both more concrete and precise designations of the phenomenon than *cutaneous stimulation* since anything a cat does can be labeled "cutaneous stimulation"—even standing on a patch of grass or lying by a fire. In the most precise empirical sense, cutaneous stimulation is an ever-present aspect of every creature's life: no animate being is ever out of touch with *something*. Aristotle recognized this fundamental meaning of tactility when he upheld the primacy of touch among all the other senses by showing it to be "the essential mark of life." "Without touch," Aristotle concluded, "it is impossible for an animal to be."[32] Two-thousand-year-old truths about the primacy of touch would be hard won in a world of cutaneous stimulation.

The question, then, is not whether the practice of analogical apperception is misplaced with respect to nonhuman animals—in effect, whether analogical apperception is to be trusted as a methodological assumption. Darwin's implicit allegiance to analogical apperception was not the result of a reflective act. It was not a choice among possible construals of animal behavior but a spontaneously and implicitly extended principle of everyday creaturely life. The question in turn is twofold: What is the evidence for analogical apperception and what are its biological roots? The paleoanthropological case studies in Part II both document its pervasive practice in nonhuman animal societies and show overwhelming evidence of analogical thinking in the evolution of hominids. In effect, the gathering of evidence in those chapters shows both the significance of analogical apperception to human evolution and how analogical apperception is rooted in corporeal life.

It should finally be noted that Darwin has never actually been shown wrong in his view of the observability of "the mental" in human and nonhuman behavior. He has only been accused of wrongdoing, either directly as by Barnett, or by a tacit boycott of his writings on mental powers in *The Descent of Man* and a relative dismissal of his writings on the expression of emotions. Neither has he ever been shown wrong in his view that mental powers and emotions have *evolved*. The evidence he presents for mental continuities has nowhere been seriously considered and methodically rebutted. It has only been sifted out in what amounts to a highly—one might even say, egregiously—selective reading of Darwin. Here, then, are added reasons a biology of mind—and a philosophy of the body—is called for: not only to open the possibility of a progressively complete human self-understanding, but to examine and elaborate a basic tenet of Darwinian evolutionary theory. If evolution is the guiding thread of life on earth, then Darwin's thesis that nonhuman animals think is directly pertinent to an understanding of our hominid kinfolk. Ancestral hominids whose discoveries and practices are integral to our humanness were *non*human. If they did not think, how is it that we do? By divine intervention? By chance genetic mutation? Given the comprehensive evidence for organic evolution, the most likely answer is that thinking evolved hand in hand with doing (which means necessarily that experience evolved hand in hand with behavior), and that it was neither a merely chance event nor in any way a separate evolutionary biological development. The integrity of the body is sustained in this Darwinian view. How otherwise explain decisions made by present-day chimpanzees as to which twig is the best for termite-fishing, for example, or decisions made by our long-ago ancestors as to which stone would be best for flaking, and where and how it would be best to flake it in order to make it into a serviceable tool? If the roots of human thinking are to be uncovered, then the viewpoint of a Darwinian observer must be taken seriously, to the extent of examining it and of taking *everything* corporeal—not just behavior but experience —as grist for the evolutionary mill.

To this end, the first step is to lay out a blueprint for a resonant and viable philosophical anthropology, and then to spell out in detail its proper methodology. On the basis of these initial steps, it will be possible to present the evidential case for tactile–kinesthetic invariants in straightforward fashion. In turn, the corporeal analyses presented in the second section of this book will be seen to be solidly anchored in a new and thoroughly substantiated genre of research: a philosophical anthropology of both evolutionary and existential dimensions and with a fully supportive theoretical and methodological backbone.

NOTES

1. For a detailed analysis of such choices and behaviors, see Maxine Sheets-Johnstone, "Hunting and the Evolution of Human Intelligence: An Alternative View," *The Midwest Quarterly* 28/1 (1986): 9–35; for a related perspective on the subject see Maxine Sheets-Johnstone, "Thinking in Movement," *Journal of Aesthetics and Art Criticism* 39 (1981): 399–407.

2. J. S. Haldane, *The Philosophical Basis of Biology* (New York: Doubleday, Doran and Co., 1931), pp. 26 and 13 respectively.

3. Stuart J. Dimond, "Introductory Remarks," in *Evolution and Lateralization of the Brain*, ed. Stuart J. Dimond and David A. Blizard, *Annals of the New York Academy of Science* 299 (1977): 2.

4. Gabriel Ward Lasker, *Physical Anthropology* (New York: Holt, Rinehart, and Winston, 1973), p. 177.

5. Aristotle, *De anima*, trans. J. A. Smith, in *The Basic Works of Aristotle*, ed. R. McKeon (New York: Random House, 1968).

6. See, for example, Derek Parfit, *Reasons and Persons* (Oxford: Oxford University Press, 1986).

7. See the correspondence between Princess Elizabeth of Bohemia and Descartes during May and June 1643 in *Descartes: Correspondence*, vols. 4–8, ed. Charles Adam and Gerard Milhaud (Paris: Presses Universitaires de France, 1960).

8. Richard M. Zaner, *The Context of Self* (Athens: Ohio University Press, 1981), p. 3.

9. See also specifically the same shortcoming in the writings of many anthropologists in *The Anthropology of the Body*, ed. John Blacking (London: Academic Press, 1977). Through the essays he has gathered together, Blacking attempts to forge a *full-scale* (see Chapters 1 and 13, this book) anthropology of the body, but until theoretical and methodological issues are clearly conceived and resolved, the prospects of achieving that goal shrivel quickly to zero.

10. Zaner, *Context*, p. 29.

11. David Michael Levin, *The Body's Recollection of Being* (London: Routledge & Kegan Paul, 1985), p. 8.

12. David Hume, *A Treatise of Human Nature*, ed. L. A. Selby-Bigge (Oxford: Clarendon Press, 1960).

13. Levin, *Body's Recollection*, p. 43.

14. Edmund Husserl, "The Origin of Geometry," trans. David Carr, in *Husserl: Shorter Works*, ed. Peter McCormick and Frederick Elliston (Notre Dame, Ind.: University of Notre Dame Press, 1981), p. 261.

15. For an in-depth discussion of this view, see the well-known evolutionary biologist John T. Robinson's "Human and Cultural Development," *Indiana Historical Society Lectures 1973–74* (Indianapolis: Indiana Historical Society, 1974).

16. Charles Darwin, *The Descent of Man, and Selection in Relation to Sex* (Princeton: Princeton University Press, 1981 [1871]).

17. Ibid., p. 62.

18. Charles Darwin, *The Expression of the Emotions in Man and Animals* (Chicago: University of Chicago Press, 1965 [1872]).

19. Darwin, *Descent*, p. 39.

20. Ibid.

21. Ibid., p. 46.

22. For a descriptive (phenomenological) analysis of analogical apperception, see Edmund Husserl, *Cartesian Meditations*, trans. Dorion Cairns (The Hague: Martinus Nijhoff, 1973), particularly the fifth meditation.

23. See, for example, Harry F. Harlow, "Development of the Second and Third Affectional Systems in Macaque Monkeys," in *Research Approaches to Psychiatric Problems*, ed. Thomas T. Tourlentes, Seymour L. Pollock, and Harold E. Himwick (New York: Grune and Stratton, 1962), pp. 209–29; Jane van Lawick-Goodall, *In the Shadow of Man* (New York: Dell, 1971).

24. Stuart A. Altmann, "The Structure of Primate Social Communication," in *Social Communication Among Primates*, ed. Stuart A. Altmann (Chicago: University of Chicago Press, 1967), pp. 325–62.

25. Conwy Lloyd Morgan, *The Animal Mind* (New York: Longmans, Green and Co., 1930), p. 22.

26. Thomas Nagel, *The View from Nowhere* (London: Oxford University Press, 1986), pp. 7–8.

27. See, for example, David Bohm, "On Insight and Its Significance," in *Education and Values*, ed. Douglas Sloan (New York: Teachers College Press, 1979), pp. 13–17, and *Wholeness and the Implicate Order* (London: Routledge & Kegan Paul, 1980).

28. See, for example, James A. Marcum and Geert M. N. Verschuuren, "Hemostatic Regulation and Whitehead's Philosophy of Organism," *Acta biotheoretica* 35 (1986): 123–33.

29. See, for example, Gunther Stent, "Hermeneutics and the Analysis of Complex Biological Systems" (Paper presented at the University of California at Davis, 14 November 1984).

30. Maurice Merleau-Ponty, *Phenomenology of Perception*, trans. Colin Smith (London: Routledge & Kegan Paul, 1962), p. 170.

31. Samuel Anthony Barnett, "The 'expression of the emotions,'" in *A Century of Darwin*, ed. Samuel Anthony Barnett (Cambridge: Harvard University Press, 1959), pp. 206–30.

32. Aristotle, *De anima* 435b16–17.

12

The Case for a Philosophical Anthropology

We can hardly expect to put our heads together if we leave our worlds apart.

WILLIAM C. WIMSATT

INTRODUCTION

Philosophical anthropology. The label conjures up a hybrid few have heard of, and for many of those, a hybrid of questionable viability. Indeed, the words sound a flat thud in the ears of most philosophers and a rude intrusion in the ears of most anthropologists, who hardly want anything to do with it. Some would in fact question the very existence of such an animal since the cross-disciplinary marriage necessary to its birth is believed never to have been consummated—at least to the satisfaction of both parties.

The estimation by most present-day anthropologists is that philosophical anthropology is mired in speculative thought and lacks any claim to empirical evidence that would make it of genuine anthropological interest, let alone elevate it to the status of science. This is in part a measure of the impressive academic growth of anthropology as a social science in the twentieth century. The critical charge is not of course aimed at the work of wayward colleagues, but at the work of philosophers, for however readily the term suggests the contrary, modern philosophical anthropology is a subdiscipline of philosophy. That the designation brings anthropologists with a philosophical bent rather than anthropologically inclined philosophers to mind easily deflects attention from a more important fact. Properly conceived and practiced, philosophical anthropology is not in the one or the other academic camp but in both equally. It is at the interface of philosophy and science, very close to the place where Darwinian bodies are found. Because it has not been positively identified as commonly held territory, but is often distantly regarded with a skeptical or pejorative eye, the potentially fertile interdisciplinary field has gone virtually untilled. There are four major correctives to the situation. Each involves effort on the part of philosophers and anthropologists alike, and each will be described in turn below.

THE FIRST MOVE

The first move by philosophers toward joint cultivation is a relatively simple one: taking evolution seriously. Humans are primates. Their primate heritage cannot be discounted—whether by choice or by default—but must figure centrally in accounts of human being. This means not merely that logical "musts" and scenarios of the irrational are inappropriate. It means that ontologies on the order of Heidegger's and Sartre's must be revised. Humans cannot sustain characterization in absolute, ahistorical terms; no *deus ex machina* ontological manipulations take place in offstage evolutionary wings. By the same token, it means that language and other present-day forms of human life are not absolute and ahistorical either. They neither began suddenly nor arrived out of the blue full-blown. Having originated and evolved in the course of hominid evolution, they have a conceptual history, one necessarily undergirded by certain experiential invariants that, like anatomical, physiological, and in general, organic invariants, have constrained certain creatures across time to membership in a certain evolutionary Family, in particular, a hominidae Family whose nature, practices, activities, predispositions, and capabilities exert as profound a pull as those of the social family in which each individual is raised. Present-day sociobiologists in fact see the two families as parts of the same genetic inheritance—though that appraisal is in no way entailed in the acknowledgment of a hominidae Family.

The correlative first move by anthropologists lies not only in the direction of welcoming philosophical studies and amplifications, and of encouraging philosophers to incorporate evolutionary thought in their work, but of doing the latter themselves. The studied fact of cultural relativism has blinded many anthropologists to the identification and study of biological invariants. Taking evolution as seriously as culture means pursuing those invariants—just as doggedly as cultural differences are presently pursued. It is more than probable that as tactile–kinesthetic invariants come to light, fundamental concepts subtending hominid classificatory systems—concepts at present taken for granted—will be elucidated and with them a detailed schema of the conceptual infrastructure subtending distinctively hominid forms of life.

Taking evolution as seriously as culture means furthermore embracing an expanded methodology. Fossil evidence apart, the lives of present-day nonhuman primates, and the practices and beliefs of people in present-day primitive societies, are regularly used comparatively to reconstruct the hominid past. They are not, however, the sole yardsticks by which to measure out *in absentia* the lives and practices of our early ancestors. Indeed, when their heuristic value is carried to ideological extremes, paleoanthropological analogies to present-day primitive societies and to nonhuman primate behavior effectively cut off recognition of those invariant corporeal realities of everyday hominid existence that necessarily came to inform the lives and practices of our ancestors—the felt hardness of teeth, for example, or the felt binary regularity of walking. It is from such mundane structures and activities that concepts subtending distinctively hominid forms of life arose—tool-making and counting, for example. Access to the conceptual infrastructure of hominid thinking and evolution is thus had not by the "comparative method,"[1] but by way of a methodology having the power to penetrate below behavioral surfaces and illuminate the standard in terms of which fundamental concepts were forged in the first place. The following two chapters demonstrate this fact in fine detail.

An especially topical and lucid example can be given of how a joint first move toward cultivation might be concretely taken and where it would lead. The example is based on current literature in both anthropology and philosophy.

In his book *Symbols: Public and Private*, the anthropologist Raymond Firth notes that while philosophical writings on symbols "may be of interest to anthropologists . . . because they offer frameworks for handling problems of symbol definition and classification," the writings are not useful because philosophers "sometimes incorporate judgments about society, resting upon assumptions which may be unstated, but which run counter to anthropological experience."[2] He gives as example Susanne Langer's theory of the evolution of dance. According to Langer, dance arose in the context of a developing mythic consciousness, namely, in the idea of Powers derived from what she identifies as "the feeling of personal power and will in the human body,"[3] and what Firth, in paraphrasing her, identifies as "subjective feelings of potency."[4] In his role as social anthropologist, Firth clearly sees the necessity of resisting priority being given to the individual in the structuring of a socio-cultural life. Hence the intrusion of the usually scientifically pejorative term *subjective,* and with it, the idea of a private over a public symbolism. After briefly describing Langer's theory, Firth goes on to say that although "anthropologists have made few contributions [to the study of dance symbolism] . . . they do have some knowledge."[5] What this knowledge comes down to is that the social import of dance far outweighs any individual import. In other words, Langer's "para-philosophic analysis of the dance" is misleading because "in the most primitive societies we have studied, dancing is a highly social activity, and not just an individual abstraction of a sense of power."[6]

For her part, Langer makes no attempt to sound out the empirical source of the idea of Power more fully, to examine how it is that "from earliest times, through the late tribal stages, men live in a world of 'Powers'—divine or semi-divine Beings, whose wills determine the courses of cosmic and human events." She says only that "the first recognition of [these Powers] is through the feeling of personal power and will in the human body."[7] Had she sounded out this feeling of corporeal power and its conceptual elaboration, she undoubtedly would have been led to an affirmation of philosopher Edmund Husserl's empirically grounded, readily verifiable analyses of bodily *I can*'s (*ich kanns*),[8] and used them to support her theory, which, in empirical terms, necessitates precisely a demonstration of how the concept of power is born in tactile–kinesthetic experience, experiences of one's own body in the course of moving. With such empirical backboning, Langer's theory could no longer be said to "run counter to anthropological experience." On the contrary, it would present evidence of pan-cultural experiential invariants. The charge of a solely private symbolism would in consequence be no longer tenable.

On the other hand, what Firth says of dance symbolism with respect to "the most primitive societies we have studied," cannot necessarily be said at all of the earliest forms of dance. Even "the most primitive" present-day societies (whatever the measure of primitiveness) are not replicas of ancestral hominid societies—any more than present-day nonhuman primates are replicas of ancestral hominid primates. As pointed out earlier, the heuristic value of analogies cannot be pushed to ideological extremes, in this instance without mocking the tenets of evolutionary theory. But furthermore, the question of whether dance originated in private or in public symbols is not at all the most interesting or critical anthropological question to pose. The one that is concerns the source of dance symbols; to wit, How is it that corporeal movement through which the symbols of power take palpable shape—symbols that, his criticism notwithstanding, Firth does *not* deny exist "in the most primitive societies we have studied" —is meaningful in generally the same way to all participants and all spectators, in effect constituting at once the source of any private or public symbolism. The anthropologist who would answer this question would be led inexorably in the same direction Langer would have been led had she sounded out the empirical evidence for the idea of Powers "from the earliest times" onward, that is, to the affirmation of invariant bodily experiences common to all hominids in virtue of their being hominids, an affirmation of the existence of *comsigns* in Stuart Altmann's terms.

THE SECOND MOVE

There is a second joint move required: taking the body and in particular tactile–kinesthetic corporeal life seriously. As might be apparent, the move is adumbrated and even prepared for in the first move. Cast in broad perspective, the first move toward rapprochement by each side is a move toward a definitive evolutionary history that identifies and analyzes concepts undergirding fundamental human practices and beliefs. Taking evolution seriously in this way means in the long run taking living bodies seriously—leaving no experiential or behavioral stone unturned, as the above example indicates. Hence the second joint move.

In general, neither philosophers nor anthropologists have shown a friendly and consistent interest in tactile–kinesthetic experience, though the latter in principle tend to ignore it more resolutely. The unspoken principle is quite simple to pinpoint: the tactile–kinesthetic body is regarded a thoroughly disreputable barometer of truth; it is vitiated through and through with "purely subjective" happenings.

Reliance on these happenings—specifically through introspection—in most instances precipitates an immediate case of methodological shudders. Introspection is in fact still the whipping dog of modern twentieth-century Western science. James L. Gould and Peter Marler, for example, two biologists writing in a recent issue of *Scientific American*, begin their article, "Learning By Instinct," with the thought that introspection is a "deceptively convincing authority,"[9] one that leads to erroneous conclusions in contrast to those true ones reached by experimental procedures. One can reasonably question why, after over fifty years of behaviorism, it is necessary to continue the flogging. The following behind-the-scenes report on the major American shift to behaviorism provides an unequivocal answer:

When these measurements [on differences in the tongue, larynx, etc. in relaxed situations and in reading situations] first came out in the early 1930's, I am told that Professor Watson, with his behaviorism, said that my findings proved his point that thinking is laryngeal behavior. . . . We do not by any means feel that Watson was correct that thinking was chiefly a laryngeal phenomenon, but that, of course, the larynx apparently is involved in the peripheral examination of thinking. A rather amusing comment was made by his colleague Karl Lashley, who was at the University of Chicago and my very close friend although we did no work together; Lashley told me with a chuckle that when he and Watson would spend an evening together, working out principles of behaviorism, much of the time would be devoted to introspection.[10]

People necessarily and regularly rely on introspection not only in attempting to determine whether thinking is a laryngeal phenomenon, but in a multitude of other situations—academic and nonacademic: in deciding how best to set up an experimental test situation (whether for humans or nonhumans), for example, particularly its procedures and overall design; in deciding which questions to answer immediately on an examination because one readily knows the answers, and which to leave to the end because they will require more time and thought; in deciding what is to count as the beginning and end of a behavior when one is studying behavior (e.g., "how large or small a segment of behavior is a primate pattern?");[11] in deciding whether to stay in bed and call in sick, indeed, in determining whether one is sick to begin with and whether to call the doctor; and so on. The problem in part is therefore to clarify just where "scientifically respectable" introspection begins and ends. This is a particularly urgent question to address since in the human sciences "introspection is still with us, doing its business under various aliases, of which *verbal report* is one."[12] The problem is also a matter of rigor: fraudulent practices in present-day "objective" science have decisively shown that any method is only as reliable as its practitioners.

In sum, the tactile–kinesthetic body is a quite reliable barometer if one comes to it at its ground floor of happenings, gives it close and painstaking attention, and is not in a rush to make higher or wished-for generalizations—whether about learning and instinct, or about thinking and laryngeal behavior. Moreover, as will be apparent in the chapters on methodology, a reflective method for securing tactile–kinesthetic truths goes beyond simple introspective reportorial techniques. What is important to emphasize once again is that a concern with behavior need not shut out experience. Indeed, a thorough understanding of behavior rests upon a clear awareness of one's own behavioral experiences—as Watson's and Lashley's introspective work on behalf of behaviorism shows, as the above examples of academic introspection also show, and as the pan-biological practice of analogical apperception, discussed in the previous chapter, also clearly shows.

Even if adhering to the tenets of behaviorism or in general aligning themselves strongly with a scientific perspective, philosophers generally take no part in the flogging. Reflection, after all, is a philosopher's stock in trade, and it readily involves introspection—a fact that incidentally explains in a further sense why Watson and Lashley necessarily had recourse to introspection in their formulation of the *principles* of behaviorism. On the strictly philosophical side, Socrates's injunction, "Know thyself," is an unequivocal testimonial to the role of introspection in the quest for knowledge in Western civilization at the least, as are all the many more current philosophical inquiries into what it means to say, "I am in pain," for example.[13]

The philosopher's self-imposed estrangement from the tactile–kinesthetic body is thus understandably not on methodological grounds at all; it is rather on epistemological ones. The tactile–kinesthetic body is not taken seriously for it is at once too intimate and too frivolous a body. It is regarded too personal a physicality and too much an intellectual lightweight. Present-day philosophers' interest in sensory experience seldom focuses on touch or on movement, for example. On the contrary, it is vision that is given priority as a gnostic system, and this even where the dismissal of, or lack of attention to, tactile–kinesthetic experience is flagrant. For example, Wittgenstein asks, "Couldn't I imagine having frightful pains and turning to stone while they lasted? Well, how do I know, *if I shut my eyes*, whether I have not turned to stone?" (italics added).[14] "If I shut my eyes" is a gratuitous contingency. The correct answer to Wittgenstein's second question—"through tactile–kinesthetic experience"—is not given, for that answer is not apparently even conceived, Wittgenstein's immediately following question being, "And if that has happened, in what sense will *the stone* have the pains?" Clearly Wittgenstein is taking as fact the idea that knowledge is tied to visuality.

The predilection for the visual is actually a culturewide bias. Whereas earlier philosophers, notably seventeenth- and eighteenth-century British empiricists—John Locke, George Berkeley, and David Hume—who had much to say on sensory experience, at least *began* their examinations evenhandedly, that is, neutrally, present-day philosophers are immediately and all too unwittingly caught up in "the addiction to visualism which marks our technological culture."[15] Although cultural historians since Marshall McLuhan have called attention to Western hypervisualism and analyzed its various forms, the addiction all the same has gone virtually unnoticed—whether because of a too-easy acceptance of an absolute cultural relativism that denies the possibility of insight into one's own culture, or a too habitual and unexamined sensory life. Foucault's painstaking analysis of the optics of power with respect to sexual behavior in Western culture is an excellent case in point. The optics of power is spelled out in detail in terms of a *scientia sexualis*—one of what Foucault calls "two great procedures for producing the truth of sex."[16] In a *scientia sexualis*, pleasure-giving sexual behavior is confessed, examined, and endlessly analyzed. In the other great, essentially non-Western procedure—what Foucault terms an *ars erotica*—sexual behavior receives no such attention. Although as experienced in an *ars erotica*, sexual pleasure is kept secret—"[it] would lose its effectiveness and its virtue by being divulged"[17]—Foucault does not discuss or even acknowledge the radical *sensory difference* between the two kinds of "truth of sex"; to wit, in an *ars erotica*, the felt pleasures of sexual experience are not made public in the manner of a visual spectacle for all to behold. *They remain in the tactile–kinesthetic body.*

Foucault comes remarkably close to grasping the essential sensory disjunction in his statement that in an *ars erotica* sexual knowledge is not broadcast but "deflected back into the sexual practice itself, in order to shape it as though from within and amplify its effect."[18] "*As though* from within": Foucault too is clearly seduced by hypervisualism. Indeed, he nowhere concretizes the internal body as he does the external one. Had he seen through the overwhelming visual bias in his often penetrating diagnostic of Western society, he might readily have seen that the all-pervasive, ever-growing optics of power he so lucidly describes is actually dependent upon a correlative and increasingly intensifying *power of optics;* and in turn that that increasingly intensifying power of optics has swollen and continues swelling in proportion to the shrinking power of a tactile–kinesthetic sensorium. What McLuhan in his popular analyses of twentieth-century Western culture characterized as "the ratio among the senses" [19] has sizable if culturally veiled epistemological consequences.

The philosopher H. H. Price called attention to the distinction in philosophical practice between vision and touch in his presidential address to the Aristotelian Society in 1943: "Some philosophers regard sight as the typical or 'model' sense and interpret other forms of sense-experience in terms of it; not that they explicitly say that this is what they are going to do, but this is what we find them doing. . . . By a kind of afterthought, they proceed to apply this analysis to the other forms of sense experience . . . treating the other senses as imperfect analogues or poor relations of sight." Other philosophers regard touch as the model sense, but as Price points out, "most Empiricists have been Visual Philosophers." [20] He explains the philosophical privileging of the visual in terms of both the rise of modern science—"without visual sensation, there could be no science, or only the faintest beginnings of it" [21]—and the related fact that since empiricist philosophers are concerned mainly with an analysis of the presuppositions of science, they have simply fallen in step with the predominantly visual modes and concerns of scientific research. In effect, seen in the context of the rise of modern science—and of most of modern philosophy— the culturewide predilection for the visual actually blots out the sharpness of the line dividing science and philosophy at the same time that it explains why Tactual Scientists, to amplify Price's designation, are as sparse as Tactual Philosophers.

It is significant to point out that the beginnings of modern science from a theoretical viewpoint were not visually oriented. Quite the contrary. There is in fact a rich irony in Galileo's original separation of "real" sense qualities from non-real ones in the interests of developing a true science of nature, for in large measure the separation distinctively marked off tactile and kinetic qualities from other sense qualities:

Now I say that whenever I conceive any material or corporeal substance, I immediately feel the need to think of it as bounded, and as having this or that shape; as being large or small in relation to other things, and in some specific place at any given time; as being in motion or at rest; as touching or not touching some other body; and as being one in number, or few, or many. . . . But that it must be white or red, bitter or sweet, noisy or silent, and of sweet or foul odor, my mind does not feel compelled to bring in as necessary accompaniments.[22]

With respect to establishing a fundamental scientific epistemology, Galileo's thought-experiment (another classic case of introspection: "*I immediately feel the need to think of it as . . .*") asserts the gnostic primacy of tactile–kinesthetic experience over visual experience. Figure, shape, and size are first given in haptic perception, as Piaget's order of experiments determining the growth of spatial concepts in young children indicates, and as Berkeley's eighteenth-century investigations of tactility and vision clearly show.[23] Descartes reduced Galileo's "real" qualities to extension, figure, and movement and designated them *primitive notions*, but said nothing of their sensory provenience; his interests were in fact elsewhere. Locke added solidity (and number) to Descartes's trio and designated them *primary qualities*. Unlike Descartes, Locke was concerned with sensory distinctions and it was he who, in his emphasis upon the priority of solidity as a felt primary quality, first directly suggested the *conceptual* primacy of the tactile–kinesthetic body:

There is no *idea* which we receive more constantly from sensation than *solidity*. Whether we move or rest, in what posture soever we are, we always feel something under us that supports us and hinders our further sinking downwards; and the bodies which we daily handle make us perceive that, whilst they remain between them, they do, by an insurmountable force, hinder the approach of the parts of our hands that press them (italics in original).[24]

(Here, in another form, is a truth about the primacy of touch that would be hard-won in a world of cutaneous stimulation.)

Berkeley went further than Locke when, as noted above, he affirmed on the basis of compelling empirical evidence that boundedness, shape, and size are all first tangible qualities. They are literally *com-prehended* before attaining visual definition. With an ever-increasing interest in the *practice* of modern science, however, and the ever-dwindling interest in theoretical matters, that is, in Galileo's original qualitative/sensory distinctions and their philosophical analyses and elaborations, burgeoning indications of the gnostic primacy of the tactile–kinesthetic body were cut short. Berkeley's *New Theory of Vision*, for example, which documents the fundamental role of touch in the establishment of basic spatial concepts, is far from being the centerpiece of present-day analyses of spatial perception—whether in science or philosophy.

On the scientific side, the failure to take the tactile–kinesthetic body seriously can have immediate and severe consequences. The validity of procedures and of conclusions in scientific research can be distorted. For example, Joel Kaplan, a primatologist, writes that "because it is generally assumed that vision is the most important sense for all primates, we decided to begin our studies by manipulating the color of our infants' surrogates."[25] From a sensory point of view, the studies begin *in medias res:* what is first in need of examination is the assumption itself. Short of that ground-floor investigation, any study methodologically and epistemologically geared to the axiological priority of the visual cannot be considered decisive or conclusive.

Failure to take the tactile–kinesthetic body seriously can furthermore hamper progress in research on vision itself. Present-day difficulties in building a visual system into an artificial intelligence[26] are a prime example. They suggest the correctness of Galileo's and Berkeley's analyses, specifically with respect to the perception of objects. As pointed out in Chapter 2, the solution to the root difficulty of determining *edges* so as to achieve specific visual-object definition may well be not in understanding the last details of an astoundingly complex visual neurophysiology, but in understanding how, in default of a gnostic tactility that provides its normal undergirdings, vision is blind to everyday spatial meanings. Again, it may be noted that in this sense, Berkeley is likely to be proved ultimately correct: what vision knows of objects in a spatial sense, it learns from touch.

THE THIRD MOVE

The third move toward joint cultivation is to take each other seriously —not only instead of ignoring each other but instead of using each other merely pragmatically as serviceable or impressive props for the case one is making or opposing. Several examples will illustrate the ultimate emptiness of both practices so far as actual interdisciplinary substance is concerned.

In what is not infrequently regarded a classic anthropology paper, "Culture: A *Human* Domain," Ralph Holloway cites the counterviews of a colleague, M. Harris, who holds that culture and learning in humans are not different in kind from culture and learning in nonhuman animals. Holloway quotes Harris's statement that "the differences are only 'a matter of degree and do not justify the Aristotelian either/or approach.' " He then proceeds to note that "Harris is guilty of Aristotelian thought himself in neglecting to consider the possibility that the rubrics he accepts, such as learning and instinct, encompass many different kinds of organized behavioral patterns based on widely different nervous systems, ecological factors, and motivations."[27] In what amounts to a game of "sully by philosophical association," Aristotle is bandied back and forth—a taint so illustrious as to magnify defilement.

An honorific but conceptually flawed use of philosophers is made by John O'Keefe and Lynn Nadel in their theory of the hippocampus as a cognitive map.[28] Here Kant's spatial *a priori* is identified with a "spatial system . . . not tied to the body but [providing] the organism with a maplike representation which acts as a framework for organizing its sensory inputs and is perceived as remaining stationary in spite of the movements of the organism."[29] In other words, a cognitive map is likened to Kant's spatial *a priori:* it is "the mechanism by which the mind organize[s] sensations." The problem here is a garbled Kantian metaphysics in which minds are reduced to material brains, the latter being defined as functional systems that produce *a priori*'s, "mindful products." In this scheme, the very thing posited—a cognitive map—while belonging unequivocally in Kantian terms to the realm of the *phenomenal* (it is a thing in the brain) functions nonempirically. In effect, a kind of metaphysical derangement obtains that is not of course present in the Kantian original. The metaphysical garbling is reinforced by a linguistic misattribution. Kant's eighteenth-century formulation of spatial *a priori*'s has nothing to do with *mechanisms, sensory inputs*—or *brains*. Similarly, it has nothing to do with genes. Sociobiologist David Barash's honorific appropriation of Kant as an impressive buttress for sociobiological theory[30] is as conceptually flawed as O'Keefe and Nadel's. Such misattributions are not unrelated to the broader issue of "conceptual assignments" in the writing of history.[31]

For their part, philosophers do not so much use scientists as the findings of scientists in their analyses and reflections on what it is to be human. In that usage, evolutionary theory is at times misappropriated, as illustrated earlier by Williard van Orman Quine's appropriation of natural selection to explain the course of human ideational history. It is also at times reduced to the point of merely providing support either for conciliating "humans and animals" or pitting the ones against the others. The support in either case is offered in such present-day terms that a bona fide hominid lineage fails to come into perspective. For example, a critical look might be taken at the possibility that analogies exist between humans and nonhumans— especially higher primates (notably chimpanzees)—specifically with respect to intelligence, language, and thought, that is, with respect to what is generally and commonly, if erroneously on the thesis of this book, designated "mental abilities." While seemingly the question is put in evolutionary perspective, it is in fact answered ahistorically. There is no concern with fossil or artifactual hominid evidence (e.g., tool-making, burial practices) that attests to certain *pre–Homo sapiens sapiens* practices, beliefs, and, in effect, concepts. There is no consideration of *Homo* forms earlier than present-day *sapiens sapiens*, not to mention earlier-than-*Homo* australopithecines who, on the basis of fossil evidence, are regarded our earliest *hominid* ancestors. Joseph Margolis and Mary Midgeley,[32] for example, are hardly alone in bypassing evidence from paleoanthropology and archaeology when they consider the propriety of ascribing intentional mental states to nonhuman animals. The same is true of philosophers' discussions of language. Nowhere is the considerable literature on the anatomical conditions necessary to the origin and evolution of language, or on primordial language, taken into account. In consequence, the pitting or conciliating of human and nonhuman animal "mental abilities," while seemingly of evolutionary moment, remains wholly synchronic. All of the presented evidence is in the here and now. Moreover analogical dimensions of the presented evidence (i.e., analogies from present-day nonhuman primates to ancestral hominid primates) are neither concretely spelled out nor suggested. In consequence the presented evidence serves simply as a test case either for affirming or disclaiming that *present-day* humans are like *present-day* higher primates (chimpanzees) with respect to their "mental abilities," or that the two extant forms are different in kind. There is not even a hint of hominid history. The science of paleoanthropology is nowhere acknowledged much less consulted.

Paleoanthropology can also be ignored at the same time that an attempt is made to educe a "scientific image of man" within a tenable historico-philosophical framework. In this instance, science is put to philosophic use in the restricted sense of a neurophysiology of the brain (or central nervous system). Again, the evolutionary study of hominids—the science of paleoanthropology—is nowhere hinted at. In fact, in Wilfrid Sellars's essay, "Philosophy and the Scientific Image of Man," the case for "Special Creation" (Sellars's phrase and capital letters) is unabashedly pressed: "the transition from pre-conceptual patterns of behaviour to conceptual thinking was a holistic one, a jump to a level of awareness which is irreducibly new, a jump which was the coming into being of man."[33] The specially created jump Sellars envisions—in effect, the giant Rubicon step—is from a speech-deficient to a speech-enabling neurophysiology, one whose processes are the physical analogue of both overt and "inner" verbal language. Given fossil evidence of Pleistocene/Pliocene hominids (human ancestors to three and a half million years ago), there are of course no grounds for asserting a virtuoso jump across an evolutionary Rubicon. Furthermore, merely given the *fact* of fossil evidence from the sciences of paleoanthropology and archaeology, the omission of a paleoanthropological/archaeological perspective is indefensible. Indeed, there is as deep an irony in the fact that the scientific image of man in much of twentieth-century Western philosophy is an image outside paleoanthropology as in the fact that Galileo's tacit distinction among sense qualities on behalf of the mathematization of science implicitly singled out the fundamental criticality of tactile–kinesthetic experience. In sum, taking each other seriously in this instance means that in reflecting upon the nature of human nature, philosophers consult the evolutionary past as it has been reconstructed by paleoanthropologists with the same sustained and studied attention they give to present-day studies of the neurophysiology of the brain.[34] (It might also be briefly noted that taking each other seriously means that apologies and justifications for taking each other seriously[35] are out of order. Though atonements and excuses are not common practice, they have no place in a *bona fide* philosophical anthropology.)

THE FOURTH MOVE

The fourth and final move toward joint cultivation is to take philosophical biology seriously. This biology is mainly the work of continental biologists who find the phenomenon of life insufficiently explained and/or not fully accounted for in the traditional Anglo-American practice of biology. For the most part, their focus is on existential dimensions of animate form, dimensions hinted at but unanalyzed in traditional accounts. For example, Adolph Portmann examines the *Weltbeziehung durch innerlichkeit* of animate life, that is, the primary inner relatedness of animals to their environment—their "centricity," as Marjorie Grene has thoughtfully translated this primary character of living creatures.[36] Helmuth Plessner examines the *positionality* of animate forms, a similar basic dimension of creaturely life that again entails the complex fact of relatedness.[37] What is at stake in both cases is clearly akin to "the mental" but is cast in a much wider and deeper mold. In the broadest purview, what philosophical biology aims at affirming and analyzing are living forms *as subjects*—subjects in the sense of both individually and phylogenetically commanding a certain world, and of being both individually and phylogenetically disposed toward it. In this view, animate form is more than a certain conjunction of bones and enabling anatomy. Its active and passive dimensions are inherently individuating. Not only size, geometric patterning, swellings, and coloration, but movement and posture serve categorial recognition of one individual by other individuals: they announce age, sex, and species, for instance. Moreover movement and posture in particular are variously expressive of mood, intent, desire, threat, fear, and so on. In short, *animate form is informative of the life of the organism in a sense far beyond what a simple comparative anatomy delineates*.

Inclusion of this dimension of biology is as mandatory to a comprehensive *and comprehensible* account of how twentieth-century humans came to be the creatures they are as it is to a complete biological explanation and understanding of living creatures generally. Short of an evolutionary history of creatures as subjects, it is impossible to explain how hominids came to make stone tools, draw on cave walls, begin counting, or conceive of death. Such acts and conceptions clearly entail a creature capable of both elaborating the world—making *more* of what is already there (as a stone into a tool)—and making sense of it—making what is there conceptually understandable, for example, lifeless bodies. A philosophical biology is thus co-terminous with a proper philosophical anthropology. A proper "science of man," as Hume termed the study of human nature, is at once philosophical, biological, and anthropological. Put in this perspective, the truth of Wimsatt's epigrammatic statement cited at the beginning of this chapter is palindromic. We can hardly expect to put our worlds together if we leave our heads apart, anymore than we can expect to put our heads together if we leave our worlds apart.

In point of fact, the bio-philosophical dimension is visible just below the surface in much traditional research on nonhuman animal life, viz., in studies where a differential "inwardness," "centricity," or subjectivity is acknowledged as exactingly as a differential morphology. Variations in subjectivity make one animal more curious and venturesome than another, one animal more strongly disposed to lead than to follow, another more clever, and so on, just as morphological variations make one animal potentially more powerful and prominent by virtue of its size, and another potentially swifter in virtue of its longer stride. Differential subjectivity is well documented both indirectly—for example in descriptions of animal behavior in the wild where the recognition of personality differences among animals motivates the very naming of the individual animals studied (e.g., "Leakey, like his namesake, was robust, high ranking, and normally good natured. Mr. Worzle, on the other hand, was always nervous, both in his dealings with other chimps and with human beings.")[38]— and directly (though not necessarily advertently) in the behavioral reports themselves, that is, quite apart from nominative labelings by field observers. The initiative taken by a female Japanese macaque to wash the sand off sweet potatoes before eating them[39] is a prime example. The novel washing practice cannot be written off as mere *behavior*. It was not a mannered aesthetic that the female—and then the macaque troop generally—began cultivating but a certain *tactile experience*.

What is critically significant about the above example of differential subjectivity—the female macaque's capacity to discern between tactile experiences and her motivation to change behavioral practice (i.e., everyday habits) in light of experienced difference—is that on a more major scale just such experiential discernments and concomitant behavioral shifts were a driving force behind much of hominid evolution. Hominid shifts that made evolutionary history—consistent bipedality and stone tool-making, for example—were not the work of neurophysiological mutations in cortical matter. Neither were they simply the result of having a certain bodily part, or of having a certain bodily part *free*—for instance the hands for tool-making as is commonly maintained. Having a certain part, or a certain part free, in no way entails the having of a certain behavior.[40] It means only having *the potential to move*, in a certain way and into certain areas and not others. (Lobe-finned fish, hypothesized to be the vertebrates to have made the key move from water to land, are an outstanding example of this fact. Only *some* lobe-finned fish made the move even though *all* lobe-finned fish had "the right part" for making the transition.) Hominid shifts that made evolutionary history were initiated by certain individuals who ventured forth in new ways—just as did the female Japanese macaque. The shifts were the work of differential Darwinian bodies, bodies differentially disposed toward the world and differentially commanding it.

Oddly enough, a description of differential subjectivity with precisely evolutionary implications, indeed, a description substantively and stylistically prescient of Darwin's own writings on the theory of natural selection, was adumbrated by Hume in his eighteenth-century analysis of what in today's terminology would be identified as differential reasoning powers. In a lengthy footnote Hume presents what closely resembles a Darwinian itemization of individual variations to explain why some persons surpass others in their capacity for understanding, and why, by analogy, persons surpass "animals" in the same respect. There are variations, Hume says, in attributes such as attention, memory, observation, the ability to infer consequences, clearheadedness, analysis, capacity for analogies, lack of prejudice, and cultural learnings.[41] What Hume specifies under all these variations are aspects of differential subjectivity.

That Darwin read Hume is a fact historians of science have documented[42] but not to the point of calling attention to Hume's "differential subjectivity" and its striking, indeed, uncanny, similarity to Darwin's first descriptions of individual variations in animals with respect to their physical features. Clearly something very like a philosophical biology appeared two hundred years ago, in an eighteenth-century "science of man" in which the principle of differential subjectivity was elaborated. That that principle is as key an evolutionary factor as the principle of differential morphology is a fact Darwin would not doubt in the least. On the thesis and evidence of this book, the two principles are inextricably bound: fundamental concepts are corporeal concepts. In effect, where philosophical biology aligns itself specifically with philosophical anthropology is in promoting investigations of conceptual origins by insisting on a thorough examination of animate life. To identify, define, and analyze a distinctively hominid subjectivity is to show how, with respect to each new major behavior—each new "form of life" as Wittgensteinians might describe it—animate form and the tactile–kinesthetic body generated those concepts fundamental to the behavior and in effect, secured the behavior as an ongoing cultural practice. As the example of the Japanese macaques' sweet-potato-washing readily indicates, the conceptual recognition of *smoothness* and of *grittiness* was necessarily engendered in the adoption of the new behavior. Mere discriminative ability, it might be noted, though obviously integral to conceptual recognition, would hardly by itself account for the perpetuation of the radically changed eating pattern as a fixed habit.[43] Moreover exclusive concern with traditional biological subject matter typically lets such conceptual aspects of creaturely life go begging. At the other extreme, neurophysiological processes can at best be translated into concepts only by way of hypothetical entities such as cognitive maps. By the latter approach, the question of where concepts come from is answered before it is asked; and the possibility—and necessity—of explaining concepts themselves by way of a conceptual standard or model is thereby ignored. In sum, forthright recognition of how corporeal experience entails corporeal concepts is theoretically foreshadowed in philosophical biology. It is precisely what is of moment in a philosophical anthropology.

NOTES

1. See Jane B. Lancaster, *Primate Behavior and the Emergence of Human Culture* (New York: Holt, Rinehart, and Winston, 1975), pp. 3–5.

2. Raymond Firth, *Symbols: Public and Private* (Ithaca, N.Y.: Cornell University Press, 1973), p. 57.

3. Susanne Langer, *Feeling and Form* (New York: Charles Scribner's Sons, 1953), p. 190.

4. Firth, *Symbols*, p. 57.

5. Ibid.

6. Ibid., p. 58.

7. Langer, *Feeling and Form*, pp. 189, 190.

8. See Chapter 2, note 8, p. 63.

9. James L. Gould and Peter Marler, "Learning by Instinct," *Scientific American* 256 (January 1987), p. 74.

10. Edmund Jacobson, "Electrophysiology of Mental Activities and Introduction to the Psychological Process of Thinking," in *Psychophysiology of Thinking*, ed. F. J. McGuigan and R. A. Schoonover (New York: Academic Press, 1973), p. 14.

11. Phyllis J. Dolhinow, *Primate Patterns*, ed. Phyllis J. Dolhinow (New York: Holt, Rinehart, and Winston, 1972), p. v.

12. E. G. Boring, "A History of Introspection," *Psychological Bulletin* 50 (1953), p. 169, quoted in Joseph F. Rychlak, *A Philosophy of Science for Personality Theory* (Boston: Houghton Mifflin Co., 1968), pp. 202–3.

13. See, for example, Ludwig Wittgenstein, *Philosophical Investigations*, trans. G. E. M. Anscombe (Oxford: Basil Blackwell, 1963); and Norton Nelkin, "Pains and Pain Sensations," *Journal of Philosophy* 83 (March 1986): 129–48.

14. Wittgenstein, *Philosophical Investigations*, p. 97[e].

15. Walter J. Ong, *Interfaces of the Word* (Ithaca, N.Y.: Cornell University Press, 1977), p. 126.

16. Michel Foucault, *The History of Sexuality*, vols. 1–3, trans. Robert Hurley (New York: Vintage, 1978), 1:57.

17. Ibid.

18. Ibid.

19. Marshall McLuhan, *Understanding Media* (New York: New American Library, 1964).

20. H. H. Price, "Touch and Organic Sensation," *Proceedings of the Aristotelian Society* 44 (1944), pp. a–ii.

21. Ibid., p. xxviii.

22. *Discoveries and Opinions of Galileo*, ed. and trans. S. Drake (Garden City, N.Y.: Doubleday, 1957), p. 272.

23. Jean Piaget and Bärbel Inhelder, *The Child's Conception of Space*, trans. F. J. Langdon and J. L. Lunzer (New York: W. W. Norton & Co., 1967); George Berkeley, *An Essay Toward A New Theory of Vision*, in *Berkeley: Essay, Principles, Dialogues*, ed. Mary W. Calkins (New York: Charles Scribner's Sons), pp. 1–98.

24. John Locke, *An Essay Concerning Human Understanding*, vols. 1–2, ed. John W. Yolton (New York: E. P. Dutton, 1961), 1:93.

25. Joel Kaplan, "Perceptual Properties of Attachment in Surrogate-Reared and Mother-Reared Squirrel Monkeys." In *Primate Biosocial Development*, ed. Suzanne Chevalier-Skolnikoff and Frank E. Poirier (New York: Garland Press, 1977), p. 226.

26. See V. Torre and Tomaso Poggio, "On Edge Detection," A.I. Memo 768, MIT, A.I. Laboratory, August 1984; see also Tomaso Poggio, "Vision by Man and Machine," A.I. Memo 776, MIT, A.I. Laboratory, March 1984; David Marr, *Vision* (New York: W. H. Freeman, 1982); and Israel Rosenfeld, "Seeing Through the Brain," *New York Review of Books*, 11 October 1984, pp. 53–56.

27. Ralph L. Holloway, "Culture: A Human Domain," *Current Anthropology* 10 (1969): 395–407.

28. John O'Keefe and Lynn Nadel, *The Hippocampus as a Cognitive Map* (Oxford: Clarendon Press, 1978).

29. John O'Keefe and Lynn Nadel, "Precis of O'Keefe and Nadel's *The Hippocampus as a Cognitive Map*," *Behavioral and Brain Sciences* 2 (1979): 488.

30. David Barash, *The Whispering Within* (New York: Penguin Books, 1982). It might also be noted that Barash confuses William and Henry James, attributing the "blooming, buzzing confusion" of the everyday world to the writings of the latter rather than the former.

31. For a discussion of this issue centering on Lamarck and Darwin vis-à-vis the concept of evolution, see Maxine Sheets-Johnstone, "Why Lamarck Did Not Discover the Principle of Natural Selection," *Journal of the History of Biology* 15 (1982): 443–65.

32. Joseph Margolis, *Persons and Minds* (Boston: D. Reidel Publishing, 1978); Mary Midgeley, *Beast and Man* (Ithaca, N.Y.: Cornell University Press, 1978).

33. Wilfrid Sellars, "Philosophy and the Scientific Image of Man," in *Science, Perception and Reality* (London: Routledge & Kegan Paul, 1963), p. 6.

34. See, for example, Patricia Smith Churchland's "A Perspective on Mind–Brain Research," *Journal of Philosophy* 77 (April 1980): 185–207.

35. See, for example, Levin, *Body's Recollection*: "Because this present study makes intensive use of anthropological material, I feel a need to point out why this use does not betray the ontological commitment of our project —why, in other words, it does not reduce our thinking to anthropologism" (p. 20). It might be added that Levin's use of "anthropological knowledge" to provide "eidetic variations" is an underhanded recognition of the need for phenomenological analyses in a *Husserlian* sense, i.e., a need for *epistemological* underpinnings in any complete ontology (see p. 19).

36. Adolph Portmann, *New Paths in Biology*, trans. A. Pomerans (New York: Harper and Row, 1964); Marjorie Grene, "The Character of Living Things, I," in *The Understanding of Nature* (Boston: D. Reidel Publishing, 1974), pp. 254–93.

37. Helmuth Plessner, *Die Stufen des Organischen und der Mensch* (Berlin: de Gruyter, 1928); see also Marjorie Grene, "The Character of Living Things, III," in *The Understanding of Nature*, pp. 320–45.

38. Jane van Lawick-Goodall, *In the Shadow of Man* (New York: Dell Publishing, 1971), p. 122.

39. M. Kawai, "Newly-acquired Pre-cultural Behavior of the Natural Troop of Japanese Monkeys on Koshima Islet," *Primates* 6 (1965): 1–30.

40. See Maxine Sheets-Johnstone, "Evolutionary Residues and Uniquenesses in Human Movement," *Evolutionary Theory* 6 (1983): 205–9.

41. David Hume, *An Enquiry Concerning Human Understanding* (La Salle, Ill.: Open Court Publishing, 1907), pp. 112–13.

42. Robert J. Richards, *Darwin and the Emergence of Evolutionary Theories of Mind and Behavior* (Chicago: University of Chicago Press, 1987).

43. Richard Rorty provides an apt illustration of the point, albeit the example runs counter to his own hard and fast thesis concerning concepts: "To say that a gadget (consisting of a photoelectric cell hitched up to a tape recorder) which says 'red!' when and only when we shine red light on it *doesn't* know what red is like is to say that we cannot readily imagine *continuing* a conversation with the gadget" (second italics added). *Philosophy and the Mirror of Nature* (Princeton: Princeton University Press, 1979), p. 189. Discriminative ability accounts for perspicacious, even sagacious, choices or responses in the moment, but by itself is insufficient to establishing and securing an on-going cultural practice—or belief. See also Claude Lévi-Strauss: "Even a classification at the level of sensible properties is a step towards rational ordering." *The Savage Mind*, trans. George Weidenfeld and Nicolson, Ltd. (London: Weidenfeld and Nicolson, 1972), p. 15.

13
Methodology:
The Hermeneutical Strand

A good interpretation of anything . . . takes us into the heart of that of which it is the interpretation.

CLIFFORD GEERTZ

To follow a history . . . is to understand a succession of actions, of thoughts, of feelings, presenting at the same time a certain direction, but also some surprises.

PAUL RICOEUR

ON PALEOANTHROPOLOGY AND
A FULL-SCALE HERMENEUTICS OF THE BODY

The paleoanthropological case studies in Part II demonstrate a full-scale hermeneutical methodology in action. It is apposite in this chapter only to illustrate in greater detail the method's central role in elucidating the roots of human thinking through corporeal analyses, and to examine in greater detail its central role in the science of paleoanthropology itself. An abbreviated look at interpretations of stone tool-making, and then of upright posture, will first demonstrate how a full-scale hermeneutics of the body is called for.

The process of tool-making presupposes certain fundamental sensory–kinetic meanings without which stone tools could never have

334

come to be forged: the concepts central to their making would be lacking. Paleoanthropologists and archaeologists speak repeatedly of *fracturing* and of *edges*[1]—even with respect to the most "crude and opportunistic"[2] tools—all the while taking them conceptually for granted in their own experience of tools and tool-making, as well as in that of the early hominids of whom they write. In describing the origin of tool-making, for example, archaeologist Kenneth Oakley states that "where no naturally sharp stones lay ready to hand, the solution was surely to *break* stones and produce sharp *edges*"[3] (italics added). To judge simply on the basis of such regularly occurring descriptive remarks, there is no doubt but that the concepts of edges and of fracturing were the conceptual *sine qua non* of stone tool-making. In brief, there are clearly concepts basic to tool-making, concepts that all acts of early hominid tool-making presuppose. The fundamental question is, Where did the elemental concepts of fracturing and of edges come from? And on what could the idea of their utility have been based?

There is a complementary conceptual point to be made. If a *gnostic tactility* can be affirmed and described by a prominent present-day neurologist[4]—and by earlier neurologists as well[5]—in terms of a blind person's ability to fashion artifacts resembling everyday objects, then the tactile–kinesthetic modality cannot in good paleoanthropological faith be underrated or ignored—certainly not indefinitely. Clearly a blind person is capable of making a tool; a sighted person deficient in tactile–kinesthetic functioning is not. The fact was brought out in the chapter on tool-making itself. It substantiates the claim that however seemingly intractable tactile–kinesthetic phenomena might at first appear, and whatever the methodological issues raised, an attempt to elucidate in a precise way the gnostic tactile structures of tool-making is demanded by the facts of the matter. A rigorously conceived and fundamental understanding of hominid intelligence ultimately hangs in the balance.

A critical methodological point arises in the context of the questions posed above concerning fracturing and edges. It concerns the necessity of attending rigorously to the exact nature of the creative tactile–kinetic transactions by which fracturing and edges are realized, and this lest too hasty interpretive conclusions be drawn concerning conceptual entailments and their degree of sophistication. Archaeologist Thomas Wynn,[6] for example, prematurely dismisses the possibility of a relationship between chimpanzee twig-stripping (for the purpose of termite-fishing) and hominid stone tool-making on the basis of the former's *"removal"* rather than *"placement"* of *"elements"*

(Wynn's terms). A less precipitous judgment would show on the contrary that in the most fundamental empirical sense, the chimpanzees' stripping manoeuvre is conceptually similar to flaking precisely in the fact that in both transactions pieces are progressively *subtracted* from an original whole, the resulting implement being in each case a *deduced* product. Sound evaluations of conceptual linkages among primates depend upon careful and thoroughgoing study of each piece of empirical evidence, that is, of each primate tool-making activity, so that in the end, what is interpretively winnowed is conceptually justified because it is empirically justifiable.

Apart from artifactual productions, a paleoanthropological hermeneutics is called for with respect to animate form itself. The hominid body requires hermeneutical analysis in its own right. Several people inside and outside philosophy have attempted to provide a hermeneutics of the human body[7]—most commonly of its upright posture—though not in every case designating the analysis a hermeneutical enterprise. The lack of a substantive evolutionary perspective and/or a complete corporeal one weakens the analysis in each case. For example, a just and thoroughgoing hermeneutics of upright posture would show initially (and in elaboration of accepted paleoanthropological theory) that an upright stance does not merely free the hands and enable one to see to greater distances. Upright posture frees the *whole* body, and in a preeminently tactile–kinesthetic sense.[8] Behaviors and perceptual possibilities routinely associated with upright posture —notably carrying objects about and seeing distant objects and events —have fundamentally to do with movement and touch, with potential *grasping* and *holding,* and with potential *approach* and *avoidance,* the sensory valencies of the latter behaviors being as tactilely motivated and ordered as the former. More than this, a just and thoroughgoing hermeneutics would show that upright posture freed the legs as well as the hands. In addition to freeing them for such actions as forward kicking and vertical jumping, it freed them—and the arms—for a binary oppositionality and an emphatically binary mode of living.[9] Because an upright body is, in an evolutionary sense, a uniquely *exposed* body and at the same time one whose spatial orientations and ordinary locomotion are radically different from those of a quadruped, an entirely new domain of sensory–kinetic meanings—particularly tactile–kinesthetic ones—becomes apparent, and with it, the possibility of radically different conceptual awarenesses. For instance, what serves as a signal of sexual readiness on an upright hominid body and what is readily available to touch on that same body are not the same as what serves as a signal or is readily available to touch on nonhominid primate bodies.[10] Philosopher Hans Jonas's essay, "The Nobility of Sight,"[11] for example, and psychiatrist Erwin Straus's "Born to See, Bound to Behold,"[12] by giving an unexamined edge to the visual and by slighting the evolutionary past, cannot discover or even approximate to the conceptual strata generated by a gnostic tactility or kinesthesia. The point of departure for their hermeneutics of the body is in each case the human present with its predilection for the visual over the tactile–kinesthetic, and its predilection for culture over biology. This approach has been justly criticized in previous chapters.

In sum, like any animate form, a consistently upright body carries with it a spectrum of certain tactile–kinesthetic possibilities and not others, possibilities actualized only in the adoption of particular behaviors, including the adoption of consistent bipedality itself. The development of a methodology to uncover and analyze the concepts embedded in the tactile–kinesthetic correlates of adopted hominid behaviors has not been of concern because by and large, the tactile–kinesthetic correlates of behavior have not been of concern. In many instances one could say they are not even conceived. Piaget's remarks upon an infant's opening of its mouth in conjunction with its attempt to open a matchbox are an apt illustration of just such blindness.[13] Why the infant opens its mouth—and why in fact Piaget bothers to note the behavior—is inexplicable apart from a certain corporeal conceptual relevance obtaining between the opening of the mouth and the opening of the matchbox. The conceptual relevance is implicitly noted by Piaget, but only by accident as it were, since the spatial/tactile–kinesthetic analogy between the two behavioral events is neither identified nor examined. In effect, a gnostic tactility–kinesthesia goes unnoticed. By the same token, it goes unnoticed from a methodological viewpoint because only a hermeneutics of the body that is grounded in paleoanthropological (and/or ontogenetical) evidence and full-scale corporeal understandings can bring the conceptual meanings of animate form and the tactile–kinesthetic body to light.

THE THEORETICAL INFRASTRUCTURE OF THE SCIENCE OF PALEOANTHROPOLOGY

SENSED RELICS

Properly understood, a full-scale hermeneutical paleoanthropology is akin to an archaeological enterprise. What is hidden or covered over is brought to the surface. Thus corporeal awarenesses and powers presupposed but unarticulated in traditional paleoanthropological ac-counts are exposed and analyzed. Insofar as these existential dimen-sions are engendered in animate form and the tactile–kinesthetic body, their presence—however veiled—in virtually every discourse on an-cestral hominid life is hardly surprising. There is, in effect, a complex theoretical infrastructure built into the science of paleoanthropology from the very beginning, one that covertly informs the hermeneutico-archaeological enterprise every step of the way. This theoretical infra-structure needs methodological elucidation and clarification.

In a quite unique way, paleoanthropology is at the interface of the natural and human sciences. Fossil bones are part of the landscape, but they are also "sensed relics"[14] of a once living form. It is this latter character of hominid fossils that motivates the paleoanthropologist's assumption of corporeal awarenesses and powers in descriptions and analyses of behavior, and that mandates a full-scale hermeneutics. To put the point in terms of ultimate interpretation, paleoanthro-pologists want to transpose into the present Hamlet's meditation on the skull of Yorick and say of the old hominid fossil they hold in their hands, "I know him [/her] well." Paleoanthropological know-ing is thus clearly not completed by a laboratory hermeneutics and epistemology—a knowing of dates, locomotor capabilities, true pelvis sizes, cranial capacities, and the like, and a building of explanatory models on the basis of such findings. Paleoanthropological knowing encompasses understandings as well as explanations, understandings having to do with the fact that, whatever the hominid fossil, it was once a living form. This dimension of *livingness* remains hidden—it is assumed but unelaborated, substantively present but virtually un-explored—in paleoanthropological reconstructions, not only because a Darwinian body has fallen from scientific grace, but because in its transfer from landscape to laboratory, the hominid fossil loses its character as a sensed relic. The livingness of the form—ancient but still potent—remains in the background, submerged in assessments of age, size, shape, and functional capacities. That this is so is clear when ancient fossils are transported to another environment, an envi-ronment in which their once consummate livingness is dramatically revealed, indeed, to the point of overwhelming for the moment any explanatory theses or questionings and any debate over laboratory measurements and interpretations. A deeper consideration of what it means to be a *sensed relic* will bring this once consummate livingness into the light.

The phrase *sensed relic* comes actually from a description of second-year medical students' reaction to a human cadaver: "Even when deal-ing with the remains of the long since dead, there is special tension involved . . . when performing investigatory medical actions involv-ing the face, the hands, and the genitalia. This thing-in-the-world that was once . . . alive [is] still encounter[ed] as once a communicating being, not quite as an object of research or instruction. [It is] a sensed relic of the human being bodily experiencing and communicating, and the body itself uniquely speaking." [15]

The reaction has a striking parallel in paleoanthropology. The cor-relative reaction was in evidence with extraordinary force and clarity at the 1984 exhibit, *Ancestors: Four Million Years of Humanity*. A *Wash-ington Post* reporter's descriptions of, and quotations from, the physi-cal anthropologist who installed the exhibit, the non-scientists who viewed it, and the attending paleoanthropologists who, by one well-known paleoanthropologist's account, "were all seasoned scientists, familiar with these bones," [16] document unequivocally the hidden but consistently assumed strata of understandings indigenous to the sci-ence of paleoanthropology. For example, "To stare into their [the ages-old skulls'] sockets is to sense the glistening eyes, and behind the eyes the brains, of those who lived before. . . . [Viewers] touch their own temples and chins as if trying to decipher the skull beneath the flesh." These are not mystical conjurations or "mumbo-jumbo," as the physical anthropologist who installed the exhibit pointed out. Nor is it a reaction peculiar to non-scientists. "Scientists often bicker. But those who gathered in Manhattan—perhaps humbled by the pres-ence of the bones they'd come to see found themselves surprised by their mutual cordiality. . . . One of them . . . observing the humility of his colleagues said, 'This is a little like discussing theology in a cathedral.' " [17]

That the exhibit subdued talk of contentious claims, antithetical explanatory models, and the like, is not explained by the publicness of the exhibit—by a socially enforced decorum—but by the fact that there is more to the fossils than meets the eye in the laboratory, and by the fact that that *more* is given full breadth when the fossils are encountered as sensed relics of once living forms. What is methodo-logically necessary to elucidating this *more* is a hermeneutics of under-standing. The palpably present existential dimensions so keenly in evidence at the exhibit—as in the medical students' lab—are initially not to be explained but understood. Indeed, they cannot be initially explained—not even on the grounds of necromancy as is clear from the above descriptions and quotations—and this in spite of the fact that their ultimate understandings are grounded in an explanatory theory, that is, in an evolutionary explanation of fossil bones.

The mandate for a hermeneutics of corporeal understandings, understandings of what it was to be an ancestral hominid body, is documented in a further way. The most impressive objects in the exhibit were not modern casts of treasured fossils but the real thing.[18] Some of the fossils were widely known from photographs, from sketches, but there, for the first time, the aura of their presence was palpably felt—hence the analogy to being in a cathedral. The character of bones as "sensed relics" was coincident with "the aura of their presence." These virtually synonymous descriptions document the same fact: an ancient but still potent livingness. When fleshed out in corporeal awarenesses and powers, that livingness is as materially grounded as determinations of age through radiometric dating, reconstructions of bodily form via measurements of condylar angles, inferences about intelligence via measurements of cranial capacities or about typical locomotor and other behavioral practices on the basis of postcranial anatomy, or specifications concerning diet on the basis of dentition. In short, understandings of livingness are not cosmetic powderings on the hard nose of science but are part of the very subject of paleoanthropology.

In any complete and credible paleoanthropological account, explanation and understanding are in fact theoretical correlatives that regularly support each other throughout the total enterprise. Explanatory theses of human origins have their roots in particular understandings of what it meant to be an ancestral hominid—to be consistently upright, for example, or to use stones as tools; and reciprocally, existential understandings, understandings of how a creature actually lived, are embedded in evolutionary explanations and models—the model of ancestral hominids as scavengers,[19] for example, or as "savanna chimpanzees."[20] The relationship between paleoanthropological explanation and understanding can be summarized in the simplest way by reference to traditional interpretational extremes: dating, on the one hand, and behavioral lifestyle on the other. Dating places fossil bones within a certain restricted evolutionary period and in so doing provides the foundation for envisioning the animated presence of a particular kind of creature. The recreation of a certain creature in turn traces out a certain restricted style of living and in so doing provides the foundation for envisioning a particular evolutionary niche or pattern of survival. In practice, the move is back and forth from understanding to explanation and explanation to understanding, the two epistemological modes being "relative moments in a complex process called interpretation."[21] The seed-eater hypothesis of hominid origins mentioned earlier succinctly illustrates the practice. The explanatory model that links early hominids to present-day gelada baboons is based on certain already observed existential relationships, for example between sitting postures and seed-eating, relationships that are in turn extrapolated to early hominid primates. In a series of interpretive steps, the paleoanthropologist's understandings of these relationships leads to a progressive broadening and detailing of the explanatory model. Postulated, for example, are preadaptations for trunk verticality, and for a precision thumb/index grip, the preadaptations being rooted in understandings of what it meant to be an early hominid.

C. Owen Lovejoy's complex model of ancestral hominid life, which is centrally rooted in fossil evidence rather than in analogy to extant nonhuman primate behavior, similarly illustrates the pendular moves from understanding to explanation and from explanation to understanding. In attempting to show the relationship among eight variables—including upright posture, mating patterns, and food-sharing, for example—Lovejoy consistently brings out the relationship between certain styles of living and certain evolutionary progressions.[22] It is not necessary then to make understanding scientifically respectable, as Paul Ricoeur points out more generally in introducing his reformulation of the place of *verstehen* in the human and natural sciences.[23] It is only a matter of acknowledging the centrality of understanding to any reconstruction of the human evolutionary past. From an evolutionary point of view, hominid history is a history of adaptations, exaptations,[24] survival, and extinction. From an epistemological as well as evolutionary view that history is necessarily a drama in which existential significations inscribed in every hominid relic and artifact discovered in the landscape are plaited into a historic narrative, and changes in the landscape—shifts in the strata of fossils and alterations in the form of the fossils themselves—are plaited into an existential one.

At yet another level the uniqueness of paleoanthropology shows itself in relation to the natural and human sciences. To reconstruct an evolutionary history from fossil bones is necessarily to bring a subject to life, in precisely the sense described earlier in the discussion of philosophical biology in Chapter 12. While it is currently common practice in biological research to write off this subject—this essentially Darwinian body—it is, ironically enough, exactly what is wanted by the paleoanthropologist, whose aim is to restore to the bones their proper individuality, to find the living body of which those bones are a mere token or memory, and at the same time to ground that living body in the actuality of the prehistory of life—to reinstall into a *living* scene the static skeletal fragments that once bore a living form. Without this full-scale reconstruction of a subject, the history written by the paleoanthropologist is only a partial record—a mere taxonomic table of items discovered in a landscape. Even at most, short of a full-scale subject, there are only truncated pieces of imagined behaviors, just as there are only fragmented pieces of actual bone, and the pieces of imagined behavior like the pieces of actual bone can be historically linked to each other only like so many beads to be accounted for and put on a string. In short, without a full-fledged subject there can be no ordering or motivating principle to explain either the provenience of such hominid hallmarks as stone tool-making, cave-painting, counting, language, and the concept of death, or the established rootedness of these practices and beliefs in hominid life. There is only a body going through the motions of hominid living without shaping or feeling them, the latter not in the simple sense of a mere ability to control movement and register sensations, but in the sense of a burgeoning gnostic system that both explains the possibility of the practices and beliefs and provides for their epistemological foundation, and at the same time unequivocally points in an evolutionary sense toward a developing rationality. In sum, an uncovering of the roots of human thinking is methodologically tied to an uncovering of the subject of hominid evolution itself, the subject that in a literal sense *made* hominid history.

STORY, HISTORY, AND THE CORPOREAL FACTS OF THE MATTER

The theoretical infrastructure also needs methodological clarification with respect to the problem posed by conflicting interpretations, for here too the dual nature of paleoanthropology is at issue. One solution of course would be to eschew all interpretations more than one step removed from fossil evidence, a solution perhaps best typified by anthropologist Tim White's dogged and pithy skepticism regarding the role of sexuality in C. Owen Lovejoy's multifaceted reconstruction of human origins: "I've never seen an estrus fossil." [25] A one-step system of double meanings, however, allows only the bare bones of an evolutionary history, one duly identified as hominid but lacking any aura of hominid presence. In effect, it allows a recognition of the natural- but not the human-science side of paleoanthropology, and thereby effectively whittles down any conflicts of interpretation to the same bare bones. Rather than finding the acknowledgment of the dual nature of paleoanthropology a threat to its status as a science, and resolutely branding middle and upper reaches in any hierarchy of interlocking interpretations with an indelible skeptical iron, it is in the long run of greater service to paleoanthropology to examine the underlying motivation for avowing an extreme skepticism, viz., why and how speculative thought is so easily admitted into paleoanthropology in the first place. In other words, only by understanding just how the traditional practice of paleoanthropology admits of highly speculative scenarios to begin with—or why, in the words of paleoanthropologist Lord Zuckerman, there is a need "to eliminate the aura of theatre from our subject"[26]—can the problem of conflicting interpretations be rightly viewed and approached, namely, in the perspective of the nature of the paleoanthropological hermeneutic enterprise itself. In such a context a healthy skepticism can be maintained without itself passing over into obtuse dogma.

As with a literary text, ancestral hominid history also presents a limited field of possible constructions in which vying interpretations may be assessed and one designated superior to others. If it is nonetheless impossible to arrive at a final and absolute verdict—a timeless truth—it is not primarily because a text is always open to further interpretations. It is because here, in paleoanthropology, the text is neither a single nor a finite text but a virtually unending number of possible texts—*there is no known end of hominid fossils*—each of them in fact *generated*. That is, each text is not a ready-made but is the initial result of a sequence of interpretations, with theoretical as well as material elements woven into the finally reconstructed individual. Moreover each generated text, or reconstructed individual, is meaningful both in itself and with reference to similar and substantively different texts or individuals. It is interpreted within the framework of an expanded, lengthier, detailed evolutionary history. Each theory of hominid evolution is thus at the same time a *story*, a composite text that interprets a given find in itself and in relation to both contemporary creatures and a contemporaneous geo-ecological scene, and a *history*, a further composite text that is an interpretation of the original in terms of far broader and more far-reaching historical meanings and relationships. Conflicting interpretations are possible at any stage in both story and history precisely because both story and history are a compound of interpretations from beginning to end.

Resolution of conflicts at any stage demands in each case a return to the things themselves, a methodological retracing of the system of constructed double meanings down to original beginnings in fossil evidence—or in analogy. But in a deeper sense, it means staying with the corporeal facts of the matter. Even further, it means analyzing those facts more deeply. Where paleoanthropology becomes theater, it is because story becomes story-telling, and history becomes a chronicle of speculations.[27] In all such cases, both story and history veer away from the path of the corporeal. Where the move should be from fossils to quasi-material/quasi-postulated individual, to behaviors, to corporeal awarenesses and powers, and thus to a full-fledged *subject* of history, the final move is from behavior to history—the subject being created out of the flimsy props provided by fancy or by speculation. The instantiation of a *bona fide* subject does not mean the end of conflict, only the end of conjectural ventures that pull paleoanthropology away from the corporeal facts of the matter, and in turn off the tracks of a credible because substantive evolutionary history. The closer paleoanthropology hews to the body, the more precise and rigorous its claim to being a scientific history. In finer methodological terms, the number of possible interpretations is reduced by putting a methodological stopper on them, in effect, plugging speculative or theatrical leaks. In so doing, more stringent methodological requirements are enforced in the construction of both story and history. Indeed, what is necessary to a proper paleoanthropology is a replacement of the aura of theatre with the aura of presence. Where paleoanthropology is methodologically grounded in the reality of the bones themselves—not just bare bones but bones rigorously fleshed out through corporeal analyses, a credible subject takes shape and a richer and more rigorous science emerges. This is essentially because a methodology is recognized and utilized that does full justice to the dual nature of paleoanthropology: hominid fossils are at once items discovered in a landscape, and sensed relics of once-living forms.

NOTES

1. See, for example, Kenneth P. Oakley, *Man the Tool-Maker* (Chicago: University of Chicago Press, 1949); André Leroi-Gourhan, *Prehistoric Man*, trans. W. Baskin (New York: Philosophical Library, 1957); Lawrence H. Keeley, "The Functions of Paleolithic Flint Tools," *Scientific American* 237 (November 1977): 108–26; Glynn L. Isaac, "The Food-Sharing Behavior of Protohuman Hominids," *Scientific American* 238 (April 1978): 90–108; Thomas Wynn, "The Intelligence of Later Acheulian Hominids," *Man*, n.s. 14 (1979): 371–

91, and "The Intelligence of Oldowan Hominids," *Journal of Human Evolution* 10 (1981): 529–41; Milford H. Wolpoff, *Paleoanthropology* (New York: Knopf, 1980); Nicholas Toth, "The Oldowan Reassessed: A Close Look at Early Stone Artefacts," *Journal of Archaeological Science* 12 (1985): 101–20.

2. Wolpoff, *Paleoanthropology*, p. 166.

3. Oakley, *Man the Tool-Maker*, p. 21.

4. Oliver Sacks, "Hands," *New York Review of Books*, 8 November 1984, p. 15; cf. *stereognosis* in Ashley Montagu's *Touching: The Human Significance of the Skin* (New York, Columbia University Press, 1971), and Jacques Monod's *Chance and Necessity*, trans. A. Wainhouse (New York: Knopf, 1971).

5. A. N. Leont'ev and N. V. Zaporozhets, *The Rehabilitation of Hand Function*, trans. B. Haigh, ed. W. R. Russell (New York: Pergamon Press, 1960).

6. Wynn, "Oldowan Hominids."

7. See in particular Maurice Merleau-Ponty, *Phenomenology of Perception*, trans. Colin Smith (London: Routledge & Kegan Paul, 1962), and *The Structure of Behavior* trans. A. L. Fisher (Boston: Beacon Press, 1963); Hans Jonas, *The Phenomenon of Life: Toward a Philosophical Biology* (New York: Harper & Row, 1966); Richard M. Zaner, *The Context of Self* (Athens: Ohio University Press, 1981); and Erwin W. Straus, "Born to See, Bound to Behold: Reflections on the Function of Upright Posture in the Esthetic Attitude," trans. Erling Eng, in *The Philosophy of the Body*, ed. Stuart F. Spicker (Chicago: Quadrangle Press, 1970), pp. 334–61.

8. See Maxine Sheets-Johnstone, "Toward an Openly Hermeneutical Paleontology," *University of Dayton Review* 17 (1984): 89–96, also in *Reflections: Essays in Phenomenology* 4 (1983): 28–36; and "Existential Fit and Evolutionary Continuities," *Synthèse* 66 (1985): 219–48.

9. See Chapter 3 of this book. A version of this chapter was first presented at the 65th annual meeting of the American Association for the Advancement of Science, San Francisco, June 1984, in a paper titled, "On the Origin of Counting: A Re-Thinking of Upright Posture." An expanded version of the paper will appear in *The Life of Symbols*, ed. Mary LeCron Foster and Jayne Botscharow (Boulder, Colo.: Westview Press, 1990) and is coincident with the version presented here.

10. See Chapters 4 and 7 of this book.

11. Hans Jonas, "The Nobility of Sight," in *Philosophy of the Body*, pp. 312–33.

12. Straus, "Born to See."

13. Jean Piaget, *La naissance de l'intelligence chez l'enfant*, 6th ed. (Neuchatel: Delachaux et Niestlé, 1968), p. 294 (obs. 180).

14. Paul Ramsey, "The Indignity of 'Death with Dignity,'" *The Hastings Center Studies* 2, no. 2 (May 1974): 59.

15. Ibid.

16. Ian Tattersall, quoted in Paul Richard's "Walking among Our Ancestors," *San Francisco Chronicle*, the "World" section, 10 June 1984.

17. Paul Richard, ibid.

18. Ibid.

19. See Lewis R. Binford, *In Pursuit of the Past* (New York: Thames and Hudson, 1983); and Pat Shipman, "Scavenging or Hunting in Early Hominids: Theoretical Framework and Tests," *American Anthropologist*, n.s. 88 (1986): 27–43.

20. For a full discussion and summary of this viewpoint see Wolpoff, *Paleoanthropology*.

21. Paul Ricoeur, "Explanation and Understanding: On Some Remarkable Connections among the Theory of the Text, Theory of Action, and Theory of History," in *The Philosophy of Paul Ricoeur*, ed. Charles T. Reagan and David Stewart (Boston: Beacon Press, 1978), p. 150.

22. C. Owen Lovejoy, "The Origin of Man," *Science* 211 (1981): 340–50.

23. Ricoeur, "Explanation and Understanding," especially pp. 150–51.

24. See Stephen J. Gould and Elisabeth S. Vrba, "Exaptation—A Missing Term in the Science of Form," *Paleobiology* 8 (1982): 4–15.

25. Tim White, quoted in Donald C. Johanson and Maitland A. Edey's *Lucy* (New York: Warner Books, 1981), p. 340.

26. Lord Zuckerman, "Closing Remarks to Symposium," in *The Concepts of Human Evolution*, ed. Lord Zuckerman, *Symposia of the Zoological Society of London* 33 (New York: Academic Press, 1973), p. 451.

27. See, for example, Glynn L. Isaac's scenario in his "The Activities of Early African Hominids," in *Human Origins: Louis Leakey and the East African Evidence*, ed. Glynn L. Isaac and Elizabeth R. McCown (Menlo Park, Calif.: W. A. Benjamin, 1976), pp. 483–85 in particular; and Richard G. Whitten's speculations in "Hominid Promiscuity and the Sexual Life of Proto-Savages: Did *Australopithecus* Swing?" *Current Anthropology* 23 (1982): 99–101.

14

Methodology: The Genetic Phenomenology Strand

"What Is It Like to Be a Bat?"

THOMAS NAGEL

"What was it actually like to be almost human . . . ?"

RICHARD LEAKEY

"What Was It Like?"

LEWIS R. BINFORD

"What Was It Like to Be Lucy?"

MAXINE SHEETS-JOHNSTONE

"How to Be a Fig"

DANIEL H. JANZEN

INTRODUCTION

Rather than begin with a summary presentation of genetic phenomenology in its role as methodological science, a summary that would require prior detailed considerations of epistemological matters as well as comparisons with static phenomenology, it is more useful to attend directly to the core methodological problem inherent in the attempt to describe experienced meanings in creatures other than one's own

347

immediate kind, and this for two reasons. First, the concern here is precisely not that of contemporary human thinking, that is, present-day human meanings, but the thinking of ancestral hominids; and second, given this paleoanthropological concern, the core methodological problem cannot be avoided but must be addressed. It should be noted that, although not discussed as such, a similar core problem is readily apparent in anthropological field studies where "the creatures other than oneself" are contemporaneous human creatures, but still are other than one's own immediate kind since they belong to a culture other than one's own. In point of fact, the epistemological question, "What is it like to be a . . . ?" consistently poses a methodological problem that must first be resolved before the epistemological question, in whatever circumstances it is asked, can be satisfactorily tackled much less convincingly answered. (The multiple citations at the head of this chapter underscore the broad, interdisciplinary circumstances in which the question is asked.) In other words, to describe what it is like to be another creature is to describe everyday meanings experienced by that creature—be it a bat, a Biamian, Lucy, or one's neighbor. To delineate or to recover those experienced meanings, if such is indeed possible at all, a mode of access must be found to them. In this sense, the starting point is always necessarily at the level of "how to be a fig": an appropriate methodology is clearly the first requirement. The need for a method akin to genetic phenomenology will be made clear in this context. "How to Be a Fig" notwithstanding, the context is actually most clearly and succinctly presented in philosopher Thomas Nagel's well-known article "What Is It Like to Be a Bat?" [1] and will be set forth in its terms.

THE METHODOLOGICAL CHALLENGE

Nagel's article originally raised interesting and difficult issues in the philosophy of mind. But it raises equally interesting and difficult, not to say more pressing issues in the philosophy of science, specifically biology and paleoanthropology. Where the intent of a discipline is to unravel the mysteries of different forms of animate life, the question, What is it like to be a . . . ? is central. Unless all of the mysteries are unlocked, an understanding of bats, baboons, bees, and even hominids—ancestral or present-day—remains necessarily incomplete. Nagel's suggestion for bridging the gap between objective and subjective *points of view* is to create an *objective phenomenology*: "a new method . . . [whose] goal would be to describe, at least in part, the subjective character of experiences in a form comprehensible to beings incapable of having those experiences."[2] Although Nagel does not spell out actual procedures or consequences of the method, it is clear that such a phenomenology would bring behavior and experience together. We would know not only how a creature lives in terms of what it does and how it does it—finds food, eats, finds a mate, copulates, defends itself, shelters itself, and so on—we would be able to conceive what the experience in each case is like from the creature's point of view. We would not merely see the kind of world it *sees*, for example, by constructing a facsimile of its visual world as has been done in the case of bees,[3] but might come to know what it means to see the world through its eyes, with *its* meanings. We might, moreover, come to know what it was like to move in ways peculiar to, and typical of, that creature. We might, in short, accede to knowledge of a sensory–kinetic domain of sensitivities and powers different from our own.

The title of his article aside, Nagel actually confronts the problem in methodological not epistemological terms. Indeed, only if the methodological problem is solved can epistemological possibilities open up. But a methodological solution leading to the expansive zoological epistemology Nagel initially has in mind seems at this moment far away indeed. In fact the idea that any approach would ever be discovered that would allow us humans access to another extant species' lifeworld appears optimistic in the extreme. Closer at hand, however, is a quite remarkable if overlooked possibility, one that is all the more outstanding insofar as it exists as a frequently assumed dimension in the practice and theory of an existing discipline. Paleoanthropologists reconstruct the human lineage not just in terms of structure and function, but also in terms of certain ways of living in the world such as by scavenging,[4] by cooperating in hunting manoeuvres and forming a single lifelong relationship with a member of the opposite sex,[5] by competing with other meat-eating species for large prey,[6] and so on. More precisely, every postulated behavioral adaptation—be it hunting, pair-bonding, bipedalism, scavenging, stone tool-making, or language—is regularly pictured in the context of certain motivations (economic or social, most usually), certain modes of interaction (cooperative or caring, most usually), certain cognitive abilities (to plan strategy or skilled sequences of action, for instance), certain enhanced sensory and/or motor capacities (visual or linguistic, most usually), and the like. To envision such needs, awarenesses, feelings, capacities, or intentions is unequivocally to assume or suggest—if not impute outright—certain "subjective" dimensions of existence. Insofar as the quest is to recreate from fossil bones the lifeworld of creatures who inaugurated a complex of new lifestyles over a period of some three and a half million to fifty thousand years ago, "what it was like to be Lucy" is a question regularly if implicitly addressed in paleoanthropology.[7] What needs examination is the legitimacy of any answers to that question short of a legitimating methodology. In brief, any speculations on what it was like to be almost human need to be put to methodological test.

Now Nagel justifiably states that "only for someone sufficiently similar to the object of ascription"[8] is it possible to adopt that object's or individual's point of view. The fundamental question then is, What constitutes "sufficient similarity"? Nagel's answer, while not fully sketched out, hinges on *types* of subjects; thus, "one person can know or say of another what the quality of the other's experience is."[9] But what of our ancestors of three million years ago? or two? or one? Are they too different from us for us to be able to adopt their point of view? And just what would the adoption entail? that is, How would we go about adopting their point of view—or know what it was in the first place?

If it were maintained that ancestral hominids are in the same category as bats so far as point of view is concerned relative to our own, then paleoanthropological research and claims to the contrary, it is likely we can never conceive or know, nor can we even come close to conceiving or knowing, what it was actually like to be almost human. We have (at present at least) no methodological means of closing the species gap. This is not to say that behavioral scenarios could not be compiled as they are presently, through informed leaps of the imagination, or through analogies made between the behavior of ancestral hominids and the behavior of present-day social carnivores, present-day hunter–gatherer societies, and present-day nonhuman primates. Paleoanthropologists could of course continue to provide these scenarios, but none of the behavioral markers—hunting, scavenging, a sexual division of labor, the having of a base camp, and the like—could any longer be taken as points of departure for conceiving "what it was actually like to be almost human."[10] On the contrary, they could tell us in comparative experiential terms no more than present-day zoological scenarios tell us of a day in the life of a bat.

On the other hand, if, relative to our own point of view, that of ancestral hominids is not taxonomically batlike but affirmed to be sufficiently similar to our own, then there is in theory nothing that stands in the way of our approximating to and describing their experiences. Insofar as our distinct but similar sensory–kinetic worlds are taken to be congruent in basic ways, we can approximate conceptually to their noticings and to their somatically felt bodies—adopt to their point of view, to use Nagel's term. But what are the grounds for affirming sufficient similarity?

The affirmative claim would have to be based on evolutionary theory itself: a structural–functional similarity, and ultimately, a general, conjectural behavioral similarity. And indeed, the world of ancestral hominids as pictured behaviorally by paleoanthropologists readily calls forth an experiential world to which present-day humans could with equal readiness relate—as they cannot relate experientially *or* behaviorally to the lifeworld of, for example, a bat. Ancestral hominids, for example, are not credited with throwing stones at eggs (or eggs at stones); they are not presumed to have marked territories by leaving urine emblems about; they are not pictured as relying on smell as a mode of recognition. Like us, they were bipedal creatures; like us, they ate plant foods and were (or eventually became) [11] large game meat-eaters; like us, they ultimately used and made tools; like us, they copulated and came at some point to form complex kinship structures that included pair-bonding. At a behavioral level, a comfortable commonality is apparent. We do indeed seem to be kindred folk. This evolutionary kindredness portends—even seems to engender—kindred points of view. The problem is that evolutionary theory, particularly in its modern dress, does not directly substantiate the latter kindredness; it says nothing about points of view. Perhaps then the affirmation is ill-founded. Paleoanthropologists only *think* they are telling us what it was like to be almost human.

Whether paleoanthropologists are actually telling us what it was like or whether they only think they are telling us what it was like, two facts cannot be ignored: (1) that the creatures in question were hominids, kindred folk, and (2) that, in Nagel's words, although "we may ascribe general *types* of experience on the basis of . . . structure and behavior . . . these experiences also have in each case a specific subjective character." [12] In consequence what first needs consideration is the possibility that, while there is similarity so far as structure and behavior are concerned, there is not *sufficient* similarity to warrant experiential ascriptions. If there is not, we must consider further whether there is a way in which sufficient similarity might be established.

ESTABLISHING SUFFICIENT SIMILARITY:
THE PROCEDURE OF BRACKETING

Certainly it is reasonable to think that a conceptual approximation to
ancestral hominid experience is not possible straight off: too much
intercedes in the way of a cultural heritage. What we notice today,
for example, is tempered by a certain epistemological tradition. It is
also tempered by a certain sensory bias. In a word, there are radical
sensory–kinetic differences between us. But of course the reverse is
also true: from an evolutionary viewpoint we are one Family—Hominidae—and thus are necessarily, by definition, "sufficiently similar." In effect, it might be said that were it not for the beliefs, attitudes,
and values that contribute to, or constitute, our twentieth-century
Western outlook, we could, if we wanted, approximate straight off to
the point of view of ancestral hominids. More specifically, we could
approximate more closely to their sensory–kinetic world if we could
in some way—and temporarily of course—feel, see, and hear things
without their typical twentieth-century Western meanings; for example, if we could see a shadow not as the shadow of a person, that
is, as an effect of the interruption of sunshine upon a certain object,
but as a singular *Gestalt* in which person and shadow were sensibly
and kinetically continuous, or if we could hear speech not in the form
of words and word patterns, but as sheer sound—an experience akin
to the hearing of a completely foreign language where a sound flow
of varying pitches, amplitudes, siblancies, and so on, has no lexical or
grammatical meanings. In brief, similarity might be enhanced to the
degree that sufficient similarity in point of view was achieved were it
possible to jettison twentieth-century culture-bound meanings.

But there is not only the problem of twentieth-century cultural
meanings in the sense of encumbering attitudes and beliefs. There
is also the problem of a culture-spawned pecking order among the
senses. Marshall McLuhan is popularly credited with pointing out
that twentieth-century media altered the ratio among the senses, but
cultural historians, anthropologists, and others since the turn of the
century have focused on and discussed the same issue at length.[13]
Sensory modalities at any given cultural period are not equal but
have privileged positions relative to one another, and this, of course,
quite apart from any evolutionary considerations—for example, that
the sense of smell in hominids has diminished relative to vision. To
establish sufficient similarity and thereby approximate conceptually
to the experienced sensory–kinetic life of ancestral hominids, would

therefore require equalizing the senses to the extent that the biases of our present-day visually dominated twentieth-century Western culture were tempered. The phenomenon of speech mentioned earlier is a case in point. Not only would speech have to be detached from its twentieth-century cultural moorings in order to be caught in the bud, so to speak, but the peculiar physiognomic form of that nascent language would itself have to be taken up and understood as such. A different kind of experience in making and living among sounds would have to be conceived and conceptually elaborated.

Sufficient similarity is clearly not there for the taking. In addition to overcoming the problem of culturally engrained meanings, sensory imbalances need to be redressed. The task is to meet these difficulties by showing a methodological path through them. By taking up the methodological problem first, and then in the following chapter, the epistemological question of what an ancestral hominid's sensory–kinetic experiences might have been like, a possible way of satisfying the criterion of sufficient similarity can be demonstrated. In this way answers can also be suggested in turn to the two questions posed earlier: How would we go about adopting the point of view of an early hominid? and How would we know what that point of view was in the first place? Satisfying answers to both questions depend on what philosophy and science jointly offer as both this and the succeeding chapter will show.

If it were agreed that the fundamental difference between our point of view and the point of view of our hominid ancestors lies in the vast overlayering of facts, beliefs, attitudes, and so on that refracts our view of the world through a particular cultural prism, then, by the same token, we would presume that our point of view was at bottom on a continuum with theirs. That is, cultural overlay aside, our most basic perceptions and movements—our fundamental sensory–kinetic sensitivities and powers, for example, lingual, manipulational, loco-motor, and the like—would be affirmed to be different, but not sub-stantively different in kind from theirs. Thus, if the play of twentieth-century cultural meanings were suspended, we might accede, and in the closest possible way, to the actual experiences of the ancestral hominids. Granted that such a procedure requires a broadening of traditional paleoanthropological methodologies, it is not in principle that far removed from common scientific practice. An example will demonstrate the theoretical methodological affinity.

For a typical twentieth-century Western adult, perception is in-formed by the correlative notions of reality and illusion. If a reflection

of an arched bridge were seen in the water, for instance, the perceived
unbroken circular form would be seen as given by what we know as
the bridge in continuity with its reflected image. But if we knew nothing of reflections or bridges, we would see the circular form *simpliciter*
and nothing more, for example, not the circular form as a real bridge
plus its reflection, not a fictional upside down bridge in the water,
and so on; indeed, we would see not two things at all but one. In a
world prior to experience that might suggest otherwise, for instance,
stepping on the circular form in the water, there is no reality and no
illusion, no fact and no fiction as such. There is only the perceived
thing itself in the form of a certain qualitative presence. Even were experience to suggest otherwise, as stepping on the circular form in the
water and discovering it to be nonsupportive, it would not necessarily
lead to a distinction between what is real on the one hand and what
is illusory on the other. A mythological form, for instance, is not an
illusory one. But furthermore, neither do optical laws nor principles
concerning the propagation of light enter into a sheer physiognomic
vision of the circular form. While regularities might be perceived relative to particular forms—the sun, for example—an entire system of
explanatory causalities—even in the form of a mythology—would be
a very long way into the evolutionary future. In brief, to approximate to an ancestral hominid's perception of a reflection in water—
or of a shadow, or of the sun disappearing into the clouds, or of any
other natural phenomenon, and not only any other natural *visual* phenomenon, but any tactile, auditory, or other sensory phenomenon
(the smell, feel, and sound of fire or rain, for instance)—requires a
bracketing of everyday twentieth-century Western adult beliefs about
the natural world and all the conceptual and explanatory theses those
beliefs entail.

     This procedure of bracketing is in principle analogous to the way
in which biologists go about investigating and understanding the beginnings of life. They first recreate the primordial soup from which the
organic universe is thought to have evolved. Only after that original
cosmic cuisine is created do they look to see what is actually given in
the way of amino acids when the soup is bombarded in ways typical of
nascent earthly processes and events. They recreate first the *conditions*
under which life is thought to have occurred. Only then do they have
a credible empirical basis for examining and describing molecular reactions relative to the possible genesis of life. In a similar way, when
certain conditions are recreated through bracketing, a credible em-

pirical basis is provided for analyzing and describing a preeminently physiognomic world, one in which perceptions and actions are not mediated by notions of reality and illusion, for instance, and where what is empirically present takes on a substantially different cast.

This different empirical cast can be spelled out more concretely in two ways—first with respect to a preeminently physiognomically perceived world itself. That world, by comparison with the normal twentieth-century Western one, is a world in which little if anything comes between perceiver and perceived. Piaget speaks of this very notion, that is, of a variable distance between subject and object, in his developmental theory of intelligence.[14] Indeed, a physiognomically oriented creature rubs up perpetually against the sheer sensuous being-there of bodily and earthly processes and forms—flesh, feces, mud, thorns, water, thunder, blood, stones, darkness, cold, and so on. This world normally remains muted, masked, or lost altogether for Western adults caught up in the profusion of everyday cultural objects such as silverware, light bulbs, shoes, raincoats, toothbrushes, toilets and toilet paper, to say nothing of language in the form of speech, shelters in the form of houses or huts, and modes of moving from one place to another apart from one's own feet. Certainly there is every reason to assume that the fundamental *tactual* immediacy of things was not masked in an ancestral hominid's world, and that any tactual meanings beyond the immediate sheer sensuous being-there of oneself and the world—beyond "the given"—would be at a very simple level of complexity. What bracketing allows is precisely an approximation to this simple level of complexity by a closing of the distance between perceiver and perceived. In fact this closing of distance and consequent change in meaning are not so strange. As suggested earlier, a preeminently physiognomic world is perceived when speech is heard in the form of sheer sound. In a similar way speech can be *seen* not as a series of linguistic gestures but as a sheer concatenation of facial and bodily movements. It can be seen in this way merely by turning off the sound on a TV. To hear or see in this way is to suspend everyday acceptances of certain sounds and movements as speech. It is to disconnect for the time being a belief that words are being uttered, that there are such things as words in the first place, and so on. To close the distance between perceiver and perceived is to take on a different sensory–kinetic stance in face of everyday objects and events, and correlatively, to enter into a different but not altogether alien sensory–kinetic world. It is in this sense that bracketing allows an experiential approximation to ancestral hominid thinking and in turn, provides the basis for conceiving–conceptually approximating to—what it was like to be almost human.

The different cast can also be spelled out more concretely with respect to meanings. As the above linguistic examples readily suggest, when everyday phenomena are transformed through bracketing, what is familiar is made strange. But the transformation can be involuntary as well as voluntary. What was on display at the 1984 exhibit *Ancestors: Four Million Years of Humanity* was spontaneously transformed. Cultural overlay disappeared to the extent that academic knowledge no longer interceded in its familiar way between fossils and professional observers. In consequence, experienced meaning was different. Fossils that professionals had observed many times, perhaps for years, suddenly had an unfamiliar physiognomy. The ability to suspend habitual or cultural meanings—the ability to bracket —thus requires no "sorcerer's apprenticeship." It is an engrained, spontaneous as well as voluntary human possibility. The meanings that come to light in bracketing are, in turn, natural to a human repertoire of meanings. Indeed as the succeeding chapter on tactile–kinesthetic invariants will show, there are good grounds for believing certain physiognomic meanings uncovered in bracketing to be fundamental not just to a human but to a *hominid* repertoire of meanings.

The methodological path to these essentially corporeal meanings can be further highlighted by an additional illustration of the difference between familiar everyday meanings and bracketed, "strange" ones. In experiences of the former kind, the formal or physiognomic aspect of things has a commonplace, enveloping cultural character about it, a character that frequently overshadows its formal aspect. Comparison with nonhuman animals—who in a general way can be said to live their lives in a preeminently physiognomic world far removed from the cultural overlay typical of Western humans—can bring this tendency toward cultural masking into relief and clarify it further with respect to bracketing. For example, although a basic similarity can be reasonably assumed in the meaning of perceived changes in female chimpanzees' sexual skin for both a primatologist and a male chimpanzee studying its morphology—both read the changes in generally the same way—during and pursuant to their observations, each will act, or not act, in a different way. Species differences aside for the moment, this is because although both are interested in the pudendal physiognomy, that is, in the sheer visual aspect of the swellings and colorations, the familiar physiognomic meanings for the primatologist leech out into non-physiognomic matrices of meaning, and in fact have their primary import in meta-physiognomic concerns pertinent to the primatologist's particular study. Were these disciplinary concerns bracketed, the primatologist would see the swellings and colorations outside their usual context of primate sexuality in general and female chimpanzee sexuality in particular. Shorn of their familiar cultural overlay of meanings, they would be seen as *strange*.

Making the swellings and colorations appear strange in this way does not mean approximating to the familiar physiognomic perceptions—the point of view—of the male chimpanzee. To re-emphasize the point discussed at the beginning of this chapter, a minimally adequate, not to say full, account of any creature's sensory–kinetic domain of experienced meanings—what Nagel more generally refers to as "types" of experience—would necessarily have to begin with the central methodological question—and mystery—of species-specific meanings, in the present case, a chimpanzee equivalent of "how to be a fig." The point coincides with biologist Johannes von Uexküll's insight that physiognomic worlds are not the same. In philosopher Ernst Cassirer's paraphrasing words, "Every organism . . . has a world of its own because it has an experience of its own." [15] The point is in fact finely illustrated by the experience of a well-known primatologist who, unlike the successful chimpanzees he so carefully and consistently observed, was unable to scan the landscape and pick unerringly —in fact *at all*—the correct spot to fish for termites. [16] Here too, bracketing would not mean approximating to a successful chimpanzee's point of view. Bracketing might or might not bring different results.

The above examples show that where human physiognomic perceptions are part and parcel of routine occupational concerns, a certain familiar, enveloping cultural context tends actually to overshadow the formal aspect of the things perceived. Occupational concerns aside, the familiar, culturally enveloped physiognomy of everyday things— the shape of a car key, the sound of a doorbell, the feel of a chair —is commonly experienced in a similar way, that is, with marginal rather than central formal attention. In other words, here too, physiognomic meaning leeches out into habitual or cultural concerns and actions. Were key, doorbell, or chair fully attended to with a bracketed attention, its formal character would be perceived in a way similar to speech when it is heard as sheer sound or seen as sheer movement, or similar to the spontaneously transformed ancient fossils. In short, like the sheer sounds and sights of speech and like the ancient fossils, key, doorbell, and chair would be perceived as strange, their once familiar physiognomy with its retinue of commonplace meanings being temporarily suspended.

The earlier examples together with these last show clearly that the basic difference between strange and familiar meanings hinges upon how the thing in question is perceived and how it is acted upon—or not acted upon. To say there is a difference in meaning is thus to say there is a difference in sensory–kinetic experience. Where this difference becomes methodologically critical is where the particular sensory–kinetic experiences of concern are not of things in the world—a landscape, a female chimpanzee's genitals, a car key, an ancient fossil—but experiences of one's own body. What is corporeally familiar through personal habit and cultural overlay—chewing, walking, striking, speaking, counting, laughing, drawing—also takes on a different cast when bracketed. The corporeal experience in each case is transformed fundamentally into a tactile–kinesthetic physiognomy whose meanings are initially strange. They no longer leech out into practical, social, aesthetic, or professional concerns, for example. Interest in the formal character of the bodily experience is not surpassed by other interests. In consequence, whatever the meanings found in the experience, they are literally *corporeal* meanings. They are *of the body* and *they remain in the body*. In this sense they are latent in any familiar act of chewing, walking, striking, speaking, counting, laughing, drawing. Bracketing brings their latent physiognomic character into the light.

Given the above extended discussion and illustrations of bracketing, it is clear that if access may be had at all to the point of view of ancestral hominids, it lies first in bracketing culturally tethered meanings and second in uncovering the residual, sedimented meanings in that bracketed world. The procedure of bracketing described here is quite similar to what Husserl terms "phenomenological reduction": a distilling of experience by suspending normal, everyday judgments about it.[17] The result is that the experience is describable at its most pristine level of perception. *Nothing is taken for granted*—whether the underside of a table or a binary gait in walking, for example. At the same time *everything normally read into the experience*—the underside of a table or a binary gait in walking, for example—*is brought to light*. Thus it is clear why the methodological elaboration of perception here is not equivalent to mere reportorial inventories on the order of "I saw a brown and white thing. It was a cow"; and why bodily movement or actions are not concomitantly mere items in a behavioral repertoire on the order of "I milked it." In a rigorous phenomenological description, perception and movement are pregnant with sensory–kinetic meanings, and are analytically resolved in those terms.

The proposed methodology is thus most aptly described not as an objective phenomenology, as Nagel suggests, but as a hermeneutical phenomenology or a phenomenological hermeneutics. Here twentieth-century corporeal realities originally discovered in a full-scale hermeneutics are in a Husserlian sense deconstructed. A return "to the corporeal things themselves" [18] eventuates in corporeal analyses that reveal the body in its full pristine physiognomy.

As indicated in the opening paragraph of this chapter, the technique of bracketing in this instance is not in the service of uncovering the ground of twentieth-century meanings to the end that knowledge is everywhere anchored in the most fundamental self-evidence —as with Husserl—but of uncovering meanings implicit in the life of ancestral hominids to the end that the roots of human thinking are elucidated. To this end a further Husserlian step is equally necessary.

THE METHOD OF CORPOREAL SCANNING OR "CORPOREAL REDUCTION"

Given access to latent experiential significations through bracketing, a methodological path is opened that makes possible an approximation to an ancestral hominid point of view. But to elucidate the roots of human thinking requires more than recovering a point of view. It requires a recovery of *origins*, conceptual origins. While bracketing allows an approximation to a world in which cultural meanings are reduced and purely physiognomic ones are ascendant, it does not allow accession to the "primal instituting" [19] of these latter meanings, in particular, to the primal instituting of meanings conceptually entailed in the establishment of such ancestral hominid practices and beliefs as stone tool-making, pictorial depiction, burial of the dead, verbal language, counting. Hence subsequent to bracketing it is necessary to find in what bodily patterns of sensory–kinetic experience fundamental hominid concepts are adumbrated. It is necessary to ask in each case: In what pattern(s) of bodily experience is (are) the concept(s) latent? [20]

The further methodological step for identifying corporeal matrices of conceptual thought is thus a scanning of corporeal possibilities. The procedure may be likened to the astronomical scanning of the universe both to narrow down the location and to specify further the nature of a stellar object theorized on the basis of all known facts. Each reflectively spawned and reflectively entertained stellar possibility is in turn examined until finally, a fit is found, that is, an object is found that answers to all known facts.[21] In like fashion, within a culturally reduced, physiognomically ascendant frame of reference, bodily experiences are methodically examined, possibility by possibility, all with respect to a particular concept—of *edges*, for example, or *numbers*. The aim is to find the experiential source of those concepts subtending and/or generated by "the facts": stone tool-using/tool-making, bipedalism, cave paintings, counting, a belief in death, primordial language. Here each reflectively spawned and reflectively entertained corporeal possibility is scanned until a corporeal experience—or experiences— is found that answers conceptually to the known facts.

Corporeal scanning is similar to Husserl's "eidetic reduction."[22] In each case what is sought is a historical disclosure of meaning. Each procedure methodologically involves a working backward to the experiential genesis of concepts. Husserl's introductory remarks in his article "On the Origin of Geometry" show in a particularly lucid way the nature of this historical undertaking and its broad anthropological/ paleoanthropological implications:

The question of the origin of geometry . . . is the inquiry back into the most original sense in which geometry once arose . . . is still present for us, and is still being worked on in a lively forward development; we inquire into that sense in which it appeared in history for the first time . . . even though we know nothing of the first creators. . . . The geometry which is ready-made, so to speak, from which the regressive inquiry begins, is a tradition. Our human existence moves within innumerable traditions. The whole cultural world, in all its forms, exists through tradition. These forms have arisen as such not merely casually; we also know . . . that tradition . . . [has] arisen within our human space through human activity . . . even though we generally know nothing, or as good as nothing, of the particular provenance . . . that brought it about. And yet there lies in this lack of knowledge . . . an implicit knowledge, which can . . . be made explicit, a knowledge of unassailable self-evidence. It begins with superficial commonplaces such as: that everything traditional has arisen out of human activity, that accordingly past . . . civilizations existed, and among them their first inventors, who shaped the new out of materials at hand. . . . From the superficial, however, one is led into the depths. Tradition is open in this . . . way to continued inquiry; and, if one consistently maintains the direction of inquiry, an infinity of questions opens up, questions which lead to definite answers in accord with their sense.[23]

Viewed from the perspective of *tradition*, numbers, language, the concept of death, bipedalism, painting, tool-making—all are open to precisely the kind of inquiry Husserl describes. All had a historical beginning; all originated in some act or insight; all have since "been worked on in a lively forward development," that is, each has been progressively elaborated over thousands or millions of years in ways that surpass the original meaning, so much so that the original meaning lies buried under layers of sedimentation. To recover the original meaning in each case is to descend through those layers and find the conceptual bedrock.

The need to recover meanings from our ancestral past has striking parallels with the need to uncover the genesis of meanings in present-day cultures studied by anthropologists. The anthropologist Roger Keesing implicitly calls attention to the need for a historical disclosure of meaning when he asks, vis-à-vis the cultural significations that symbolic anthropologists write about, Who creates these meanings? [24] Clearly, where it is a question of hominid traditions or artifacts, the question of where meanings come from cannot be indefinitely ignored nor its answer(s) indefinitely taken for granted. On the contrary, the question of meaning must in each case be taken up methodologically and a path found that leads back to its primal instituting.

Corporeal possibilities entertained in scanning center on complex aspects of bodily life: animate form; bodily conformations such as teeth, orifices, hair, nails; bodily exudings; bodily postures; bodily acts such as chewing and walking. The process of scanning thus involves more than merely filling out an inventory sheet, more than a mere narrowing down of possibilities to a specified aspect or aspects —say, animate form in the context of an analysis of the origin of counting. Only by closely examining what a particular aspect presents in the way of possible experiences, in effect, by examining its possibilities assiduously, thoroughly, and without haste, is it in turn possible to determine which aspect or aspects of bodily life are conceptually linked to a particular practice or belief.

The process of corporeal scanning thus results in a sense of how the body in each case is not simply *implicated* in meanings through its very acts but is the very source or standard upon which those meanings are forged in the first place. The process might be termed *corporeal* rather than "eidetic" reduction in the sense that there is a distillation of meaning down to the experiencing and experienced body that generates it. What is elucidated through corporeal reduction are different faces of a bodily logos. With each corporeal analysis, one aspect of an on-going, evolving bodily logos is brought to light.

It should be explicitly pointed out that corporeal possibilities entertained in scanning are always tightly controlled by the concept(s) implicit in the particular practice or belief being investigated and analyzed. Corporeal possibilities are thus "free variations" (as Husserl calls them),[25] but free variations on a particular theme. The theme itself in some instances closely dictates the specific corporeal possibilities to be explored: with respect to the origin of language, for example, lingual (tactile–kinesthetic) and aural experiential possibilities. Such closely directed instances differ from ones in which the practice examined does not conceptually originate in the bodily act(s) constituting it. An example is counting. The bodily act of counting assumes the conceptual existence of numbers. Thus the practice of counting must be corporeally explored not with reference to the act of counting itself but with reference to the question, Where do numbers come from?

A hewing to the corporeal facts of the matter through both bracketing and corporeal scanning sustains the phenomenological strand of the methodology as it sustains the hermeneutical strand. Here too imaginative scenarios not derived from a controlled examination of corporeal evidence are not evidentially legitimated. Again, the long-term result is that the science of paleoanthropology is secured, theoretically and methodologically, and thereby also is its claim to being a *scientific* history. Hewing to the corporeal facts of the matter leads to the roots of human thinking and hominid evolution.

NOTES

1. Daniel H. Janzen, "How to Be a Fig," *Annual Review of Ecology and Systematics* 10 (1979): 13–51; Thomas Nagel, "What Is It Like to Be a Bat?" *Philosophical Review* 448 (1974): 435–50.

2. Ibid., p. 449.

3. Karl von Frisch, *Bees: Their Vision, Chemical Senses, and Language* (Ithaca, N.Y.: Cornell University Press, 1950).

4. Lewis R. Binford, *Bones: Ancient Man and Modern Myths* (New York: Academic Press, 1981); "Objectivity—Explanation—Archaeology 1981," in *Theory and Explanation in Archaeology*, ed. Colin Renfrew, Michael J. Rowlands, and Barbara Abbott Segraves (New York: Academic Press, 1982), pp. 125–38, and *In Pursuit of the Past: Decoding the Archaeological Record* (New York: Thames and Hudson, 1983). See also Pat Shipman, "Scavenging or Hunting in Early Hominids: Theoretical Framework and Tests," *American Anthropologist*, n.s. 88 (1986): 27–43.

5. See, for example, Milford H. Wolpoff, *Paleoanthropology* (New York: Knopf, 1980); Glynn L. Isaac, "The Activities of Early African Hominids: A Review of Archaeological Evidence from the Time Span Two and a Half to One Million Years Ago," in *Human Origins: Louis Leakey and the East African Evidence*,

ed. Glynn L. Isaac and Elizabeth R. McCown (Menlo Park: W. A. Benjamin, 1976), pp. 483–514, and "The Food-Sharing Behavior of Protohuman Hominids," *Scientific American* 238 (April 1978): 90–106; Richard E. Leakey and Roger Lewin, *Origins* (New York: E. P. Dutton, 1977); Sherwood L. Washburn and C. S. Lancaster, "The Evolution of Hunting," in *Perspectives on Human Evolution* 1, ed. Sherwood L. Washburn and P. C. Jay (New York: Holt, Rinehart, and Winston, 1968), pp. 213–29; David R. Pilbeam, *The Ascent of Man* (New York: Macmillan, 1972).

6. See, for example, Roger Peters and L. David Mech, "Behavioral and Intellectual Adaptations of Selected Mammalian Predators to the Problem of Hunting Large Animals," in *Socioecology and Psychology of Primates*, ed. Russell H. Tuttle (The Hague: Mouton, 1975), pp. 279–300.

7. Lucy is a three-and-a-half-million-year-old female hominid reconstructed from her fossilized remains, which were discovered by Donald C. Johanson and Tom Gray: See the former's *Lucy*, with Maitland A. Edey (New York: Warner, 1982). A paper titled, "What Was It Like to Be Lucy?" was presented by Maxine Sheets-Johnstone at the 58th annual meeting of the American Philosophical Association, Long Beach, California, March 1984. It should be noted that in both the paper and in the present context "Lucy" is being used rhetorically to designate not Lucy per se (or the species *Australopithecus afarensis* per se), but ancestral hominids in a general sense.

8. Nagel, "What Is It Like to Be a Bat?," p. 442.

9. Ibid.

10. Leakey and Lewin, *Origins*, p. 84.

11. See Lewis R. Binford, *In Pursuit of the Past*.

12. Nagel, "What Is It Like to Be a Bat?" p. 439.

13. Marshall McLuhan, *Understanding Media*, 2nd ed. (New York: American Library, 1964). See, for example, Lucien Lévy-Bruhl, *How Natives Think*, trans. Lilian A. Clare, (New York: Arno Press, 1979 [1926]), and *The Notebooks on Primitive Mentality*, trans. P. Rivière (New York: Harper and Row, 1975); Walter J. Ong, *Interfaces of the Word* (Ithaca, N.Y.: Cornell University Press, 1977); Joseph Smith, "A Critique of Visual Metaphor in Philosophy and Music," in *The Experiencing of Musical Sound* (New York: Gordon and Breach, 1979), pp. 27–64; H. H. Price, "Touch and Organic Sensation," "Presidential Address," *Proceedings of the Aristotelian Society* 44 (1944): 1–30; William C. Johnson, Jr., "Literature, Film, and the Evolution of Consciousness," *Journal of Aesthetics and Art Criticism* 38 (1979): 29–38; and Marshall McLuhan, *The Gutenberg Galaxy* (New York: New American Library, 1969).

14. Jean Piaget, *La psychologie de l'intelligence* (Paris: Librairie Armand Colin, 1967).

15. Ernest Cassirer, *An Essay on Man* (New York: Bantam Books, 1970), p. 25; Johannes von Uexküll, *Theoretische Biologie*, 2nd ed. (Berlin: J. Springer, 1928).

16. Giza Teleki, "Chimpanzee Subsistence Technology: Materials and Skills," *Journal of Human Evolution* 3 (1974): 575–94.

17. Edmund Husserl, *Ideas Pertaining to a Pure Phenomenology and to a Phenomenological Philosophy, First Book,* trans. F. Kersten (The Hague: Martinus Nijhoff, 1983), hereafter referred to as *Ideas I*; See also his Cartesian Meditations, trans. Dorion Cairns (The Hague: Martinus Nijhoff, 1973).

18. This phrase is a paraphrase of Husserl's *"zu den Sachen selbst"* (to the things themselves). The phrase is one Husserl often used to plead the need for, and the way to, a sound and consummate epistemology, and it is regularly associated with him and his work.

19. This phrase too is Husserl's. See, for example, "The Origin of Geometry," trans. David Carr, in *Husserl: Shorter Works,* ed. Peter McCormick and Frederick Elliston (Notre Dame, Ind.: University of Notre Dame Press, 1981).

20. It might be noted that the design of educational toys for children hangs on this very premise of a relationship between sensory–kinetic experience and conceptual awareness, and that theory to the contrary, experimental studies of the development of intelligence in children, such as those of Piaget and his followers, also assume concepts to be latent in sensory–kinetic experience.

21. The television program *Nova,* in "Countdown to the Invisible Universe," documented the procedure of astronomical scanning quite fully. It focused on the attempt to identify a planetary system in the process of formation through information supplied by the Infrared Astronomical Satellite—a space-based telescope.

22. See Husserl's *Ideas I;* see also his *Cartesian Meditations.*

23. Husserl, "Geometry," pp. 255–56.

24. Roger Keesing, "Anthropology as Interpretive Quest," *Current Anthropology* 28/2 (1987); see particularly pp. 161–62.

25. Husserl, *Ideas I,* see, for example, pp. 157–60; see also his *Cartesian Meditations.*

15

The Case for Tactile–Kinesthetic Invariants

We experience behavior.

ANTHONY STEVENS

The acquisition of basic concepts requires the actual recognizing of instances. . . . Recognition is a *pre-verbal* process in the sense that it is not dependent on the use of words.

H. H. PRICE

INTRODUCTION

Epistemological justification of sufficient similarity answers the second question posed in the last chapter, namely, How do we know what the point of view of ancestral hominids was in the first place? The justification rests ultimately on the body. If present-day humans can approximate to the point of view of their hominid ancestors, then explicit corporeal grounds exist for affirming that approximation. Tactile–kinesthetic invariants obviously provide the strongest and most direct way of demonstrating those grounds. Rather than taking up these invariants straightaway, however, a more circuitous epistemological route will be followed, and this in order to demonstrate how certain unexamined biases might unwittingly prejudice a clear understanding of the ultimate justification. In particular, precisely because language may unwittingly be conceived in a misleading way with respect to point of view, it is particularly instructive to consider it beforehand. What might inadvertently be assumed is not only that nascent language-users articulated and sounded speech in the same way we articulate and sound speech as twentieth-century Western adults (a view discussed at length and in fact severely challenged in Chapter 6), but further, that speech dominated and anchored their point of view in the same way that it is thought to dominate and anchor our twentieth-century Western point of view. These assumptions are erroneous for three reasons, two of them historical in nature and the third stemming from current studies of primordial language. A brief examination of each in turn will suggest what the point of view of nascent language-users was actually like and in a progressively more detailed way.

ON NASCENT LANGUAGE AND LANGUAGE-USERS

To begin with, if the received evolutionary picture is correct, then everything in the lifeworld of our hominid ancestors was a matter of survival, that is, in an individual sense, a matter of eking out a successful livelihood in a dog-eat-dog, cut-throat world such that one passed on one's genes. How things looked, smelled, felt, sounded, and tasted was therefore of primary significance. Since paying attention and noticing differences between a dead animal and one playing dead, for example, or between a toxic seed and a nontoxic one, or between a cry for help and a cry of alarm, were at all times critical, physiognomic perception—awareness of the sheer qualitative aspect of the event, process or thing—was necessarily paramount. From this evolutionary perspective, speech could not have been any mere social chit-chat or abstract musings on the world but must have been a way of securing or enhancing survival within it. As articulated and heard, speech—like everything else in our ancestral hominids' world —would have gained its acceptances and meanings in relation to a physiognomically perceived world. Hence, language could not at this time have been experienced as a distancing or separation of oneself from the immediacy of concrete relationships, objects, and happenings in the world. On the contrary, if the received evolutionary picture is credible, then what was spoken would have had to have been intimately and literally bound up with all of those processes, things, and events that mattered and that demanded virtually eternal vigilance.

In short, the physiognomically centered point of view of the nascent language-user could not have been semantically offset or imbalanced by an *intercession* of language in the form of speech, but would have incorporated speech as a way of fastening upon and battening down perceived physiognomic meanings.

The received evolutionary picture validates both the primacy of physiognomic perception in ancestral hominid life generally and the physiognomic character of nascent speech in particular. This evolutionary view is strengthened and brought into finer focus by studies of cultural historians mentioned earlier. Although the present-day non-Western and pre-twentieth-century Western cultures to which they make comparison are eons removed from those of paleoanthropological concern, the cultures are nevertheless historically, and certainly one has reason to believe, qualitatively, closer to earlier ancestral hominid societies than are technology-laden twentieth-century Western ones. Accordingly, insofar as the emphatically visual orientation— or hypervisualism—of present-day Western societies has been shown to be preceded by tactile–kinesthetically focused cultures, and, more pointedly so far as language is concerned, insofar as present-day non-literate cultures are tactile–kinesthetically and aurally oriented rather than visually oriented to speech, that is, they have no *written* form of speech, there are further reasons for believing the nascent language of our hominid ancestors to have been different in a sensory-kinetic sense from what we experience as speech today. The verbal meanings that anchored an almost human point of view (and were themselves sustained by it) were more than likely rooted in a tactile–kinesthetically centered lifeworld. It might be noted that from this perspective, the point of view and nascent speech of language-using ancestral hominids would be as analogically comparable to the point of view and speech of members of present-day nonliterate societies as the hunting behavior of ancestral hominids is in present practice taken to be analogically comparable to that of present-day hunter–gatherer societies.[1] Similar reasoning supports both analogies, and indeed their methodological substantiations would be identical since in each case comparison is being made to the same kind of, if not literally the same, present-day society.

The above evolutionary and cultural perspectives on language are supported and further crystallized by recent studies of primordial language. These studies show a spatial physiognomic analogy between the tactile–kinesthetic articulatory gestures of primordial speech and the process, event, or thing referred to. In other words, they show a correspondence between articulatory gestures and their referents.[2] Further study has suggested that a three-way physiognomic congruency existed.[3] In addition to the above-noted spatial congruency between articulatory gesture and referent, a physiognomic congruency obtained between articulatory gesture and sound, and between sound and referent (see Chapter 6). Thus, in an ancestral hominid's nascent speech, articulatory gesture, sound, and referent were physiognomic cognates of one another. The advent of spoken language was in consequence a literally *lingual* discovery, a discovery of the *tongue:* first and foremost as locus of tactual powers and maker of tactile objects, the latter in the sense of bringing potential tactile apparencies—the hardness of teeth, for example—to life; then as locus of aural powers and maker of aural objects such as the sound *m* or the sound *p;* and finally as locus of visual powers and maker of visual objects in the naming of things seen in the world. Through touch, movement, and sound, the immediately richest and most corporeally distant of public worlds is corporeally appropriated. To adopt the point of view of a nascent language-user would thus mean to approximate to the tactile–kinesthetic/auditory/visual meanings of speech, and to experience as part of the global experience of those meanings, their physiognomic correspondence to each other.

THE CASE FOR TACTILE–KINESTHETIC INVARIANTS

However brief the foregoing exposition of reasons for disavowing certain assumptions about nascent speech vis-à-vis ancestral hominids' point of view, it clearly indicates that articulated significations were once intimately tied to experiences of one's own body. In consequence it strongly suggests once again the idea that a proper conception of what it was like to be almost human is rooted in knowledge of a preeminently physiognomic world in which tactile–kinesthetic values were primary. It is in this context that the central, epistemologically critical dimension of the proposed methodology is most clearly evident. As pointed out in Chapter 1, present-day hominids have two legs of a certain form, teeth of a certain kind, a tongue of a certain shape, all of which are, in *essential* respects, no different from those of ancestral hominids said to be capable respectively of bipedal locomotion, of chewing, of speaking. Such corporeal uniformities are the foundation of *fundamental* tactile–kinesthetic invariants. As with anatomical and physiological hominid invariants, short of tactile–

kinesthetic invariants it could not justifiably be claimed that present-day humans and ancestral hominids belong to the same Family. The point merits further elaboration in three respects.

In the first place, it is a question of semantical truth. One cannot say on the basis of anatomical structures and relationships that Lucy walked,[4] for example, and at the same time deny to her the tactile–kinesthetic experience of walking. To walk means not merely to have a certain anatomy or to put one leg in front of the other in a certain way for all to see, but to experience a quite particular gait—one readily distinguishable in a tactile–kinesthetic sense from hopping, leaping, running, skipping, or sliding. The same criterion of semantical truth holds for any constructive activity attributed to ancestral hominids—stone tool-making, for example. One cannot say that a certain creature made a tool, and at the same time deny the creature the tactile–kinesthetic experience of making the tool.

In the second place, it is a question of matching tactile–kinesthetic and visual experience in a regularly ordered way: for instance, the felt striking of stone on stone and the visible fracturing of the latter stone. The conjunction of sensory meanings is rooted in the perception of tactile–kinesthetic regularities, in a broad sense in the causal relationships of corporeal praxis: "If (I do) this, then this (is felt) and this (is visually perceived)"—precisely as when a stone is hit and seen to fracture.[5] A creature finding no connection between the felt impact of stone on stone—the experienced action—and the visible shattering of stone—the experienced result—could hardly have been a tool-maker. It could hardly have structured its world to begin with since it would have been at a loss to anticipate certain dynamic regularities with respect to its own behaviors—the gradual disintegration, juiciness, and diminution of food pieces as a result of putting food in the mouth and chewing it, for example—or even to explore actively a new visibly observable object or terrain. In default of tactile–kinesthetic regularities, and especially those giving rise to a gnostic tactility (and kinesthesia),[6] the behavioral possibilities of approach and avoidance—the cornerstones of all animate behavior[7]—would be rendered meaningless. So also would the notion of adaptation since barring the possible evolution of purely visual minds or disembodied spirits, if the tactile–kinesthetic correlates of visual experience were lacking, behavior would necessarily be arbitrary and capricious. It would lack the systematic motivation that carries through any project, supposing any project were somehow conceived and initiated to begin with.

Finally, it is a question of something akin to a logical truth. A thing cannot be what it is and at the same time be something else. A creature cannot both be a hominid and fail to be *essentially* hominid. To have two legs of a certain form, teeth of a certain kind, or a tongue of a certain shape is more than taxonomically and functionally definitive. It is, as pointed out above, experientially definitive. However much and for whatever reasons one might argue against experience and self-awareness in a nonhominid world,[8] one cannot argue against them in a hominid one without thereby nullifying the very hallmarks of a developing rationality, the latter attested to surely by the systematic reasonableness of meaning evident in the sequential fracturing of even the simplest of stone tools, and in any case regularly invoked to mark the separation of hominids and nonhominids. The issue warrants extended commentary and analysis, for a fundamental error commonly exists in estimations of self-awareness, an error that, if not attributable to it outright, appears indissolubly linked to hypervisualism.

A LOGICAL ONTOLOGY, THE TACTILE–KINESTHETIC BODY, AND SELF-AWARENESS

Self-awareness is consistently assumed to be a visual phenomenon, and in effect is consistently conceived in visual terms. Gordon Gallup's experimental research on self-recognition and self-awareness in non-human animals provides an excellent illustration. In Gallup's experiments self-awareness is operationally defined as self-directed behavior with a mirror. That is, since self-recognition in a mirror implies a self-concept, it is taken as a criterion for self-awareness. Thus when a chimpanzee makes "self-directed . . . attempts to groom parts of the body while watching the results and guiding the fingers in the mirror, . . . [or when it manipulates] food wads with the lips while inspecting the reflection," or when it blows bubbles or makes faces "with the help of mirror feedback,"[9] the animal's self-recognition is taken to imply the existence of a self-concept, and the self-concept in turn is taken as coincident with self-awareness.

Now curiously enough, Gallup states that there is "reason to suspect that the capacity for self-recognition in chimpanzees may be influenced by certain kinds of early experiences," and he goes on to say specifically that "to the extent that one would require *an already integrated concept of self before he could learn to recognize himself in a mirror*, it seemed reasonable to suppose that the development of self-awareness could be influenced by early experience, and that it, too, might be an acquired phenomenon" (italics added).[10] Gallup gives reasons for believing these early experiences to center on interpersonal relationships. An individual's concept of him/herself is in other words the result of social interactions. The idea that the "already integrated concept of self" derives from the tactile–kinesthetic body never arises. Its absence is peculiar in that an infant's visual experiences of its own body—in the sense of investigations of its own body as an *object*—come after a basic gnostic system of tactile–kinesthetic sensibilities and powers has begun to be forged in such acts as opening and closing the mouth, bringing the hand or thumb toward the mouth, flexing and extending body parts, reaching, closing the hand over an object placed in it, and so on. An infant's ultimate coordination of visual and tactile–kinesthetic bodies is from this perspective a transposition of meanings from an original datum to a second, *a transfer of sense* in the double meaning of the latter word. Through this transfer what is seen and what is touched or moved comes to coincide in such a way that what was *felt*—in flexing or extending, opening or reaching, for example—comes to be perceived as a *visual* phenomenon in much the same way that pointedness or smoothness come to be *visually* perceived.

Visual self-awareness is undoubtedly learned as Gallup suggests. Visual self-awareness may be socially dependent as he also suggests. But *tactile–kinesthetic* self-awareness, if present at all, comes semi-automatically with being an animate body. It seems in fact biologically axiomatic that, *to the degree an animal has to learn to move itself, it is self-aware.* Such an animal is not just aware of discrete movements and disjunct points of contact, it is globally aware of itself as the source of certain tactile–kinesthetic possibilities. It forges these possibilities itself. This primary form of self-awareness develops autonomously and incrementally in many primate species. If it did not, infants and young children would not likely survive to maturity. Young chimpanzees, orang-utans, and gibbons, for example, who do not learn to comport themselves intelligently in the trees by making life-enhancing judgments of distance, solidity, and the like, are not likely to live to reproductive years, or be in a condition to enjoy them should they do so.

Animals who must learn to move themselves learn spontaneously and over a period of time. In the process they come to forge the *I can*'s [11] of a personal and species-specific existence. The *I can*'s comprise a personal repertoire of movement possibilities ordained and limited by a certain biological heritage. The "already integrated concept of self" is thus a corporeal concept conditioned by an evolutionary history. It is this primary, phylogenetically informed tactile–kinesthetic self-awareness that gives the visual body, the body the chimpanzee sees in the mirror, or the body the infant inspects when it discovers its hand as a visual object, its meaning. In other words, what is done with mirrors, social ones or literal ones, involves a secondary form of self-awareness. Confirmation of this fact is found in the experimental research itself. When a chimpanzee, previously exposed to a mirror for a period of time and tested for self-recognition, is then anaesthetized and marked on its face with a spot, it gives a "mark-directed response," touching the spot or trying to expunge it when confronted with a mirror. [12] The unasked question—and unremarked upon fact—concerns the animal's unerring movement to the spot. How does it know where this spot is in a tactile–kinesthetic sense, and how does it know how to reach it straightaway—in the same sense? Clearly the same fundamental self-awareness informs its unerring mark-oriented movement as informs its self-grooming movements in front of the mirror. Indeed, if the mirror is actually used as a *guide,* as Gallup reports, it is an exceedingly tricky one to learn from. Right/left mirror reversal demands that an individual always return to the felt, tactile–kinesthetic body as the standard.

Wherever the tactile–kinesthetic body is passed over, the visual body is necessarily conceived as in a sentient vacuum. It is no longer anchored in *animate* form. It is a surface over which a glance or even a hand may pass, but always from the point of view of a detached outsider. The concept of self-awareness that comes with this visual vacuum is thus necessarily a third-person conception. As Gallup in fact notes in speaking of philosopher G. H. Mead's "speculations" that support his own notion of a social origin for self-awareness, "In order for the self to emerge as an object of *conscious inspection,* . . . it requires the opportunity to examine one's self from another's point of view" (italics added). [13]

Clearly there is a difference in self-awareness between this looking and inspecting with a third person orientation and concept, and moving and noticing—or simply *being* and noticing—in the first person. The latter kind of self-awareness does not eventuate in an object in the conventional, public and visual sense of that word. The self of which one is aware in the latter instance is not equatable to a material body having such and such unique surface, inner, or microscopically determinable visual features, and such and such visually determined positions with respect to other material bodies in the world—not even in an ultimate coordination of the visual and tactile–kinesthetic bodies, as when a young child learns to use a fork to pick up food on its plate. The self of which one is fundamentally aware is a spatially resonant locus of animate possibilities, a felt center of dynamic motivations and voluntary actions. Perhaps the strongest confirmation of this corporeal self-awareness in nonhuman animals comes from reports of chimpanzees who use tools to groom their teeth—without the help of mirrors—who, like orang-utans, use leaves to wipe themselves after defecating—without the help of mirrors—and who make a point of scratching themselves in those places inaccessible to visual self-grooming—without the help of mirrors.[14] All such actions give evidence of a repertoire of *I can*'s grounded in a self-awareness unequivocally anchored in the tactile–kinesthetic body.

The foregoing commentary on, and critical analysis of, Gallup's experimental studies should emend any notion of ancestral hominids either as devoid of experientially resonant bodies or as incapable of self-awareness. Moreover it should be clear that, whatever the construal of their respective lineages, neither experience nor self-awareness, not to mention rationality itself, could have arisen *ex nihilo*. If evolutionary theory is correct, both would have had to have developed within the context of tactile–kinesthetic awarenesses and a concomitant gnostic tactility and kinesthesia. Gallup's operational definition notwithstanding, it is possible to conceive of a self that is blind but not of one that is thoroughly devoid of a tactile–kinesthetic world.[15] *In terms of hominid evolution, learning to move oneself and noticing tactile–kinesthetic aspects of oneself are historical facts that are not contingent.* A creature by its very nature self-aware—or evolving into progressively greater stages of self-awareness—cannot be denied the very ground of its distinctiveness and still be what it is. In sum, tactile–kinesthetic invariants of hominid experience are bona fide evolutionary characters. They are as much sustained by a logical ontology as they are sustained by a common and singular Familial membership, guaranteed by semantic truth, and upheld by an intelligible regularity of corporeal experience.

NONLINGUISTIC CONCEPTS

Tactile–kinesthetic invariants are of course entailments of animate form. The invariants or the form itself may give rise to corporeal concepts, a fact demonstrated extensively and in depth in Part II. The immediate concern here is to show further that these concepts are not language-dependent.

It is important to validate and thus vindicate the claim of non-linguistic corporeal concepts since prominent people in a variety of disciplines, particularly those wedded to a coherentist (or relativistic) rather than foundationalist epistemology, maintain that short of language there are no concepts.[16] Were these people correct, ancestral hominids would have been cognitively disadvantaged to the point that many behaviors—stone tool-making, caring for injured individuals, or even big-game hunting with all the intellectual abilities it presupposes—would hardly have been feasible undertakings. Nonlinguistic corporeal concepts will in consequence be examined in some detail in order to show how and why they would have come into awareness. Of course justification of nonlinguistic concepts could easily be avoided by arguing, and quite compellingly, that stone tools, for instance, were made before language originated (and that care-giving behavior apparently did also.)[17] Indeed, as pointed out in an earlier chapter, the period in which language arose is generally taken as considerably later than that in which stone tools were first fabricated. To take refuge in this reasoning, however, would skirt the very points at issue, namely, that there are *corporeal* concepts, and that they are not on that account in any way inferior to their linguistic relatives. The nonlinguistic corporeal concept of hardness will be used to exemplify the justness of these claims.

To begin with, consider the concept of hardness in terms of a human infant's world. That world is in great measure an oral one: an infant takes things into its mouth, runs its tongue over its lips, makes sounds, and so on. Intrauterine life aside and first support/holding contacts notwithstanding, an oral world is the locus of its first meanings. In sucking, an infant is buccally focused and in a purely tactile sense since taste buds are not yet functioning.[18] Given their lingual explorations, it is absurd to think that infants do not feel the hardness of their toothless gums or developing hard palates.[19] Apart from the inner surfaces of their lips, which indeed stand out in contrast, the items discovered in their lingual explorations are palpably hard. The buccal cavity of any human adult reveals the same invariant hardnesses. No word or words is or are necessary to the recognition of this humanly universal tactile quality.

Human infants and adults are not ancestral hominid infants and adults. Yet the line of reasoning that connects certain as-

pects of the one life with certain aspects of the other is not spe-
cious or unwarranted. In broad terms, and echoing the earlier-given
evolutionary justification of tactile–kinesthetic invariants, a sensory–
kinetic evolutionary continuity between ancestral and present-day
hominids—infants or adults—cannot be denied any more than can
an anatomical–physiological evolutionary continuity. Standard paleoanthropological behavioral analogies [20] would fall by the wayside
should such sensory–kinetic evolutionary continuities be denied. One
cannot both make comparison to extant hunter–gatherer peoples, for
example, to reconstruct ancestral hominid hunting behavior and at
the same time deny ancestral hominids a concomitant sensory–kinetic
world of experience. Nor can one say that with respect to the hunting
behavior studied that that world is essentially different from that of
extant peoples. Or rather, one can do both, but only at the expense
of logical probity [21] and accepted taxonomic classifications. In brief,
sensory–kinetic continuities are entailed by anatomical–physiological
continuities, and are assumed if unacknowledged in every paleoanthropological reconstruction where behavioral comparisons are
made. In lingually recognizing the hardness of teeth, present-day and
ancestral hominids are and were recognizing what any present-day
paleoanthropologist or archaeologist tacitly recognizes *manually, and
anticipates recognizing manually,* the moment he/she picks up an old
hominid tooth or tooth-filled jaw from the fossil-bearing landscape: a
hard material substance.

The likening of ancestral hominids to human infants and young
children need not be tethered to estimations of intelligence. [22] It can
simply be a comparison between two worlds without speech and thus
without the visual biases that Western language entails in the form of
human speech. Naming, after all, is patently oriented toward a visual
world, that is, toward what is experienced in common, hence what is
furthest removed from any one individual. Human infants and very
young children, in spite of their exposure to language, are apt models
for ancestral hominids insofar as they share a similar ratio among
the senses. In neither can nonlinguistic conceptual understandings or
tactile–kinesthetic awarenesses such as an awareness of hardness be
underestimated. [23]

There is a second major reason for claiming that the corporeal concept of hardness would arise naturally, apart from language: teeth call
attention to themselves. Whatever the hardnesses felt prior to their
eruption, the original appearance of teeth is an event not likely to go
tactilely unperceived. Moreover the fact that original teeth are lost and

others take their place is further occasion for remarking upon their tactile quality. Since loss and replacement affect a young hominid's experiences in the course of eating, an awareness of teeth can hardly be denied. In fact, while other bodily features such as hair or nails might be lost and eventually grow back, the loss and replacement of teeth are, in contrast, wholly natural happenings. Along with eruption, they are all chronologically consistent events. Surely a creature who grooms its teeth is aware of their hardness in the same way that it is aware of the hardness of the nut shell it must crack in order to eat the nut. By the same token surely a creature said to be capable of making a stone tool—to say nothing of the attributions frequently made relative to stone tool-makers, such as cooperative hunting, a division of labor, the having of a base camp [24]—could not be unaware of such regular corporeal processes.

Teeth are not only a new item in the mouth when they erupt, they are also a *peculiar* new item. They are both similar to and radically different from other buccal apparencies. Like palate and gums, teeth are hard, but the textural quality of their hardness is distinctive. This peculiar textural hardness is thrown into starker relief by the fleshy, pulpy softness of the lips and tongue. In fact, teeth are like stones in this respect. They do not feel like the "typical" felt body at all. On the contrary, they feel like worldly objects—precisely those devoid of organic material.

Such natural differences and similarities give rise to perceptual discriminations—as the proverbial snow distinctions made by Eskimos and plant distinctions made by gatherers further indicate. Lest it be thought that such distinctions are language-dependent, one need only think back to the question of how different names could be applied unless each variety of snow or plant named was once noticed as similar to others and different from still others. In other words, a *concept* of the thing to be named must precede the naming. There is otherwise nothing in conceptual particular to name. It is not helpful to argue that linguistic designation gives the thing an enduring recognizability, a kind of abstract placement in the world, for with respect to the body—teeth, for example—any time one wishes to validate a certain quality—hardness, for example—there it is. Abstract placement in the world in the sense of specifying an enduring object is thus fundamentally guaranteed not by language but by a tactile–kinesthetic freedom to observe (or to do actively or desist from acting), a freedom derived from the *I can*'s of a personal existence.[25] The moment one thinks in terms of the *origin* of concepts—how they could have arisen

—one realizes that they neither drifted down from the blue into the mouths of waiting hominids nor were they spawned *causa sui* by a brain. They were rooted in creaturely experience.

The significance of differentiation to the development of sensory perception has been studied in humans and nonhumans alike.[26] It is reasonable to conclude from the evidence that the greater the difference of a thing from the normal, typical, or expected, or the greater the difference between types, the greater the likelihood of its being remarked upon. There is thus a third reason for maintaining that the corporeal concept of hardness would have arisen naturally. If hominid evolution is distinguished by increasingly refined sensory perception, then discriminatory sensitivities and powers would have been progressively heightened in reference not only to the external world but to the individual's own felt body. In effect, at the same time the normal fleshy feel of the body would have been recognized, so also, in substantial contrast, would have been the quite un-bodylike feel of teeth.

If any aspect of the validation of nonlinguistic corporeal concepts presented thus far is deemed preposterous on the grounds that ancestral hominids would not have sat around on lazy afternoons feeling their gums and teeth, or that such awarenesses are "purely speculative," or that such aspects of oneself are trivial and would not have been noticed, then surely the notion of a greatly expanding cortical representation of tactility, the notion of a developing self-awareness, and the notion of lingual/buccal awarenesses and powers developing to the point of language in the form of speech—to name only a few of the classically claimed characteristics of hominid evolution— are equally preposterous in one way and another. It is not reasonable to claim, for example, in interpreting the significance of a greater cortical representation of tactility and movement, that it had no actual resonating sensory–kinetic living reality, in effect, that tactility was all in the head (or is all in the experimental laboratory) rather than part and parcel of the actual lifeworld of the creature in question. The considerable tactile–kinesthetic shift must have counted for something in the actual evolutionary world of the creature in whom such cortical sensorimotor representation came to exist. The sensorimotor homunculus [27] attests in fact to the prominence of highly differentiated tactile–kinesthetic experiences, that is, to the importance of tactile– kinesthetic discriminations to normal human development.[28] A similar prominence cannot be denied a consistently bipedal ancestral hominid whose hands are everywhere characterized as being "free." The neuroanatomist R. W. Sperry's evolutionary view of the brain as an organ of and for movement is not inappropriate to recall in this context.[29] If thinking is fundamentally a motor act as he suggests, and if tactility like movement itself is a basic way of exploring the world and coming to know it, then the evolutionary basis of a gnostic tactility is transparent, and its evolutionary importance is equally so. An awareness of the hardness of teeth is a simple but far-reaching example of this tactility—as the paleoanthropological case study of stone tool-using/tool-making (Chapter 2) further demonstrates.

Two final validations may be adduced that spell out these evolutionary dimensions in greater detail. Nonlinguistic corporeal concepts are substantiated as much by the received evolutionary picture as by the notion of a developing rationality.

In the first instance, the received evolutionary picture is one of a world in which everything matters; in essence, a world demanding vigilance and sensory-kinetic acuity. In such a world, noticing is not a casual or willy-nilly occurrence but in good measure what everyday living hinges upon. A quite modest but significant tactile example of this acuity is the distinction between the hardness of earth and the comparative softness of leaves, especially as concerns resting or sleeping nests—a distinction difficult to deny ancestral hominids in light of present-day chimpanzee nesting behavior.[30] That the feel of objects in the environment is regularly explored by extant nonhuman primates[31] is further indication of an attentive noticing and strong tactile acuity. More convincing still is the literature on primate play[32] which, at the same time that it affirms the didactic value of play as primary, just as strongly (if at times implicitly) affirms that tactile noticings and explorations are paramount—that pokings, probings, grapplings, and the like, are the foundation of a gnostic tactility vital to normal development and adaptation.

A creature capable of initiating new behaviors on the basis of its noticings often gives active evidence of a gnostic tactility. Sand, for instance, is a tactile datum: a granular irritation in the mouth, an abrasive against the hands. Although not recognized and analyzed as such, the Japanese macaques' act of washing sand off the skins of sweet potatoes[33] is basically a tactile act. The macaques' intentional transformation of the potatoes' tactile values from grittiness to smoothness makes empirically evident the acuity and prominence of their tactile discriminations and powers. Such acts further validate the received evolutionary picture by substantiating both the existential centrality of noticing and its possible phylogenetic implications with respect to both adaptation and culture. Noticing the somatic feel of one's own body and the feel of things with which it comes in contact can in other words have potentially far-reaching evolutionary as well as existential significance.

Particularly in the context of stone tool-making, the received evolutionary picture documents an ever-increasing discriminatory ingenuity on the part of *Homo faber*. The basis of that developing ingenuity has to do with tactile–kinesthetic perceptions, the kind that distinguished a sharp edge from a blunt one, for example, one kind of blow or flaking technique from another, and one stone material from another. In brief, beyond vigilance and sensory–kinetic acuity, the received evolutionary picture documents the importance of tactile–kinesthetic differentiation and tacitly documents the importance of tactile–kinesthetic concepts as well. This is because barring conditioned or otherwise primitive recognitory responses,[34] sensory differentiation is potentially concept-laden (in a way similar to the way in which typical observation is theory-laden),[35] most fundamentally at the level of *difference* itself as studies of infant perception would seem to indicate.[36] The perceptions that actively shaped hominid stone tool-making attest to evolving discriminatory concepts. The idea of an *intentional* transformation of a material object would otherwise be meaningless and the ultimate standardization of tools would otherwise have been impossible since conceptual recognition of sensory–kinetic differences, samenesses, and similarities would never have occurred, and neither, of course, would conceptual recognition of oneself as the center of possible actions and experiences.

A developing hominid rationality is necessarily tied to this evolving system of tactile–kinesthetic meanings. In the first place, a developing rationality means increasingly refined powers of discernment, insight, and action. In other words, it is tied to a creature whose sensory–kinetic awarenesses and behaviors demonstrate ever-increasing conceptual acumen. Certainly palpable examples of this acumen are had in the earlier Oldowan as well as later Acheulian stone tools, in cave paintings, and in burial practices that attest to a concept of death and thus to a distinction between two possible guises of the same visual body: one anchored in animate form and one in inanimate form. From this perspective, a developing rationality defines not a privileged state of mind but a progressively astute way of being conceptually present to the world. Such an understanding of rationality is the only one possible if "it is no mere coincidence that the rational being is also the one who holds himself upright or has a thumb which can be brought opposite to the fingers.[37]

Given the above evolutionary context for rationality, nonlinguistic corporeal concepts such as hardness cannot be misconstrued as merely trivial conceptions. Tactile–kinesthetic discriminations would indeed have been at the heart of a developing, corporeally articulate rationality. At the same time, a gnostic tactility–kinesthesia is not either to be misconstrued as being of only "practical" significance, unless understood as such within the context of an epistemology that upholds all reasoning to be practical reasoning,[38] or practical reasoning to be at the core of *all* reasoning,[39] not in a Piagetian developmental sense as a stage surpassed, but as substantively entwined in, and presupposed by, the theoretical.

Lastly, tactile–kinesthetic concepts such as hardness are clearly not speculative entities. They are empirically evident, and they are empirically evident across all hominid cultures, diachronically as well as synchronically. A given group of hominids, past or present, could hardly speak the same language were there not a tactile–kinesthetic uniformity of felt articulations, ones in which distinctions between hardness and softness—of tongue against teeth or lip against lip, for example—are critical to the intelligible and consistent production of sound. By the same token, there could hardly be agreement on present-day pan-cultural classification of lingual phenomena: fricatives, plosives, and so on, are accepted classificatory designations possible only in virtue of a pan-hominid tactile–kinesthetic uniformity of possible felt articulatory gestures.

Being pan-cultural, fundamental tactile–kinesthetic concepts are of course open to corroboration by any hominid, anywhere. It would be possible in fact to turn the empirical evidence of tactile–kinesthetic invariants into an inductively reached "proof" by questioning subjects and validating the uniformity of their experience—the touching of lips in sounding the letter *m*, for example, or the binary rhythm of a normal bipedal gait. Induction procedures here would seem, however, only to underscore the obvious. Indeed, one could rightfully insist that the same kind of empirical generalization is at work in the case of acknowledging tactile–kinesthetic invariants as it is in acknowledging fossil bones. *Analogical reasoning—not induction*—in each case cements the empirical generalization. Fossil bones are taken as *bones* on the basis of dissection, or something effectively akin to it. That is, when stripped of their outer flesh, many creatures have been seen uniformly to have a skeletal frame. In consequence (and quite apart from the question of acknowledging *fossil* bones in default of observational evidence of the process of their fossilization), those unattached items in the landscape are taken as tokens of once-living creatures. Though never observed as such, they are believed to have been attached to once-living flesh.

A similar analogical inference sustains the empirical generalization regarding tactile–kinesthetic invariants. Although no one today has ever observed an early hominid running his or her tongue over his or her teeth, for example, or chewing and thereby transforming material substances, it can be justifiably inferred on the basis of analogy that the teeth of ancestral hominids were felt as hard and that a disintegration of material substances was felt in chewing. Moreover the *analogical* inferences that taxonomically unite all hominid creatures morphologically and functionally cannot stop short of fundamental tactile–kinesthetic experience. As emphasized earlier, the essentially "same" bodies and the essentially "same" behaviors cannot give rise to essentially different tactile–kinesthetic awarenesses. Hence, unless it were literally waltzing across the plains or hobble-gaited in some unnatural way, for instance, there is no way a two-legged functionally upright hominid could walk (or run) and not feel the cadence of its gait as binary.

Just as no inductive procedure has ever been used—or sought—to validate or invalidate the conclusion (and belief) that some fossil items in the landscape are the bones of once-living but never-observed creatures, so no inductive procedure need be used—or sought—to validate the claim that the hardness of teeth, or the articulatory gesture of the sound *m*, or the binary cadence of walking is among the tactile–kinesthetic invariants of hominid experience. Sound analogical inference upholds the empirical generalization in each and every case. In like manner, although no inductive procedure can be used to validate the claim that sufficient similarity in point of view obtains between present-day humans and their ancestral kinfolk through pan-hominid tactile–kinesthetic invariants, sound analogical inference upholds the epistemological claim. To insist that fundamental tactile–kinesthetic concepts are all the same objectively unsubstantiated, that is, to deny the existence of fundamental experiential pan-hominid evolutionary characters, is to stop short of a full elaboration and appreciation of evolutionary theory, and in so doing ultimately to deny to paleoanthropological reconstructions—and our own twentieth-century human selves—their full measure of completeness.

The paleoanthropological case studies have exemplified the richness of that measure. Our own twentieth-century living bodies do likewise if we but listen. The corporeal turn, like the linguistic turn, requires paying attention to something long taken for granted.

NOTES

1. See, for example, Glynn L. Isaac, "The Activities of Early African Hominids: A Review of Archaeological Evidence from the Time Span Two and a Half to One Million Years Ago," in *Human Origins: Louis Leakey and the East African Evidence*, ed. Glynn L. Isaac and Elizabeth R. McCown (Menlo Park, Calif.: W. A. Benjamin, 1976), pp. 483–514, and "The Food-Sharing Behavior of Protohuman Hominids," *Scientific American* 238 (April 1978): 90–108; Sherwood L. Washburn and C. S. Lancaster, "The Evolution of Hunting," in *Perspectives on Human Evolution I*, ed. Sherwood L. Washburn and P. C. Jay (New York: Holt, Rinehart, and Winston, 1968), pp. 213–29; and Richard E. Leakey and Roger Lewin, *Origins* (New York: E. P. Dutton, 1977).

2. Mary LeCron Foster, "The Symbolic Structure of Primordial Language," in *Human Evolution: Biosocial Perspectives*, ed. Sherwood L. Washburn and Elizabeth R. McCown (Menlo Park, Calif.: Benjamin/Cummings, 1978), pp. 77–121, and "Reconstruction of the Evolution of Language," in *Handbook of Symbolic Evolution*, ed. A. Lock and C. Peter (Oxford: Oxford University Press, in press); and E. G. Pulleyblank, "The Beginnings of Duality of Patterning in Language," in *Glossogenetics*, ed. E. de Grolier (New York: Harwood, 1983), pp. 369–410. See also Ivan Fonagy, "Preconceptual Thinking in Language," ibid., pp. 329–53.

3. Maxine Sheets-Johnstone, "On the Origin of Language," *North Dakota Quarterly* 51/2 (1983): 22–51.

4. See Donald C. Johanson and Maitland A. Edey, *Lucy* (New York: Simon and Schuster, 1981); and C. Owen Lovejoy, "Locomotor Anatomy of *A. afarensis*" (Paper presented at the conference, "The Evolution of Human Locomotion," Institute of Human Origins, Berkeley, California, April 1983).

5. For an analysis and discussion of these "kinestheses," see Edmund Husserl, *Ideen zu einer reinen Phänomenologie und phänomenologischen Philosophie, Zweites Buch*, ed. Marly Biemel (The Hague: Martinus Nijhoff, 1952), hereafter *Ideas II*; and *The Crisis of the European Sciences*, trans. David Carr (Evanston, Ill.: Northwestern University Press, 1970).

6. See Oliver Sacks, "Hands," *New York Review of Books*, 8 November 1984, p. 15; A. N. Leont'ev and N. V. Zaporozhets, *The Rehabilitation of Hand Function*, trans. B. Haigh and ed. W. R. Russell (New York: Pergamon Press, 1960).

7. T. C. Schneirla, "An Evolutionary and Developmental Theory of Biphasic Processes Underlying Approach and Withdrawal," in *Nebraska Sympo-*

sium on Motivation, 7, ed. M. R. Jones (Lincoln: University of Nebraska, 1959), pp. 1–42.

8. See, for example, Susanne Langer, *Mind: An Essay on Human Feeling*, 3 vols. (Baltimore: Johns Hopkins University Press, 1967 and 1972), vols. 1 and 2. See also Donald R. Griffin, *The Question of Animal Awareness* (New York: Rockefeller University Press, 1976), for a full discussion of the view that only humans *experience* and are *self-aware*.

9. Gordon G. Gallup, Jr., "Towards an Operational Definition of Self-Awareness," in *Socioecology and Psychology of Primates*, ed. Russell H. Tuttle (The Hague: Mouton, 1975), pp. 309–41.

10. Ibid., pp. 330–31.

11. See Husserl, *Ideas II* and *Crisis*.

12. Gallup, "Towards an Operational Definition," pp. 331–32.

13. Ibid., p. 331.

14. Jurgen Lethmate, "Tool-Using Skills of Orang-utans," *Journal of Human Evolution* 2/1 (1982): 49–64; Claudia Jordan, "Object Manipulation and Tool-Use in Captive Pygmy Chimpanzees (*Pan paniscus*)," ibid., pp. 35–39; and Jane van Lawick-Goodall, "The Behaviour of Free-Living Chimpanzees in the Gombe Stream Reserve," *Animal Behaviour Monographs*, vol. 1, pt. 3, 1968.

15. Aristotle, *De anima*, trans. J. A. Smith, in *The Basic Works of Aristotle*, ed. R. McKeon (New York: Random House, 1968); and Albert Johnstone, "The Corporeality of the Cartesian Thinking Subject or What Descartes Should Have Conceded Princess Elizabeth of Bohemia" (Paper presented at "Giving the Body Its Due: An Interdisciplinary Conference," Eugene, Oregon, 5 November 1989). Also in Johnstone's manuscript, *Does the World Exist?*

16. See, for example, Jean Piaget, *La construction du réel chez l'enfant* (Neuchatel: Delachaux et Niestlé, 1967), and *Genetic Epistemology*, trans. E. Duckworth (New York: Columbia University Press, 1970), wherein Piaget does not insist on language exclusively but does insist on "semiotic function," i.e., some form of symbolizing; Richard Rorty, *Philosophy and the Mirror of Nature* (Princeton: Princeton University Press, 1979); Ludwig Wittgenstein, *Philosophical Investigations*, trans. G. E. M. Anscombe (Oxford: Basil Blackwell, 1963); Williard van Orman Quine, *Word and Object* (Cambridge: MIT Press, 1970); Dorothy Lee, "Conceptual Implications of an Indian Language," *Philosophy of Science* 5 (1938): 89–102; Claude Lévi-Strauss, *The Savage Mind*, trans. G. Weidenfeld and Nicolson Ltd. (London: Weidenfeld and Nicolson, 1972); Edward Sapir, *Language*, 2nd ed. (New York: Beckman, 1979); and Benjamin Whorf, *Language, Thought, and Reality* (Cambridge, Mass.: Technology Press, 1956).

17. Australopithecines (representing a genus preceding *Homo*) are credited with caring for injured individuals on the basis of healed fractures: "A broken leg is much more serious for a biped than it is for a quadruped, and the fact that the break *healed* indicates that the individual was taken care of by others." See Milford H. Wolpoff, *Paleoanthropology* (New York: Knopf, 1980), p. 150.

18. Ashley Montagu, *Touching: The Human Significance of Skin* (New York: Columbia University Press, 1971).

19. Cf. studies of sound perception and cognition in infants. For example, Peter D. Eimas, "Developmental Studies of Speech Perception," in *Infant Perception: From Sensation to Cognition*, 2 vols., ed. L. B. Cohen and P. Salapatek (New York: Academic Press, 1975), 2:193–231; Philip A. Morse, "Speech Perception in the Human Infant and Rhesus Monkey," in *Origins and Evolution of Language and Speech*, ed. Stevan R. Harnad, Horst D. Steklis, and Jane B. Lancaster, *Annals of the New York Academy of Sciences* 280 (1976): 694–707; James E. Cutting and Peter D. Eimas, "Phonetic Feature Analyzers and the Processing of Speech in Infants," in *The Role of Speech in Language*, ed. James F. Kavanaugh and James E. Cutting (Cambridge: MIT Press, 1975), pp. 127–48.

20. See, for example, Sherwood L. Washburn, "The Analysis of Primate Evolution with Particular Reference to the Origin of Man," *Cold Spring Harbor Symposia on Quantitative Biology* 15 (1950): 67–77; and Jane B. Lancaster, *Primate Behavior and the Emergence of Human Culture* (New York: Holt, Rinehart, and Winston, 1975).

21. Discussed more fully in Maxine Sheets-Johnstone, "What Was It Like to Be Lucy?" (Paper presented at the 58th annual meeting of the American Philosophical Association, Long Beach, California, March 1984).

22. The practice is in many cases the result of wedding Piagetian theory with evolutionary anthropology. See, for example, Sue T. Parker, "Piaget's Sensorimotor Series in an Infant Macaque: A Model for Comparing Unstereotyped Behavior and Intelligence in Human and Non-Human Primates," in *Primate Biosocial Development*, ed. Suzanne Chevalier-Skolnikoff and Frank E. Poirier (New York: Garland Press, 1977), pp. 43–112; Sue T. Parker and Kay R. Gibson, "Object Manipulation, Tool Use and Sensorimotor Intelligence as Feeding Adaptation in Cebus Monkeys and Great Apes," *Journal of Human Evolution* 6 (1977): 623–41, and "A Developmental Model for the Evolution of Language and Intelligence in Early Hominids," *Behavioral and Brain Sciences* 2 (1979): 367–408; Kay R. Gibson, "Brain Structure and Intelligence in Macaques and Human Infants from a Piagetian Perspective," in *Primate Biosocial Development*, pp. 113–57; Thomas Wynn, "The Intelligence of Later Acheulian Hominids," *Man*, n.s. 14 (1979): 371–91, and "The Intelligence of Oldowan Hominids," *Journal of Human Evolution* 10 (1981): 529–41; and Suzanne Chevalier-Skolnikoff, "The Ontogeny of Primate Intelligence and Its Implications for Communicative Potential," in *Origins and Evolution*, pp. 173–211.

23. See the earlier-cited study on concept development in very young children (note 16). See also the literature on concept development in infants and young children cited in Chapter 9.

24. See, for example, Wolpoff, *Paleoanthropology*; Leakey and Lewin, *Origins*; Sherwood L. Washburn and C. S. Lancaster, "The Evolution of Hunting," in *Perspectives on Human Evolution 1*, ed. S. L. Washburn and P. C. Jay (New York: Holt, Rinehart, and Winston), pp. 213–29.

25. This seminal insight undergirds Albert A. Johnstone's article, "The Role of '*Ich Kann*' in Husserl's Answer to Humean Skepticism," *Philosophy and Phenomenological Research* 46/4 (1986): 577–95. See also his book, *Rationalized Epistemology: Taking Solipsism Seriously*, forthcoming from State University of New York Press.

26. See, for example, E. J. Gibson, *Principles of Perceptual Learning and Development* (New York: Appleton-Century Crofts, 1969); Eimas, "Developmental Studies"; Peter D. Eimas, E. R. Siqueland, P. Juszyck, and J. Vignito, "Speech Perception in Infants," *Science* 171 (1971): 303–6; Joel Kaplan, "Perceptual Properties of Attachment in Surrogate-Reared and Mother-Reared Squirrel Monkeys," in *Primate Biosocial Development*, pp. 225–34; and Kay R. Gibson, "Brain Structure."

27. Wilder Penfield and T. Rasmussen, *The Cerebral Cortex of Man* (New York: Macmillan, 1950).

28. See Montagu, *Touching*.

29. R. W. Sperry, "Neurology and the Mind–Brain Problem," *American Scientist* 40 (1952): 291–312.

30. Jane van Lawick-Goodall, *In the Shadow of Man* (New York: Dell, 1971), and "Free-Living Chimpanzees."

31. Ibid. See also, for example, Harry F. Harlow, "The Effect of Rearing Conditions on Behavior," in *Sex Research: New Developments*, ed. J. Money (New York: Holt, Rinehart, and Winston, 1965); K. R. L. Hall and I. De Vore, "Baboon Social Behavior," in *Primate Patterns*, ed. Phyllis J. Dolhinow (New York: Holt, Rinehart, and Winston, 1972), pp. 125–80.

32. See, for example, Jane van Lawick-Goodall, "Chimpanzee Locomotor Play," and "Mother Chimpanzees' Play with Their Infants," in *Play—Its Role in Development and Evolution*, ed. Jerome S. Bruner, Alison Jolly, and Kathy Silva (New York: Basic Books, 1976), pp. 156–60 and 262–67 respectively; S. J. Suomi and Harry F. Harlow, "Monkeys Without Play," ibid., pp. 490–95; Harry F. Harlow, "Development of the Second and Third Affectional Systems in Macaque Monkeys," in *Research Approaches to Psychiatric Problems*, ed. Thomas T. Tourlentes, Seymour L. Pollack, and Harold E. Hemwick (New York: Grune and Stratton, 1962), pp. 209–29; and Phyllis J. Dolhinow and Naomi Bishop, "The Development of Motor Skills and Social Relationships among Primates through Play," in *Primate Patterns*, pp. 312–37.

33. M. Kawai, "Newly Acquired Precultural Behavior of the Natural Troop of Japanese Monkeys on Koshima Islet," *Primates* 6 (1965): 1–30; Junichiro Itani and A. Nishimura, "The Study of Infrahuman Culture in Japan: A Review," in *Precultural Primate Behavior*, ed. Emil W. Menzel (Basel: Karger, 1973), pp. 26–50.

34. See, for example, Jacques Monod on stereospecific interactions in *Chance and Necessity*, trans. A. Wainhouse (New York: Knopf, 1971).

35. See Norwood R. Hanson, *Patterns of Discovery* (Cambridge: Cambridge University Press, 1958).

36. Eimas, "Developmental Studies"; and Morse, "Speech Perception."

37. Maurice Merleau-Ponty, *Phenomenology of Perception*, trans. Colin Smith (London: Routledge & Kegan Paul, 1962), p. 170.

38. See, for example, Robert Hollinger, "Practical Reasoning and Hermeneutics" (Paper presented at the 58th annual meeting of the American Philosophical Association, Long Beach, California, March 1984).

39. Martin Heidegger, *Being and Time*, trans. John Macquarrie and Edward Robinson (New York: Harper and Row, 1962); see also C. B. Guignon, *Heidegger and the Problem of Knowledge* (Indianapolis, Ind.: Hackett, 1983). Guignon strongly argues in favor of this interpretation of Heidegger.

Name Index